Innovative Applications of Artificial Intelligence 4

Innovative Applications of Artificial Intelligence 4

Proceedings of the IAAI–92 Conference

Edited by A. Carlisle Scott and Phillip Klahr

AAAI Press / The MIT Press
Menlo Park • Cambridge • London

445 Burgess Drive
Menlo Park, CA 94025

Copublished and distributed by The MIT Press, Massachusetts Institute of Technology, Cambridge, Massachusetts, and London, England.

ISBN 0-262-69155-8

The chapter, "Intelligent Decision Support for Assembly System Design," (Hernandez et al.) was funded by the Defense Advanced Research Projects Agency, contract MDA972-88-C-0027, and was approved for public release with unlimited distribution under OASD(PA) 2/7/91.

Trademarks

Contents

IAAI–92 Program Committee

Jan Aikins, *AION*
Bruce Buchanan, *University of Pittsburgh*
Elizabeth Byrnes, *Banker's Trust Company*
Ed Feigenbaum, *Knowledge Systems Lab, Stanford University*
Mark Fox, *University of Toronto*
Philip Klahr, *Inference Corp*
Alain Rappaport, *Neuron Data*
Earl Sacerdoti, *The Copernican Group*
Herb Schorr, *USC/ISI*
Carli Scott, *Expert Support, Inc.*
Howie Shrobe, *Symbolics*
Reid Smith, *Schlumberger Lab for Computer Science*
Richard J. Wood, *AICorp.*

Preface

Innovative Applications of Artificial Intelligence 4 is the fourth volume in a series highlighting the successful application of artificial intelligence (AI) techniques to real-world problems. The applications selected this year illustrate that AI has matured as a set of commercially viable technologies. AI technology has infiltrated a huge number of companies around the world and has enabled these companies to solve significant business problems and achieve major business benefits.

In the initial volume of this series, most of the applications represented the first attempts by various organizations to put AI to practical use. In this volume, we see the next generation of applications developed in organizations that no longer view AI as risky, but rather as stable technology. American Express and Swiss Bank Corporation, for example, are each working toward a corporate computing environment in which cooperative AI applications interact. In the first volume, we saw many applications by companies that traditionally have been early adopters of new technology; this year we see that AI applications are appearing also in companies that traditionally have waited to use proven technologies.

The book presents AI applications in a variety of industries such as finance and banking, telecommunications, automotive and transportation. The applications address a variety of tasks such as customer service, data analysis, design, and planning. As computer scientists, we are particularly interested this year to see AI applied to our own field. Three applications address different aspects of software development:

automatic program generation, inspection and analysis of source code, and analysis of core dumps. Although many applications are aimed as solving problems local to a single organization, the PHAROS system, developed by National Westminster Bank, illustrates how AI can be used to help companies adjust to more global changes, such as the formation of a single European market.

The applications described in this book not only demonstrate the commercial value of software systems employing AI techniques but also delineate the process by which these software systems are developed and deployed. The book points out the techniques or combination of techniques that are useful in particular circumstances or the difficulties encountered in applying or integrating different techniques. It teaches about project management, for example, the steps required in planning and coordinating the many activities that lead to the finished software product. It illustrates the importance of understanding and addressing the needs of the user community. Each application presents a case study that contains valuable lessons for those who will develop future AI applications.

– Carlisle Scott & Phil Klahr

Customer Service Applications

SMART: Support Management Automated Reasoning Technology for Compaq Customer Service

Timothy L. Acorn, Compaq Computer Corporation, and Sherry H. Walden, Inference Corporation

Because of the increasingly competitive nature of the computer manufacturing industry, Compaq Computer Corporation has made some trend-setting changes in the way it does business. One of these changes is the extension of Compaq's call-logging system to include a problem-resolution component that assists customer support personnel in determining the resolution to a customer's questions and problems.

Recently, Compaq extended its customer service to provide not only dealer support but also direct end user support; it is also accepting ownership of any Compaq customer's problems in a Banyan, Microsoft, Novell, or SCO UNIX operating environment. One of the tools that makes this feat possible is SMART (support management automated reasoning technology). SMART is part of a Compaq strategy to increase the effectiveness of the customer support staff and reduce overall cost to the organization by retaining problem-solving knowledge and making it available to the entire support staff at the point it is needed.

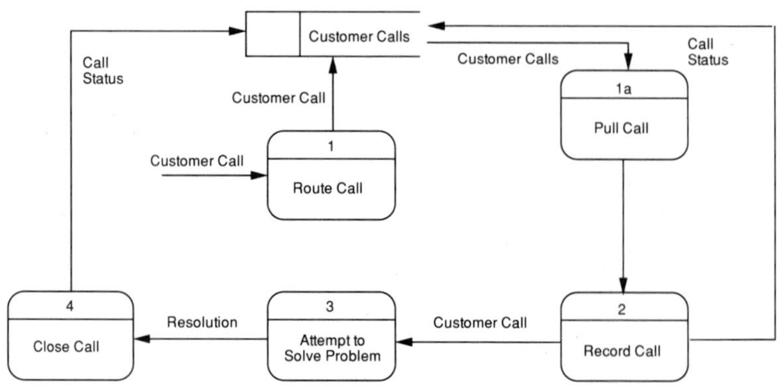

Figure 1. Problem-Resolution Work Flow.

Business Problem

Compaq is a multibillion dollar, Fortune 500 company listed on the New York Stock Exchange. Compaq is a manufacturer of personal computer systems, ranging from laptops to high-end systems. Compaq has gained a reputation for superior products, such as the Compaq LTE 386/20 notebook-sized computer and the high-end Compaq SYSTEM PRO.

In addition to providing high-quality products, one of Compaq's strategic business objectives is to provide quality support. Customer satisfaction is recognized as one of the company's top objectives.

With a tactical approach to providing customer satisfaction, personnel manning the telephone lines are required to respond to technical support requests in real time, online. The mission of the telephone support groups is to elate every customer by being accessible, responsive, enthusiastic, courteous, helpful, and caring.

Compaq utilizes an automatic call distributor to route support requests to its technical support engineers. The support engineer is required to answer the telephone, gather caller and support request information, log the call into the call-logging system, analyze the information or problem-resolution request, conduct research or perform problem duplication or resolution, and deliver the information or solution. The engineer uses various electronic and hard-copy resources as well as works with his/her peers in responding to support requests (figure 1).

As with most computer manufacturers, Compaq's price for each unit is continuing to decrease to remain cost competitive. A reduction in the price translates into fewer dollars available to implement support programs to keep up with the ever-increasing user support requirements.

Many corporations are moving from mainframe environments to distributed, local area network (LAN)–based architectures. In a recent *COMPUTERWORLD* analysis of management information system organizations, 8 of the 10 industry groups surveyed identified LANs as one of their top three critical technologies (Premier 1991).

Companies that are evaluating the use of local area network computer systems in lieu of larger computer systems still expect the level of support that is traditionally available in the mainframe world. To meet this expectation, Compaq's Customer Service Department employed a strategy using AI to develop a system that will improve the quality of support by putting known solutions at the fingertips of its technical support engineers.

Members of the Compaq customer service telephone support organizations are required to provide technical support, ranging from product information requests to problem resolution in complex network environments on a vast array of product offerings. Support requests include inquiries about product specifications as well as requests for assistance to resolve technical issues. Needless to say, there are no typical questions and no typical day.

Traditionally, Compaq provided technical support to its dealer channels, which, in turn, provided support to the millions of computer users. In an effort to enhance customer satisfaction, in March 1991, Compaq opened a Customer Support Center. The Customer Support Center provided end users with the ability to call Compaq directly to request technical support.

The implementation of a Customer Support Center has more than doubled the number of support requests received by the telephone support groups. Compaq's telephone support groups handle thousands of support requests each day. With the introduction of an ever-expanding product line to meet user support requirements in a high technology area, staffing levels to support these products would continue to grow. The Compaq Customer Service Department needed a means to more effectively and efficiently handle the increasing volume of support requests.

In anticipation of the increase in the number of calls with the advent of the new customer support services, the customer service telephone support groups grew by 100 percent. Such a significant increase in staffing levels brought with it training considerations and requirements.

Economic conditions, the cost of providing technical support, the complexity of the support environment, customer requirements and expectations, an increase in call volume, an increase in training requirements, staffing levels, desired service levels, as well as other factors, were all considerations in deciding to build additional support tools.

Business Requirement

To meet its technical support objectives, the Customer Service Department must provide the following: information at the point of need; continuous availability of expertise; consistency in answers and responses; accurate, technically sound answers and responses; a reduction in the need to resolve problems multiple times; a learning aid for employees with limited domain knowledge; and retention of corporate knowledge.

Traditionally, hotline organizations can receive the same support request numerous times each day. A mechanism was required that could capture information—or the resolution to a problem—and provide this information to the technical support engineers, who, in turn, could supply the information or resolution to the customer in real time. The information or resolution needed to be in a format similar to the way technical experts receive the support request.

Compaq's technical support organization has been in place for several years. In 1989, the Customer Service Department installed a new problem management and reporting system (call-logging system). The new problem-resolution system would need to interface with the call-logging system, as well as all existing, associated software. Also, Compaq has one of the largest LANs in the world. The problem-resolution system would need to reside in, and be compliant with, the existing network environment.

The SMART Solution

To meet the company's objective of customer satisfaction, Compaq's Customer Service Department, in conjunction with Inference Corporation, developed and installed the SMART system.

Compaq implemented a problem-determination and problem-resolution assistant, SMART, using knowledge-based system technology. The technical approach applies a case-based reasoning, problem-solving paradigm to solve the customer problems. *Case-based reasoning* is a technique that adapts stored problem solutions (as cases or examples) to solve new problems.

Work Flow

SMART is now an integral part of the customer support engineer's work flow (figure 2). Each call received by a support engineer is recorded in the call-logging system.

The phases of technical support are (1) answer the phone, (2) gather caller and support request information, (3) log the call, (4) analyze the information or resolution request, (5) conduct research or prob-

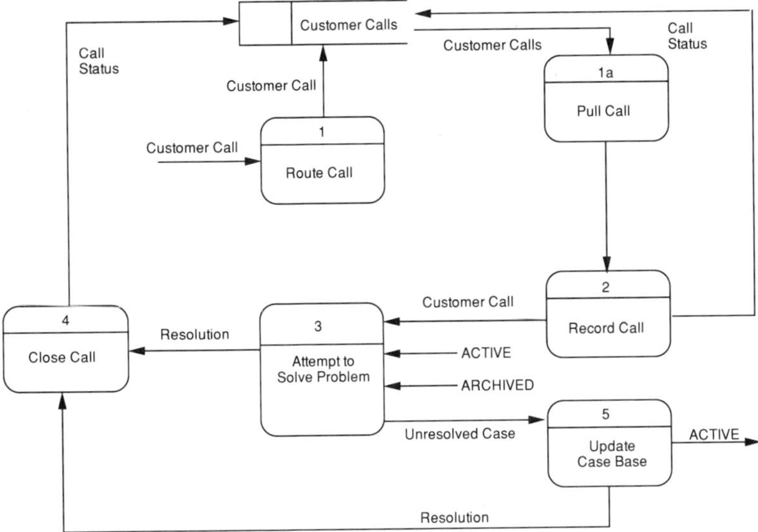

Figure 2. Problem-Resolution Work Flow Using SMART.

lem resolution, and (6) deliver information or solution.

Initially, the support engineer collects basic customer or dealer, information, that is, name, address, dealer identification, and so on. The support engineer then types a textual description of the information request or problem into the summary field of the call log. If the support engineer knows the answer based on its initial description, he/she relays it to the customer, records it in the call log, and closes the call log. If the support engineer needs further information or is unfamiliar with the domain the customer is inquiring about, he/she selects the SMART button on the call-logging screen (figure 3).

The summary description is automatically extracted from the call log and propagated to the description field of the SMART screen. An initial search is then performed. SMART looks for a case that matches the information request, or problem description, by analyzing the description string at a subword level using a trigram-matching algorithm (Inference 1991) that compares the contents of the information request against the description fields of previously stored cases. A case is a problem-scenario–problem-resolution pair consisting of a textual description, relevant questions and their corresponding answers, and a recommended resolution or action (figure 4).

After the first search, the support engineer is presented with a list of

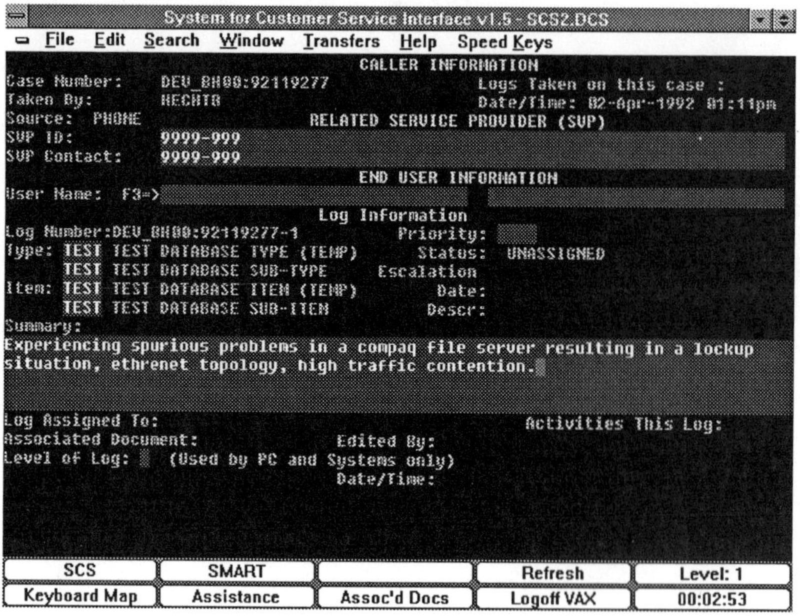

Figure 3. Call-Logging Screen through WINDOWS*-Based Terminal Emulator.*

the best matching cases. Additionally, SMART displays the questions associated with these cases. The support engineer uses this list of questions to request additional information from the customer to better define the problem. As the answer to each question is provided to SMART, a new search is performed. As more information is provided, SMART provides an increasingly accurate set of relevant cases and associated questions. At any time in the process, the support engineer can browse through supporting information associated with the question, matching cases or associated actions (figure 5).

The numbers from 0 to 100 located to the far left of each case title represent the degree of relevance given to the case by SMART. The *degree of relevance* represents the percentage of this case's information that matches the information provided by the support engineer on the problem definition. The degree of relevance considers the worth of the description with respect to accurately representing the problem scenario, the match and mismatch weights of answered questions, and the worth of unanswered questions. In the Compaq case base, a degree of relevance equal to or greater than 70 alerts the support engineer (through a textual color change of the matching cases) to a case that is similar or identical to the one presented by the customer (figure 6).

Once a case representing the current customer problem is located,

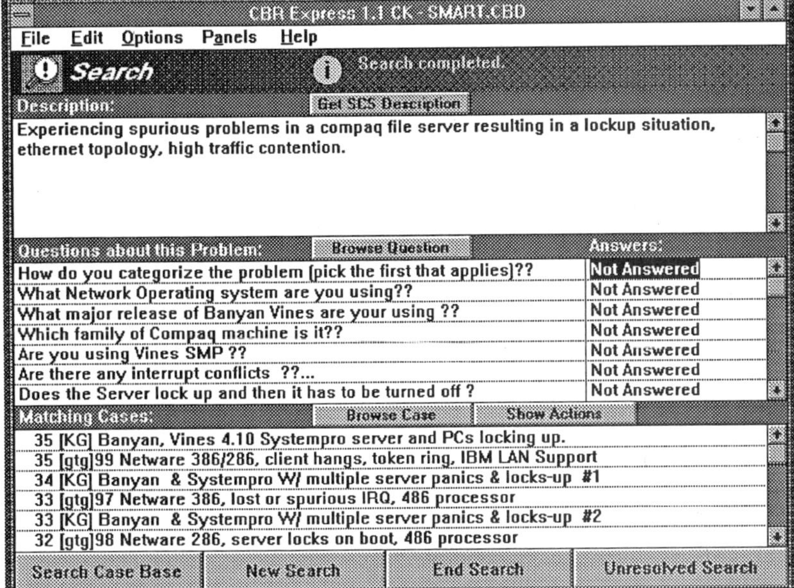

Figure 4. SMART *Screen after Initial Search.*

the support engineer relays the information, or solution, to the customer. To complete the exercise, the support engineer highlights the case and presses the end-search button.

The *session information*, which includes the contents of the description field, all answered questions, and the selected matching case and its corresponding resolution, is copied to the WINDOWS clipboard. The support engineer then returns to the call-logging screen. The support engineer completes the call log by pasting the session information into the resolution portion of the call log and closing it (figure 7).

If a matching case is not located, the support engineer presses the unresolved-search button. The session information is then stored in a case format in the case base with a status of unresolved. A reference to the call log number, the name of the support engineer, and a time stamp are stored with the case. Unresolved cases are later developed into actual cases by the case builders.

SMART has had the most impact on the fifth technical support phase (conduct research or problem resolution) of the process. SMART has enhanced the engineer's ability to provide timely, accurate information to customers, with minimal duplication of effort.

Justification for the SMART system was based on the ability to retard growth of the staffing levels. Based on Compaq's capital model analysis

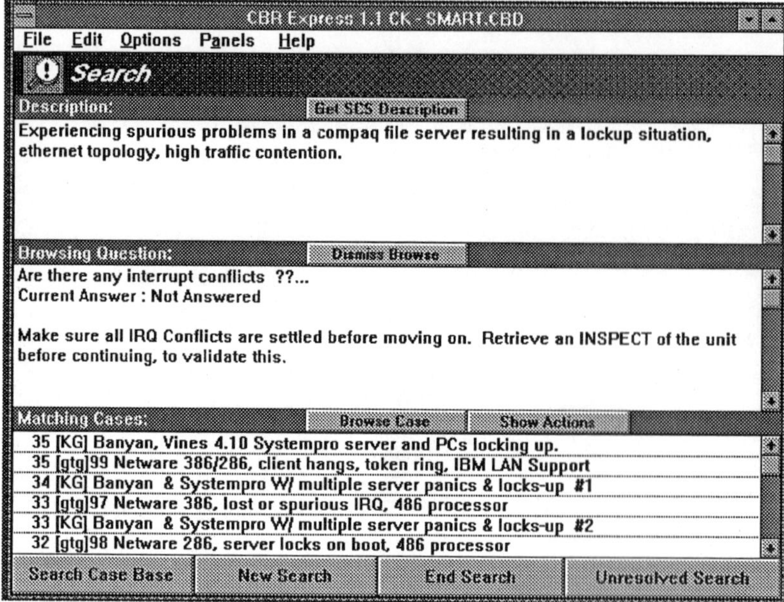

Figure 5. SMART *Screen Browsing for Supporting Information.*

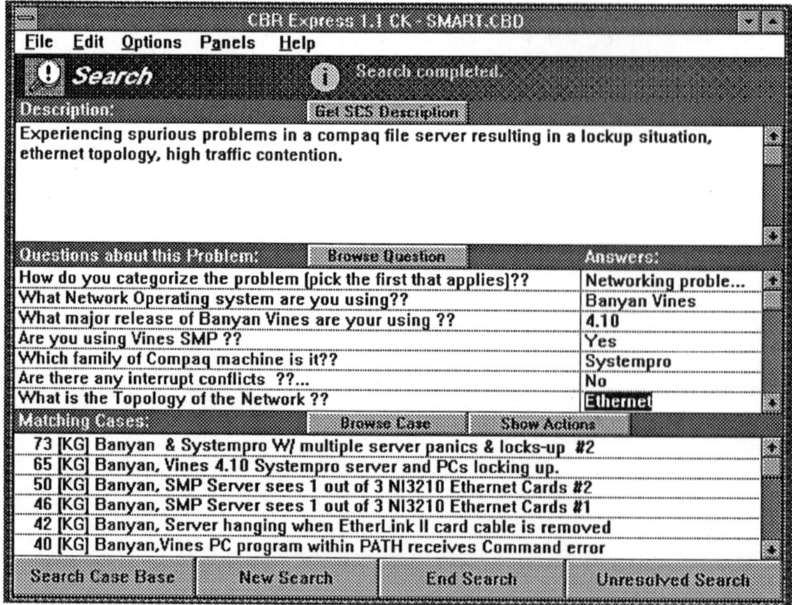

Figure 6. SMART *Screen after Matching Case Is Located.*

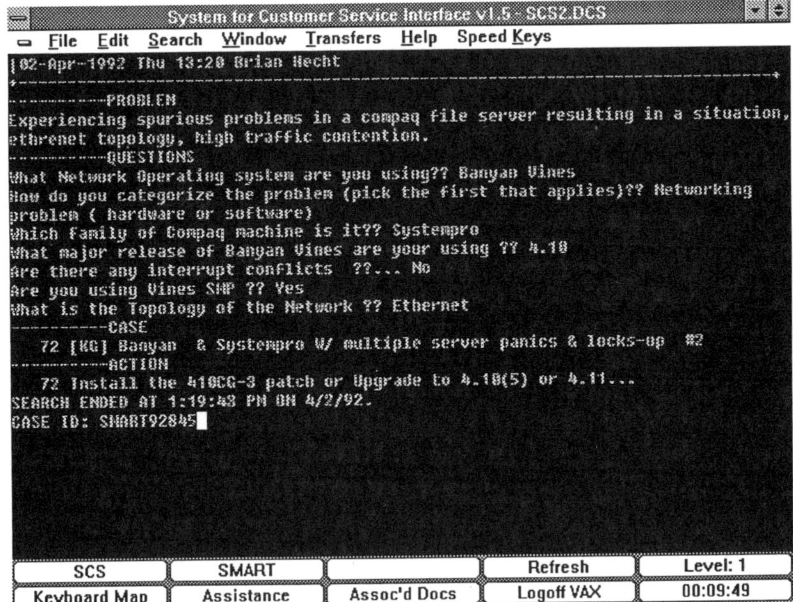
System for Customer Service Interface v1.5 - SCS2.DCS
File Edit Search Window Transfers Help Speed Keys
02-Apr-1992 Thu 13:20 Brian Hecht
PROBLEM
Experiencing spurious problems in a compaq file server resulting in a situation,
ethrenet topology, high traffic contention.
QUESTIONS
What Network Operating system are you using?? Banyan Vines
How do you categorize the problem (pick the first that applies)?? Networking
problem (hardware or software)
Which family of Compaq machine is it?? Systempro
What major release of Banyan Vines are your using ?? 4.10
Are there any interrupt conflicts ??... No
Are you using Vines SMP ?? Yes
What is the Topology of the Network ?? Ethernet
CASE
72 [KG] Banyan & Systempro W/ multiple server panics & locks-up #2
ACTION
72 Install the 410CG-3 patch or Upgrade to 4.10(5) or 4.11...
SEARCH ENDED AT 1:19:43 PM ON 4/2/92.
CASE ID: SMART92845
SCS
SMART
Refresh
Level: 1
Keyboard Map
Assistance
Assoc'd Docs
Logoff VAX
00:09:49

Figure 7. Call-Logging Screen with Resolution Pasted in Call Log.

of SMART, payback of the system was one year, with a high internal rate of return and net present value. Once installed, the SMART system changed the way technical support engineers perform their jobs. The work flow was enhanced with the advent of the SMART system.

The SMART Architecture

In this section, we discuss the various parts of the SMART architecture: the initial deployment architecture and the current subnetwork architecture and case base architecture.

Initial Deployment Architecture

SMART is a client-server architecture with user workstations running in a WINDOWS environment (figure 8).

As mentioned in Business Requirements, it was Compaq's desire to integrate SMART with existing software, that is, the VAX-based call-logging system, without modification to existing applications. To accomplish this task, Compaq upgraded from a DOS-based terminal emulator for VAX to a WINDOWS-based VT220 terminal emulator. Propagation of information between the call-logging system and SMART is accomplished

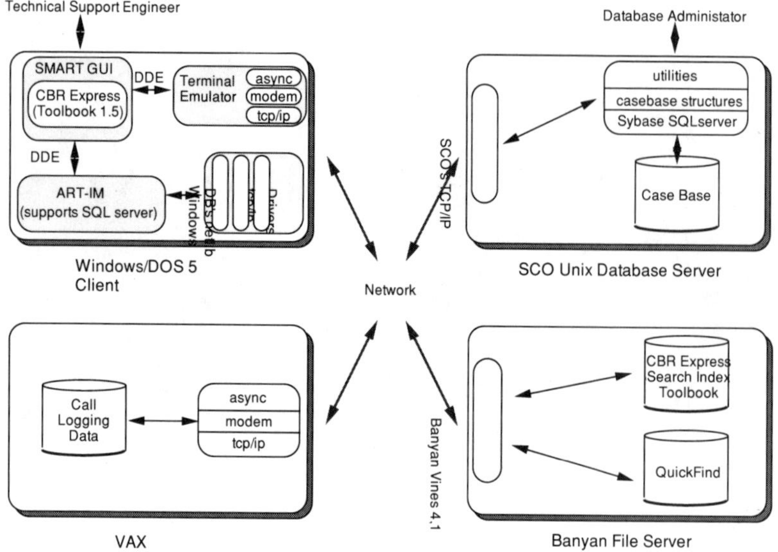

Figure 8. SMART System Architecture.

using the terminal emulator's scripting capability and communication with WINDOWS dynamic data exchange without any modification to the call-logging application.

Compaq promotes use of off-the-shelf products that provide an open architecture to avoid customization when additional or modified requirements are established. Therefore, cases are stored in a standard relational database, and the transport protocol between the user workstations and the case base is TCP-IP.

Multiple-Subnetwork Architecture

The system is currently deployed on two subnetworks. The Compaq campus network uses Banyan VINES. The campus LAN is composed of many subnetworks connected through a spine. To ensure consistently good network performance, each organization, which is usually located in close proximity, has its own subnetwork.

All the subnetworks travel the length of the campus. Each subnetwork supports more than 50 users, all of which are SMART users. Any user of the Compaq campus network can access the SMART system. SMART users access network files from their local subnetwork Banyan file server, and they access the case base from a local subnetwork, UNIX-based database server.

As additional Compaq departments begin using the SMART system, the Banyan file server–based files and the database server–based case base can be duplicated on each local subnetwork. A synchronization program, called SYNC SMART, synchronizes the case bases each evening to ensure they are identical, never taking SMART offline entirely.

Case Base Architecture

Compaq's case base currently consists of nine domain partitions. A domain partition is a collection of cases, all regarding a specific product line. The domain partitions include NOVELL, LAN Manager, BANYAN, Unix, DOS, Windows, OS/2, and general hardware and software. To ensure consistency among cases, high-reuse, or focusing, questions were established that are used in all cases in which they apply. Examples of this type of question include, Which network operating system are you using? Which processor does your machine use? Which family of Compaq products are you using? What operating environment are you using?

The SMART Case-Building Process

The case building model is a tiered approach, providing a mechanism of checks and balances to ensure accurate cases (figure 9). Designated senior support engineers have been trained as case builders. The list of unresolved cases is reviewed daily, and cases are assigned to the case builders based on domain specialty. The case builders review the session information captured during the call, research the problem, incorporate the session information into a case complete with resolution, change the status to active, and save it in the case base (figure 10). SMART is in continuous operation during this process, and once saved as active, the cases are immediately accessible by all users of SMART.

Results

This section discusses SMART's acceptance, deployment, and performance.

User Acceptance Criteria

The customer support organization—the user community—established acceptance criteria in the following areas: user interface, functions, performance, documentation, and maintenance.

The Compaq Human Factors Organization conducted a usability test of SMART in October 1991. The results of the study indicate that the probability of resolving a case is much higher when using the SMART sys-

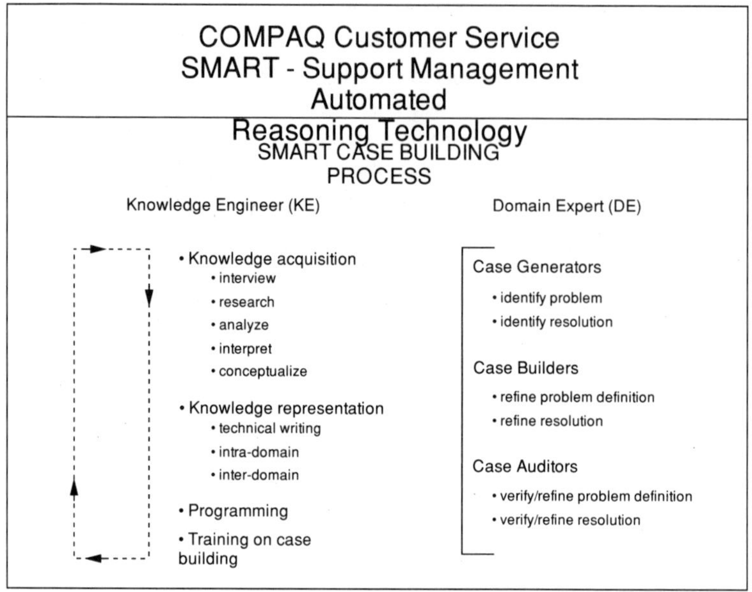

Figure 9. Case-Building Model.

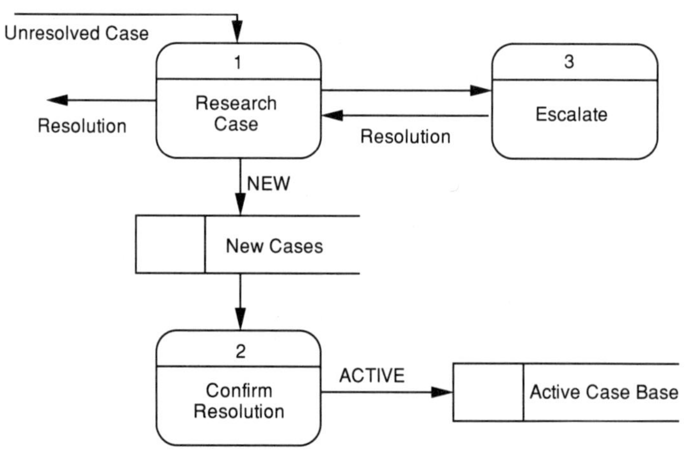

Figure 10. Case Base Update Work Flow.

tem. Altogether, less than 50 percent of the test cases were resolved without using the SMART system. When using the SMART system, 87 percent of the test cases were resolved.

Specific results of the test show the acceptance and usability of the SMART interface to be high and identify areas of SMART that require improvement. These areas include the transitions between the call-logging system and SMART and the advice-giving aspects of some of the cases.

As a result of this analysis, the functions of SMART were extended to provide more automated propagation of information between applications: For example, the call log number is now stored with unresolved cases, and SMART session information is captured for use in the call log. In addition, more specific information on creating consistent and complete cases was documented.

A follow-on study will be conducted by the Human Factors Organization after the January multi-subnet deployment.

SMART Deployment Timeline

1991

August: Lab online to support case building

September: Multiuser access in lab

November: Case base migrated to relational database; case builders online (12 users); phase 1 users (20 additional users)

December: First LAN completed (50+ users)

1992

January: Second LAN completed (50+ users)

SMART Performance

smart's performance is measured using two perspectives: time to resolution, where actual search speed is a factor, and probability of resolution. The performance criteria require less than two minutes for a problem resolution, assuming an average of five questions answered to reach a reasonable match. Currently, smart is taking three to five seconds for each search, depending on the hardware configuration of the user workstation. The minimum configuration is a 386-based computer with 6 megabytes of memory and a 10-megabyte swap partition.

The development of SMART included an analysis of the case base after it reached reasonable coverage, approximately 600 cases. Tools were used that automated the testing of the case base by constructing search strings that included variable amounts of randomly generated text and automated answering of questions. During the test, if questions are presented that are not associated with the case being tested, a randomly generated answer is provided. The tool also permits the tester to specify a percentage of questions that have the wrong answer provided. These tools have assisted the case builders in identifying cases that could be defined better.

Innovative Techniques and Aspects of SMART

Although the mechanics of case development are straightforward and actually trivial to grasp, effective case base development requires analysis of the domain and adherence to a style of case building. Early in the process of case development, Compaq realized a need for the development of a Case Construction Style Guide. The style guide establishes conventions and principles for case development, including the following areas: when to use list, text, yes-no, or numeric answers; what information the case description should include to increase the effectiveness of the first search; how many questions are associated with each case; how the questions are phrased; and which questions are included with each case.

As an example, one principle included in the Case Construction Style Guide is as follows:

When asking a related series of questions about an object, ask the most general questions first, and the most specific questions last (the Principle of Progressive Disclosure). If any of the specific questions make sense only for a particular answer of the more general question, make sure to use elimination scoring (Inference 1991) on the more general question (Compaq 1991).

In addition to establishing a case construction style, the style guide documents a methodology for the case-building process itself. Compaq is responsible for addressing a rapidly evolving platform of issues. The case-based reasoning paradigm provides the architectural flexibility that is required to adapt to this dynamic environment. The methodology outlines the logistical process that ensures the timely inclusion of cases that address even the most recent issues.

A bottleneck in the development of knowledge-based systems has traditionally been the knowledge-acquisition process. The SMART system is designed to permit the users to populate the knowledge themselves in the form of cases. Knowledge engineers were instrumental in the development of Compaq's Case Construction Style Guide, but case building and maintenance is the responsibility of the user community.

Compaq has always made important information available to its support engineers in the form of product manuals, technical reference notes, service advisories and bulletins, an online information resource, electronic mail, and so on. SMART is not only an information resource in a format more useful for a support organization (that is, in the form of resolutions to problems); it also ensures that information is available to the support engineer at the point it is required. Application of knowledge at the time of need reduces time to resolution significantly.

Finally, the SMART system is a real-time, online production, knowledge-based system built with off-the-shelf products on general-purpose hardware, all Compaq, of course. Compaq is committed to empowering its employees with the tools required to excel in the industry as a service provider. SMART is an innovative, leading-edge example of one such tool.

Summary

Using AI technology, Compaq now captures the knowledge its support engineers use to solve customer problems and folds it back into SMART, making it available for reuse. In addition to facilitating the business of servicing its customers, Compaq now has this information in a tangible form as well as a means of continuing to collect this information.

Compaq is now investigating methods of extending the automation of SMART in two ways: (1) adding intelligent parsing mechanisms that deduce the answers to questions from information contained in, and implied from, free-form text entries and (2) answering new questions from previously answered questions.

Acknowledgments

We would like to thank our case builders Jose Bolua, Robert Brimer, Larry Edington, George Gayle, Ken Githens, Robert Jellison, Nick Kostoff, Eddie Martinez, Erwin Nicolau, Robert Proffitt, John Sawyer, and Mike Wideman; the Compaq Computer Corporation knowledge engineers Brian Hecht and Trung Nguyen; and the Inference Corporation knowledge engineers David Coles, Gary Vrooman, and Steve Lindner. A special thanks goes to Melvin Lyon and Dick Kleven of Compaq and Daniel Lee and Lewis Roth of Inference for making it happen.

References

Compaq Computer Corporation. 1991. Case Construction Style Guide. Compaq Computer Corporation, Houston, Texas.

Inference Corporation. 1991. Case-Based Reasoning in ART-IM. Inference Corporation, Los Angeles, Calif.

Inference Corporation. 1991. CBR Express User's Guide. Inference Corporation, Los Angeles, Calif.

The Premier 100: Analysis of the Top 100 MIS Organizations in the United States. 1991. *COMPUTERWORLD,* Sept. 30, 1991.

A Knowledge-Based System within a Cooperative Processing Environment

Dale B. Danilewitz, Whirlpool Corporation, and
Frederick E. Freiheit IV, Technology Solutions Corporation

CADS (consumer appliance diagnostic system) is a diagnostic and advisory knowledge-based system that provides advice through call-taking representatives to consumers calling the Whirlpool Consumer Assistance Center (CAC). Even though this application is not an original AI application, valuable lessons can be learned from the process that was followed during its development and integration into a revolutionary support system for a customer service operation (the Consumer Assistance Center System [CACS]). Whirlpool CACS was developed and implemented over a 3-year period with a financial investment of over $20 million. Whirlpool recognized the necessity of pursuing an advanced technological solution to the problem of handling an ever-growing number of customer calls. Over 250 call-taking representatives are currently handling as many as 1.7 million calls annually, which is projected to grow to approximately 9 million calls by 1995. This chapter focuses on CADS and how it will strengthen Whirlpool's ability to respond to customer requests as well as create a front-line source for quality information on Whirlpool products. CADS plays a synergistic role in CACS by either accessing other components to enhance its decision-making

Taking a Call from a Consumer and Consulting the CACS.

ability or providing it with additional information from which to efficiently support the consumer.

CADS is intended to support the call-taking representative when he/she responds to a variety of calls being taken through a toll-free telephone line. A call usually takes one of the following forms: asking for help with an appliance that seems to be malfunctioning, soliciting advice on using or installing an appliance, asking for information on an appliance, or requesting a technician to service the appliance. Two levels of representatives are dedicated to supporting these calls. The initial call takers, or *front-end representatives*, can respond to general calls about appliance information, schedule a service call for the consumer, order replacement or additional parts on request, or screen the consumer before transferring him/her to a more technically adept representative. The *technical representative* is on hand to guide the consumer through a diagnostic procedure that leads to a successful resolution to the consumer's problem.

The Need for CADS

One of the most important roles of CADS is to bridge the knowledge chasm that exists between the two levels of representatives. The front-end representative is usually a person who recently joined Whirlpool and has little knowledge or experience with Whirlpool products. The representative is hired into this position based on the ability to communicate over the telephone with a confident, yet compassionate attitude. Training consists of an elementary introduction to Whirlpool products with emphasis on how to expeditiously access sources of detailed information. The technical representative is an extension of the front-end representative with at least five years of experience (usually from the field) in handling appliance problems. Unfortunately, there are insufficient technical representatives to support the growing number of technical calls, with limited prospects for adding more because of the reluctance of experienced technicians to take desk jobs and the disparity of the skills required of the technicians who take this position.

CADS also presents more tangible benefits to the company by helping to eliminate unnecessary service calls. Before CADS, the call-taking representative would condense the consumer's problem to a one-line description when calling to schedule a service. The technician responding to the request for assistance would travel to the consumer's home and diagnose the problem. The technician would then do one of the following: inform the consumer of the incorrect use of the appliance, replace a malfunctioning part in the appliance, readjust a consumer's unsuccessful attempt at fixing the problem, or reschedule a return to the consumer's home to replace a previously unavailable part. The consumer is inconvenienced by the additional call, and Whirlpool incurs the expense of additional service calls, especially when the appliance is under warranty.

The following is an analysis of the anticipated savings that were mapped out as a justification for developing CADS: It was conservatively estimated that 15 percent of repeat calls would be eliminated with the effective use of CADS. If the cost for a call remained static over the next five-year period, and the number of calls requesting service increased by about 10 percent annually, the approximate savings obtained during this period would be $1.5 million for in-warranty calls and $2.5 million for out-of-warranty calls. This figure excludes the approximately $2 million that would be saved by eliminating in-warranty calls that occur because of incorrect use or installation of the appliance.

Further intangible benefits were anticipated and are now being realized. These benefits are discussed in Current Status of CADS.

Functional Overview of CADS

CADS was implemented as a standard graphic user interface with the capability of coexisting as a component of the larger application, CACS. The user selects a response from a list of answers to a question displayed in a question window. Each question is offered to the caller in a paraphrased form by the user. The customer responds with an interpretation of what can be observed about the problem with the appliance. The answers are not necessarily mutually exclusive but often overlap to provide the user with the confidence of not misguiding the system by entering an inappropriate answer. The knowledge base is structured so that qualifying questions are offered if the response is not specific enough.Different entry points in the knowledge base address the problem created by the system of having to support many levels of technical competency among consumers. For example, one consumer might suggest a problem with dishes not coming out clean after completing a dishwasher cycle, but another consumer might have already performed some simple tests to determine that the dishes are dirty because the dishwasher dispenser is not opening at certain points in the cycle. Both situations might lead to the same diagnosis, but the first consumer will be asked more questions and go into a greater amount of detail than the second consumer.

The questions used by CADS are designed to prevent the consumer from performing any mechanical or electrical testing of the appliance. The consumer is asked to report on what is observed either during the initial running of the appliance when the problem was first observed or after running certain tests. The consumer might realize the answer by seeing, hearing, feeling, or smelling the problem.

CADS then suggests one of three scenarios after diagnosing the probable cause of the malfunctioning appliance: The system might explain to the user how to resolve the problem that occurred because of incorrect use of the appliance (consumer instruct), the system might recognize that the problem was caused as a result of a bad installation or electric problems in the home and have the consumer first call the installer or electrician or plumber to resolve the problem, or the system might identify a part or list of parts that could have caused the problem and suggest servicing the unit. In the last case, suggested part names and corresponding part numbers are placed on the technician's service work order, and control is transferred to a scheduling system to schedule the service call.

Certain utilities were added to CADS to improve the accuracy of the diagnosis and offer subsequent advice to encourage consistent use of the system.

Receiving Context-Sensitive Help

At any stage during a consultation, the user can request more information about a question or how to interpret an answer if it does not match one of the responses provided. When the help button is depressed, the system displays text directly related to the question and its effect on the reasoning of the system. This technique has been beneficial when using the system with live calls and adds a level of credibility to the reasoning process. It also acts as a supplemental training tool.

Accessing an Image System

A second level of help is provided by one of the cooperative systems within CACS, an image system. Technical and user documentation on all models of appliances is provided directly to the users through an image-retrieval system that contains over 175,000 scanned pages stored on a CD-ROM. The image-retrieval system allows users to acquire information directly through a menu-driven interface or indirectly through an application such as CADS.

CADS was built to diagnose problems for over 12 appliance types at a level at which the consumer would be able to provide diagnostic input. It became apparent that it would not be feasible either functionally or financially to have model-specific diagnoses for over 20,000 appliance models. Precision is compromised by the generality of the rules, with the lowest level of questions discriminating between brands (Whirlpool owns the three brands Whirlpool, KitchenAid, and Roper) and major functional differences between the appliances, such as side-by-side versus top-mount or bottom-mount refrigerators.

This problem of gaining specificity existed at both the question and advisory levels. For example, the consumer might be asked whether the refrigerator thermostat is set to the middle setting. The consumer might respond that he/she is not familiar with what the middle setting of his/her particular model of refrigerator is. The call-taker will access, the system accesses the literature on the specific model through an image button associated with the CADS question, which will display the location of the thermostat and what the middle setting should be. Direct access to image is also especially beneficial when a diagnosis refers to use and care instructions. These model-specific instructions are found by selecting an image button from the resolution screen.

Having a Familiarity with a Model's Features and Components

CADS has access to a database arranged by model number that consists of all the features and some of the components contained within every appliance. This database eliminates the need to ask questions about features or components that do not apply for the appliance model being diagnosed. Thus, CADS will not ask a question specific to top-mount refrigerators if the refrigerator model is a side by side, or suggest a defrost timer as a part that might have failed if the refrigerator is not frost free.

Rules about features that certain types of appliances will or will not have are also contained in the knowledge base (see later discussion). Once the system recognizes that it is not dealing with a KitchenAid trash compactor, for example, then all questions associated with charcoal air filters (specific only to KitchenAid) are avoided.

Suspending a Diagnostic Session

Certain situations require that the consumer be able to call back to resume a suspended consultation. A CADS session might be suspended because the telephone line was disconnected, the consumer could not answer a question because he/she was calling at a location remote from the appliance, or the consumer had to run a test and call back with the results. The architecture of CACS is defined around a series of local area networks (LANs) that are connected over multiple locations to form a wide-area network (WAN). The return call is directed to any one of 250 representatives at a site in either Knoxville, Tennessee, or Benton Harbor, Michigan, that is transparent to the consumer.

When the consumer suspends a CADS session, the session is stored in a mainframe database associated with the consumer's current profile. CACS detects the origin of the call through an automatic telephone number identification facility and alerts the representative that the consumer might be calling back to resume a previously suspended session. Once confirmed, the session is automatically reloaded onto the representative's machine, and the CADS session is restored without loss of context.

Rescinding a Selection

CADS allows a user to back up to a previous question if he/she wants to change an answer. This change might result from an incorrect user selection or a change of heart by the consumer. The system then pursues an alternative path of reasoning based on the new answer. All previously asserted answers that were system implications are undone to maintain the validity of the consultation.

This facility has the additional benefit of allowing a trainee to learn about hypothetical cases and what the answer would have been if an alternative selection had been made.

Handling Uncertainty

If the consumer is unsure of an answer, the user selects "don't know." Currently, the system is set up to follow a path that leads to the most general solution in the current context. This approach is being modified to force the system to traverse all the alternative paths and either lead to a conclusion that contains more than one suggested solution or lead to a solution that was not contradicted by subsequent questions.

More Precise Scheduling of Service Calls

Once the solution has been determined and a list of probable faulty parts identified, CADS searches a central database for the part numbers that correspond to the replacement parts. The consumer is informed that a service call might be necessary to correct the problem and is immediately transferred within CAC to a scheduling system to plan the call. The scheduling system identifies the most appropriate technician to run the call and checks the inventory of parts that the technician has in stock. One of the factors influencing when the technician is available to run the call is the availability of parts suggested by CADS. Ideally, the technician makes the call once he/she has all the parts that CADS suggested as necessary to successfully complete the call.

The parts suggested by CADS are usually high-turnover parts, and if not used on this particular call, they will most probably be used on a future call. This process establishes a store of inventory for each technician and location that contains the parts with the highest turnover, thereby creating a customized and more manageable inventory system.

Prioritizing the List of Parts

The user decides whether to schedule the service call if only a subset of parts is available to the technician. CADS helps by prioritizing the list of parts according to the rate of failure for each part for the model number or model group.

For example, CADS might suggest the following three parts as possibly causing the consumer's problem: defrost heater, defrost timer, and thermostat. CADS lists these parts in descending order of failure rate for the specific model number. Suppose that for this model, the defrost timer contributes 50 percent of all part failures, the defrost heater contributes 20 percent, and the thermostat contributes 5 percent. If the user is informed that the technician does not have the correct thermostat in stock but does have the other two parts, then the chances are that the user will proceed with scheduling the service call. However, this case might not be so if the defrost timer is the unavailable part.

These failure rates are specific to the model number and might show completely different results for a different appliance model. The part failure rates are accessed from a central database that is continually being updated. Therefore, this heuristic is dependent on current failure rates that reflect a snapshot of the pattern of part failures corresponding to particular models at any point in time.

Creating a Diagnostic Trace for the Technician

The diagnostic system generates and stores a trace of the consultation, including the resolution, the correct procedure to follow (including service pointers), and a list of suggested parts and corresponding part numbers. As soon as a technician is scheduled to service the appliance, these results are linked to the corresponding service work order that is available to the technician in the field through a hand-held computer.

Once the service call is completed, a failure code and the parts that were replaced are resubmitted to the system database through a modem from the hand-held computer. This procedure acts as a validation check of the knowledge base and an assessment of the part failure rates.

Development Details

All texts on successful knowledge-based system deployment (Prerau 1990; Irgon et al. 1990; Bahill, Harris, and Senn 1988) emphasize the need for management sponsorship and the assessment of management and user expectations. Early sponsorship was easily obtained because of the insights that upper management brought to the early specifications. The original project was conceived by upper management, which established a solid ground on which to proceed. It was the responsibility of the CADS development team to sustain this positive attitude. This task was achieved by decomposing the project into manageable tasks that would produce demonstrable results.

We chose a rapid application-development approach by proceeding through successive cycles of modeling a problem, implementing the resultant model, and then testing it. Prototypes were developed and tested for every new product type added to the knowledge base.

The CADS architecture and coding were developed by two knowledge engineers and a system programmer. The tasks of knowledge acquisition and representation were separated from that of implementation to develop a sound knowledge model that was not reliant on the characteristics of the expert system shell.

A knowledge engineer worked with the experts and users to extract the relevant information and formalize the knowledge into a decision tree–like structure that could be encoded into the expert system shell. An expert in the ADS development tool dealt with the nuances of the shell and translated the acquired knowledge into a supportive representation (discussed later). He was also responsible for manipulating the shell to address the needs suggested by the system (trace and backing up) and domain requirements (forward chaining on model features). The system programmer was responsible for creating the interfaces from CADS to the other components of the larger system and ensuring that accurate data were being transmitted to and from the applications and databases. He was also responsible for developing the user interface in PRESENTATION MANAGER that was to interact with the underlying ADS tool.

Fundamental expertise for the system was supplied by a 25-year veteran technician whose skills spanned Whirlpool brands and products as well as the delivery of technical advice over the telephone. In conformance with advice and insights provided by Prerau (1990), this technician was appointed lead expert. He was selected because of his knowledge and experience, his demonstrated ability to communicate, his vision of the benefits that could be realized through such a system, his willingness to work on the project, and the respect afforded him by his peers. His most valuable trait that had the greatest bearing on the outcome of the project was his modesty, which allowed him to recognize weaknesses in his knowledge. This trait was surmounted by his research of other knowledge sources to supplement his own. It is doubtful that the system would have succeeded without his outstanding contribution.

We were fortunate in acquiring the assistance and commitment of three other experts: a second field technician, a technical representative, and a front-end representative. The field technician was used to verify the knowledge in the system to ensure soundness and completeness. He accomplished this task by generating hundreds of hypothetical and bona fide cases and testing them against the system. The technical and front-end representatives were instrumental in periodically authenticating and refining the wording of the questions. Questions were disambiguated and customized to address the subtle differences in the wide range of callers that are Whirlpool consumers. Proposed users were involved in prototyping the iterative design of the user interface.

CADS development spanned approximately 11 months from its inception to the first phase of deployment.

Knowledge Maintenance and Problem Detection

An infrastructure was created to address the future maintenance needs of the knowledge. As with any manufacturing company, products are frequently introduced, and new problems surface with these and existing products. Therefore, *knowledge maintenance* was defined as "maintaining knowledge integrity, adding depth and breadth to the knowledge, and removing irrelevant or obsolete knowledge."

The user community appointed respective users to coordinate with a knowledge engineer to manage these tasks. This user ownership was critical to supporting the creation of a communication channel between the manufacturing and servicing segments of the business. Thus, the flow of knowledge about new appliances and problems to CADS was achieved.

The integrity of the knowledge base is divided into two sections: ensuring that correct parts and advice are provided within a problem context and ensuring that the appropriate sequence and wording of questions are maintained. For every service call, the technician records the failure and the parts that are replaced. These reports are submitted directly to the central database, which is checked against the suggested diagnosis from CADS. A CADS failure to suggest the correct parts and diagnosis might result from incomplete or inaccurate knowledge or from an invalid consumer response to a question. As a check, selected technicians transmit a comparison of the appliance status against the trace of the CADS consultation to ascertain where the problem occurred. If this check produces incongruous results, then the questions are reviewed for ambiguities; otherwise, the knowledge base itself is updated.

CACS Environment

CADS is a subcomponent of a large cooperative processing application, CACS, operating over various networks and at remote sites. We are concentrating on CADS as a subprocess within the overall CAC system, noting which services are supplied by CACS and those that are supplied

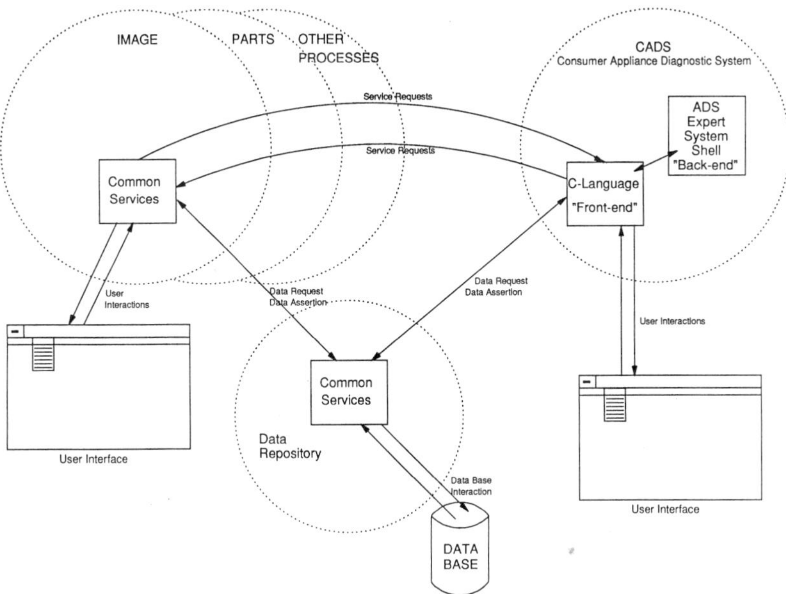

Figure 1. CACS *Distributed Environment.*

from within CADS.

Figure 1 illustrates the configuration of CADS and CACS within the cooperative environment, demonstrating that each has independent and dependent functions to facilitate communication between other processes and the user.

CACS Architecture

The user interfaces to CACS consist of two main forms: the hand-held field unit and the workstation. CADS is not intended to operate on the hand-held device, which is a DOS-based machine using a cellular modem to communicate with mainframe databases. The workstations are PS/2s running OS/2 CICS and operating off token ring networks. The LANs are linked by mainframe-based WANs. Database services are provided from a number of locations and are intended to be transparent from the view of the workstation (although, in practice, the location of the database is considered because of communication time constraints). The CACS user interacts with CACS through a standard CUA graphic interface. Functions are provided in logical units encapsulated as screens. Screens can operate independently of each other and are constrained by the interdependence of the specific business function being provided.

An incoming telephone call is routed to a workstation where a front-end representative, the user, interacts with CACS and the consumer to resolve the problem. If a consumer requests servicing of an appliance, the user is (optionally) routed through CADS to help determine what the problem is. Basic information, such as the make and model number of the appliance, is gathered from the consumer, if it does not already exist within CACS databases, before invoking CADS. This information is made available to CADS on invocation (CADS requests additional information directly from the user). After a diagnosis is derived, CADS places it into a data repository. The data repository resides on the workstation and is responsible for routing data to and from appropriate CACS databases. Data in the repository are immediately available to all processes residing on the workstation. If CADS recommends that a service call be scheduled, the recommended repair parts are accessed directly by the CACS scheduling subsystem.

CADS Architecture

CADS is divided into two asynchronous components: a front end implemented in C and a back end implemented in Aion's expert system shell ADS. The C-based front end provides the means by which the ADS back end communicates with the rest of the world. The front end consists of components that deliver the following functions: PRESENTATION MANAGER windowing user interface, file handling, imaging interface, backup, diagnostic tracing, suspension and restoration of a diagnostic session, and database interfacing.

Figure 2 presents the Ptolemaic view of CADS within CACS. The primary components of CACS that CADS interacts with are image, consumer services, service work orders (SWOs), and parts.

The ADS back end is the expert system shell that the diagnostic rules are implemented in. ADS was chosen from the shells that run under OS/2 because it supplies a rich set of required capabilities, including object-oriented programming; forward and backward chaining; extendibility through a C interface; the ability to run under DOS, OS/2, and several mainframe environments; and support of direct interfaces to various database formats.

The ADS object-oriented properties were used to implement CADS. A hierarchy of question, answer, and solution objects incorporates common methods and data. The expert's diagnostic knowledge is represented as standard production rules (if-then rules), where each rule

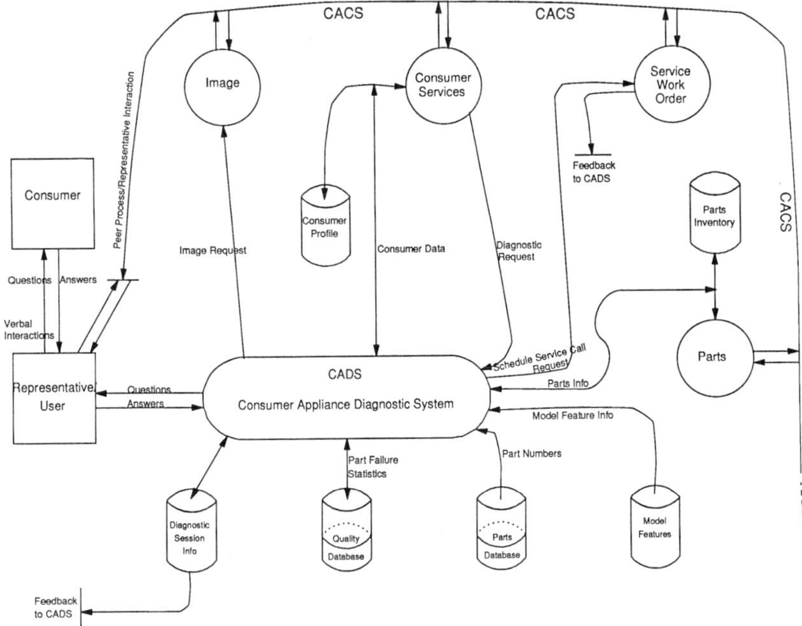

Figure 2. Ptolemeic View of CADS and CACS.

corresponds to a specific diagnosis. Rules are classified into a hierarchy of rule classes or states, each state containing related rules.

The *solution object* is the superclass for diagnostic solutions within CADS. It consists of a method to fire the rule and slots containing the attributes of the particular solution, including the solution ID, the diagnostic result text, recommendations about whether to schedule service or do it yourself, a recommended parts list, and a reference to any corresponding image indexes. Descendant classes of instances for specific appliance types are created primarily for efficiency and ease of maintenance, such as "air conditioner" and "refrigerator" classes. Question and answer object classes are similarly constructed. See figure 3.

CADS Reasoning

CADS uses a mix of forward and backward chaining to arrive at a diagnosis. When firing a rule, all the question-response pairs (conditions) of the rule (the if part) must be confirmed. CADS forward chains when a question is flagged as having an implies relationship. The implies relationship defines the interdependence of question-response pairs. For example, after recognizing that the refrigerator is frost free, CADS up-

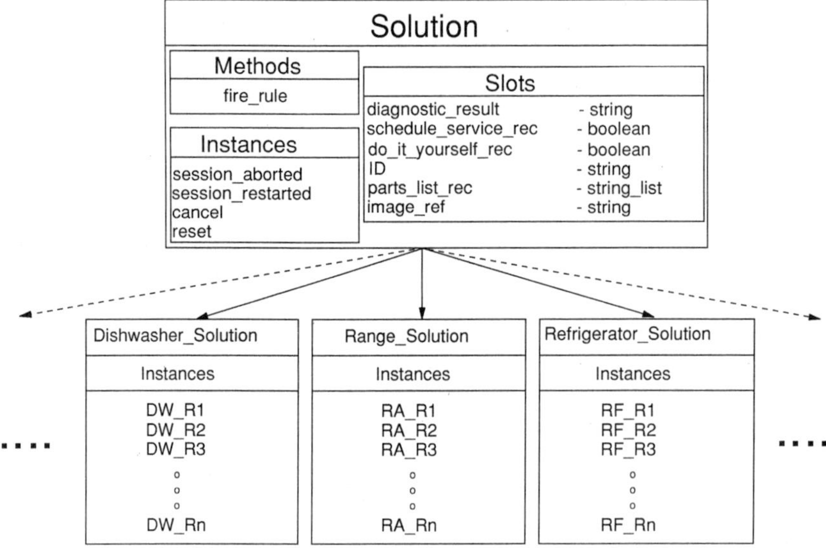

Figure 3. Solution Class Hierarchy.

dates the working memory by asserting facts common to all frost-free refrigerators, such as that they only contain compact model ice makers. These implications can be compounded such that a combination of facts leads to further assertions of facts. When a response to a question is flagged as implying further information, it fires an attached ADS demon method to resolve the implied relationship. This method forward chains across a state containing rules that represent the implied relationships. A chain reaction of new fact assertions can propagate across the implies rule set because one assertion can imply new assertions.

The rule body (the then part) constitutes either a call to a subclass of rules (more specific diagnosis) or instantiates a resolution to terminate the reasoning. A method attached to the corresponding solution instance is responsible for instantiating all resultant values (see later discussion) when a final resolution is found. The qualifying subclass of rules is invoked by backward chaining over a newly established goal that is more specific than the prior one.

When the user is prompted for an answer, the ADS back end passes the identification of the question object to the front end, which contains the following attributes: the text of the question, the set of possible response texts, the type of the question, an indicator of whether the question is a model feature (system driven), a help reference, and an image reference. The front end populates a window with the relevant details and displays it. If the user selects one of the responses to the question, the question is pushed onto a stack of question-response values, and the response is passed to the ADS back end. If another action is selected, such as a request for help or image, the front end services these requests and then returns to the original question to await a response.

If the user requests backing up to a previous question, the ADS back end is sent a message indicating the user's intention. The session is restarted, and the front end pops the questions off the stack until the requested question is reached. All question-response pairs and implications made after the selected question are retracted and present a state consistent with the new selections. (A similar method is used for suspended sessions that are being restored.)

Current Status of CADS

At the time this chapter was written, CADS had been deployed for 11 months. During this period, Whirlpool was shifting the operation of scheduling service calls from the field branches to CAC. Thus, CADS was initially used in stand-alone mode in the field and as a support tool for the call-taking representatives and was slowly phased in to CACS. A tracking system was installed to compute the frequency of use of CADS during this transition phase and was found to be used by about 150 representatives approximately 4000 times each month, with the greatest concentration of calls being advice to consumers on incorrect use of their appliances. During this period, an estimated savings of over half a million dollars was realized.

CADS has been fully integrated in CACS for two months, with data being transferred directly between CADS and the other business systems. The technicians are currently using the data to assist them when running service calls and ordering parts. The feedback from the technicians is still manual because their use of the hand-held systems has not been implemented.

The following is a list of benefits (based on formal and informal surveys) that we have realized from running CADS both as a stand-alone and an integrated system:

Consumer satisfaction has improved because we have demonstrated that we are sincerely willing to help consumers eliminate unnecessary service calls and, therefore, save them time and money. When a service call was warranted, the consumer revealed to us that the information provided over the telephone boosted their confidence when conversing with the technician, who they then felt would not deceive them.

Reasoning about appliance problems has been standardized. Consumers are confident in our ability to help them because they hear consistent approaches to resolving their problems when speaking to multiple representatives.

CADS contains the most detailed assemblage of formalized information about diagnosing appliance problems that exist at Whirlpool. The knowledge has been extracted from the most experienced technicians at Whirlpool and has been made available not only to the call-taking representatives but also to other groups within the organization. These groups apply CADS in stand-alone mode to help with consumer mail correspondence, training, and engineering.

The first line representatives are gaining greater confidence in dealing with consumers who call about problems with their appliances. The representatives have never had immediate access to this level of detailed support and relish the independence they are being afforded when working with consumers. The representatives are also learning more about the functioning of appliances and reasoning about defects.

Results generated by CADS will be used as a resource for quality control with appliances and user documentation. The database fed by CADS is constructed to associate rule firings with model numbers, failure history, appliance location, serial numbers (containing manufacturing and engineering details), and subsequent technician support. Therefore, the potential exists for querying the database about patterns of recurring product defects. These patterns might appear in common geographic locations with similar climates; products manufactured at the same facility and, possibly, along the same manufacturing line; products with a similar history of failures; certain working environments; and more. CADS is playing a significant role in closing the loop between engineering, manufacturing, and servicing operations at Whirlpool. We will also be able to detect weaknesses in consumer use and care documentation for each model number or product type. This is becoming evident now with the online database that is concurrently being updated.

Limitations and Potential Enhancements to CADS

The greatest limitation of CADS is the unreliability of the responses provided by consumers. The knowledge base might be considered sound, but it will never be complete until we can preclude inaccurate diagnoses from being generated because of bad input. Therefore, the knowledge base needs to be updated to compensate for this weakness by adding rules to verify consumer responses.

An underlying assumption when developing CADS was that we would not expect the consumer to perform any mechanical or electric analysis of the appliance. This shallow depth of knowledge often leads to a more general diagnosis. A planned enhancement is to qualify the consumer and follow a path of reasoning that most reflects his/her level of competency with handling appliances, thus allowing mechanical and electric analyses for those consumers who are qualified and willing to perform them.

CADS is currently designed to follow a reasoning path that closely matches a problem with an appliance. This path is generated in a stepwise fashion, with each new question being proposed based on the developing context of the problem—a typical backward-chaining approach. The users, however, are complaining that the consumer volunteers much of the information at the front end that causes breaks in the conversation while the user proceeds through the system. We are planning to address this problem with a more hybrid approach to the reasoning (integrating forward and backward chaining) by emphasizing forward chaining early in the consultation. A constrained natural language interface might also be considered.

User acceptance of the system is critical to its success. CADS is not intended to replace expertise that currently exists but rather augment what is already known. The users have been educated to understand the distinction so that it will not appear threatening to them. The users' productivity has always been assessed on the rate of taking calls. Because of quality initiatives that Whirlpool is implementing, call rate is less important than quality of call. CADS is helping to adjust this mindset by measuring the frequency of its use.

The plan is to demonstrate to the representatives that the additional time spent using CADS will generate greater payback to Whirlpool and is directly attributable to them.

Management also has to be convinced that using CADS will not adversely affect the ability of the users to take an acceptable number of calls each hour. This result could be achieved by using the utility provided by CACS that monitors the number and frequency of incoming calls. CADS could be customized to control the depth of the decision trees such that it is inversely proportional to the size of the queue of incoming calls being placed on hold. This approach would speed the use of CADS during busier periods, with a sacrifice in the reduction in specificity of the results. The capability exists for CADS to report on its effectiveness through feedback about its use and the accuracy of its results. Management can monitor these results and devise a threshold that corresponds to the knowledge level at which the marginal returns are optimal.

Concluding Remarks

These and other enhancements will be considered and prioritized by the users once they have had the opportunity to investigate the system more fully. They will also recognize the benefits that are being gained from using the system and those places where they could potentially add to these benefits. As soon as the users start benefiting directly from using CADS, they will realize that their ownership of the system allows them greater control over its evolution. They will be motivated to discover areas where CADS could be improved to enhance their ability to earn Whirlpool (and themselves) greater revenues. CADS has provided Whirlpool with a genuine opportunity for making inroads into the AI and expert system arena after years of tentative investigation into the virtues and pitfalls of the technology for business. We have successfully demonstrated that AI can be rewarding if applied effectively. CACS and CADS, in particular, have been receiving much exposure throughout the company, and with positive results starting to emerge, other departments within Whirlpool are inquiring about using the technology. Certain areas have been identified for expert system development and are currently being explored and developed. We have managed to leverage the momentum gained from the development of CADS at Whirlpool and establish AI as a viable technology in the hands of users, management, and analysts.

Acknowledgments

We want to acknowledge the loyalty and significant effort afforded by Mark Douglas and Karen Kenworthy during the development of the system. We are ever grateful to Loren Schaus, the lead expert, for his undivided support and attention to the intricate details of the knowledge contained within the system. They were all instrumental in attaining the technical requirements of the system in an ambitious time frame. Finally, thanks to Jeff Reinke and the upper management at Whirlpool Consumer Services for their perseverance and unwilting support, which provided us the momentum to successfully accomplish our mission.

References

Bahill, A. T.; Harris, P. N.; and Senn, E. 1988. Lessons Learned Building Expert Systems. *AI Expert* 3(9): 36–45.

Irgon, A.; Zolnowski, J.; Murray, K. J.; and Gersho, M. 1990. Expert System Development: A Retrospective View of Five Systems. *IEEE Expert* 5(3): 25–40.

Prerau, D. S. 1990. *Developing and Managing Expert Systems.* Reading, Mass.: Addison Wesley.

HELPDESK: Using AI to Improve Customer Service

Debra Logan and Jeffrey Kenyon, Carnegie Group, Inc.

HELPDESK is a software solution that enables a customer service organization to expand its first-tier problem-resolution capabilities without adding additional personnel or requiring additional training. It is an integrated approach to customer support, encompassing a diagnostic expert system, a hypertext reference facility, and a trouble-ticketing database system. The effectiveness of the system in meeting its goals has been verified through user surveys, showing its acceptance in everyday use. Its success is attributed to the tight integration of its modules, a phased deployment strategy, and local maintenance.

Introduction

In many organizations, the task of supporting a product or service is performed by a hot line or help-desk support group. All these groups share certain characteristics. They receive calls from internal or external customers and must track and resolve these calls. The calls are resolved by either the support staff or referral to another organization. Most help desks use some type of trouble ticket, either on paper or computer, to record calls and maintain a central status board listing the calls that have not been resolved and any information of general interest to the group. Many help desks support multiple domains, sev-

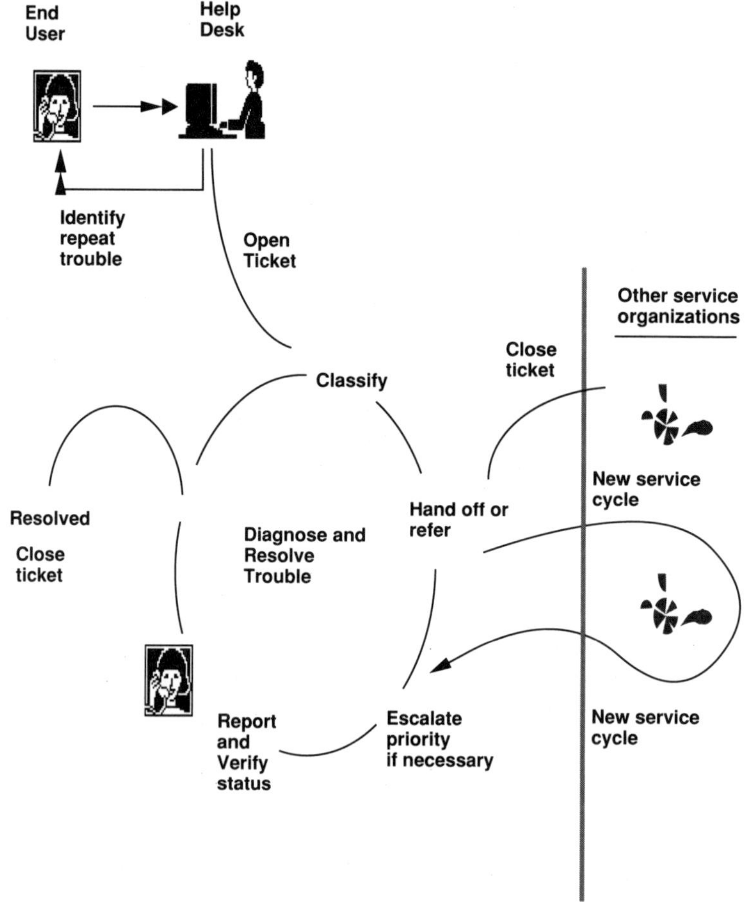

Figure 1. HelpDesk Service Cycle.

eral software programs, a variety of hardware, or a family of products. Just as most help desks share a set of characteristics, they also share a set of problems:

First, because many help desks support multiple domains, individuals develop expertise in particular domains over time, and the help desk comes to depend on this expertise, referring all difficult problems in the domain to a particular expert. If the expert is unavailable, then so is the expertise. The customer must then wait for an answer or rely on a less experienced individual. If the expert leaves the group or the company, much of the expertise is lost.

Second, help desks often have high turnover rates because of the stressful nature of the job. This turnover has the effect of draining the group of expertise. The experienced staff members remaining must take on the additional task of training replacement staff members.

Third, the number of users supported by a help desk often increases, but the number of help-desk staff members remains constant because of economic constraints.

Fourth, help desks are being asked to support increasing numbers of products and services. Learning everything there is to know in today's help-desk environment is a virtual impossibility for the help-desk staffers.

To alleviate these problems, U S West, a large telecommunications company,[1] began exploring ways of increasing their operational effectiveness while maintaining service quality, maintaining or decreasing staffing levels, and adding to the user base. AI technology suggested itself as a natural way of solving some of the problems that the help desks at this company were experiencing.

In studying the problem of help desks, it was discovered that they all carried out three basic functions: administrative, diagnostic, and reference. Two of the functions, administrative and reference, were determined to be functions of conventional technology; the third, diagnosis, required the application of AI technology.

A software solution tightly integrating these functions was then designed and deployed. A phased approach was taken to development, allowing staffers to begin using the software within a week after the start of development and realize benefits. At the conclusion of the development phase, the responsibility for maintenance was transferred entirely to local control.

In this chapter, we present a complete description of the HELPDESK software solution, its development and deployment within U S West Communications, and its emphasis on user empowerment.

Problem Description

The function of a help desk is to resolve the technological problems encountered by product users. These problems are usually reported verbally by telephone, although electronic mail, paper mail, and personal visits can also be used. The help-desk personnel must then track the information given by the customer until the problem is resolved. The service cycle is illustrated in figure 1.

In the service cycle, three basic job functions can be identified: information tracking, reference, and diagnosis. Each function is problematic.

To track information, the help-desk staffers are required to fill out a trouble report. These reports, or *trouble tickets*, can either be on paper or online. Tickets are used to track a problem until it is resolved. They can also serve as input to daily status postings and monthly status reports.

This trouble-ticketing function can lead to several kinds of difficulties. If the tickets are of a paper variety, they can be easy to fill out, but paper makes it difficult to disseminate critical information among members of the group. In addition, the data on paper tickets do not make ready input to reporting mechanisms or status posting. In the paper environment, writing the information on the status board is a manual process, and it is only useful if (1) everyone checks the status board regularly and (2) everyone can see the status board.

Online tickets present problems of their own. Internal Carnegie Group assessments found several types of online tickets in use, maintained with older databases on large mainframe computers in a central location. The ticket format tended to be inflexible, and using the data-storage and data-retrieval facilities was time consuming (Logan, Kenyon, and White 1991).

The reference function also proved to be complex. The information that help-desk staffers need to resolve problems is often paper based. In some environments, there can be several thousand pages of paper documentation. Keeping the material current is a problem; updates are frequent and difficult to track. Telephone numbers, contact names, product release data, and procedures are other examples of information that the help-desk staffer must track and have available for users. Finding a way to efficiently organize and access all the diverse types of information that a typical help-desk staffer must have available proved to be a challenging problem.

As a third job function, a help-desk staff member must diagnose complex problems. Typically, help desks support many different products; end user computing is one example. One help desk Carnegie Group worked with supported office automation software on a network of minicomputers in different geographic locations. When a user calls the help desk with a log-in problem, the problem can potentially be in the host computer, the network, the application software, or the user's procedure. Diagnosing such a problem requires a high degree of expertise. Generally, expertise in particular domains tends to develop around certain individuals; learning the details of troubleshooting over 20 different applications is beyond the scope of most people. When users call, problems are referred to the expert on a particular application. The difficulty arises when an expert is temporarily or permanently unavailable (Logan, Kenyon, and White 1991).

These three functional areas represent the staff member's perspective on the help-desk problem. From the manager's viewpoint, there are different problems associated with running a help desk. The manager's primary concern is to maintain a consistently high level of support to customers calling the organization, using people with varying levels of experience or ability, possibly in multiple locations.

All help desks face economic constraints. If the number of customers calling the help desk is increasing, the manager might be faced with the need to add new support people, who will need to be trained, or help the existing staff members to manage an increasing work load. The training of a new staff member can take between 1 and 12 months, depending on the complexity of what is being supported (Logan, Kenyon, and White 1991).

Managers must also deal with the problem of replacing staff members. Often, the most experienced members of the help desk have grown beyond their support roles and are ready to move on to other assignments. In addition, burnout is common because the stress of listening to customer problems all day takes its toll. The loss of accumulated expertise can be devastating; with the experienced support people gone, training replacements becomes even more difficult.

Application Description

After studying the operations of help desks, an architecture for computerizing help-desk support operations was developed using a mix of conventional and AI technology.

The HELPDESK software solution consists of three integrated modules. The first is a trouble-ticketing system for reducing the administrative overhead associated with paper trouble tickets. The trouble-tracking system is a straightforward database application. The second HELPDESK module is the diagnostic adviser, for increasing the range and number of problems solvable by the support staff without assistance. This component of the software is an expert system based on the Carnegie Group product TESTBENCH. The final module of the software suite is a hypertext reference system designed to simultaneously consolidate and distribute a standard body of information needed by the support staff. These modules are collectively referred to as the HELPDESK software system. Figure 2 shows these components in graphic format.

Application of AI Technology: THE Diagnostic Adviser

The diagnostic adviser addresses the issue of scarce, distributed, or vanishing expertise within a help-desk organization. It also addresses the problem of ever-increasing levels of complexity of products and ser-

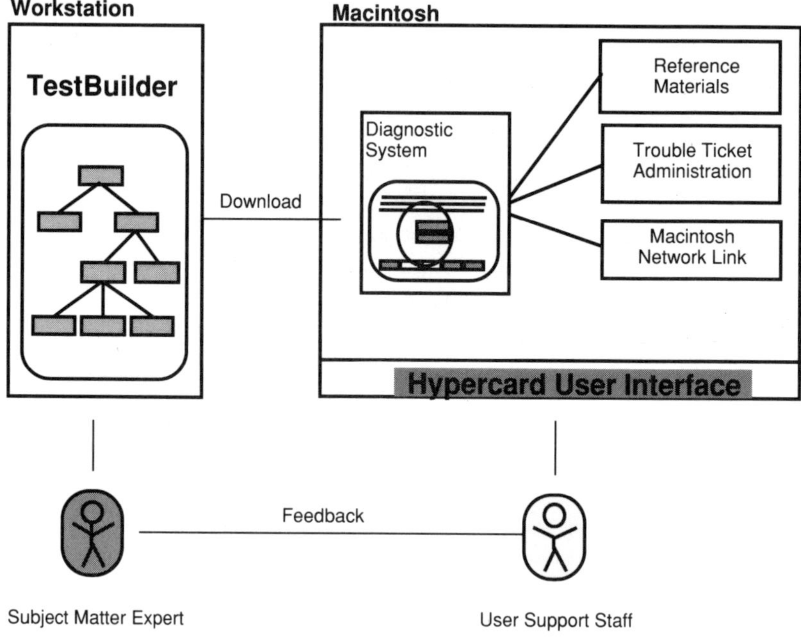

Figure 2. HELP DESK *Components.*

vices to be supported. By capturing knowledge in an expert system, it remains available even when the individuals who possess it are not.

The adviser, built using TESTBENCH, offers a method of capturing expertise as a permanent asset of the group and distributing this expertise to all the support staff. It was chosen because it matched the task of software and hardware diagnostic problem solving faced by help desks.

TESTBENCH (Carnegie Group 1991) is made up of three modules. TESTBUILDER is the workstation-based development environment; it comprises a graphic knowledge editor (figure 3) and an inference engine called the DIAGNOSTIC PROBLEM SOLVER (figure 4). When ready for deployment, the knowledge base is moved to the delivery environment and compiled into binary form using the TESTBRIDGE module. The third module is TESTVIEW, the delivery diagnostic environment available on a number of platforms, from which end users can run the compiled knowledge base.

The value of TESTBENCH is in its knowledge representation. Instead of programming languages or rules, knowledge in TESTBENCH is captured in objects specific to the diagnostic domain. At the top level are *category objects*, which are used to logically group the *symptom objects* the

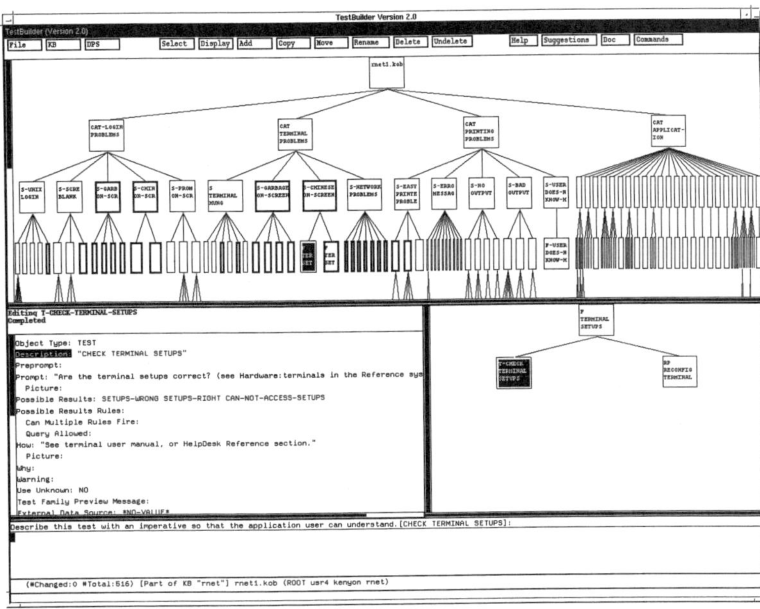

Figure 3. TEST BUILDER *Knowledge Editor.*

system is capable of diagnosing (for example, in the category Printer Problems might be the symptoms No Printer Output and Printer Error Message). Attached to each symptom are the *failure objects* that are possible causes; when a symptom is selected by an end user for diagnosis, these failures are each considered in turn and either confirmed or disconfirmed based on data gathered from the end user. Data are collected through the use of *question objects* and *test objects*, presented to the user as required. Questions and tests can be combined into logical families (so that all tests on a subject are asked at one time) and in And or Or relationships. When a failure is confirmed, it is either repaired (if it is a component-level failure) using the procedure contained in the *repair object* attached to the failure, or the system continues to isolate the failure down to the component level by investigating those failures that are possible causes for the confirmed failure. Although the diagnostic behavior is established by the developer, it can be altered at run time, using rules to change the order of failure investigation or recommend a different repair.

Development proceeds by acquiring the necessary knowledge from the domain expert, programming the knowledge into TESTBUILDER, demonstrating the diagnostic behavior to the expert, then refining the

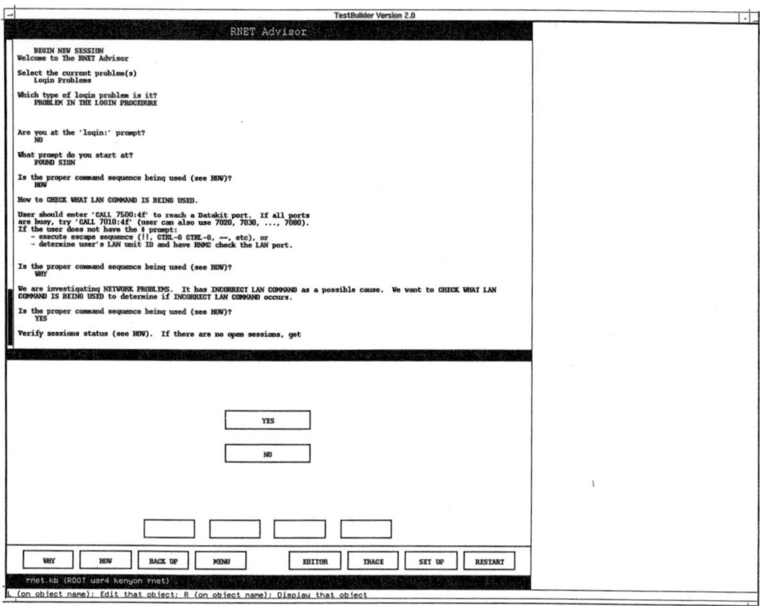

Figure 4. TEST BUILDER DIAGNOSTIC PROBLEM SOLVER.

behavior as needed. Figure 4 shows the TESTBUILDER DIAGNOSTIC PROBLEM SOLVER, which is used by the developer to examine and demonstrate the diagnostic behavior. The DIAGNOSTIC PROBLEM SOLVER uses the knowledge base to engage the user in a question-and-answer dialog. This approach is natural for the help-desk environment, in which the user is often at the other end of the telephone, and the help-desk staffer is trying to determine what the problem is by querying the user.

There are several alternatives to TESTBENCH's fault-isolation strategy, but none met the needs of the HELPDESK application. The most obvious alternative is the classic *rule-based system*: Using rules and data gathered from the user, the system attempts to reason to a conclusion. The difficulty of maintaining a large rule base, especially for a nonprogrammer, was a major factor in deciding against this approach. The use of a deep causal model was also ruled out because of the difficulty in creating the number of models required (some help desks offer service over a dozen or more discrete systems). Decision trees, another option, lacked the needed flexibility and were seen as too difficult to maintain, especially in a large knowledge base. The last alternative, case-based reasoning, was assessed as too slow for the requirements of HELPDESK (response within 2 to 3 seconds) and the diagnostic behavior too difficult to control. The advantage of TESTBENCH is that it allows a diagnostic knowledge base to be built by a nonprogrammer in a format that facilitates maintainability.

HELPDESK'S diagnostic adviser is a TESTBENCH application, developed and maintained locally by a knowledge engineer working with one or more experts within the help-desk group itself. Once the diagnostic behavior is verified and validated on the development platform, a runtime version that cannot be modified is delivered on the MACINTOSH platform. The ability to maintain the diagnostic adviser locally, without the help of a programmer or a knowledge engineer, is vitally important; help desks, as a group, are dynamic environments, with knowledge assets requiring regular updates. Rather than turning the responsibility for maintenance over to a programmer, the task can instead be given to a senior member of the customer support team, who modifies the system in response to his/her colleagues. By keeping maintenance under local control, the probability that the system will evolve over time to meet the needs of the users increases dramatically.

A traditional approach was inadequate for help desks because of the many different interacting components of the environment. Most help desks must have multiple experts to support the multiple areas of their responsibility. AI's approach of separating knowledge base from inference engine was a natural choice; multiple knowledge bases could be constructed, but the same diagnostic inference engine could be used for each one. The ability to incorporate the knowledge of multiple domain experts was a critical element in the success of the software. In addition, because domain knowledge is different for each help desk, the paradigm of a general problem-solving method (diagnosing) used over a variety of different domains matched the nature of the environment.

TESTBENCH was chosen for its proven record of success in building diagnostic expert systems, its knowledge representation, and its graphic user interface.

The diagnostic adviser alone was not sufficient to solve the problem. The other technologies (database and hypertext) used to solve the administrative and reference lookup function are described in the following sections.

Application of Other Technology: Trouble-Ticketing System and Reference

The Trouble-Ticketing System (TTS) replaces paper trouble tickets with computerized versions of the same tickets. These electronic tickets are easily passed between members of the help-desk staff; are used to automatically maintain a central, electronic status board; and can be used to provide a variety of administrative reports. The software is MACINTOSH based, with a hypercard interface to an OMNIS 5 database.

TTS is based on a client-server architecture, with the server containing a central database of tickets. Any number of client workstation users can log onto the server over local area networks (LANs) or wide-area networks (WANs). These clients are able to create and store unopened tickets on their own machines, but once a ticket is opened, it is saved on the central server and appears on the central status board.

The *central status board* is a computer-based version of the standard chalk or white board maintained by most help-desk operations. It is automatically updated and is instantly available to all users on the system, anywhere on the LAN or WAN. Users are able to select tickets directly from the status board and continue call resolution from the point where the last support person left off without having to re-request basic information from the caller.

The REFERENCE DESK module of the HELPDESK software is a MACINTOSH-based hypercard stack developed from the ground up according to the needs of each help-desk organization. In addition to containing detailed descriptions of various procedures routinely performed by the help desk (for example, changing a password) or lists of often-used telephone numbers, reference information can include such items as maps, tables, or textual or graphic information on hardware or software. The designer of the reference material is limited only by the development software.

A hypertext approach (Conklin 1987) was seen as superior because of the eclectic nature of the information to be captured. Each organization would require the ability to include any type of information, textual or graphic, and establish unique links between items to navigate through the information effectively.

A fourth module, the TTS ADMINISTRATOR, is used only by developers and maintainers of HELPDESK systems. The TTS ADMINISTRATOR is used primarily to create and modify the electronic versions of the tickets and the layout of the central status board in an icon-based, WYSIWYG (what you see is what you get) interface.

Technology Integration

Only by integrating these three software components was it possible to deliver a total solution that met the needs of diverse groups of users doing similar jobs. The help-desk problem was solved by integrating three shell technologies (diagnostic expert system, database, and hypertext). Each shell was selected to match the demands of a specific job function and then populated with domain-specific knowledge. This integration of conventional and AI technologies is an innovative way of solving a real and pressing business problem.

To be successful, it was felt that a tight integration of the modules was key. It would not be sufficient to have separate applications handling each of the needed functions; instead, the movement between expert system, database, and hypertext modules had to be as seamless and natural as possible. The HELPDESK software is not viewed as an AI application; it is a solution where AI has a key role but is working in concert with other technology.

Application Development and Deployment

The average software life cycle proceeds along a linear course through the preliminary exploration and requirement analysis to development, validation, implementation, and maintenance (Tuthill 1990). Although true in the case of the individual modules of HELPDESK, the design of the software invites a parallel and sometimes overlapping development process. It is precisely this process that allows the system developers to introduce change as an evolutionary (rather than a revolutionary) process and to build user acceptance at each phase.

Typically, development of a custom HELPDESK begins with the application assessment. After determining that the HELPDESK software is appropriate for a support group, the appropriate hardware is purchased and deployed. The first software module to be developed is the trouble-ticketing software because its design is copied (at least initially) from an existing paper ticket. The ticket can be designed, implemented, and the users trained within the first week of development. The support staff becomes acclimated to both the MACINTOSH and the trouble-ticketing software while development on the other modules continues.

The REFERENCE DESK is easily implemented in stages as needs become apparent, and time becomes available. It might begin as nothing more than an electronic list of telephone numbers, then expand to cover a number of basic procedures. As the help-desk staffers gain familiarity with the system, they will often be vocal about what they would like to see included in the reference materials. The REFERENCE DESK, more so than any other module, continues to expand and grow over the software life cycle.

The diagnostic adviser is the most difficult portion to develop because it often involves learning both new hardware and new software.

It also involves knowledge acquisition, verification, and validation to ensure that the system meets the demands of the real world.

The initial development of the TTS system took approximately one person-year and occurred over a period of six months. The development staff consisted of two developers and a project manager. Averaged over the five subsequent deployments, the cost for each deployment was roughly the annual cost of one help-desk staff member. Because the system has allowed at least one group to expand the hours of coverage and the number of systems they support without adding to the head count, the system has proven its ability to pay off for U S West (Logan, Kenyon, and White 1991).

Deployment

Deployment of the HELPDESK software required the purchase of MACINTOSH II computers for the help-desk staff members, an additional MACINTOSH as the central file server, and cable sufficient to connect the clients and server on the APPLE TALK network.

Training on the HELPDESK software was minimal, consisting of an initial 4 hour session with all the help-desk staff members and short one-on-one sessions (usually 15 minutes or less) when new functions were added to the system.

At the initial site, the system was deployed with approximately 15 MACINTOSH workstations. For a subsequent deployment, the system was installed on approximately 10 workstations. In addition, the diagnostic adviser was made available to all end users through the UNIX server used for a variety of office automation tasks. At the conclusion of a diagnostic session, if the outcome of the session is unsatisfactory, the end user has the option of mailing a log of the session to the help desk's electronic mail address along with a text description of why the resolution was unsatisfactory.

Deployment of these systems has become a short process, taking from one to four weeks. The variation is accounted for by whether the site has hardware already in place or whether the hardware must be installed as a part of the process of deploying the software.

Maintenance

The concept of local maintenance is a key element in the design philosophy of the HELPDESK. Using the TTS Administrator software, TESTBUILDER (the development environment for the adviser system), and hypercard, each module of the HELPDESK system is maintainable on a local level by domain experts with little or no programming expertise. One or more staff members of the help desk perform all HELPDESK maintenance, and their training is an important part in the delivery of each HELPDESK application.

Local maintenance also allows a faster resolution of errors or gaps in the domain knowledge base. Help-desk environments are constantly changing, and releases are made on an as-needed basis; if needed, the domain knowledge can be updated as often as once a day.[2] Local control of the maintenance process significantly reduces the development and testing cycle for changes and extensions. A feeling of ownership is another advantage stemming from the emphasis on local maintenance. A software system that is maintained by a local administrator quickly becomes tailored to the group's environment and becomes their software rather than an externally imposed software package that they must use and conform to.

The drawbacks of local maintenance are few and can be avoided by the group's management. The problems observed were primarily because of the assignment of maintenance responsibilities to a staff member with a variety of other, more pressing responsibilities. The diagnostic system was not updated in response to the staff's suggestions, and as a result, it became outdated quickly. Staff members stopped consulting the system once they had learned its contents, and eventually it became little more than a training tool for new staff members. In a changing environment, the HELPDESK domain knowledge must be updated on a regular basis; otherwise, it becomes an outdated snapshot from the past.

Before releasing new versions, the domain knowledge must be verified and validated. *Verification*, or confirming that the knowledge in the system is in agreement with the expert's knowledge, is a simple matter because it is the expert who placed the knowledge into the system. *Validation*, or ensuring that the knowledge is in agreement with the real world, is a more complex affair. For the TTS and REFERENCE DESK modules, validation is carried out by recruiting a user (if possible, the user who requested the modifications) to evaluate the changes. For the diagnostic adviser, the preferred way of performing validation is to induce the failure in the real world and then ask a third party to use the adviser to solve the problem. In cases where induction of a failure is too dangerous or costly, a third party reviews the transcript of the user-adviser dialog. The preexisting knowledge should also be reexamined to ensure that the new knowledge has not corrupted the existing knowledge in some way.

The validation of the preexisting domain knowledge was facilitated by the use of the TESTBENCH diagnostic shell. With TESTBENCH, a library of user-adviser dialogs can be developed and rerun automatically, providing an effective means of automated regression testing.

Application Use and Payoff

The HELPDESK software developed over the course of these projects is in use by five different user groups; approximately 50 people use the software on a daily basis to perform their job function. A help desk responsible for office automation support has deployed the diagnostic adviser module on a regional network, enabling hundreds of users to troubleshoot some of their own problems. HELPDESK systems at U S West have been deployed and in use since September 1989 and have produced multiple benefits.

In the first deployment, at a help desk supporting a number of software applications, the PREDICTOR application with approximately 3000 end users was targeted for HELPDESK development; all calls regarding this application were automatically referred to the domain expert. The HELPDESK software was delivered and deployed in 20 person-weeks. The diagnostic adviser enabled the help-desk personnel to respond effectively to 80 percent of the incoming calls in the first 4 months of its deployment in which the help desk received, on average, 30 calls each month. For this 80 percent, the time required to resolve the problem was reduced by approximately 30 minutes; this savings was the result of eliminating the average time between the referral to the domain expert and the expert returning the call and resolving the problem (Logan, Carey, and Hayes 1990).

A second benefit that resulted from the introduction of the HELPDESK software had to do with the increase in support capabilities that the help-desk personnel were able to provide. In the first help-desk organization where the software was deployed, there were 10 help-desk analysts supporting 7 computer systems. The help desk operated from 6:00 A.M. to 8:00 P.M. Over the course of a year after the HELPDESK software was installed, the number of systems supported rose to 12, and the hours of operation increased from 14 to 20. According to U S West management, the increase in support capabilities was accomplished without an increase in head count because of the deployment of the HELPDESK software. With the preexisting manual procedures, this expansion of service would have required a minimum of one to two additional support personnel.

The HELPDESK system also improved the quality of service provided by the help-desk staff. Daily users of the HELPDESK software were asked the question, Do you feel that the HELPDESK software has improved the quality of customer service that your group provides? Of the 21 respondents, 17 said yes. They also reported that the HELPDESK software had decreased call turnaround time and attributed this decrease to the software itself. Finally, users of the expert system portion of the system re-

port that it has decreased the number of calls that they must refer to domain experts (Logan, Kenyon, and White 1991).

Conclusions

The success of the HELPDESK projects at U S West is the result of three factors. First, the application modules provide a total software solution for help-desk groups. By mixing conventional and AI technologies, the users were given what they needed to become more efficient at their jobs. In the original vision of automated help-desk support, the expert system was the only component that was needed. In gathering user requirements as part of the original application assessment, however, it soon became apparent that there were other needs, such as an online trouble-tracking system, that were far more pressing than the need for expert system technology. By listening to the users and providing them with all the component pieces that they needed, user support was gained as well as user acceptance of the technology.

Managing the initial introduction of new software technology for help-desk groups and working toward final deployment and acceptance of the system is a difficult task in the best of times. The evolutionary approach toward software development is a positive influence on

this process. Introducing components individually enables users to familiarize themselves with the software more gradually and allows the organization to realize benefits sooner. The sequence of deployment of the components can be based on ease of use, required development time, and potential for high visibility and most dramatic effect on productivity. For example, the HELPDESK REFERENCE DESK is the easiest to understand and use of the three components. Although the TTS system involves some pain—that is, it is not as fast as paper—the payback (in terms of increased efficiency) is large and readily appreciated by a group that might have been laboring under a paper system or a conventional system with cumbersome restrictions.

Finally, the notion of local maintenance is critical. The most common complaint that users had about older trouble-ticketing systems and, indeed, telephone company software in general was its inflexibility and often its inability to meet their needs. Older, monolithic systems still widely used in the telecommunications industry are not easily changed. Users are forced to adapt to the software, not the other way around. Teaching the expert to maintain the diagnostic system using TESTBENCH allows the expert system to be constantly changed and updated as the parameters of the environment change. The same philosophy is extended to the ticketing and reference components of the HELPDESK, allowing users to add new ticket families and new reference materials as the need arises. In the dynamic environment of the help desk, this approach was the only way to ensure that the system would continue to be useful after the developers were out of the picture. Further, when a system can be maintained locally and when changes and extensions proposed by the group are quickly realized, the pride of ownership enforces the acceptance climate.

Notes

1. All the data in this chapter were obtained in working with different help-desk groups at U S West.
2. On average, REFERENCEDESK is updated once a month, but both the trouble-ticketing system and diagnostic adviser are updated every six months.

References

Carnegie Group. 1991. TESTBUILDER User's Guide, Software Version 2.0. Pittsburgh, Penn.: Carnegie Group, Inc.

Conklin, J. 1987. A Survey of Hypertext, revision 2, Technical Report STP-356-86, Microelectronics and Computer Technology Corporation, Austin, Texas.

Logan, D.; Kenyon, J.; and White, J. 1991. Help-Desk Support Systems to Improve Service Quality. Paper presented at 1991 NEC ComForum: Customer Service: Strategy for the '90s, Orlando, Florida, 9—12 December.

Logan, D.; Cary, J.; and Hayes, S. 1990. The PREDICTOR HELPDESK Assistant: Software Problem Diagnosis and Resolution. In Expert Systems Conference and Exposition Proceedings, 35–46. Detroit, Mich: Engineering Society of Detroit.

Tuthill, G. S. 1990. *Knowledge Engineering: Concepts and Practices for Knowledge-Based Systems.* Blue Ridge Summit, Pa.: Tab Books.

Data Analysis

Making Sense of Gigabytes
A. C. Nielsen

TFP Dump Analyzer
Covia Technologies

MARVEL
Jet Propulsion Laboratory, California Institute of Technology

Making Sense of Gigabytes: A System for Knowledge-Based Market Analysis

Tej Anand and Gary Kahn, A. C. Nielsen Company

Market researchers are looking more and more to point-of-sale scanners in retail outlets as a rich source of high-quality and timely sales data. Unfortunately, the sheer volume of such data makes analysis and interpretation an overwhelming task. Consequently, there is a demand for software tools that can automatically provide an analysis of large volumes of data. SPOTLIGHT is a knowledge-based product that enables A. C. Nielsen clients to understand what is significant in databases of point-of-sale scanner data. Using SPOTLIGHT, manufacturers and retailers track the sale and movement of products, assess the effectiveness of various promotional strategies, and compare the performance of competing products and product segments.

SPOTLIGHT provides an alternative to the classical approach, where market analysts provide custom interpretations and reports, typically using spreadsheet tools such as Lotus as aids. SPOTLIGHT turns a task that takes 2 to 4 weeks into a task of 15 minutes to several hours depending on data volumes. Although previous attempts were made to automate the analysis of market data, within this domain, SPOTLIGHT represents the first commercial use of an expert system shell and the first deployment of sophisticated analytic capabilities directly onto a large number of widely distributed personal computer (PC) platforms.

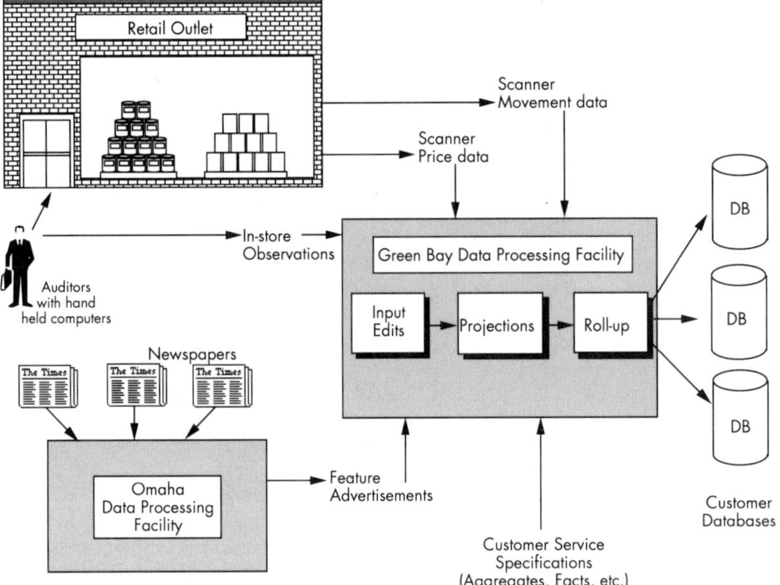

Figure 1. The Information Factory.

Task Description

Over 1 billion dollars a year is spent by consumer-packaged goods companies to understand why their products are succeeding or failing in the marketplace. Proctor and Gamble, Kraft/General Foods, and others devote significant resources to purchasing and analyzing market data pertaining to thousands of products sold across hundreds of retail organizations to millions of consumers. A. C. Nielsen addresses the needs of such companies by providing custom and syndicated data services.

Among the most significant data collected are universal product code (UPC) volumes and prices taken from cash register scanning systems in a representative sample of grocery stores. In addition, data are collected by field auditors visiting individual stores to record in-store promotional conditions such as displays, discounts, shelf placements, and coupons. Data about market conditions, such as retailer advertising in newspapers and flyers, are also collected.

Sample data are projected to a market-level assessment using statistical techniques and are made available through online databases typically organized by four dimensions: product, market, period, and measure.

The lowest level of granularity at the product dimension is UPC; at the market dimension, an individual store; and at the period dimension, a week. The measure dimension consists of facts such as price and distribution. Nielsen organizes its product databases into categories such as coffee and carbonated beverages. Figure 1 provides an overview of the flow of data from the retail outlet through Nielsen's information factory.

Nielsen databases are customized according to its clients and contain aggregated facts over the product and market dimension based on knowledge supplied by the client. Examples of aggregates over the product dimension are brand totals and totals over product characteristics, such as total caffeinated coffee. Examples of aggregates over the market dimension are totals for user-defined geographic boundaries. These boundaries are usually arranged hierarchically, for example, total United States, northeastern region, New York, and Buffalo. A user can define custom aggregates over the product and market dimensions and also request facts to be aggregated for any number of weeks.

The databases described here have over 100 factual measures for thousands of products across hundreds of geographic areas for at least 125 weeks. These are large databases with millions of records. Nielsen has over a terabyte of online data. Some clients regularly review several gigabytes of data, some megabytes.

Extracting meaningful information for decision-making purposes is a difficult task. As scanners make the collection of high-quality data possible, the analysis and interpretation of the resulting volumes of data becomes an overwhelming task. Consequently, there is a growing demand for software tools that aid in interpreting marketing data.

Application Description

SPOTLIGHT is a knowledge-based product that enables A. C. Nielsen clients to understand what is significant in large databases of point-of-sale scanner data. SPOTLIGHT recognizes significant shifts among product segments (share of caffeinated coffee decreased while share of decaffeinated coffee increased), the impact of promotional programs, and changes in distribution and price that lead to a reportable shift in market share or volume. SPOTLIGHT also tries to find patterns of common behavior across a set of competing products.

SPOTLIGHT processes large amounts of data into five brief, clearly understandable reports. These reports allow manufacturers and retailers to track the sale and movement of their products, assess the effectiveness of promotional strategies, and compare the performance of competing products and product segments.

Insightful Analysis from the Executive Overview

Executive Overview *Nielsen Spotlight*™

Butter Pop
Total US Over $4 Million - Unpopped Popcorn - Microwave
13 Weeks Ending March 30, 1991

- ***Butter Pop share is 34.9, down 3.7 points vs. last year.***

  Butter Pop volume is 2,059.2 M Eq Units, down 2.4 percent versus last year. Unpopped Popcorn - Microwave, however, improved 8.1 percent to 5,905.6 M Eq Units.

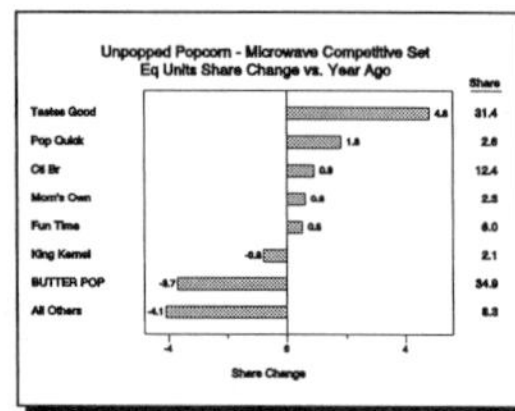

- **Butter Pop** ***Share Change Explanation:*** Price increased $0.20, or 9.6%, to $2.28 per Eq Unit. In contrast, Unpopped Popcorn - Microwave average price decreased 0.6%. Share of display volume decreased 3.7 points to 25.2. Share of feature volume decreased 4.3 points to 30.5.

- **Butter Pop** share of Unpopped Popcorn - Microwave promo volume (27.3) is below its share of total Unpopped Popcorn - Microwave volume (34.9).

- **Tastes Good** gained the most share, up 4.8 points to a 31.4 share. ***Share Change Explanation:*** Price decreased $0.21, or 10.4%, to $1.81 per Eq Unit. Unpopped Popcorn - Microwave average price also decreased, however, at a lesser rate (-0.6%). Display support increased 7 ACV points to 19 ACV. As a result, share of display volume increased 5.3 points to 31.1. Share of feature volume increased 4.6 points to 45.5.

Butter Pop Top Item Summary

	Share	Share Change
Butter Pop	**34.9**	**-3.7**
Gainers		
Bp Mw Lt Gm Lws Bt Bx 6ct 21 O	3.8	+2.8
Bp Mw Lt Gm Lws Nt Bx 6ct 21 O	2.0	+1.4
Decliners		
Bp Mw Gm Bt Bx 3ct 10.5 Oz	5.3	-2.0
Bp Mw Gm Nt Bx 3ct 10.5 Oz	2.4	-1.4
Bp Mw Lt Gm Lws Bt Bx 3ct 10.5	5.9	-1.1
Bp Mw Lt Gm Lws Nt Bx 3ct 10.5	4.4	-0.8
Bp Mw Gm Nt Bx 6ct 21 Oz	1.4	-0.4
Bp Mw Gm Bt Bx 6ct 21 Oz	3.6	-0.4
All Other Butter Pop	6.1	-1.8

Butter Pop Exceptional Markets
(Based on Share Change)

	Share	Share Change
Top Performers		
Minneapolis	36.4	+7.8
St. Louis	34.2	+5.0
Des Moines	25.1	+4.3
Memphis	35.3	+3.6
Milwaukee	41.9	+2.6
Bottom Performers		
Baltimore	38.3	-22.5
Washington D.C.	36.0	-20.1
Miami	34.4	-11.6
Albany	31.4	-10.0
Richmond/Norfolk	36.5	-9.9

 Page 1

Nielsen Marketing Research
a company of
The Dun & Bradstreet Corporation

Figure 2. Example SPOTLIGHT *Report Photo.*

Each report is one to two pages and has a specific role to play in supporting the analysis of product behavior:

Executive overview: This report provides key information that is further detailed in subsequent reports.

Product profile: This report summarizes sales and merchandising information for a selected product and category and identifies significant segment shifts.

Competitive profile: This report summarizes and explains sales and merchandising performance of competitive products.

Exceptional market profile: This report summarizes events in the most volatile markets and identifies events that might explain volatility across markets.

Product trend chart: This report encapsulates a factual summary of merchandising volume, distribution, price, and promotional events.

The first four reports are output as composite documents with text, tables, and business graphics (see, for example, figure 2). The fifth report is a complex table.

SPOTLIGHT Characteristics

SPOTLIGHT uses expert heuristics to determine possible causes for the sales of a product. An example of a heuristic is, If the share of a product has increased over a time period and its distribution has also increased during that period, then the increase in share can be attributed to the increase in distribution. All these heuristics are parameterized such that they can be customized by the user for a particular category. Default parameters are built into the system for categories where customization is not necessary. Where customization is desired, the user can control SPOTLIGHT's selection criteria for key competitors, key product segments, and volatile markets.

Users of SPOTLIGHT have different needs based on their role within marketing or sales. SPOTLIGHT accommodates different analytic needs by providing the user with the flexibility to select the granularity of analysis along the product and market dimensions. The product targeted for explanation might be a unique product UPC, but it could also be a brand grouping or all of a manufacturer's products, that is, many brands, each containing many UPC items. Similarly, the user can select the target geography to be the total United States, a particular region, or an individual city market. In addition, SPOTLIGHT has limited interactive capabilities that allow the user to start at one level of granularity and then drill down to the next, as needed, for example, going from a brand to its UPCs to further isolate reasons for poor performance.

Differences in information and presentation needs are addressed by providing a selection of reports and display formats. Reports produced by SPOTLIGHT can be used to generate status reports for the performance of various products, evaluate the impact of promotional programs, or diagnose the performance of products. The graphs and tables incorporated into SPOTLIGHT reports can be generated individually in enlarged formats to assist the user in making effective presentations.

SPOTLIGHT Innovations

SPOTLIGHT provides an alternative to the classical approach where market analysts provide custom interpretations and reports, typically using spreadsheet tools such as Lotus as aids. SPOTLIGHT turns a task that can take 2 to 4 weeks into a task of 15 minutes to several hours depending on data volumes. Although previous attempts have been made to automate the analysis of market data, within this domain, SPOTLIGHT represents the first commercial use of an expert system shell and the first deployment of sophisticated analytic capabilities directly onto a large number of widely distributed personal computer (PC) platforms.

By using a modular rule-based architecture, SPOTLIGHT provides more functions and higher-quality reports and achieves greater maintainability than previous efforts to develop similar products.

SPOTLIGHT is innovative as well in its tight integration with third-party software, distributed architecture, and approaches to product development, as discussed below.

SPOTLIGHT System Description

The SPOTLIGHT system architecture is designed to access large mainframe databases, provide an untethered report-generation capability, take advantage of a low-cost central processing unit that processes millions of instructions per second, and minimize mainframe connect time. SPOTLIGHT achieves these objectives by downloading a filtered set of data to PC for extended analysis and report generation. Filtered data sets typically measure about one one-hundredth of the original data file. Once they are downloaded, a variety of SPOTLIGHT reports can be run untethered from the mainframe.

The PC component of SPOTLIGHT is delivered on 286- and 386-based PCs and PC compatibles. The system runs under conventional memory; that is, extended memory is not needed. After the downloading of data from the mainframe, the system completes the analysis and output generation phases in approximately one minute on a 386-based 33-MHz PC.

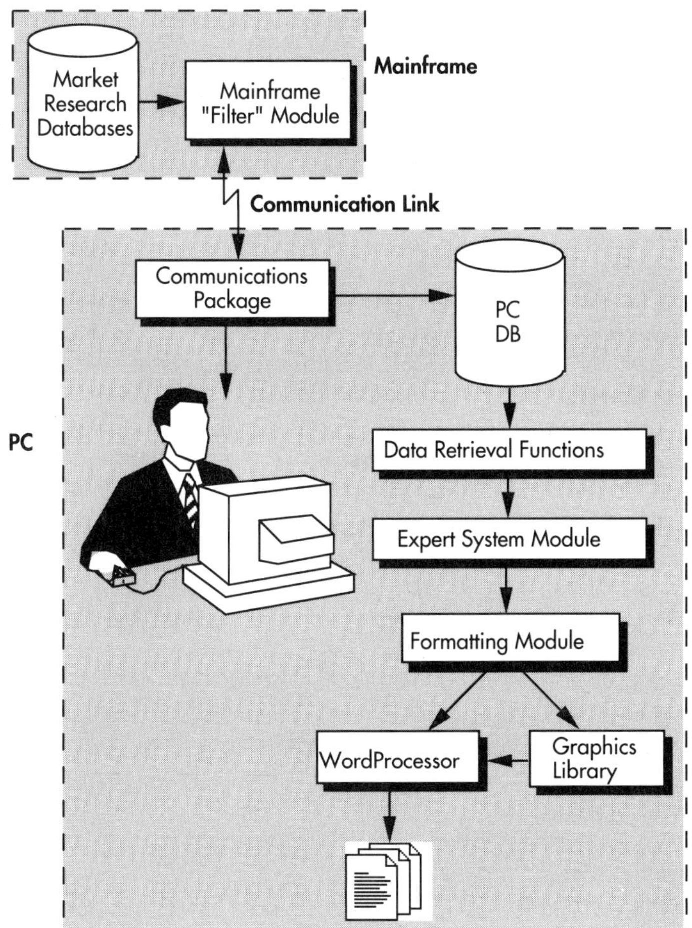

Figure 3. System Overview.

System Overview

The major components of the SPOTLIGHT system are shown in figure 3.

Mainframe Filter Module: This module extracts data about the products and the key competitors in the target geographies. It can automatically determine key competitors and exceptional geographies. Important product segments and aggregates are also identified. The extracted data are stored in a binary indexed file and downloaded to PC.

Communication: SIMPC, a commercial communications package, provides the cooperation between the mainframe and PC. Both messages and files are transferred.

User Interface: The user interface in SPOTLIGHT is mouse driven, with the user making selections from pick lists. The user is guided through the selection of a target product and a target geography by the system. All other selections are made at the user's initiative. The user can access and change the default selections in a SPOTLIGHT analysis by selecting menu items.

Data-Retrieval Functions: These functions are a library of access functions that allow the expert system to query the database that is downloaded from the mainframe to the PC disk. The expert system module queries for data, as needed, depending on dynamic needs.

Expert System Module: This module incorporates heuristic rules for analyzing the data extracted from the mainframe, selecting among graphs to present these data, and generating text to describe results of the analysis. This module is implemented with a rule-based expert system tool. The role and design of this module is described further in the next subsection. Additional detail is provided in Anand and Kahn (1992).

Formatting Module: This module generates the final SPOTLIGHT output. Currently, this module uses CHARTMAN, a proprietary Nielsen graphics package, to generate the graphs and WORD PERFECT to generate the compound document. This module makes all the composition and layout decisions. Integration with third-party word processing and graphics software allows users to customize the reports using editors that they are familiar with.

Expert System Module Discussion

The functional breakdown of the expert system module is shown in figure 4. The architecture of SPOTLIGHT is similar to applications that use the PENMAN system (Mann 1983; Springer, Buta, and Wolf 1991): An expert system is supplemented by text-generation and control utilities. In addition, SPOTLIGHT is modular with respect to the analytic and output-generation components. As a result, the user can configure reports with different contents without changing the underlying approach to analysis.

The result of a SPOTLIGHT analysis is a series of reports consisting of text, tables, and graphs. Within the expert system module, the contents of the reports are represented as instantiations of bullet objects, paragraph objects, graph objects, and table objects. Each of these objects has a *condition attribute,* which specifies when the object is relevant, and a *parts attribute,* which defines the contents of the object; for example,

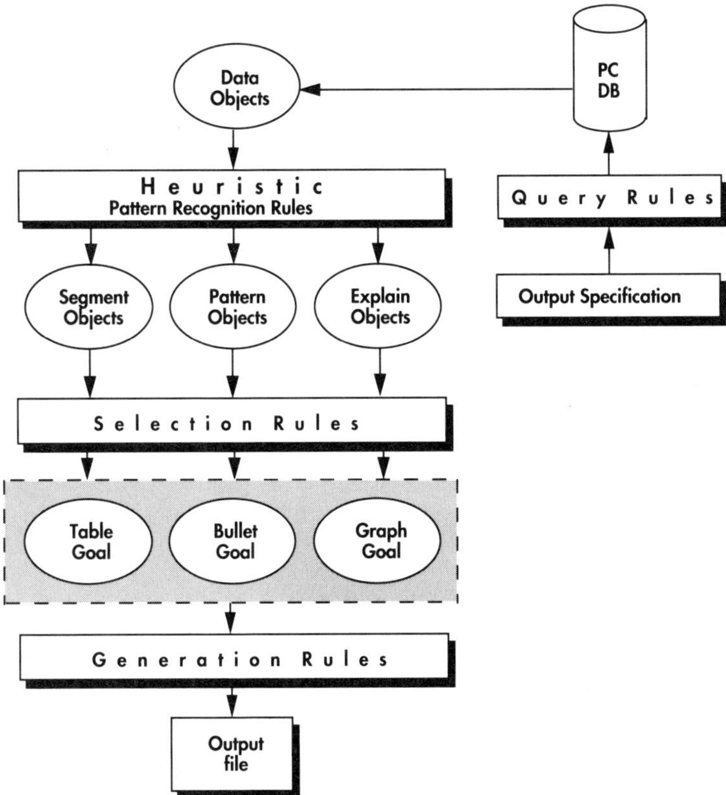

Figure 4. Expert System Module.

the value of the parts attribute of a particular bullet instance is one or more sentence types.

A report is defined within SPOTLIGHT by specifying instances of bullets, graphs, and tables, including values for the condition and parts attributes of each of these instances. These instances are loaded into a working memory agenda. Query rules take the instance on the top of the agenda, determine the data needs of this instance, and formulate queries to the database. Once the data are retrieved, the system enters the analysis phase.

Data retrieved from the database are mapped onto data objects. The internal representation of a data object is such that the relationship between the target product and its competitors, the target product and its component products, and the target geography and its component geographies is preserved. The system forward chains on these data objects and uses heuristics to produce explain, pattern, and segment objects. *Explain objects* represent causes for the performance of products. *Pattern objects* represent correlations among market share and causal factors across the set of all products. *Segment objects* represent a significant shift in volume among product segments.

Associated with a data object representing a product, there might be one or more explain objects representing causes for the performance of the product. These explanations are represented as a *directed acyclic graph* of interrelated concepts. This graph is a model of how the causal factors affect the performance of a product. The product performance in need of explanation is attached to a top-level entry node. Subordinate nodes represent explanations for the entry node. Links from the entry node represent a partial preference ordering of explanations. Nodes closer to the top are stronger explanations. Once the strongest explanation is found, weaker explanations are not considered.

When all relevant explain, pattern, and segment objects have been created, the system shifts from the analysis phase into the output-generation phase. This phase is driven by the specification of the report and controlled by the objects produced in the analysis phase.

Based on the data, explain, pattern, and segment objects in memory, the system selects a bullet, table, or graph instance whose condition attribute is satisfied and establishes this instance as a goal. The values of the parts attributes of this goal then constitute subgoals recursively until one or more generation rules is fired to generate the necessary output. Only subgoals whose condition attributes are satisfied are established as goals. Selection rules determine whether a condition attribute is satisfied. For example, the parts of a bullet are various sentences that can be produced conditioned on the presence or absence of specific data and explain objects. If the conditions are satisfied, then the appropriate sentences are output.

SPOTLIGHT includes rules that are capable of producing a variety of sentences that describe the performance of a product, explanations for the performance, and so on. These rules generate text by completing a wide variety of context-dependent templates. The output of this module is a file of report contents and format commands. The formatting module reads this file and generates WORD PERFECT files for display and printing.

Similarly, SPOTLIGHT includes rules that are capable of producing different types of graphs and tables. The system selects among alternative graphs based on the relationship between the objects produced by the analysis phase. For example, a pattern object that represents a correlation between market share and price generates a substantially different graph than a pattern object that represents a correlation between market share and distribution.

The expert system module consists of approximately 200 parameterized rules, 70 different sentence types, 10 different graph types, and 10 different table types. These units can be controlled flexibly to produce selected reports or define new reports.

Why Knowledge-Based Techniques?

The heuristics changed as the expert validated the results of initial implementations. We used rule-based techniques to facilitate representation of the domain knowledge and allow iterative refinements. As we expected, a rule-based representation also made it easy to allow user customization of key parameters: Custom values instantiated parameterized rules.

A commercial forward-chaining expert system tool, ECLIPSE (Haley 1991), greatly reduced the development cycle by providing an inference engine that enabled experts' rules to be encoded in a straightforward manner. In addition, the use of ECLIPSE reduced the complexity of the code relative to a procedural language. ECLIPSE is a commercially supported, more efficient version of CLIPS (Giarratano 1991). ECLIPSE was preferred to alternative products because it uses a standard (CLIPS-ART) syntax, requires substantially less memory, and is faster. ECLIPSE enabled delivery on a conventional PC/286, 640K platform.

Application Use and Payoff

SPOTLIGHT was released on 15 July 1991. Response from customers in the marketplace has been overwhelming. A large number of Nielsen clients have taken delivery of SPOTLIGHT. As a result, development costs were recovered in six months, and product revenues are currently growing ahead of plan. With the success of SPOTLIGHT, Nielsen is planning further knowledge-based applications.

Most users have found that SPOTLIGHT provides a quick, effective overview of the market and pinpoints areas for richer, in-depth analyses. Client feedback includes comments such as "we have an effective tool to realize incremental benefits of the data we are purchasing from Nielsen" and "our analysts do not have to spend all their time browsing through data and making pretty graphs and tables."

SPOTLIGHT is designed for easy installation and minimal training. Nielsen field representatives provide training for clients, usually lasting no more than a day. Because of its ease of use, SPOTLIGHT is rapidly spreading through client organizations. For example, one major manufacturing organization has already deployed SPOTLIGHT to 250 field sales representatives and 19 regional centers. The regional centers produce reports for hundreds of other sales representatives that need the information to understand brand behavior in their territories. It appears that this client is saving hundreds of hours a month relative to the time it used to take to analyze data with spreadsheet tools.

Application Development and Deployment

About 48 person-months were spent on SPOTLIGHT over a period of 7 months from concept to delivery. The developers, a core of six, were split into three teams. One team had responsibility for the expert system module, one for mainframe extraction, and one for conventional PC software. The efforts were cost justified by expected revenues and client demand for interpretive tools that could enhance the value of Nielsen data.

Validation of the application was done by running dozens of case studies for review. The development team worked closely with the marketing organization. Domain experts from marketing were responsible for validation. SPOTLIGHT might be one of the first systems to explore a unique relationship between marketing and product development—one that goes beyond traditional roles of requirement generation and system analysis to those of domain expert and knowledge engineer. Approximately three months of effort were required to roll the product through Nielsen's entire sales organization.

Maintenance

We are already realizing the tremendous advantages of using knowledge-based techniques in the ease with which we maintain the system and the rapidity with which we respond to requests for enhancements. Based on client feedback, two new releases were made within six months of the original release.

SPOTLIGHT's design addresses maintenance and upgrade needs in several ways. For example, a clear separation exists between analytic capabilities and presentation generation. This design makes it possible to embed SPOTLIGHT capabilities in other delivery vehicles, such as planned interactive decision support systems. In addition, text is clearly separated from the rules that decide which concepts to express. This separation between text and rules makes it easier to package SPOTLIGHT for international delivery.

Maintenance requires the ability to produce subsequent releases with minimal costs. One area of concern, particularly for rule-based systems, is regression testing. Because rules are evoked depending on the state of data, it is difficult to guarantee regression with large databases. Consequently, we created a continually growing library of test cases that were manually validated by the experts. This library includes cases that account for all possible input combinations. We developed utilities to ensure that this library of test cases leads to 100-percent coverage of the rules.

Whenever changes are made to the rules, all cases in the library are run in a batch mode. The resulting output is compared with the previous output, and the differences are presented to the expert. If these differences are acceptable, the library is updated. After every change, the library is reviewed to ensure coverage of all the rules. If necessary, new cases are added to the library.

Finally, attempts were made to enable limited end user maintenance. Where possible, the behavior of the expert system can be controlled by using an interactive setup facility that allows custom definitions of key concepts and threshold values.

References

Anand, T., and Kahn, G. 1992. SPOTLIGHT: A Data-Explanation System. In Proceedings of the Eighth IEEE Conference on AI for Applications, 2–8. Washington, D.C.: IEEE Computer Society.

Giarratano, J. C. 1991. *CLIPS Reference Manual.* Houston, Tex.: National Aeronautics and Space Administration.

Haley, P. 1991. *ECLIPSE Reference Manual.* Sewickley, Pa.: Haley Enterprise.

Mann, W. 1983. An Overview of the PENMAN Text-Generation System. In Proceedings of the Third National Conference on Artificial Intelligence, 261–265. Menlo Park, Calif.: American Association for Artificial Intelligence.

Springer, S.; Buta, P.; and Wolf, T. 1991. Automatic Letter Composition for Customer Service. In *Innovative Applications of Artificial Intelligence 3,* 67–83. Menlo Park, Calif.: AAAI Press.

TPF Dump Analyzer:

A System to Provide Expert Assistance to Analysts in Solving Run-Time Program Exceptions by Deriving Program Intention from a TPF Assembly Language Program

R. Greg Arbon, Laurie Atkinson, James Chen, and Chris A. Guida, Covia Technologies

The TPF dump analyzer (TDA) was conceived in an effort to create an intelligent programming assistant for the transaction-processing facility (TPF) programming environment where IBM System/370 assembly language is used. This particular program represents the first component of the system, which provides expert advice in the domain of solving run-time control dumps (software exceptions) in the TPF environment. This program is used by the application development, run-time coverage, and stability staff members at Covia Technologies to provide more rapid problem diagnosis and resolution to a set of common TPF programming errors. The system has an installed base of nearly 750 users and has proven to be a useful tool in diagnosing commonly occurring errors in the TPF environment.

Covia operates and maintains the APOLLO computer reservation system (CRS) for United Airlines. The APOLLO reservation system, the world's largest airline computer facility, supports over 60,000 terminals in 45 countries, which generate message rates of as much as 1700 messages per second. APOLLO uses IBM's TPF as the operating system (IBM, 1987) that executes thousands of programs written in IBM 370 assembly language. A staff of approximately 750 programmers write and maintain the reservation system software. The software supports functions such as searches for the lowest fare, airline services, hotel services, car services, airport check in, and the tracking of lost baggage. TDA was developed by Covia to aid in solving run-time control dumps in this environment. To better describe the function of TDA, a brief description of the TPF operating system is necessary.

TPF is used by data processing environments requiring remote access to a large common database, such as airline reservation systems, banking systems, and insurance companies. The units of work in a TPF system are called *entries* and are initiated by commands made by a user such as a travel agent. A typical entry flows through the system in the following way: After the user inputs a command and hits the enter key, the TPF scheduler or control program is ready to process the message. The control program reads the command and determines which set of programs is required to process it. The correct programs are moved from disk to main memory, and a block of storage called the entry control block (ECB) is initialized. (ECB is the primary control medium for an entry in the TPF system and is used by the application programs until processing of the entry is completed.) The execution of the application program then begins. Based on the contents of the input message, control is transferred from one program to another until an output message is formatted and returned to the initiating user's computer terminal.

Problem Domain

When a software exception occurs on the APOLLO system, a program interrupt is generated, and sections of memory are written to tape. This information is postprocessed into a readable format called a *dump* and is generally sent to a programmer for analysis. Hundreds of different types of dumps can occur in TPF, with countless variations of each different type. To identify the problem that is the root cause of the dump, the programmer uses dump-solving strategies and debugging techniques. Experienced programmers can solve a typical dump in minutes, but a novice programmer can require days to solve the same problem. Also, a novice programmer might require assistance from a senior programmer to determine the proper strategy for analyzing the dump.

The objective of TDA was to develop an intelligent application that could examine a dump, diagnose the error, and recommend a correction. TDA is used by programmers and coverage and stability staff members to reduce the time required to solve a common set of problems. TDA reduces the average time required by analysts to solve these problems and increases the reliability of TPF software testing. These types of systems are thoroughly discussed in Rich and Shrobe (1978), Waters (1982), Green et al. (1983), and many others. TDA is an implementation of a system that is based on these early concepts. TDA is part of a larger ongoing effort to continuously improve the quality of Covia's product and productivity.

The rationale for applying AI to this problem domain was based on previous experience with other applications and on knowledge of the current state of the technology. Previous attempts to create analysis tools were stymied by the difficulty of maintaining complicated procedural code; the lack of necessary skills required to build sophisticated AI programs; and the cost and complexity of the available hardware, languages, and development shells used to produce AI solutions.

Many of the previous analysis tools stopped short of performing any analysis and were actually data-manipulation tools that massaged and translated information into a more useful format for the human analyst. TDA uses some of these existing tools and then proceeds to apply AI to perform intelligent problem analysis.

Application Description

The architecture of TDA is innovative in that it uses a hybrid approach, mixing evidential forward chaining, model-based reasoning, and focused opportunistic search.

TDA Architecture

The architecture of TDA, shown in figure 1, consists of three distinct components: information-gathering utilities, assembly program reconstruction, and problem diagnosis. The *utilities component* reads the dump file and instantiates objects defined within the class hierarchy for use by the diagnostic component. The *assembly program reconstruction component* takes the program from the utilities component in the form of a flat set of hex data and constructs a model of a System/370 assembly code listing. This model contains all the assembly instructions as well as flow relations between different sections of code (we describe it in more detail later). The *diagnostic component*, which includes forward-chaining rules and model-based reasoning, then analyzes the vari-

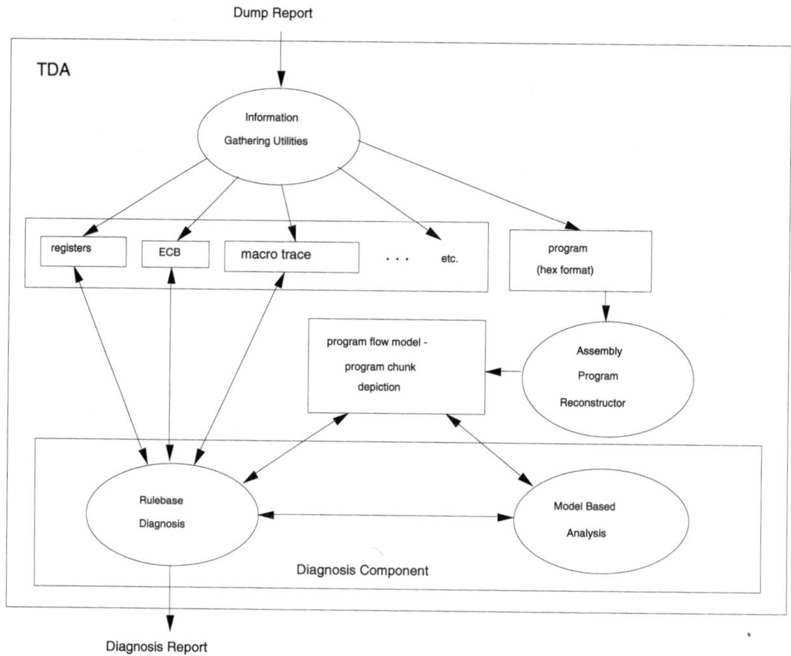

Figure 1. High-Level Architecture of TDA.

ous data, as well as the program model, to identify the root cause of the problem and provide a recommendation for a solution. A report, consisting of relevant parts of the data, organized by the utilities component and the diagnosis component, is then presented to the user. The intelligent components of TDA include the reconstruction of the program and the execution of the diagnosis component.

Information-Gathering Utilities

TDA was designed and constructed using an object-oriented approach to organize the data given in the dump. The file containing the dump is read once, and each part of the dump that is of use to TDA is instantiated as an object. Specifically, information from the dump that TDA uses includes the following:

General registers: The *general registers* contain the values of the 16- to 32-bit general registers at the time the dump occurred. These registers can be used for base addresses, indexes, or accumulators.

Control registers: Sixteen 32-bit *control registers* are available to the operating system but not the application programs. TDA uses these registers to determine which system functions were active at the time of the dump.

Program status word: The *program status word* (PSW) contains information about the status of the program currently being executed. It includes the instruction address, condition code, and other information used to control instruction sequencing and determine the state of the central processing unit. The PSW is used by TDA to determine the failed instruction.

Storage protection keys: A *storage protection key* is associated with each 4K block of memory. A store instruction is permitted only when the program-access key matches the memory storage key. A protection exception occurs when this action is attempted, and the keys do not match. The dump contains a partial listing of the storage keys associated with each 4K block.

Macro trace: A *macro trace* is a list of the last 250 macro calls executed by the system. This list includes any macro call executed by any program (TPF is a multiprocessor system). TDA extracts the macro calls relevant to the current problem being analyzed. This listing of macro calls is also provided to the user in the output report.

Core blocks (levels): *Core blocks* are data within the blocks of memory currently being accessed by this entry.

Entry control block: The *entry control block* (ECB) is the primary control medium for an entry into APOLLO. One ECB is assigned to each entry into the APOLLO system and represents the entry while in the system. The ECB contains such items as register save areas, error indicators, information regarding related core and file locations, program enter and return addresses, and work areas.

Program: *Program* refers to the program in which the entry failed in hexadecimal format. This information provides the basis for the program flow model, which is described later.

Assembly Program Reconstructor

The reconstruction of the assembly language program consists of stepping through the file of hex data and extracting each instruction. As this extraction is performed, all branch instructions are identified to determine the addresses of labels that exist within the program. These addresses then enable TDA to build the labels that delineate the program into program chunks. TDA must also determine the length of macro calls within the program that are of unknown length. This determination is accomplished by constructing different potential macro call lengths and checking for valid instructions based on these lengths. Known locations of labels further ahead in the listing are used to en-

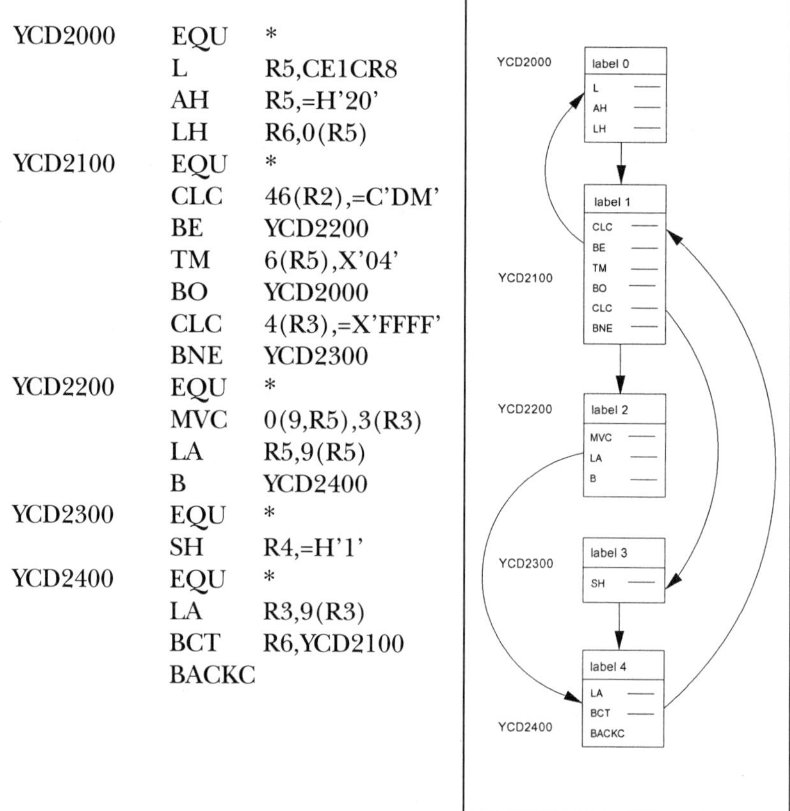
YCD2000 EQU *
L R5,CE1CR8
AH R5,=H'20'
LH R6,0(R5)
YCD2100 EQU *
CLC 46(R2),=C'DM'
BE YCD2200
TM 6(R5),X'04'
BO YCD2000
CLC 4(R3),=X'FFFF'
BNE YCD2300
YCD2200 EQU *
MVC 0(9,R5),3(R3)
LA R5,9(R5)
B YCD2400
YCD2300 EQU *
SH R4,=H'1'
YCD2400 EQU *
LA R3,9(R3)
BCT R6,YCD2100
BACKC
YCD2000
label 0
L
AH
LH
label 1
CLC
BE
TM
BO
CLC
BNE
YCD2100
YCD2200
label 2
MVC
LA
B
YCD2300
label 3
SH
label 4
LA
BCT
BACKC
YCD2400

Figure 2. Section of an Assembly Program and the Associated Program Chunks.

sure that no instructions overlap the address of any label.

An example of the translation of an assembly language program into a set of program chunks is shown in figure 2. The labels seen in the assembly version do not exist in the hex representation of the data because references to them are replaced during compilation with specific addresses. A typical program contains approximately 1000 instructions, which are translated by TDA into approximately 250 program chunks.

By constructing these program chunks, the program can be represented by TDA as a directed cyclic graph (Aho, Sethi, and Ullman 1986; Pearl, Verma 1988), with the program chunks as the nodes and the flow relations (to-from relations) as the arcs. Each program chunk consists of the instructions contained in the particular section of code and flow pointers indicating possible paths of execution both to and from the current chunk. The combination of these chunks forms the set of possible logical flows of the program. It is the model that the reasoning system uses when identifying possible paths of program execution to isolate the root cause of a dump. TDA begins by examining the program chunk that contains the failed instruction. The search space can then be expanded by following possible paths of program execution.

Problem Diagnosis

The diagnosis component of TDA uses a combination of reasoning techniques to determine the solution to the current problem, including evidential forward chaining, model-based reasoning, and focused opportunistic search. It begins with the use of a set of forward-chaining rules that identify evidence of interesting situations that might explain the problem. Sometimes, the solution is determined simply by firing this rule set. Other times, however, these interesting situations require more sophisticated reasoning techniques. For such cases, a search is begun to ascertain further evidence of a problem type by perusing the flow model of the program to follow possible paths of execution. Sometimes TDA identifies a situation where previous assumptions need to be changed and the analysis restarted.

Different sequences of instruction types indicate different types of problems. The objective of the model-based reasoning component of TDA is to step through the program model (represented by the interrelated program chunks) to identify the interesting instructions that identify a problem type. This reasoning is guided by the values of the registers at the time the dump occurred and utilizes the concept of focusing on probable diagnoses to limit the potential scope of the search.

For example, a possible dump type is a *protection exception*. This dump occurs when a program attempts to access an area of memory that the program does not have the authority to access. That is, the storage key for the block of memory does not match the key associated with the application program. One of the problem types that would cause a protection exception is the presence of a loop that contains an increment of a base register combined with a loop that is executed too many times. Once this loop is exited, the base register addresses a new block of memory with a different storage protect key. Thus, when the base register is used in a subsequent instruction and is addressing an area of memory with a different protect key, a protection exception dump occurs. In this case, TDA detects the presence of the loop, finds the instruction that increments the base register, and determines the reason

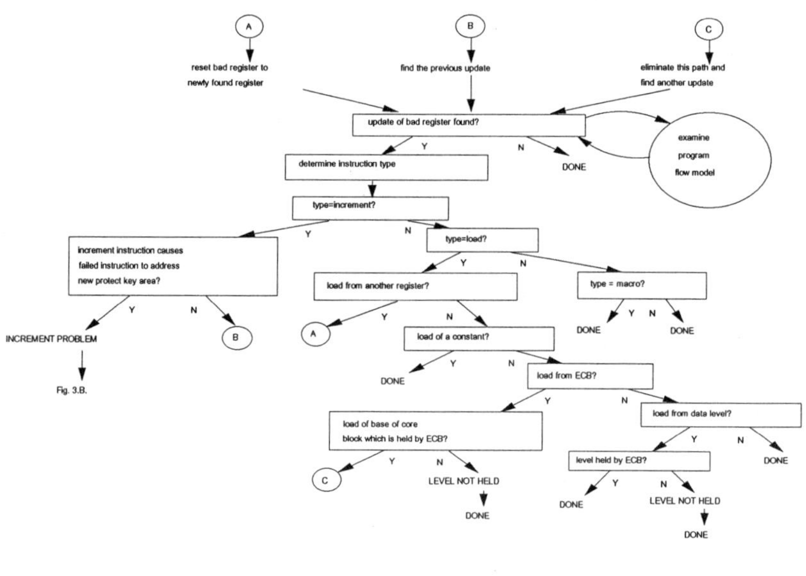

Figure 3a. Decision Tree Used When a Register Contains a Bad Value.

that the loop was executed too many times.

Depending on the type of programming construct for which TDA is searching, different opportunistic search strategies are used that focus on the most probable diagnosis first, as described in de Kleer (1991). For example, when searching for the update of a register that seems to contain a bad value, TDA steps back through the previous program chunks, scanning for the use of this bad register. The search space is then expanded to include each chunk that references the bad register in order of proximity to the current chunk and continues in a breadth-first search manner.

However, when searching for a looping construct, TDA scans forward through the program chunks looking for the presence of a connection that creates a loop. Although it is impossible to determine if a program terminates (the halting problem [Harrison 1978]), it is possible to look for localized sequences of instructions that provide evidence of an incorrect looping construct (for example, decrementing a counter from zero and checking for zero to terminate or not initializing a register correctly.)

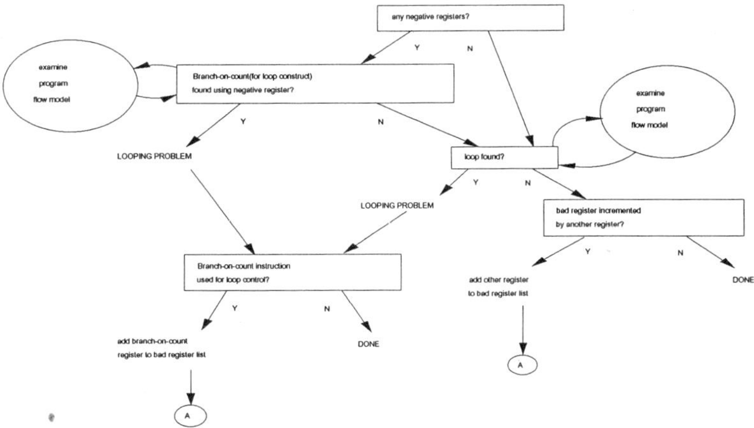

Figure 3b. Decision Tree Used When a Register Contains a Bad Value.

Different types of program dumps are distinguished by different flavors of problems. This distinction between dump types allows for different search methodologies when deriving a diagnosis of the particular problem.

These methods include both the selection of where to search and the choice of what parts of the search space to prune. For example, when searching for the solution to a protection exception dump and determining the path that the program was executing before the dump occurred, a path is eliminated for two reasons: (1) a previous instruction is found that would have caused a protection exception before executing the failed instruction and (2) a load of a valid value to a register known to contain a bad value is found.

An example of the reasoning logic for a particular problem is given in figure 3a. If TDA has determined that a dump occurred because a register was being assigned a bad value, then this section of the rule base is used. First, the model-based reasoning component is invoked to find the instruction that last updated this bad register. If such an instruction is found, then the forward-chaining can continue, and the type of the update instruction (that is, increment, load) determines which set of rules fires next. If, for example, this instruction increments the bad register, then TDA attempts to confirm that the increment instruction caused the register to contain a bad value. If an increment problem is detected, then TDA continues to look for a looping problem, as illustrated in figure 3b. During this diagnosis, TDA might alter the target of its search. For example, if an instruction is found that loads the bad register with a second register (as shown in figure 3a), TDA begins searching for the update of this second register. Another example of TDA altering the target of its search is given in figure 3b, where a looping problem has been detected, and a branch-on-count instruction is being used to control the loop. That is, a register is decremented and tested for zero on each iteration through the loop. In this case, TDA updates the target register to be this loop control register and begins the analysis again. This capability allows TDA to find a root cause of a problem rather than simply the most recent symptom of the problem.

The forward-chaining logic, as well as the methods used to search the program model, were derived from the TDA Expert Group. This group consisted of a select group of TPF analysts considered to be experts in solving dumps or persons with a broad range of knowledge about the TPF system.

During the problem diagnosis, as facts are determined relating to the problem being solved, the report is updated. These facts include such results as there is a looping problem, or register 2 contains a bad value, and it was updated by register 4 at displacement 100 in the program. Other useful information is added to the report. This information includes such items as the instruction that was being executed when the dump occurred, registers that contain bad (or potentially bad) values, and an ordered list of macros executed by this entry. TDA constructs these items through straightforward operations on data in the dump so that the programmer does not have to spend time with these mundane tasks. The programmer is thus freed to work on a more sophisticated analysis of the problem, and the potential for computational errors is eliminated.

Implementation and Development Issues

The actual implementation of the dump analyzer was preceded by a number of analyses to determine where the use of AI could provide a high return on investment. These analyses included a study to determine which of the problems that were being solved by the analysis groups could be automated and solved by an intelligent, online software system.

Many problems can occur within the System/370 architecture. Criteria for the inclusion of a problem in the analysis capabilities of TDA encompassed problem complexity, problem frequency, availability of data to determine a solution, and computational complexity of the determination of a solution. With these criteria in mind, a group of experts was selected that represented the diverse application, operations, and support groups within the company. These persons determined which dump types should be addressed and in what order. The overriding criteria for selecting the first dump type were high problem frequency and ease of determining a solution.

Another factor in the design of the system was the impact on the company computer network that would be caused by transferring the data required to solve the problem to TDA and then back to the analyst. This factor led to the decisions to process only minidumps, which are limited to approximately 200K (A full TPF dump on the System/370 can be as large as 32 megabytes.), and to deploy TDA on a mainframe computer using the MVS operating system as opposed to each programmer's workstation (thus maintaining the volume of traffic on the local area network [LAN] at current levels and avoiding potential LAN performance problems).

The development team that constructed TDA consisted of three people: a project lead; and two developers, one full time and the other part time. The development team worked with a group of TPF experts to construct and validate the knowledge base of TDA.

The development effort used a prototyping approach that allowed for early validation of the system requirements and functions and provided the opportunity to include or remove features from the system. The prototypes were continually extended, leading to a final installed system that met the system requirements. The expert group assisted in the validation of each prototype. This process ensured that the analyses that TDA performed were similar to what an expert would do and, most importantly, that the analyses were correct.

The total development time from inception to system installation was 8 months and took approximately 2800 hours.

Application Deployment

Deploying TDA for use by the user community was discussed with the expert group to determine the various impacts associated with bringing a new utility into the analysis environment. It was agreed that among the most important considerations was to minimize the impact to both the existing dump postprocessing utilities and the user community itself.

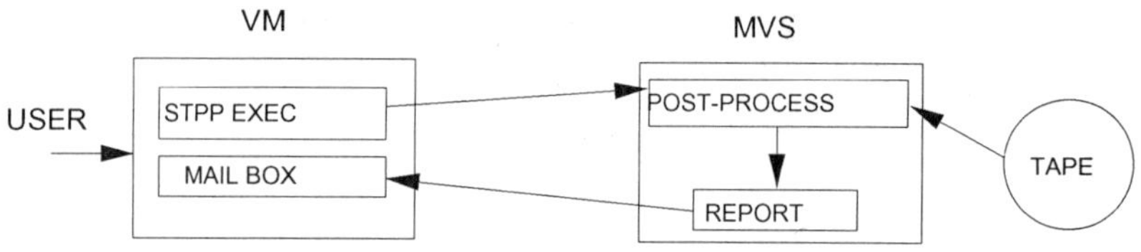

Figure 4. Previous Dump Postprocessing Architecture.

With this goal in mind, an architecture for installation was derived that would simply intercept the dumps as they were processed.

Previous Dump Architecture

As illustrated in figure 4, the previous dump process involved a user request through the STPP program (run under the VM/CMS operating system), which invokes the MVS dump postprocessor. On completion of the dump processing, the output report (minidump) is sent to the user's mailbox or an output device defined by the user.

New Dump Process, Including TDA

The current process for TDA (figure 5) uses the previous postprocessing architecture. The output report (minidump) from the MVS dump postprocessor is provided to TDA as input. The report is then analyzed, and a TDA analysis report is attached to the beginning of the minidump. This final report is then sent to the user's mailbox or an output device defined by the user.

Delivery Benefits

Many benefits have been derived from this development effort, in problem-solving methods as well as increased programmer productivity.

During the course of the knowledge-acquisition process, experts from diverse application, operation, and support groups were gathered to discuss problem-solving methodologies. This process was educational to all the participants in that it allowed the normalization of each group's analysis techniques as well as the derivation of new techniques owed to the synergistic nature of the meetings. The TDA project provided a formal mechanism for this gathering of experts that did not previously exist.

Prior to approving the TDA project, a detailed cost-benefit analysis was performed that identified a potential for nearly a half a million dollars in annual personnel savings because of the automation of the

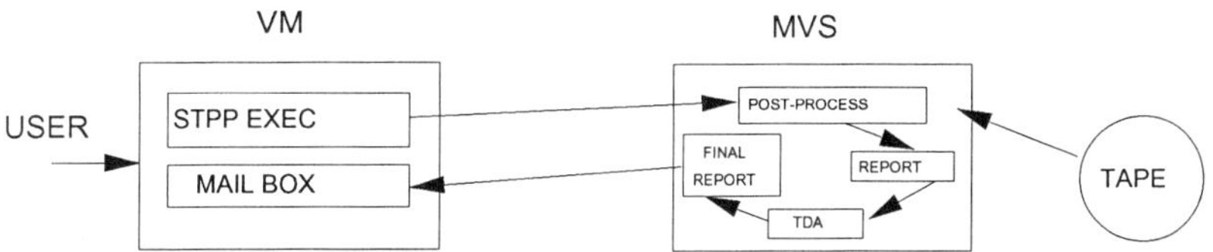

Figure 5. The Current Process for Dump Analysis.

dump analyses during both the development process and normal operations. These savings have been documented and justify the development of the system.

It was determined that TDA saves an experienced TPF programmer an average of one hour during the analysis process and a novice TPF programmer an average of a full day (eight hours). TDA also reduces the amount of supervision required by less experienced programmers when analyzing a TPF dump, freeing senior personnel to focus on more complex problems. (The average time savings for each dump was estimated at approximately six hours.)

TDA has provided productivity improvements in four separate areas of the development and operations process: (1) the analysis of problems occurring on the online APOLLO system, (2) system testing during new project development, (3) general testing of system operations and existing application enhancements, and (4) the installation and loading of new software segments onto the APOLLO system.

Roughly 1000 TPF dumps occur on the online APOLLO system that are analyzed each year. TDA reduces the amount of time required to solve these dumps by 6000 hours (6 hours for each dump, on average). Dumps that occur during new project development are usually encountered during the system-testing phase of the project. On average, 20 development projects occur during a year. Each of these projects encounters approximately 25 dumps during system testing. TDA reduces the total time required to solve these problems by 3000 hours (20 projects x 25 dumps each project x 6 hours each dump). There are 25 application areas, each of which generates 4 dumps each month, on average, during ongoing application enhancement and testing. This process adds another 7200 hours in time savings (25 projects x 4 dumps each month x 12 months x 6 hours each dump). Finally, the time saved during the installation and loading process comes to about 1500 hours each year. There are typically 250 installation and load cycles each year, with an average of one dump each cycle (250 installation and load cycles x 1 dump each cycle x 6 hours each dump).

Additional nonquantifiable benefits, such as improved customer goodwill and greater system reliability, were also identified, but it is impossible to quantify actual cost savings in these categories.

Highlights of TDA Benefits.

Automated dump analysis: Automated control dump analysis results in increased up time, cost savings, and efficient use of programming resources. These factors are especially critical when viewed from the maintenance perspective. As newer, high-level languages are introduced into our environment (C, PL/1), the level of expertise related to the TPF assembly language programming environment is inexorably deteriorated. An automated analysis system significantly reduces the personnel required to support the tremendous amount of TPF assembly code that has been created over the last 20 years (~ 10 million lines of code).

Rapid problem resolution: The TPF dump analyzer reduces the time required for programmers to diagnose and resolve common programming errors.

Quantified productivity improvements: The greatest savings is nearly half a million dollars annually in personnel costs. These costs savings are realized by saving time and increasing productivity; there has been no actual staff reduction at Covia. The productivity improvements were quantified by determining the amount of time that the programming staff would have spent performing the tasks now done by TDA.

Maintenance Issues

The initial maintenance of TDA will be performed by a member of the Artificial Intelligence Group. It is planned to train a member (or members) of the development staff to maintain the system in the future.

TDA has generated a great deal of interest and excitement in the user community, especially because it provides an analysis aid in an environment that is intimidating and complex. Numerous suggestions have been made, however, for further enhancement of the system to automate the processing of other problem types. These suggestions are being collected and will be addressed during a subsequent development phase.

TDA will also be a continuing effort, which will allow the system to handle a wider variety of dump types. This enhancement and others are discussed in the following section.

Future Enhancements

This section outlines future system enhancements. Such enhancements include extending the diagnostic capabilities, using the system as a code analyzer, and adding a tutorial.

Extend Diagnostic Capabilities

The dump analyzer will be extended to diagnose a wider range of problems than are currently addressed. This task will be accomplished by performing ongoing knowledge acquisition with the community of analysts who use TDA. As further problems are given sufficient description to allow a solution to be encoded in TDA, these newly identified diagnoses will be added. This knowledge-acquisition–TDA enhancement process is envisioned to be a continuous, ongoing effort.

By adding additional problem types that TDA will need to solve, the computational complexity of the reasoning system within TDA will increase. These additions will most likely require the simultaneous assessment of many possibly contradictory solutions, suggesting the addition of a truth maintenance system (Forbus and deKleer 1991) to enable TDA to perform these more sophisticated analyses in an efficient manner.

Use with Other Languages

TDA can be used with the assembled output of any language, such as C or COBOL, that generates native System/370 code because TDA constructs its internal representation of the offending program from the actual System/370 hex representation.

Use as a Code Analyzer

Based on the unanimous comments received from our expert group, we concluded that it would be appropriate to use TDA as a preventative measure, not just as a means of diagnosing existing errors. Thus, TDA would serve a purpose similar to the UNIX LINT utility, although not nearly as extensive as LINT because it has been incrementally improved for most of two decades.

The use of TDA as a code analyzer would not remove the need for the analysis of real-time program exceptions because the body of code being exercised spans 20 years of development and will be replaced slowly over time, if at all. Also, computational restrictions, such as the halting problem and the postcorrespondence problem (Harrison 1978), limit the capability of determining program correctness. Thus, there seems to be a long-term use for a system that diagnoses problems ex post facto.

Provide Tutorial Services

Another enhancement planned for TDA is to include a sophisticated hypertext-based tutorial system that can be used to teach the basics of the dump-solving process to novice programmers.

Conclusion

TDA is the first component in what will be a larger set of programming assistants that will improve the efficiency of the development and operations functions within Covia. To maintain the high levels of service and system up time and stay competitive, it is essential to develop processes and tools that assist existing programming and support staff members in performing their jobs more efficiently.

The objective of TDA was to develop an intelligent application that could be used by both programmers and coverage staff members to reduce the time required to solve a common set of problems. TDA is just one component of a larger ongoing effort to improve quality and reduce costs and time to market.

About Covia and TDA

Covia is an information systems company serving the travel industry in 45 countries.

TDA was developed on IBM PS/2s using OS/2 and DOS. The expert system was developed using Aion Corporation's Aion Development System (ADS). The system is deployed on a mainframe computer running MVS and interacts with other mainframes running VM/CMS.

Acknowledgments

We would like to thank our experts who provided the knowledge and intelligence that was encoded in TDA: Atul Amin, Tammy Homan, Bryan Karr, Steve Murphy, Ky Slickers, Steve Schoenstein, and Jerry Tyra. Additionally, we would like to thank Pierre Campbell, Ralph Henning, and Greg Mally for their help during the installation process; John Bray, Kip Henderson, Kyung Lee, Jerry Looney, Tom Osborne, and Jeannie Smith for their insightful comments during the design and development process; and Phil Marie, Rich Lee, and Brad Boston for supporting our efforts.

Suggestions for Further Reading

Balzer, R. 1990. AI and Software Engineering, Will the Twain Ever

Meet? In Proceedings of the Eighth National Conference on Artificial Intelligence, 1123–1125. Menlo Park, Calif.: American Association for Artificial Intelligence.

Bobrow, D. 1985. *Qualitative Reasoning about Physical Systems.* Amsterdam: Elsevier Science Publishers, North Holland Publications.

Fikes, R. 1990. AI and Software Engineering—Managing Exploratory Programming. In Proceedings of the Eighth National Conference on Artificial Intelligence, 1126–1127. Menlo Park, Calif.: American Association for Artificial Intelligence.

Fox, M. S. 1990. Looking for the AI in Software Engineering: An Applications Perspective. In Proceedings of the Eighth National Conference on Artificial Intelligence, 1128–1129. Menlo Park, Calif.: American Association for Artificial Intelligence.

Hayes-Roth, F.; Waterman, D. A.; and Lenat, D. B. 1983. *Building Expert Systems.* Reading, Mass.: Addison-Wesley.

McDermott, J. 1990. Developing Software Is Like Talking to Eskimos about Snow. In Proceedings of the Eighth National Conference on Artificial Intelligence, 1130–1133. Menlo Park, Calif.: American Association for Artificial Intelligence.

Soloway, E. 1990. The Techies versus the Non-Techies: Today's Two Cultures. In Proceedings of the Eighth National Conference on Artificial Intelligence, 1123–1125. Menlo Park, Calif.: American Association for Artificial Intelligence.

Stallings, W. 1987. *Computer Organization and Architecture: Principles of Structure and Function.* New York: Macmillan.

References

Aho, A. V.; Sethi, R.; and Ullman, J. D. 1986. *Compilers: Principles, Techniques, and Tools.* Reading, Mass.: Addison-Wesley.

de Kleer, J. 1991. Focusing on Probable Diagnoses. In Proceedings of the Ninth National Conference on Artificial Intelligence, 842–848. Menlo Park, Calif.: American Association for Artificial Intelligence.

Forbus, K., and de Kleer, J. 1991. Building Problem Solvers: Program Notes on Truth Maintenance Systems. Presented at AAAI-91 Tutorial on Truth Maintenance Systems, 15 July, Anaheim, Calif.

Green, C.; Luckham, D.; Balzar, T.; Cheatham, T.; and Rich, C. 1983. Report on a Knowledge-Based Software Assistant, Technical Report RADC-TR-83-195, Rome Air Development Center, Rome, New York.

Harrison, M. A. 1978. *Introduction to Formal Language Theory*. Reading, Mass.: Addison-Wesley.

IBM. 1987. IBM System/370—Principles of Operation, 11th ed. Yorktown Heights, N.Y.: IBM T. J. Watson Research Center.

Pearl, J., and Verma, T. 1988. The Logic of Representing Dependencies by Directed Graphs. In Proceedings of the Sixth National Conference on Artificial Intelligence, 374–379. Menlo Park, Calif.: American Association for Artificial Intelligence.

Rich, C., and Shrobe, H. 1978. Initial Report on a Lisp PROGRAMMER'S APPRENTICE. *IEEE Transactions on Software Engineering* SE-4(6): 456–467.

Waters, R. 1982. The PROGRAMMER'S APPRENTICE: Knowledge-Based Editing. *IEEE Transactions on Software Engineering* SE-8(1).

MARVEL: A Distributed Real-Time Monitoring and Analysis Application

Ursula M. Schwuttke, Alan G. Quan, Robert Angelino, Cynthia L. Childs, John R. Veregge, Raymond Y. Yeung, and Monica B. Rivera, Jet Propulsion Laboratory, California Institute of Technology

Real-time AI is gaining increasing attention for applications in which conventional software methods are unable to meet technology needs. One such application area is the monitoring and analysis of complex systems. MARVEL (multimission automation for real-time verification of spacecraft engineering link), a distributed monitoring and analysis tool with multiple expert systems, was developed and successfully applied to the automation of interplanetary spacecraft operations at the Jet Propulsion Laboratory (JPL) of the National Aeronautics and Space Administration (NASA). In this chapter, we describe MARVEL implementation and validation approaches, the MARVEL architecture, and the specific benefits that were realized by using MARVEL in operations.

MARVEL is an automated system for telemetry monitoring and analysis. It has been actively used for mission operations since 1989. It was first deployed for the *Voyager* spacecraft's encounter with Neptune and has remained under incremental development since this time, with new deliveries occurring every 6 to 10 months. MARVEL combines stan-

Figure 1. The JPL Mission Operations Environment.

dard automation techniques with embedded rule-based expert systems to simultaneously provide real-time monitoring of data from multiple spacecraft subsystems, real-time analysis of anomaly conditions, and both real-time and non–real-time productivity enhancement functions. The primary goal of MARVEL is to combine conventional automation and knowledge-based techniques to provide improved accuracy and efficiency by reducing the need for constant availability of human expertise. A second goal is to demonstrate the benefit that can be realized from incorporating AI techniques into complex real-time applications.

The traditional spacecraft operations environment at JPL, shown in figure 1, has not relied heavily on automation because until fairly recently, software technology was insufficient for meeting many of the complex needs of this application. The traditional approach has involved large teams of highly trained specialists and support personnel for each spacecraft subsystem and each mission. (Each JPL spacecraft has seven subsystems: attitude and articulation control, command and data, power, propulsion, telecommunications, thermal control, and science instruments.) There have been separate teams for uplink (commanding), downlink (monitoring and analysis), and science activities. The downlink teams for the individual spacecraft subsystems include both real-time personnel and non–real-time personnel who are responsible for routine telemetry monitoring and more detailed analysis, re-

Figure 2. Voyager *at Neptune, with the Moon Triton in the Background.*

spectively. When system-level analysis is required to handle events that affect more than one spacecraft subsystem, a separate set of individuals coordinates the efforts of the relevant subsystem analysts. The total operations staff for the two *Voyager* spacecraft during peak activity periods (such as planetary encounters) consisted of over 100 individuals. This traditional approach was used successfully for the *Voyager* mission, resulting in enormous volumes of scientific data from brief flyby encounters with Saturn, Jupiter, Uranus, and Neptune. The success of *Voyager* has helped to enable new orbital missions to other planets, such as *Magellan* to Venus, *Galileo* to Jupiter, and *Cassini* to Saturn. Figures 2 and 3 show artist renditions of *Voyager* at Neptune and *Galileo* at Jupiter.

Despite the past successes, the increasing number and complexity of missions cause this operations approach to become less feasible for two reasons. First, the work force costs for supporting this style of operations for multiple simultaneous missions are too great to be sustained by current NASA budgets. Second, with the exception of *Voyager*, missions will be returning significantly higher volumes of engineering and science data on a more continuous basis than in the past.

MARVEL provides user interface functions, data access, data manipulation, data display, and data archiving within an X WINDOWS–MOTIF envi-

Figure 3. Galileo Orbiter and Probe at Jupiter, with the Great Red Spot at Upper Right.

ronment. The detailed expertise for anomaly analysis is supplied by embedded knowledge-based systems. In the event of anomalies, the appropriate knowledge bases provide an analysis and recommendations for corrective action. Conventional processing is implemented in C functions. The knowledge bases are embedded within the C program and are implemented in data-driven and goal-driven rules using a commercial expert system shell. The shell is written in C, which allows easy integration with the conventional code. MARVEL makes it possible for an analyst to effectively handle significantly more demanding real-time situations than in the past because it automatically performs numerous tasks that previously required human effort. As a result of MARVEL, it has become possible for individual analysts to be responsible for several spacecraft subsystems during periods of low and moderate spacecraft activity. Thus MARVEL reduces both the level of training and the cognitive load that are required to perform routine mission operations.

MARVEL hasdemonstrated that the use of automation enhances mission operations. Individual spacecraft analysts are no longer burdened with routine monitoring, information gathering, or preliminary analysis functions. They are able to view the results of the automation of these activities on displays associated with individual spacecraft subsystems at the click of a mouse button. This approach resulted in a reduced need for staffing, less work force dedicated to routine tasks, earlier anomaly detection and diagnosis, leverage of scarce and valuable expertise, and reduced impact from personnel turnover. As a result, a MARVEL system for the *Galileo* mission (to Jupiter) is now under way, and MARVEL for the *Cassini* mission (to Saturn) is being considered.

Achieving Real-Time Performance

Fast systems are not necessarily real-time systems; however, in many applications, fast response time can be essential for meeting real-time constraints. *Real-time systems* have been defined as systems that have the "ability to guarantee a response after a (domain-defined) fixed time has elapsed" (Laffey, et al., 1988, p. 27) or that are "designed to operate with a well-defined measure of reactivity" (Georgeff and Ingrand 1989, p. 209). In other words, real-time systems must be able to reliably and predictably process data at rates as fast or faster than they are arriving. According to these definitions, knowledge-based systems have not yet been sufficiently demonstrated for complex real-time applications because in such applications, the amount of computation is nondeterministic, even in the presence of constant input data rates. This limitation is already being recognized as the primary limitation of AI systems, making it difficult to apply AI approaches where they might otherwise prove useful.

Although future approaches might make it possible for intelligent systems to adapt more flexibly and dynamically to real-time situations (Horvitz, Cooper, and Heckerman 1989; Hayes-Roth 1990; Schwuttke and Gasser 1992) without becoming overloaded, it is unlikely that any single new method will be able to handle all real-time situations. However, judicious use of existing AI methods can make it possible to obtain improved performance, both in current systems and in more dynamic systems of the future. The following paragraphs describe some of the methods used in MARVEL that enable knowledge-based techniques to enhance the capabilities of a real-time system without causing a negative impact on performance.

Knowledge-Based Methods Used Only Where Essential

For certain functions, such as diagnostics and anomaly correction, expert systems provide better implementational paradigms than more efficient conventional approaches. However, expert systems usually use interpreters to perform inferencing on the knowledge base rather than compile the knowledge base into native code. This approach tends to compromise performance and can pose difficulties in applications where the fastest possible response time is a critical factor in meeting real-time constraints (Barachini and Theuretzbacher 1988; Bahr 1990).

MARVEL achieves adequate response time by placing as much of the computing burden as possible into conventional algorithmic functions written in the C language. For example, C processes handle the initial tasks of allocating telemetry to a monitoring module and detecting anomalies. If a potential anomaly is found, the corresponding telemetry is passed to the appropriate expert system for verification. If the expert system concurs that the telemetry appears to be anomalous (without actually diagnosing the specific anomaly at this point), the subsystem monitor then performs an algorithmic check to determine if the anomalous telemetry is merely the result of data noise or corruption. After these preliminary tests are done, and a probability of anomaly occurrence is established, the subsystem monitor invokes knowledge-based processing for diagnosis of the anomaly and recommendation of corrective action. In MARVEL, knowledge-based processing is used only for knowledge-intensive tasks for which it is essential. All other tasks are implemented with C routines. This technique contributes to an overall response time that is sufficient for real-time monitoring.

Hybrid Reasoning for Improved Performance in Knowledge-Based Methods

MARVEL augments several types of reasoning with conventional software methods to improve performance. For example, MARVEL uses hybrid reasoning for detecting data that are uncertain or corrupted or of decaying validity. In the MARVEL system, there are two mechanisms for detecting data-integrity problems. The first mechanism is algorithmic: It uses algorithmic calculations to check the validity of incoming telemetry-based quantities, such as telemetry values and data modes, so that obviously noisy data can be eliminated from further processing. This technique is implemented at the level of the data management process and is used to monitor simple data types. The second mechanism is knowledge based in nature and is implemented in rules. This mechanism uses the method of expectation-based data validation (Chandrasekaran and Punch 1984). Data of questionable integrity are verified by cross-checking them with other data sources for correlation and corroboration. If an anomaly is indicated by a new incoming telemetry word, one can validate this hypothesis by examining known related data to see if they have values that one would expect if the hypothesis were true. If the related data corroborate the initial indication, then the knowledge-based system can conclude that the new data are valid, and the anomaly hypothesis is confirmed. Conversely, if the related data do not appear to be consistent with the new data, then the anomaly hypothesis is not proven. MARVEL's expert systems have been designed explicitly so that they do not disregard the new data, which might provide the first evidence of a true anomaly that will eventually be confirmed by subsequent telemetry. Thus, whenever possible, the conclusions of the expert systems are based on patterns of consistent data rather than on a single piece of data in isolation.

Temporal Reasoning with Minimal Impact on Real-Time Processing

Real-time systems often need to reason about past events and the order in which they occurred. The MARVEL expert systems respond to events (symptoms) indicated in the spacecraft telemetry by attempting to identify and diagnose specific subsystem anomalies that caused an event. To make this response, the expert system might need to know about other spacecraft events that have occurred in the past and the sequence of their occurrence. This knowledge process involves temporal reasoning, which is implemented in MARVEL using dynamically updated structures, as shown in Figure 4.

The structures contain the name of the event, the name of an anomaly that might have caused the event, a Boolean flag indicating whether the event has occurred and is currently relevant, and an integer specifying the sequence in which the event occurred relative to other events. The anomaly identifier is necessary because a particular event can have bearing on the diagnosis of more than one anomaly (that might or might not have occurred). Thus, a single event can point to multiple structures that are each associated with a different anomaly. The Boolean flag in a structure is set when the event associated with the structure is detected from telemetry. When this flag is set, the relative time of the event is recorded in the structure. The validity of a Boolean flag expires after its corresponding anomaly is resolved, causing the flag to be reset so that it cannot contribute to the detection or diagnosis of the same anomaly unless the associated event occurs again.

These structures are intended to have minimal impact on performance. Once an event is detected, a structure is created for each anomaly whose diagnosis might depend on this event. Thus, the multiple pieces of evidence that confirm the occurrence of an event need only be evaluated once, regardless of how many anomalies might be related to this event. Also, event structures are not retained indefinitely. There is a time limit beyond which an event structure is considered no longer useful for identifying and diagnosing new anomalies. After this time limit expires, a structure's Boolean flag is reset to false, regardless of whether its associated anomaly has been diagnosed. This approach minimizes the number of event structures that are active or relevant at any one time, which, in turn, reduces the number of event structure comparisons that must be performed during a rule-evaluation cycle.

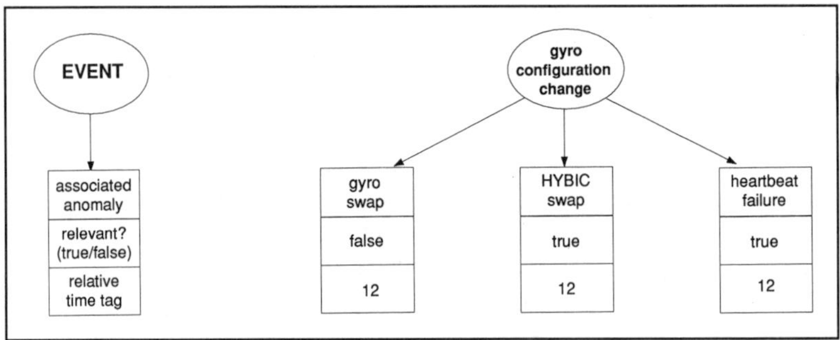

Figure 4. The Event Structure.
The figure on the left depicts the general form of the structure; the figure on the right shows a specific instance of an event associated with three different anomalies.

Multiple Knowledge Bases for Improved Focus of Attention

When significant events occur, real-time knowledge-based systems must focus their attention and resources on relevant parts of the search space to achieve adequate performance. Many expert system environments do not have an efficient method for focusing attention. One standard way to enable focus of attention is to apply different subsets of the domain rules within different contexts. MARVEL accomplishes this task with separate knowledge bases for each spacecraft subsystem and with rule contexts (mini-experts) within the individual knowledge bases.

A top-level data management process identifies incoming telemetry and determines which subsystem monitoring module to invoke for anomaly detection. When an anomaly is found, the subsystem monitor then invokes its corresponding expert system to perform the necessary analysis. This logical partitioning of input data among reasoning modules enables more rapid traversal of the search space and helps to ensure that conclusions and responses that are not relevant to the current analysis are not pursued. This approach has also contributed to the maintainability of the knowledge bases: Several smaller knowledge bases are easier to maintain than a single large one.

Knowledge-Based Reasoning and Transfer of Interprocess Control: An Example

To illustrate the mechanisms that are used in the process of anomaly detection and diagnosis in MARVEL, we give a specific example based on the partial rule network shown in figure 5. Initially, data representing

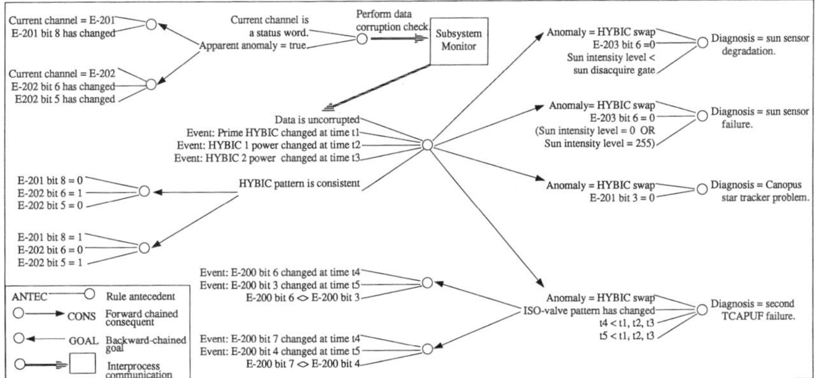

Figure 5. A Partial Rule Network for the Analysis of a Voyager *Articulation Control Subsystem Anomaly.*

the telemetry channel identified as status word E-201 is received by MARVEL's top-level data management process. This module recognizes that the channel is from the attitude and articulation control subsystem (AACS) and routes it to the AACS subsystem monitoring module. It is important to note here that this particular channel is received only if one or more of its bit values has changed from its last known value (in other words, redundant data are suppressed by an external telemetry processing system).

The subsystem monitor compares the given octal value of the status word to the current predicted value of the status word contained in a file. If the two values match, then the status word is ignored, and no further processing occurs (all appears to be well). If the two values are not equal, then a potential anomaly has arisen, and the subsystem monitor passes the status word to the AACS expert system using the C-to-expert-system interface functions.

The AACS expert system checks the bit values of the status word to see if, in fact, they would indicate an anomaly if they were valid (as opposed to corrupted during data transmission). The knowledge base contains domain knowledge that quickly enables it to recognize both anomalous and normal miscompares. If the status word appears to represent an anomaly, then the expert system sends a message back to the subsystem monitor through a call-back function, informing it of this fact. The subsystem monitor at this point initiates an algorithmic check to determine if the change in the status word was the result of data corruption or if it was caused by an actual anomaly.

Two facts are used by the subsystem monitor to examine whether data corruption has occurred: Redundant status data are suppressed by the ground system, and status problems cannot be remedied without ground intervention. If the anomaly resulted from a mere corruption, then a new correct status word follows, but if the anomaly resulted from a problem on the spacecraft, then no new status word follows. If the monitor determines that the status word is valid (that is, not corrupted), then it notifies the expert system of this fact.

On receiving this final signal that knowledge-based reasoning is appropriate, the expert system initiates the diagnosis of the exact anomaly. From the example status word, E-201, the expert system deduces that the spacecraft has automatically swapped out a possibly faulty AACS component and switched to its backup unit. This event can be corroborated by examining two related values in status word E-202. Because the value of E-202 is not in the knowledge base, the expert system calls back to the subsystem monitor for the last known value of this status word. The expert system confirms that the values of E-202 do corroborate the indicated component swap. If the E-202 data had not borne out this conclusion, processing would have stopped, and control would have passed back to the subsystem monitor with no anomaly messages.

Next, the expert system attempts to deduce the cause(s) of the component swap. Such a swap usually occurs when *Voyager* detects an impairment in its ability to maintain its attitude. The cause of the impairment is normally indicated by the value of one or more other telemetry channels. The expert system retrieves the relevant channels from the subsystem monitor and searches for the cause. Based on these channels, the expert system concludes that the cause of the component swap was an abnormally low sun-sensor intensity value (which could mean that the sensor is bad or that the spacecraft is going off course). The expert system sends a message back to the subsystem monitor, indicating the nature of the anomaly and its cause. Control is then transferred back to the subsystem monitor, which relays this information to the MARVEL system operator by displaying a red window on the workstation screen and displaying the anomaly message (figure 6). At this point, the anomaly diagnosis cycle is completed, and control reverts to the subsystem monitor, which continues to monitor incoming data that are allocated to it by the data management process.

Implementation and Performance of the Distributed Architecture

MARVEL has previously monitored three of the most complex spacecraft subsystems (the computer command subsystem, the flight data subsys-

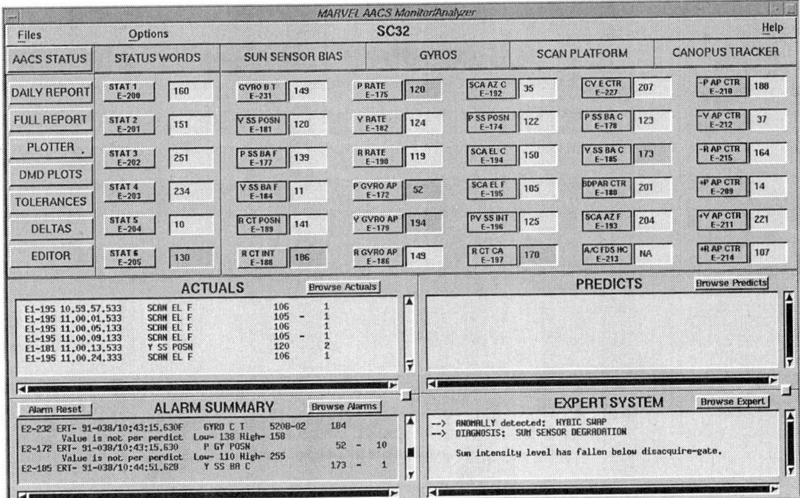

Figure 6. The Main Attitude and Articulation Control Subsystem Real-Time Display and Expert System Dialog.

tem, and AACS) for both *Voyager* spacecraft on a single workstation. However, there are a total of seven spacecraft subsystems that could ultimately be monitored. In addition, the incoming *Voyager* data are sparse compared to the data rates that will need to be handled by future applications of the MARVEL system. Therefore, we pursued a distributed implementation of MARVEL to improve performance for future application to more complex spacecraft.

There are many reasons for distributed problem solving (Bond and Gasser 1988). For example, distributed systems are often characterized by greater computational speed because of concurrent operation. Also, a distributed system can be significantly more cost effective because it can include a number of simple modules of low unit cost. Further, distributed systems can offer a more natural way to represent certain classes of problems that contain subtasks that can be naturally partitioned. Each of these reasons is considered important in the mission operations environment, and as a result, a distributed MARVEL environment was implemented.

Implementation of the Distributed Architecture

The distributed MARVEL architecture shown in figure 7 is based on a central message-routing scheme. The various software modules are allocated among a configuration of UNIX workstations. The data management module receives telemetry data from JPL's ground system. Each of the three subsystem monitors provides functions such as validation of telemetry, detection of anomalies, diagnosis of causes, and recommendation of corrective actions. The latter two functions are provided through intelligent reasoning modules that are embedded within each of the individual subsystem monitors. The remaining modules include the display processes for each of the three subsystem monitors, the system-level reasoning module for diagnosing anomalies that manifest themselves in multiple subsystems (and therefore cannot be analyzed completely by any one subsystem alone), and the data-routing module for interprocess communication.

The interconnectivity of the distributed system is provided by a transmission control protocol–internet protocol (TCP-IP) central router program and a set of messaging routines that are linked to the subsystem processes. All MARVEL processes are connected to the central router by UNIX sockets. Each process registers with the router under one or more aliases (names) and a systemwide, unique group name. This approach allows several instantiations of MARVEL with different group names to operate simultaneously and independently. The router delivers each message according to the destination's alias(es) and group name only, allowing a message to be sent to one, some, or all processes within a group, depending on which processes share the destination alias. In MARVEL, each subsystem has a subsystem-specific alias of *<id>_subsystem* for receiving messages sent to one or more instances of the same subsystem. Each subsystem also has a generic alias of *subsystem* to receive global data sent to all subsystems. This characteristic allows an arbitrary number of processes to be included in MARVEL at run time. Furthermore, different copies of distributed MARVEL can be supported by the same router through the use of distinct group names. (These features are important when more than one analyst needs access to the same subsystem display at his/her own workstation.)

The implementation of the distributed MARVEL system involves the installation of a set of remotely executed functions that act as data and event handlers for the appropriate data types. For example, the data management module sends a message to a subsystem module that tells the subsystem to analyze newly arrived telemetry data. This analysis involves sending a message to the destination alias of *name_of_subsystem* with the event descriptor *data_analysis*. The telemetry data to be analyzed are buffered in the body of the message. After receiving this message, the network process registered as *name_of_subsystem* takes the data carried in the message and calls the function *data_analysis(data)*. This implementation scheme was shown to be compatible with (and integrated well with) both the SUN VIEW and X WINDOW systems.

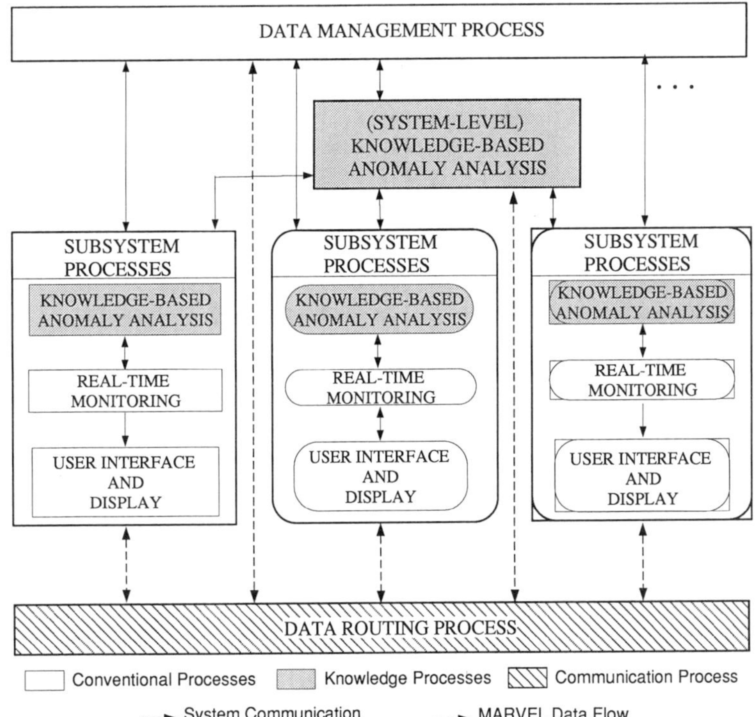

Figure 7. The Distributed MARVEL *Architecture.*

Performance of the Distributed Architecture

A general critical measure for evaluating computer systems is cost-per-unit performance versus fixed-total performance. This curve usually rises at a steeper than linear rate. Thus, in the uniprocessor domain, acquiring additional computing power is expensive. However, for some applications, the cost can be minimized through distributed processing. For distributed systems having tasks of identical work load and requiring negligible communication overhead, the critical measure curve is constant. For realistic systems with nonnegligible communication overhead, the critical measure curve is related to the speedup $S(N)$ (Fox et al. 1988), defined as

$$S(N) = T_{seq} / T_{conc}(N) .$$

In this equation, N denotes the number of processors, and T_{seq} and $T_{conc}(N)$ refer to the execution times of the sequential program and the distributed program on N processes, respectively. Distributed systems with speedup $S(N) = 0.8N$ are considered efficient (Fox et al. 1988); the minimum desired speedup for a distributed MARVEL system is $0.6N$.

The basic measurement of performance for the distributed MARVEL is the speedup $S(N)$. However, it was not possible to measure a unique value of speedup because of the heterogeneous nature of the MARVEL modules. This heterogeneity arises because the processing loads of the four basic components (the data management module and the three subsystem modules) are not identical. Thus, the logical alternative to this measurement was defined as the worst-case estimate of speedups for the individual subsystems. With a four-processor implementation, a speedup of 3.6, or $0.9N$, was observed. This result indicates that the MARVEL environment is a highly efficient distributed system. Two factors contribute to the success of these results. The first is the modularity inherent in the application (as is common in many other complex applications). The second factor is a distributed design that effectively minimizes the need for interprocess communication.

Distributed AI Research in Progress

Distributed AI involves coordinating the knowledge, goals, and plans of several independent, intelligent systems to solve problems that cannot easily be solved by any of the independent units acting alone. The MARVEL expert systems exchange information to cooperatively solve *system-level analysis problems.* These are problems that affect or are manifested in more than one spacecraft subsystem and, therefore, cannot be solved by any one of the subsystem monitors acting alone. To achieve this end, a higher-level expert system is being developed that coordinates the activity of the subsystem experts.

This system-level expert responds to input from the subsystem experts in a data-driven mode that begins with the arrival of telemetry. Anomalous telemetry is detected by the subsystem monitor and analyzed by the corresponding subsystem expert. The latter is invoked by the arrival of the anomalous data. The subsystem experts have knowledge of subsystem anomalies that could have possible system-level impact. When such an anomaly is recognized, the relevant information is communicated by the subsystem expert(s) to the system-level expert. The system-level expert then requests additional information as needed (from the subsystem experts and subsystem monitors) to perform the appropriate analysis.

Discussion

The development of MARVEL has shown the value of a rapid development approach that emphasizes top-down design and bottom-up implementation. The implementation was modular and incremental, with frequent deliveries (every 5 to 10 months) of new or enhanced capabilities. The result is an automated tool that began as a simple software module for automating straightforward tasks and that evolved over a period of five years into a sophisticated system for automated monitoring and analysis of multiple spacecraft subsystems. The initial modular design enabled MARVEL to be developed incrementally, with each subsequent delivery providing greater breadth to the application. This approach was instrumental to the success of the effort because it was compatible with available budgets and encouraged user and sponsor confidence with frequent demonstration of results. In addition, the approach influenced the validation and use of MARVEL, as described in the next two subsections.

Validation of MARVEL

The validation of MARVEL was ad hoc largely because of a lack of formal procedures for testing AI systems. Two methods were used: carefully engineered test cases and online validation (involving parallel operations with human analysts). Most problems were detected with the use of test cases, but some were not detected until the software was used in an online mode. Newly delivered modules were subject to an online validation period, typically on the order of one month. The purpose of the validation period was to continually compare the results of manual approaches with those obtained by MARVEL, so that reasonable levels of confidence in the automated system could be obtained without risk to ongoing operations.

The primary advantage of this approach was its minimal impact on development costs. However, there were several disadvantages, which under ideal circumstances would cause us to avoid the ad hoc testing approach in the future. On isolated occasions, minor bugs in MARVEL went undetected until the end of the parallel-operations phase. Not detecting these bugs temporarily undermined user confidence, particularly with users who were not enthusiastic about automation. A second disadvantage is that without formal validation procedures, there were occasional questions about whether MARVEL should be accepted formally as official ground software for mission operations. The current lack of solid answers in this area would prevent the use of MARVEL's AI modules for certain tasks that are considered mission critical but has not prevented the use of these modules in an advisory mode.

Use and Benefit of MARVEL

MARVEL has been in active use since it was first deployed in 1989. In its current version, it performs real-time monitoring functions for the three subsystems for which it was developed. These functions previously required the presence of human analysts for a minimum of 8 hours for each subsystem every day; during planetary encounters, human presence was required on a 24-hour basis. In addition, MARVEL automatically performs a variety of non–real-time functions that previously required analyst attention. These functions save anywhere from 30 minutes a week (for clock drift analysis) to 2 hours a day (for daily report generation). During the time that MARVEL has been online, it has not failed to detect any anomalies that occurred within its domain. During parallel operations, several of these anomalies were detected by MARVEL prior to their being detected by the human analyst. On two occasions, MARVEL detected anomalies that operations personnel believe might have been overlooked completely by human analysts because the quantities of data that were being transmitted at these times were larger than could reasonably be handled without automated assistance.

Initial emphasis on productivity enhancement resulted in an early version of MARVEL that (according to the responsible operations supervisor) would have made real-time CCS subsystem work force reductions of 60 percent (3 out of 5 analysts) possible during the Neptune encounter had MARVEL been approved for stand-alone, rather than parallel, operations. Subsequent to the Neptune encounter, significant work force reductions were implemented for all spacecraft subsystems, not primarily because of MARVEL but because of postencounter budget cuts. However, it should be noted that MARVEL played a substantial role in simplifying the transition to reduced work force for the subsystems for which it was available.

The initial emphasis on productivity enhancement temporarily curtailed the development of MARVEL's expert systems because it was perceived that the presence of expert systems did not improve efficiency of operations. This perception stemmed from the correct observation that anomaly analysis was only required in the presence of spacecraft anomalies, which did not occur with sufficient frequency to warrant an automated approach, particularly because human confirmation of the expert system analysis would still be required.

However, the postencounter work force reductions brought about renewed interest in expert system development. However, the goal of this development is no longer work force reduction but the preservation of mission expertise. The current analysts are new to the mission and, for the most part, do not have the experience of the previous staff members. In addition, the new personnel will have little opportunity to gain such experience: Although the *Voyager* interstellar mission is scheduled to continue until approximately 2018, spacecraft activity is at a relatively low level. Thus, there are far fewer opportunities for learning about the spacecraft and its operation than during planetary encounters. There is concern that analysts with the experience to handle future anomalies will be less readily available or that they will have retired. As a result, MARVEL's expert systems are being expanded to provide information to the current analysts that is based on the expertise of former analysts. The system-level anomaly analysis work that was described previously is part of this effort.

Summary

This chapter presented methods for combining conventional software with AI techniques for use in real-time problem-solving systems. The methods described were presented in the context of the MARVEL system for automated mission operations, which has provided a continuous and evolving demonstration of the success of the approach since *Voyager*'s Neptune encounter in August 1989. These techniques were implemented in a distributed environment that will accommodate the more rigorous real-time demands of NASA's more recently launched interplanetary missions.

Acknowledgments

The research described in this chapter was carried out by the Jet Propulsion Laboratory, California Institute of Technology, under a contract with the National Aeronautics and Space Administration. The authors want to acknowledge discussions with John Rohr; encouragement from Dave Eisenman and Jim Marr; mission expertise provided by Roy Otamura, Gene Hanover, Ralph Ellis, and Enrique Medina; and support from JPL's *Voyager* Project, Flight Project Support Office, and Director's Discretionary Fund.

References

Bahr, E., and Barachini, F. 1990. Parallel PAMELA on PRE. In *Parallel Processing of Engineering Applications,* ed. R. A. Adey, 209–219. New York: Springer-Verlag.

Barachini, F., and Theuretzbacher, N. 1988. The Challenge of Real-Time Process Control for Production Systems. In Proceedings of the Seventh National Conference on Artificial Intelligence, 705-709. Menlo Park, Calif.: American Association for Artificial Intelligence.

Bond, A. H., and Gasser, L. 1988. *Readings in Distributed Artificial Intelligence.* San Mateo, Calif.: Morgan Kaufmann.

Chandrasekaran, B., and Punch, W. 1987. Data Validation during Diagnosis: A Step beyond Traditional Sensor Validation. In Proceedings of the Sixth National Conference on Artificial Intelligence, 778–782. Menlo Park, Calif.: American Association for Artificial Intelligence.

Fox, G., et al. 1988. *Solving Problems on Concurrent Processors,* volume 1. Englewood Cliffs, N.J.: Prentice Hall.

Georgeff, M. P., and Ingrand, F. F. 1989. Monitoring and Control of Spacecraft Systems Using Procedural Reasoning. In Proceedings of the Space Operations-Automation and Robotics Workshop, 209–217.

Hayes-Roth, B. 1990. Architectural Foundations for Real-Time Performance. *Artificial Intelligence Journal* 26: 251–232.

Horvitz, E. J.; Cooper, G. F.; and Heckerman, D. E. 1989. Reflection and Action under Scarce Resources: Theoretical Principles and Empirical Study. In Proceedings of the Eleventh International Joint Conference on Artificial Intelligence, 1121–1127. Menlo Park, Calif.: International Joint Conferences on Artificial Intelligence.

Laffey, T.; Cox, P. A.; Schmidt, J. L.; Kao, S. A.; and Read, J. Y. 1988. Real-Time Knowledge-Based Systems. *AI Magazine,* 9(1) (Spring 1988): 27-43.

Schwuttke, U. M. 1991. Intelligent Real-Time Monitoring of Complex Systems. Ph.D. diss., Dept. of Electrical Engineering, Univ. of Southern California.

Schwuttke, U. M., and Gasser, L. 1992. Real-Time Metareasoning with Dynamic Trade-Off Evaluation. In Proceedings of the Eleventh National Conference on Artificial Intelligence. Menlo Park, Calif.: American Association for Artificial Intelligence. Forthcoming.

Finance Applications

PHAROS

Ernst & Young Management Consultants & National Westminster

The Credit Assistant

American Express & Inference Corporation

Mocca

Swiss Bank Corporation

CRESUS

Carnegie Mellon University & Norsistemas Consultores S.A.

PHAROS—The Single European Market Adviser

Ebby Adhami, Ernst & Young Management Consultants, Michael Thornley, National Westminster, and Malcolm McKenzie, Ernst & Young Management Consultants

The formation of the single European market (SEM) will create a new business environment in Europe. The competitiveness and, indeed, the survival of many United Kingdom businesses depends on how well they understand and react to the threats and opportunities presented by opening up Europe and associated industry restructuring. Expertise in single-market issues and legislation is scarce and expensive, making it difficult for many organizations to obtain. In addition, the recession has prompted many organizations, particularly the smaller ones, to concentrate their efforts on improving short-term profitability. Most of these organizations cannot afford the resources needed to assess the impact of SEM on their business. This chapter describes PHAROS, an expert system designed to assess the impact of SEM legislation on businesses in the United Kingdom. PHAROS was developed by National Westminster Bank (NatWest) and Ernst & Young Management Consultants. It will be used by 70,000 medium-sized businesses, resulting in millions of pounds of savings for the United Kingdom business community yet offering the bank a competitive advantage. This section discusses the importance of SEM. This importance is assessed in relation to business in the United Kingdom in general and NatWest in particular. How PHAROS was conceived is also discussed.

Why Is the Single European Market Important?

The creation of SEM is one of the greatest challenges that European industry has faced in nearly half a century. The changes it brings will shape the way business will be conducted across the Continent for decades to come. As trade barriers are removed, and business legislation across member states is harmonized, European companies will have access to a market of over 380 million consumers. Markets and industries are likely to undergo progressive restructuring similar to the American deregulatory experience of the last 10 years.

The formation of the single market presents tremendous opportunities, as well as significant threats, to businesses in the United Kingdom, and there will inevitably be major winners and losers. However, with less than 12 months to go, many United Kingdom companies do not appear to have developed robust business plans and operational strategies to effectively meet these changes. Indeed, a recent survey by the Department of Trade and Industry (DTI) showed that although 98 percent of British firms were aware of the creation of SEM, only 41 percent have taken any action, 10 percent are still thinking about it, and a further 28 percent remain convinced that they will not be affected.

Why Is the Single Market Important to National Westminster Bank?

As a major European bank, NatWest was concerned about the degree of indifference within its customer base and the United Kingdom business community in general. Its own strategies for Europe are well advanced, but pivotal to these is the recognition that the success of these strategies is inextricably linked to the business success of its client base. The facts of life for corporate banking in the 1990s mean that it is impossible to sustain a position as a successful financial services organization with a customer base deteriorating in quality and a loan book experiencing significant levels of default.

The difficulty facing NatWest was how to help its customers in a cost-effective manner. The provision of individual consultancy for each of its customers would be prohibitively expensive and time consuming. General exhortation by existing bank executives had not brought about the required level of change. A more unusual and radical method had to be identified that would capture the imagination of NatWest's customers.

How Was the Idea of PHAROS Conceived?

The process that eventually led to the development of PHAROS began with research done in mid-1990 by NatWest among its small- and medium-sized enterprise customers. This research found that the biggest problem facing these organizations was a lack of appropriate information on SEM issues. Nearly one-third of the firms surveyed were prevented from taking any action for this reason alone.

At first, the result was puzzling. From NatWest's perspective, the problem appeared to be precisely the reverse because traditional awareness-raising activities had resulted in an excess of information from countless sources. However, further analysis revealed that the real problem centered on lack of time to identify and analyze this information. This time deficiency, combined with the state of the economy, had pushed SEM down on their list of priorities.

As a direct result, the idea of developing a disk-based means of delivering business-related information about SEM was conceived. This information could be structured to make it easily accessible and simple to use. It would also have an updating mechanism to ensure that the knowledge base remained up to date.

An off-the-shelf product was located in mainland Europe that could provide a solution. This product offered a database of SEM legislation on a disk that could be run on any IBM-compatible personal computer (PC). The user could access the database using either a hierarchical menu or a keyword search.

A limited field trial of the prototype was arranged to evaluate the concept by a representative number of NatWest customers. The results of this exercise, however, were mixed:

First, the database was recognized to be comprehensive, but the information was not business oriented, and key issues could not easily be identified and assessed.

Second, users found it difficult to navigate through the tree structure easily, and virtually all got lost in the hierarchy. Additionally, this structure was unnatural and did not fit in with their way of thinking about the problem.

Third, the keyword search facility relied on a prior knowledge of the terminology used by the developers of the product, causing difficulties.

Fourth, doubts were expressed about a bank's ability to support such a product in the field.

However, if NatWest could arrange for the information to be business oriented and accessed more quickly than a paper-based substitute, users would receive a value-added service of this sort enthusiastically.

Given this positive response to the concept, new objectives for the product were drawn up. These objectives were the following:

First, the product needed to be custom built for NatWest and targeted at decision makers who are typically not computer literate and, thus, demand complete ease of use.

Second, it should be capable of delivering advice specific not only to the relevant industry sector but also to the business itself.

Third, the knowledge base contained within the system must extend across the spectrum of single-market issues for a business and not be limited to banking topics.

Fourth, the advice must be accessible and delivered shortly after starting to use the system.

Fifth, the system itself should not appear too glossy. It must be a practical, functional business tool and not contain overt marketing material.

It was becoming clear that these objectives could only be achieved by arranging a joint venture of some form with another organization. This organization must have wide-ranging business skills outside the traditional banking environment combined with leading-edge system capabilities. These skills were identified as those typically possessed by large firms of management consultants, particularly those with significant experience with both United Kingdom and European business issues. After an appropriate selection process, Ernst & Young Management Consultancy was engaged to undertake the project.

The initial brainstorming sessions identified expert system technology as a strong contender for delivering the required solution. The combination of Ernst & Young's skills and NatWest's market position, its knowledge of its customer base, and its direct distribution system to over one-third of the United Kingdom business community provided the foundation for an ambitious marketing program. In this way, NatWest could deliver a true value-added service to its customers and create significant competitive differentiation for itself in the United Kingdom banking sector by being in the lead toward this 1992 change.

A Description of PHAROS

This section introduces PHAROS. It describes what PHAROS does, what is innovative about PHAROS, why expert system technology was used, how PHAROS was implemented, and how users interact with it.

What Does PHAROS Do?

PHAROS was developed to help organizations in the United Kingdom compete in SEM. It identifies and assesses the issues arising from SEM legislation that directly affect a business and its markets. This information provides valuable input to the business planning process.

Through a series of consultation sessions, PHAROS builds a detailed profile of a business by capturing the key aspects of its current and planned activities. The following areas are covered:

Suppliers: This area elicits information about key suppliers and the major purchases made by a business, including imported goods.

Own Operations: This area is concerned with the internal operation of an organization and covers such facets as logistics, finance, production, marketing, human resources, and information systems.

Products: This area captures information about the nature of the products or services offered by an organization.

Customers: This area covers the key markets for a business, including exports, and issues such as pricing policies as well as the specific needs of customers.

With this unique profile of a business, PHAROS does the following: (1) it identifies SEM legislation that affects a business and that could be important to its future operations; (2) it assesses and highlights the potential business implications of legislation in terms of threats and opportunities; (3) it suggests possible strategic and operational actions that a business can take to minimize the threats and maximize the opportunities; (4) it provides additional detail on particularly complex or technical SEM topics; and (5) it directs the business to sources of information, such as trade associations or government bodies, where further guidance can be obtained.

At any stage during the consultation, intermediate results can be viewed on the screen. At the end of a consultation, PHAROS produces a comprehensive report, which can be printed out, on its conclusions and recommendations.

What Is Innovative about PHAROS?

The expert system techniques used to develop PHAROS represent the best practice in the field, but they do not break any new ground as far as technology is concerned. What is innovative about PHAROS is that it demonstrates how knowledge-based systems can be used to deliver an area of expertise to a large number of users at a low cost.

From NatWest's perspective, PHAROS opens a new chapter in business-to-business marketing. The key to innovation has been to link an ambitious technology project with a marketing strategy to deliver a true value-added service to a major share of the United Kingdom business community. Other considerations that qualify PHAROS as an innovative AI application are as follows:

First, PHAROS will be the most widely distributed operational expert system at least in the United Kingdom, saving the business community millions of pounds of effort.

Second, it represents the first successful attempt at wide-scale retailing of expertise to external organizations using expert systems as a delivery mechanism.

Third, it demonstrates the feasibility of combining diverse sources of expertise to synthesize a new product.

Why Did We Use Expert System Technology?

The following requirements influenced the design and development of PHAROS:

Relevance: Identifying SEM legislation relevant to a particular business is a difficult and time-consuming task. PHAROS would succeed if it could quickly guide a business to information that is directly relevant to its operations.

Business focus: Information sources currently available on SEM legislation are mainly of a technical nature and require expert interpretation to relate them to the specific circumstances of a business. The advice given by PHAROS had to be focused on the business implications of legislation, with technical detail provided as supporting information.

Simplicity of use: The target user population of PHAROS is 70,000 and might eventually grow to be over 100,000 users. For this reason, it is difficult to make many assumptions about the user population and its knowledge of using decision support tools. PHAROS had to be easy to use and understand.

Ease of maintenance: SEM legislation is evolving rapidly, and there would be a need to keep users informed of any developments that affect their businesses. An update of PHAROS is planned every six months until legislation begins to stabilize. The architecture of PHAROS had to facilitate the updating of information without the need for system reconstruction.

These requirements seemed to render a conventional software solution unmanageable. Table 1 summarizes the justification for adopting an expert system approach.

Requirements	Issues	Expert System Solutions
Relevance	Large Search Space	Heuristic Search
	Complex Queries	Partial Pattern Matching
	Incomplete Search Criteria	
Business Focus	Heuristic Knowledge	Rule-Based Representation
Simplicity of Use	Large Number of Questions	Dependency Network
	Complex Dependencies	Truth Maintenance
Ease of Maintenance	Evolving Legislation	Declarative Representation
	New SEM Topics	

Table 1. Justification for Using Expert System Techniques.

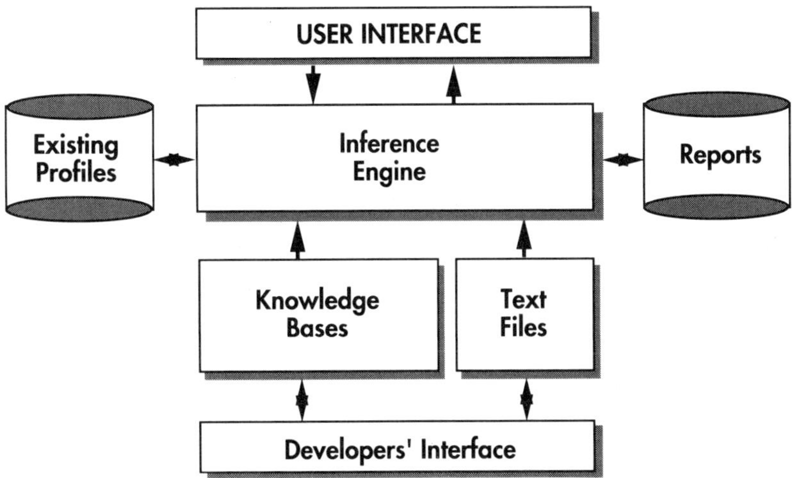

Figure 1. An Overview of the Architecture of PHAROS.

The remaining subsections outline how these requirements are satisfied by applying expert system techniques.

How Is PHAROS structured?

The architecture of PHAROS is illustrated in figure 1. This architecture makes a clear separation between the user interface, inferencing mechanism, and knowledge bases. This separation offers the flexibility to modify the content of the knowledge bases without needing to make major software modifications. This feature is facilitated by the *developers' interface,* which enables knowledge coordinators to view and edit the content of the knowledge bases and textual information, such as context-sensitive help messages.

The inference engine supports backward and forward chaining. The structure of knowledge bases and other related information is shown in figure 2. The knowledge and data bases consist of three components: working memory, knowledge bases, and textual information.

Working memory: The working memory is populated as a user progresses through a consultation. This component includes information supplied by the user about the nature of his/her business, SEM legislation that has been identified as relevant, and the business implications that arise.

Knowledge bases: The core of PHAROS consists of three separate but related knowledge bases. First is the *p*rofiling knowledge base, which includes a dependency network that models the relationship between

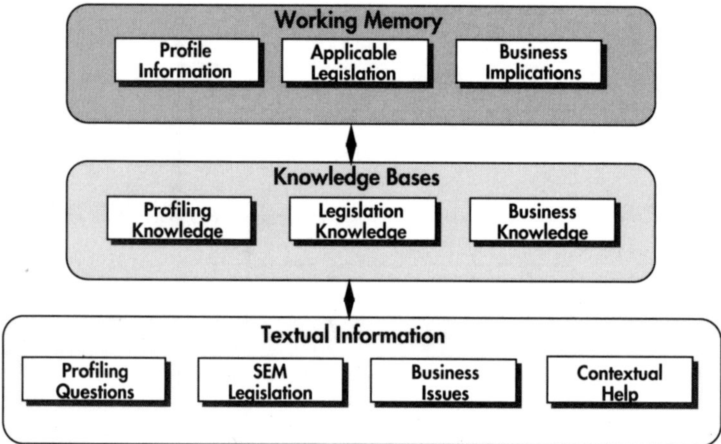

Figure 2. Overview of the Knowledge Base Structure.

all the questions in the system. This approach ensures that only questions that are relevant to a user's business are asked. Second is the *legislation* knowledge base, a set of rules that specify the circumstances under which a piece of legislation becomes relevant to an organization. SEM legislation is grouped under 20 topics, as shown in figure 3. Third is the business knowledge base, which consists of a set of production rules that determine the business impact of a piece of legislation in the context of the individual circumstances of a business. These rules represent the expertise of numerous individuals with both a knowledge of specific industries and a good understanding of changes that will result from the formation of the single market.

Textual information: PHAROS compiles its recommendations using a database of canned text paragraphs. Variables are embedded within text paragraphs that enable PHAROS to tailor its recommendations to the individual circumstances of a business. In addition, help information is stored as a set of text files. PHAROS consists of 720 rules, 120 questions, 551 text files, and 150 help files.

How Is PHAROS Implemented?

PHAROS is implemented using crystal, which is marketed by Intelligent Environments in the United Kingdom. Our choice of development tool was influenced by the following factors:

Technical requirements: Our requirements included support for rule-based representation, good user interface facilities, support for text manipulation, and interfaces to databases and external procedures.

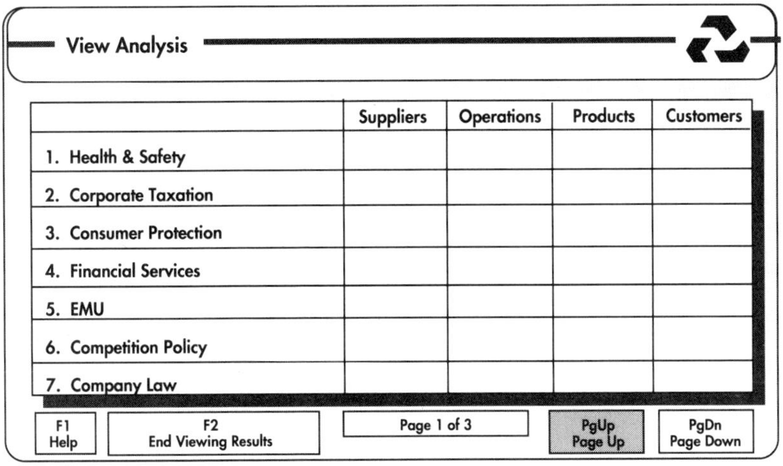

View Analysis

	Suppliers	Operations	Products	Customers
1. Health & Safety				
2. Corporate Taxation				
3. Consumer Protection				
4. Financial Services				
5. EMU				
6. Competition Policy				
7. Company Law				

F1 Help | F2 End Viewing Results | Page 1 of 3 | PgUp Page Up | PgDn Page Down

Figure 3. Summary Matrix Screen.

Hardware requirements: Because PHAROS is aimed at a large number of users, it was of paramount importance that it be able to run on IBM PCs or compatibles under DOS.

Productivity: The productivity of the developers was a key factor that influenced the selection of the development environment. The facilities that were required included screen painting, graphic display of knowledge bases, and good debugging and tracing facilities.

Robustness and performance: PHAROS will be installed on a range of PCs with different configurations and processing capabilities. It was therefore important for the development environment to run reliably on different platforms and perform adequately on a range of PCs.

Licensing and pricing: Initial discussions with tool vendors resulted in a wide range of prices and licensing conditions. Our requirements included an unlimited number of run-time licenses and further development of the application without incurring new license charges.

Other considerations that influenced our final choice included the ability of the vendor to provide training and technical support, the financial stability of the vendor, and the existing development skills of the project team.

How Do Users Interact with PHAROS?

PHAROS is intended for use by a wide range of individuals with varying levels of expertise and experience in using computer-based tools. The system will be used by the top managers within an organization whose time is scarce. Their first impressions are crucial to the success of

PHAROS. Any initial difficulties in understanding the tool and the way it works could deter users and affect their perception of the value of its advice. Hence, a great deal of emphasis was placed on structuring the dialogue and designing the user interface. The key requirements that were addressed are as follows:

Ease of navigation: At any stage during the interaction, information is provided that indicates where the user is and what he/she can do next. In addition, context-sensitive help is available throughout the system, and a tutorial provides example interactions with the system. Field trials proved that most users could learn to navigate through the system with ease.

User versus system control: Given the diversity of the user population, it was important to strike a balance between system-driven and user-driven dialogue. At one extreme, the system needs to guide novice users through all the steps, but experienced users should be offered more control. That balance was achieved by providing a menu-based dialogue with shortcuts for more experienced users. In addition, the consultation is structured to provide the user with maximum control over the sequencing of the dialogue.

Presentation of information: Depending on the nature of a business and the complexity of its operations, PHAROS could identify a large number of issues affecting it. In a complex case, the final report with the supporting technical details can be as large as 100 pages. The way this information is presented to the user was seen as a major determinant of its impact. PHAROS presents its findings on three levels: The first level is the *summary matrix*, a concise summary that highlights the key areas of a business that are affected by a particular SEM topic (figure 3). On this matrix, the rows represent the SEM topics and the columns the four key areas of a business. A tick in a cell indicates that a particular topic affects the corresponding area of the business. This matrix provides a useful summary that at a glance indicates how significantly a business is affected. The second level is *business i*mplications. Behind each tick in the matrix are detailed implications for the particular business with potential actions to be taken. The screen, as shown in figure 4, indicates the number of likely implications and the area of the business that will be affected. Third is *ad*ditional detail. Where necessary, additional background information and technical details are provided on complex topics. This information can relate to the underlying legislation from which a particular business implication derives or provide further detail to clarify a specific issue. The availability of additional detail is indicated by a button marked "detail" that appears next to an implication. The detail can be viewed simply by highlighting the detail button and pressing return.

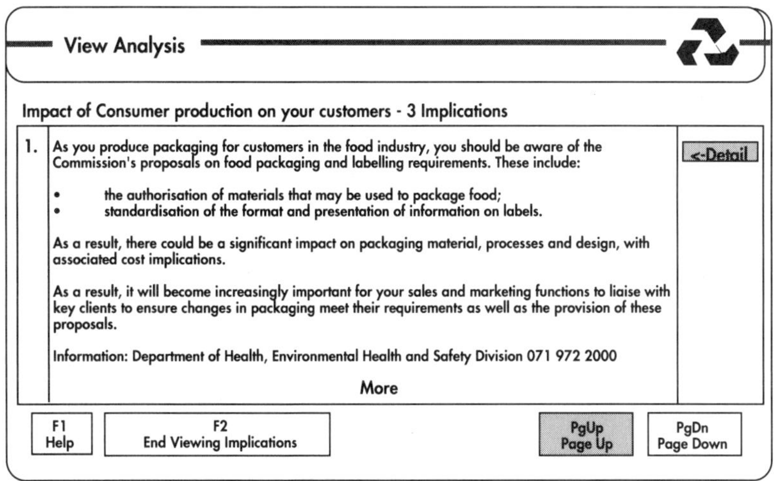

Figure 4. Business Implications Screen.

Feedback: At each stage during the interaction, PHAROS provides feedback in response to users' actions. The provision of feedback is important for maintaining users' confidence, particularly when there are possible delays while PHAROS is performing a complex analysis.

Finally, judicious use of color was made to improve the aesthetics of the product as well as to focus users' attention.

The Commercial Benefits of PHAROS

The benefits of the system were assessed from two perspectives: the benefits to the users and the benefits to NatWest.

What Are the Benefits to Users?

The field trials highlighted that PHAROS will be valuable for most organizations regardless of their level of awareness of single-market issues; for example:

First, for businesses that are already well aware of the single market and the way it will affect their operations, PHAROS provides a check that all the relevant issues, particularly those that are cross-sectoral, were identified.

Second, for businesses that are not significantly affected by the formation of the single market, PHAROS provides a comfort factor by confirming their own assessment of the situation.

Third, for businesses that are unaware of the implications of the single market for their operations, PHAROS provides a detailed analysis of how they will be affected.

For businesses that for whatever reason believe they will not be affected by the single market and are taking no action, PHAROS might indicate new issues not previously considered and, therefore, could prove to be crucial.

For any organization, even a cursory analysis of SEM issues has a considerable cost associated with it. Based on the field trials, such an analysis could cost a minimum of £1000 ($1,767) in resources.

PHAROS provides a comprehensive analysis, and therefore, the market value of its advice could represent a savings of over £70 ($123) million for the United Kingdom business community.

From the users' point of view, PHAROS represents a virtually zero-cost route for accessing major ongoing business research programs, yielding results that are specific to their business and can be achieved rapidly.

What Are the Benefits to NatWest?

Benefits to NatWest include the following:

The first benefit is promoting the image of NatWest as a forward-thinking organization. In the past, NatWest has been proactive in responding to customers' needs, and PHAROS provides it with a new tool to sustain this drive.

The second benefit is providing a competitive edge. Most banks in the United Kingdom have embarked on some program to create awareness of SEM within the business community through seminars and the distribution of brochures. PHAROS offers a marketing tool that enables NatWest to maintain its lead among the United Kingdom banks. We are not aware of any other financial organization in the United Kingdom that provides or plans to provide such a service to their corporate customers.

The third benefit is winning new customers. PHAROS is an integrated part of a marketing program that is aimed at penetrating competitors' customer bases. Linked with a planned sales campaign, this benefit will potentially lead to new business conversions in the corporate market.

Finally and most importantly, NatWest's philosophy is based on a recognition that the success of its customers is fundamental to its own profitability. The outlook over the medium to long term is bleak if customers do not compete successfully in Europe. PHAROS supports this philosophy by placing the single market firmly on the agenda of its corporate customers.

Most of these benefits, although not tangible, are extremely important from NatWest's viewpoint. Compared with other marketing strategies, such as an advertising campaign, PHAROS offers a more effective tool at a comparable cost. One objective of the field trials was to establish the reaction of clients to the provision of such a service by NatWest and the type of followup service they would welcome. The general response was extremely positive, and in every case, clients expressed an interest in such a service.

Two postlaunch activities have been planned to monitor the success of PHAROS. The first is the provision of an update service for a nominal fee. The number of businesses that subscribe to this service will be a further indication of success. In addition, a survey will be conducted to establish what actions were taken by organizations as a result of using PHAROS.

The Development Process

PHAROS was developed using the Ernst & Young methodology for structured techniques for analysis and generation of expert systems (STAGES). STAGES provides a framework for managing the development of expert systems with a strong focus on business requirements.

The components of STAGES support an entire project, from application selection through the investigation phase to delivery and maintenance of an operational system. The core of the methodology is project structure, which gives guidance on organization and staffing; project life-cycle management, and project activities.

How Was PHAROS Developed?

An overview of the project organization showing the key roles and their relationships is shown in figure 5. The project was managed and controlled using the STAGES life-cycle model. This model is based on a spiral model of development that ensures adequate attention is paid, in appropriate proportions, to quality management, project control and reviews, risk management, definition of objectives, and planning and estimating as well as development. The project was conducted in four phases, with formal reviews at the end of each phase and other check points at appropriate stages during each phase. Governed by this life-cycle model were the project activities. The diagram in figure 6 shows the configuration of STAGES activities for the project.

During the development, a number of prototypes were constructed to validate the key deliverables, decisions, and assumptions. The objectives for each prototype were clearly defined and were used to plan the field trials. These prototypes were as follows:

Sampler: The objectives of the sampler were to establish the technical, business, and organizational feasibility of the approach and estimate the level of funding needed for the full development project.

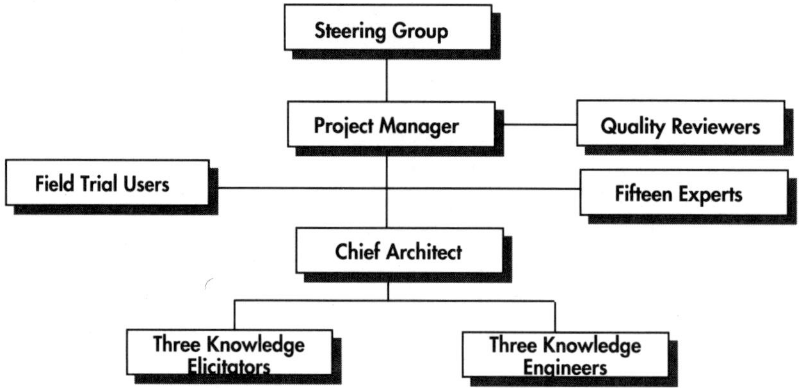

Figure 5. Project Organization.

Prototype 1: The objectives for the first prototype were to assess the efficacy of the user interface and the appropriateness of the advice given by PHAROS in terms of the level of detail and emphasis.

Prototype 2: The objectives for the final prototype were to establish how well PHAROS performed compared to professional management consultants and evaluate the total packaging of the system.

Each prototype was carefully evaluated through field trials with NatWest's customers and internal validation. The outcome of each field trial was used to plan and focus subsequent phases. An important outcome of field trials was the identification of the need by users for an update service.

Work on PHAROS started in April 1991 and finished in January 1992. A summary of project costs is given in table 2.

Cost Category	**Costs (£)**
System Development	220,000
Knowledge Elicitation and Expert Resources	200,000
Production	175,000
Distribution, Marketing, and Support	270,000
Total	**865,000**

Table 2. Summary of Costs.

How Were Costs Justified?

The costs were justified based on maintaining a low unit cost and obtaining new customers.

Low unit cost: The unit cost of PHAROS is approximately £12 for each customer, and the cost of the project can be justified on this basis

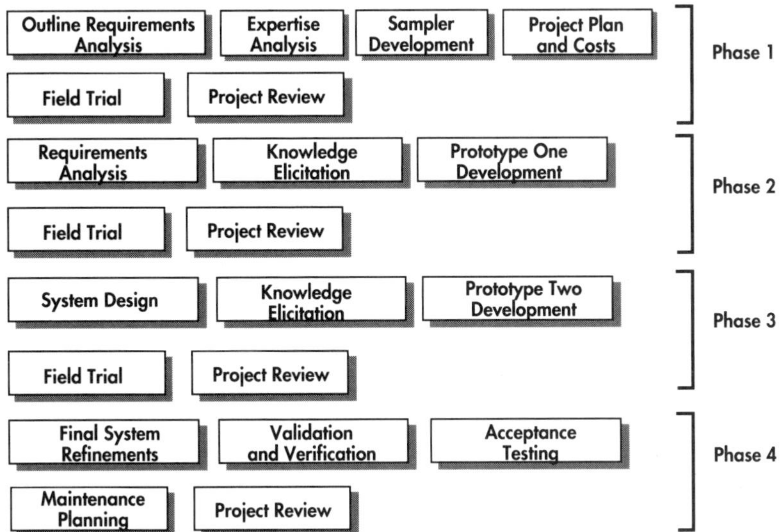

Figure 6. Project Phases and Activities.

alone. This amount is considerably lower than the cost of alternative services NatWest could provide as part of its normal corporate customer care program. In addition, other benefits might be realized.

New customers: Any new customer attracted as a result of PHAROS represents a profit-making opportunity.

Therefore, NatWest was convinced of the benefits of PHAROS, but it was concerned about the project's feasibility and whether it could deliver within acceptable time scales. For this reason, the project was structured to address the major risk issues early in the development process. The investigation phase was instrumental in demonstrating the feasibility of the project and creating confidence that the project could deliver.

How Was PHAROS Validated?

Because PHAROS will be distributed so widely, it is paramount that the advice it gives is valid and correct. In addition to internal system verification and destructive testing, a number of activities were undertaken to validate the advice provided by PHAROS:

Walkthrough by experts: The knowledge bases of PHAROS were documented using specially designed rule charts that ease validation. Experts on each SEM topic conducted a detailed walkthrough of each topic to ensure completeness and correctness.

External validation: The rule charts were further validated by European specialists who were not involved in knowledge elicitation. This validation not only provided an additional comfort factor but also ensured that recent changes in legislation were reflected in the rule charts.

Field trials: Three separate field trials were carried out to validate the assumptions underlying the system. In total, 15 representative NatWest's customers were visited. The final field trial included a comparison of the advice given by PHAROS and that of a SEM expert. In each case, PHAROS identified a larger number of issues that included those identified by the human expert. However, experts were able to prioritize the issues where PHAROS could not.

Dynamic validation: The system was worked through by over 50 people within NatWest and Ernst & Young. This work involved presenting PHAROS with case studies and reviewing the relevance of its recommendations.

Acceptance testing: The system was formally acceptance tested by NatWest staff members.

How Will PHAROS Be Maintained?

An update of PHAROS is planned on a biannual basis. In addition to updating the knowledge contained in PHAROS, each update will include a new module. The module that is currently being investigated for the first update is an in-depth analysis of environmental legislation that is a rapidly emerging area of importance for businesses.

The updates to the existing knowledge bases will be carried out by a team of knowledge coordinators who have some training in expert systems. Stringent change control procedures were put in place to ensure the integrity of the knowledge bases. The updates of PHAROS will highlight the recent SEM developments affecting users since they last consulted PHAROS.

Planning for Deployment

The deployment process for PHAROS commenced as soon as its feasibility was established. The deployment process was just as important as the development process in ensuring the success of the product. This process involved formulating tactical marketing and deployment strategies to support the launch of the new product.

The thrust of the marketing drive centered on the following key issues:

Identifying Competitors' Response Routes

The first stage was a forward study to identify likely competitor response routes to the proposed outline marketing plan. The main conclusion was that a straight "me too" response was unlikely. A successful retaliation would be possible through a joint venture with other major players in the wider United Kingdom business arena, particularly if partners could bring enhanced credibility to the product. These partners included government bodies such as DTI or a major alternative distribution channel such as the Confederation of British Industry (CBI). A series of activities were undertaken to involve all potential joint venture partners in the distribution process: First, negotiations took place with CBI, which resulted in it becoming involved. Second, as a co-partner and with an agreement to promote and distribute PHAROS to its membership base, DTI was kept fully advised, and the involvement of users of government advisory units throughout the country was secured. Third, sponsorship deals with other major players secured additional distribution arrangements.

Deciding a Pricing Policy

It was recognized that the level of sustainable competitive advantage was directly linked to the level of distribution. A pricing policy was devised both to support this arrangement and yield an acceptable return on investment on the following basis: First, the initial package was to be provided free of charge to all businesses regardless of whether they were NatWest customers. Second, the price of the biannual update service was to reflect value and give preference to customers through a differentiated annual charge of £40 ($70) for customers and £125 ($220) for noncustomers.

Creating Internal and External Awareness

Internal and external awareness and promotional campaigns were developed in parallel with the system project. These campaigns included the development of a combined leaflet and application form that outlined the capabilities of the product and solicited the data required to drive NatWest's central database and provided the information needed to support a help-line service.

Detailed press, advertising, and distribution arrangements were also put in place to coincide with the target launch date. These arrangements included an internal briefing and demonstrations of the system to NatWest's regional sales managers and the preparation of a specially designed training and awareness guide for NatWest's managers and staff to provide information on SEM, its importance to NatWest, the rationale for PHAROS, and their role in making it a success.

Addressing the Logistics of Distribution and Technical Support

Concerns about NatWest's ability to support a software program of this nature in the field were addressed by commissioning NatWest's computing subsidiary, CentreFile Ltd., to provide software support and manage disk reproduction.

Launching the Product

PHAROS was formally launched on 18 February 1992. At the time of writing this chapter, April 1992, requests for 15,000 copies of the system have been received.

The marketing objectives for this campaign are demanding, and targets have been set at ambitious levels. For the first stage of the project, it is intended to send out 70,000 copies of PHAROS. However, the true measure of success will hinge on how many subscribers sign up for the update service. The target is 35,000 users at a minimum.

Conclusions

In conclusion, PHAROS demonstrates how expert system technology can be used to gain competitive advantage. The main factors contributing to the success of the project were as follows:

- A strong focus on business objectives and users' requirements as opposed to technical issues
- An effective combination of a strong marketing program and advanced technology to develop a unique product reaching a significant proportion of the United Kingdom business community
- Management commitment and support throughout the project, reflecting its belief in the objectives of the project
- An appropriate project structure bringing together skills and roles necessary for a successful project
- A structured approach to development with strong emphasis on risk, project, and quality management
- A well–thought-out deployment plan paving the way for the introduction of the product

In summary, all the indications are that PHAROS will achieve its primary twin objectives—competitive advantage for NatWest and true added value for the customers.

The Credit Assistant: The Second Leg in the Knowledge Highway for American Express

James Dzierzanowski, American Express, Eric Hestenes, Inference Corporation, and Susan Lawson, American Express

This chapter describes the development and deployment of the credit assistant (CA), a knowledge-based system to support credit operations for Travel-Related Services (TRS) of the American Express Company. CA was developed using ART-IM, a rule-based programming environment from Inference Corporation. American Express developed this application under a UNIX environment (SUN and RS/6000) and deployed it into a high-volume real-time mainframe environment. CA was designed to be fully cooperative across business operation units with the authorizer's assistant (AA) and other knowledge-based systems currently under development. CA also reflects advances in technology and general trends in the AI industry that have taken place since AA was implemented in 1989. This chapter also introduces the *knowledge highway* concept, the design and construction of a series of cooperative knowledge-based systems to support a global operational strategy of authorizations, credit operations, fraud detection, new account processing, and customer service at American Express.CA was designed to support online credit analysis of card members within the credit operations environment of American Express and to synergistically interact with AA (Dzierzanowski et al. 1989). Credit Operations reviews accounts for the Personal, Gold, Platinum, and OPTIMA card products for credit risk and potential fraud situations. The review process is driven by internal American Express risk management statistical models, which set up risky accounts to be reviewed by analysts. Accounts in question could be set up for many reasons, for example, those showing a delinquency or a history of past due balances. When an account is queued to an analyst for inspection, CA is invoked to support the review by denoting interesting features on the card member's account and recommending actions. Previous to the implementation of CA, a case required, on the average, 22 transactions to achieve resolution. With CA, one transaction can review data, synthesize information, annotate an account, and provide advice and recommendations to a credit analyst. Advice ranges from setting the account up to be reviewed again in several weeks to recommending the cancellation of a card in serious situations. To support continuous training, scripts are also generated if interaction with the card member occurs. In addition, CA ensures that credit policies are consistently enforced. For example, state laws vary on permissible collection activities. Collection procedures allowed in Minnesota might be illegal in Maine. CA takes all the different statutes into account and guarantees that the analyst is in compliance. As scheduled enhancements are rolled out, the system autonomously makes decisions on some cases, composes letters to card members, orders additional information when necessary, and routes accounts into queues for specific actions by analysts.

Designed as components in the knowledge highway of cooperative expert systems, CA and AA have been built for compatibility and allow for the real-time exchange of data. Results from one system can be incorporated into the decision process of the other. AA is part of American Express's front line of service in credit authorization at a point of sale. It interfaces with the TRS credit authorization system (CAS), which is based on a transaction-processing facility–based system built for high volume and transaction rates. AA handles transactions referred by CAS. Those charges that are not resolved by AA automatically are then sent to an authorizer with supporting advice and recommendations, thus serving as a decision support tool.

Credit Assistant Expertise and System Review

The CA expertise is segmented into components that analyze accounts across a number of dimensions. These components include the credit-analysis expertise; expertise to recognize fraudulent use of the card (that is, mail-order fraud); a component to recognize misuse of the card by the card member or supplemental card members; expertise to recognize administrative errors on accounts and remove outdated information; a component to recognize special customer service situations; a component to generate scripts if interaction with the card member occurs; and a dimension that determines the reason the statistical models set up the account for review.

When an account is set up, it can remain in review for weeks and be reviewed a dozen or more times by many analysts before the issue with the account is resolved. Therefore, the expertise must support handling the account over time and consider the actions already taken by CA and analysts on the account. For example, suppose the initial recommendation was to talk to the card member to obtain additional financial information. Accordingly, the analyst attempts to telephone the card member but is unsuccessful. In this situation, CA aids the analyst in deciding what to do: for example, send a letter, fax the card member, or wait and try to telephone the card member at a later time. Also, depending on which of these actions is taken, CA decides what date to set for the account to be brought back up for a continuation of the work effort. These decisions vary depending on the account status (that is, whether the account is delinquent or perhaps has an unusually high balance), previous experience with the card member, and the credit laws where the card member resides that regulate how often contacts can be made with the card member. When the account is activated again to continue the work effort, CA must take into account the actions already taken or attempted as well as spending activity that has occurred in the interim.

In making a decision on an account, CA accesses a large source of internal and external information about the card member. Depending on what is available for each card member, these data can include card member banking information; statistical risk management model account evaluation; card member information (occupation, income, and so on); history of the account, including payments, delinquencies, and types and amounts of purchases; AA's evaluation of the account; history of the Credit Operations current and previous interactions with the card member, and the credit bureau report

CA is invoked when an analyst working at a 3270 terminal pulls a case out of a work queue from the work-flow management system. To fit into the MVS-IMS environment, CA is embedded into a transaction, which is controlled with a COBOL driver program. Part of the COBOL code maps data directly from IMS databases to a screen. The driver program also passes the IMS data, AA's evaluation of the account, and the CAS information to the knowledge-based system portion of the CA transaction. The flexible advice and recommendations region is built by the knowledge-based system portion of CA and passed back through a buffer to the driver program for display. To further refine the information that is presented to the analysts through the advice and recommendations portion of the screen, rules were designed to select and prioritize account information for display. Therefore, the best of both technologies is used: COBOL for transaction control in a mainframe environment and display of static data and the knowledge-based system for the reasoning component and flexible display of account control information and analytic results. CA operates in a real-time environment and has become the primary credit review and analysis transaction.

Development and Deployment Strategy

The knowledge-based system industry has moved away from the requirement of highly specialized development hardware to more conventional environments such as UNIX workstations, personal computer (PC) platforms, and mainframes. In many cases, knowledge-based system vendors now fully support platform portability that allows application developers to select development and deployment options based on cost-benefit business issues. CA took advantage of these trends. The rule-based expertise was developed using ART-IM and MOTIF on a UNIX platform (both the SUN and the RS/6000 were supported). The rules were then deployed in a mainframe environment. Tools were specifically built on the workstation to represent American Express–specific data structures, address technology transfer issues, support context-sensitive help, and speed interactive development and testing. As a graphic user interface standard, MOTIF was selected to support portability, and resource languages were used to ease maintenance. The knowledge-based component of CA was designed for performance; therefore, a forward-chaining, data-driven approach was selected with rules to control expertise and the overall system.

Strengths and Weaknesses

As with any project, there are aspects that the developers recognize as accomplishments and issues with the system that would be handled differently in the future. Some of the strengths of the CA environment are as follows:

Regression test bed: CA has the ability to verify, validate, and statistically measure the expertise in terms of its impact on the credit operations environment.

Control panel: CA has the ability of a manager to control various aspects of the CA expertise to support the management of daily operations. For example, if volumes are unexpectedly high, CA can be empowered with greater decision-making authority to resolve certain cases without human intervention.

Information overload: CA handles the information overload situation by reviewing and subsequently presenting only the necessary account information with recommended actions, thus turning data and information into knowledge.

Ability to reason over time: CA can reason about previous actions that it recommended on an account, analyze effectiveness, and subsequently recommend new actions.

Weaknesses embodied in CA include the following:

Mainframe deployment: Because of mainframe release cycles and procedures, rapid change to the knowledge base is difficult.

3270 interface: Given the nonconversational IMS mainframe environment, the screen design and overall flexibility of the user interface is diminished.

Project Team, Timelines, and Cost

The project team comprised members from TRS Advanced Technologies, Business Systems Development, Credit Operations (business analysts were the domain experts), and Risk Management, as well as external contractors, to support one-on-one training. The project spanned a period of 18 months from conception to deployment. Although it might seem that this duration is lengthy, the time required to develop business requirements and achieve consensus from all U.S. operation centers demands such project length. It is the perspective of corporate American Express that knowledge-based systems have matured from a risky technology (as prevailed when the development of AA was undertaken) to a stable technology. Therefore, the corporate technology strategy currently funds knowledge-based system R&D projects to support a technology paradigm shift and infuse this technology into conventional system development and maintenance organizations. The project team consisted of one technical project manager, one senior knowledge engineer, 2 system development programmers, one knowledge engineer for technology transfer and rule development, one UNIX-MOTIF ART-IM developer for the construction of the workstation development environment, two business representatives, and one risk management representative.

Implementation Strategy for Knowledge-Based Systems

When management decided to continue the construction of knowledge-based systems based on the success of AA, a case study of the success of AA was initiated, and the results were applied to other portions of the business. The study indicated that systems of this type can broadly be applied in operations such as (1) work-flow management, (2) referral reduction, and (3) advice and recommendations.

Knowledge-based system technology can be applied to the work-flow management of card member accounts as cases are moved from one area to another for work and can perform a series of simple actions on the account. Referral reduction is a goal in a high-volume, transaction-oriented environment. Systems such as AA and CA allow for the automation of many decisions that previously would have been referred to an analyst for action. Finally, when a card member's account cannot be handled automatically by a knowledge-based system, advice and recommendations are generated and provided to the analyst on how to handle the account. With these three broad strategies, knowledge-based systems support growth of the business while they control expenses, help enforce compliance with regulatory laws, help implement American Express best business practices, decrease training time, and provide consistent quality service to the card member.

Knowledge Highway Concept

The knowledge highway is the concept of a series of cooperative knowledge-based systems that utilize the results of each component member of the highway to support company-wide service to the card member. An example from the medical domain illustrates the concept of the knowledge highway: Imagine a patient undergoing medical treatment by a general practitioner, who consults with an orthopedic surgeon and a neurologist for diagnosis of spinal pain. In consulting with specialists and using their expertise, the general practitioner accesses specialized expertise outside his/her own realm of expertise. He/she taps into a cooperative human network (knowledge highway) that he/she has established with a number of medical specialists to help properly diagnose and treat the patient. In a comparison of this notion with the business of American Express, a card member can call in with a customer service issue, which invokes a knowledge-based system to support the interaction between the card member and the customer service analyst. In resolving the customer's concern, other knowledge-based systems can be invoked to review a possible fraud or credit-related issue.

The deployment status of the knowledge highway in American Express is as follows:

Authorizer Assistant
U.S.–wide production, November 1989

Credit Assistant
Initial production operating center, August 1991
Full U.S.–wide Production, December 1991

New Accounts Assistant
Expected deployment, November 1992

Information Technology Issues: Waterfall Versus Modified Spiral

The waterfall development methodology has been used successfully in traditional large system development; however in a practical sense, the waterfall methodology was not designed to support largely heuristically based systems. In contrast, the spiral methodology is most often used in object-oriented programming systems, but it does not explicitly denote the incorporation of management control and review. Therefore, a blend of the best of both approaches was used to develop a methodology that would support knowledge-based system development in our corporate environment.

The spiral methodology was modified to incorporate an empowered user into the technical development team for immediate decisions and, most importantly, couple the development process with the appropriate management checkpoints to ensure development was meeting user requirements and expectations. This modified spiral approach supports the rapid prototyping concept that contributes to faster time to market and improved developer productivity with the appropriate management controls often required in large corporations.

Maintenance

CA was designed to rapidly add expertise enhancements and provide legacy. The members of the system development organization that is responsible for the support and enhancements to American Express applications were part of the CA development team. One of the major goals of the project was to facilitate the technology transfer process of knowledge-based systems from an advanced technology group to the system development organization. The system group is now responsible for all CA changes and enhancements.

Conclusion

CA was successfully deployed to provide online interactive support to the credit operations business of American Express. From a technology perspective, one accomplishment of CA was to develop a system on a UNIX workstation using industry-standard products (ART-IM and MOTIF), supporting developers with a fast, portable, and flexible environment, and deploy the knowledge base into a mainframe environment for economies of scale. Finally, from a higher corporate business view, CA is the second leg in a continuing strategy to build and deploy cooperative knowledge-based systems (the knowledge highway), provide improved customer service, manage business operations and growth, and reduce credit and fraud losses.

Acknowledgments

The authors want to thank Neil Goldsmith, Corporate Technology Strategy, and Edward Hatler, Advanced Technology, American Express, and Eric Stablow, Expertec Corporation.

References

Dzierzanowski, J.; Chrisman, K.; MacKinnon, G.; and Klahr, P. 1989. The Authorizer's Assistant—A Knowledge-Based Credit-Authorization System for American Express. Presented at 1989 Innovative Applications of Artificial Intelligence Conference, Palo Alto, Calif., 28–30 March.

MOCCA: A Set of Instruments to Support Mortgage Credit Granting

Steve Hottiger and Dieter Wenger, Swiss Bank Corporation

Mortgage credit granting has to be supported by task-oriented instruments (highly interactive support tools that enable cooperative problem solving) because of increasing competition and unfriendly economic circumstances. MOCCA (mortgage controlling and consulting assistant) provides instruments for decision support, customer consultancy, and management. Most of the underlying models in MOCCA are innovative in terms of being either completely new or operative for the first time. The implementation of the application is based on a combination of different knowledge-based techniques, such as agent-based processing, generic application building blocks, fuzzy measure, data-driven paradigm, and a two-layer windowing system. MOCCA (mortgage controlling and consulting assistant) is now being used in the major branch offices of Swiss Bank Corporation (SBC). The development of the application required two person-years.

Task Domain

Mortgage credit granting is a central activity in the Swiss banking business. More than $35 billion or nearly one-third of all SBC assets are

covered directly or indirectly by real estate. Based on decades of high real gross national product and a restricted amount of real estate set against growing demand, investments in property were considered nearly risk free for a long time. In the last couple of years, however, the economic stagnation has affected the real estate market. Traditional models and techniques are no longer able to provide support in defending against growing risks, such as the interest rate risk and business and customer risks, or competing better given the unfriendly economic circumstances.

The interest rate risk became important when mortgages could no longer be refinanced by favorable long-term savings. This situation led to more and more money being absorbed on the interest volatile and expensive markets. As a consequence, mortgage rates had to be adjusted several times, which caused solvency difficulties for more customers. Because no operative models were available for the prediction of credit worthiness, no workable management policy could be developed. There was also no cost-calculation instrument to separate the profitable deals from the others. Recently, the decreasing demand resulted in a remarkable reduction in prices, causing anxiety among some local financial institutes engaged mainly in mortgage lending. The value of the real estate had been estimated too high; therefore, the invested money was no longer fully covered. To complicate matters, these valuations were often done by external architects whose judgments couldn't be checked sufficiently.

Global banks such as SBC have to compete on the mortgage market with a range of specialized financial institutions that are able to provide more attractive mortgage rates and services. Moreover, today's customers are used to having connections to more than one financial firm, depending on the service and the security provided. Therefore, like any other company, a bank is forced to offer attractive and competent consulting services, including areas that are not traditional for a bank, such as tax and budget consultancy. A global bank has the advantage of a large variety of products compared with more specialized competitors. By promoting cross-selling at each point of sale, this advantage can be transformed into higher profits. Acquiring knowledge of the variety and complexity of the offered products is a great challenge to a customer consultant. With the complexity of the products growing, it is nearly impossible for him/her to offer all the products without the support of a computer, especially if he/she cannot invest more time in the consultation. The supporting tools must be graphically attractive, self-explanatory, readily understandable, and flexible in any situation. They have to motivate the user to explore the underlying models. Furthermore, they have to be efficiently adaptable to new banking products.

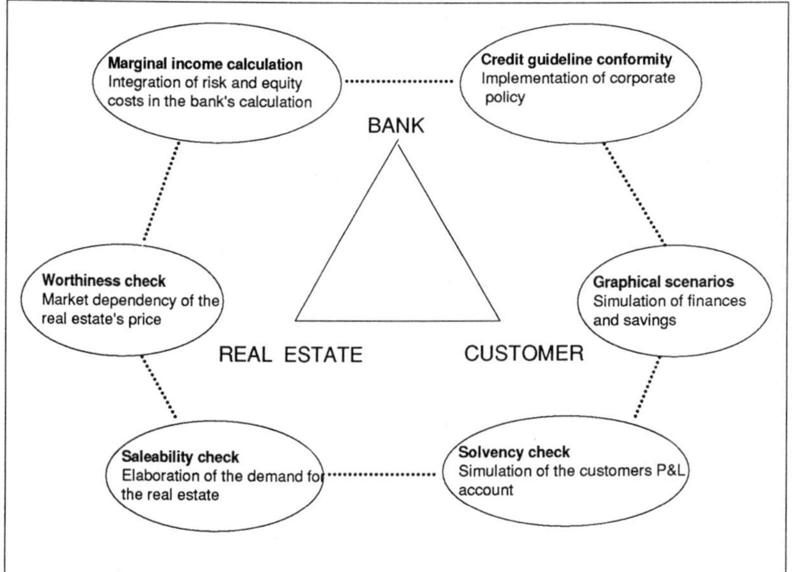

Figure 1. Overview of MOCCA.

The use of knowledge-based techniques promised several advantages compared with more traditional approaches in the modeling of the complex, incomplete, and heterogeneous task domain. Today, this assumption has been confirmed completely. In the following sections, we introduce MOCCA and elaborate on the combinations of knowledge-based techniques on which the application is built.

Overview of MOCCA

MOCCA broadly covers the areas of decision support, risk control, customer consultancy, and management support. It appears as a homogeneous application based on a set of heterogeneous instruments.

MOCCA is decision oriented. It is based on a model that collects, relates, and evaluates all components of the decision process based on their importance. MOCCA guarantees that depending on the complexity of the case, the most critical and economically important elements are always examined, elements such as a positive marginal income for the bank, degree of conformity with internal credit guidelines, customer solvency, worthiness of the real estate, and salability (figure 1).

Besides the decision process, MOCCA also models the mortgage business in various dimensions (figure 2). Each dimension has different levels of abstraction that require different methods and information.

They are represented by an object hierarchy in which the different processes can be attached according to the level of abstraction.

MOCCA is not an expert system in the sense of imitating the expert's problem-solving behavior. It is a system for cooperative problem solving. The occasion to develop a new system has allowed SBC to implement models based on theory as well as knowledge from other banking sectors, particularly if they provide better information and are acceptable to the expert (see the following section). The intention behind MOCCA is to shape the future, not rebuild the past.

The implementation of the selected models was driven by the requirements of flexibility, self-explanation, and easy handling. Thus, the expert was motivated to explore the models, test their usefulness, and develop decision-oriented measures for the evaluation. If no existing models were available, they had to be developed in an iterative prototyping process in close cooperation with the expert. Examples of these models include solvency check and salability investigation.

The set of customer consulting instruments is closely attached to the decision models. In this way, MOCCA encourages the user to work with the customer and analyze his/her financial background to get better decision quality. In the following section, we present some of the economic innovations of MOCCA.

Economic Innovations in MOCCA

With MOCCA has come some economic innovations, including task-oriented application, the ability to make theory operational, and the use of interactive simulation instruments. These innovations are discussed in the following subsections.

Task-Oriented Application

MOCCA is completely task-oriented. It is used as an intelligent assistant at different levels of the mortgage credit-granting process (figure 3).

MOCCA allows the different levels (management and front) to work closely together, primarily because it facilitates communication.

The architecture of MOCCA is multidimensional, based on a system-oriented approach where several subsystems are integrated into one system. The user is driven by the critical points of the current case and not by the structure of the user interface. To carry through each manipulation automatically, MOCCA makes use of the data-driven paradigm.

MOCCA is strongly decision oriented. The evaluations of all aspects are related to a scale. In this way, deals become comparable, and the

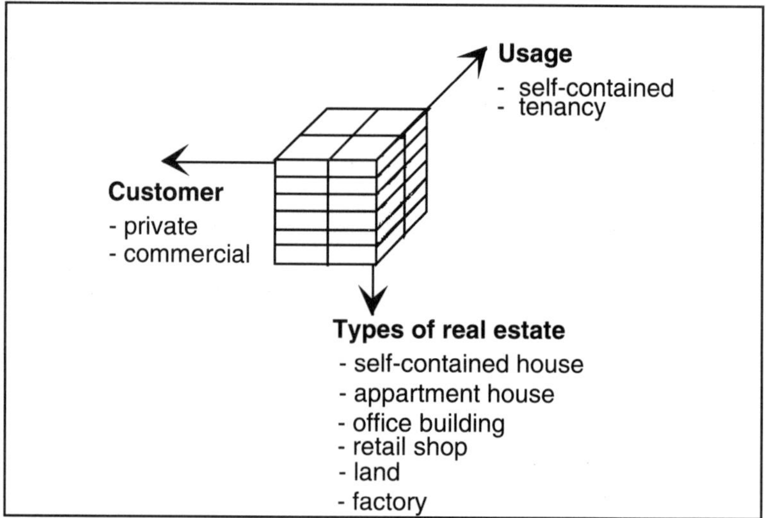

Figure 2. Dimensions of the Mortgage Business.

results are prepared for classification. In addition, MOCCA supports multiperson decisions. It enables the user to add information in an informal way when he/she wants to change an evaluation of the system.

Theory Becomes Operative

There are several ways in which MOCCA has turned theory into operation. The property-worthiness analysis is based on two competitive models: the Lageklassenmodell of Nägeli (1980) and the Strukturwertmodell of Fierz (1987). Although both were regarded as valuable, they were never used because of the large effort required to perform one single evaluation. In MOCCA, the models are implemented efficiently and in a flexible way.

Now, the strengths and weaknesses of these models have been explored widely.

The model for the marginal income calculation was developed in another banking department. With the implementation in MOCCA, it was possible to develop decision-oriented standards for the evaluation of the results. Interactive simulation instruments proved to be an excellent medium to bring different experts together for the elaboration of such standards. Now that the model is decision oriented, it is really operative.

Interactive Simulation Instruments Replace Rules of Thumb

The solvency check for private customers was based on a simple rule of

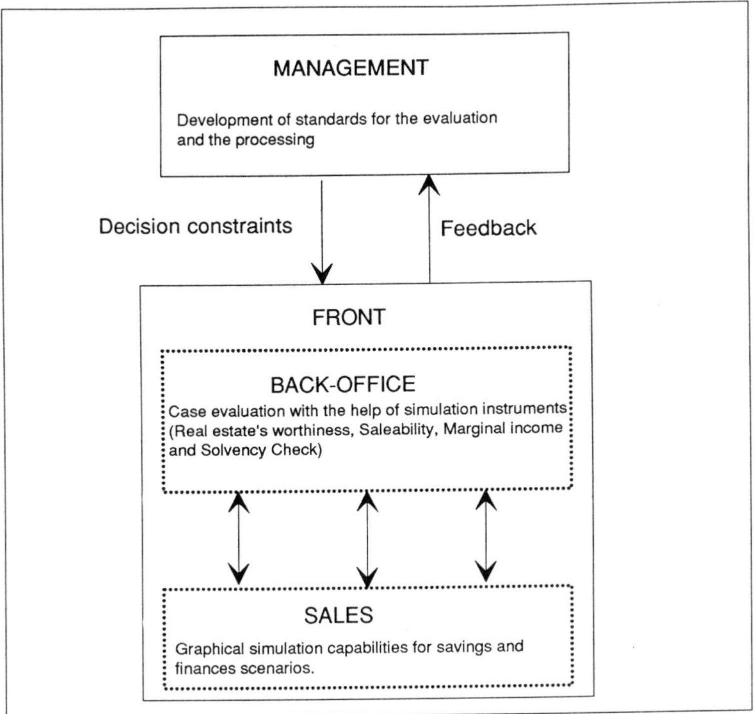

Figure 3. Levels of Mortgage Credit Granting.

thumb: If the costs for mortgage interest, repayment, and maintenance exceed one-third of the income, then solvency is considered critical. It is obvious that for higher incomes, this rule is too restrictive, whereas for lower incomes, it is not restrictive enough. The new solvency check in MOCCA is the result of an intensive prototyping process conducted during the first few months of the project. Expert and developer met once every week for at least two months until the credit section was satisfied with the new model. The evaluation is now based on the balance between income after mortgage interest, repayment of principal, maintenance and utilities, other interest and taxes, and a family budget that guarantees a reasonable standard of living (figure 4). The budget can be customized separately, as is the tax calculation. Although a larger base of information must be examined, the model is easy to understand and, therefore, is much better accepted than the initial rule of thumb.

New Decision Parameters Reduce Risk

The salability investigation is crucial for the credit decision because it

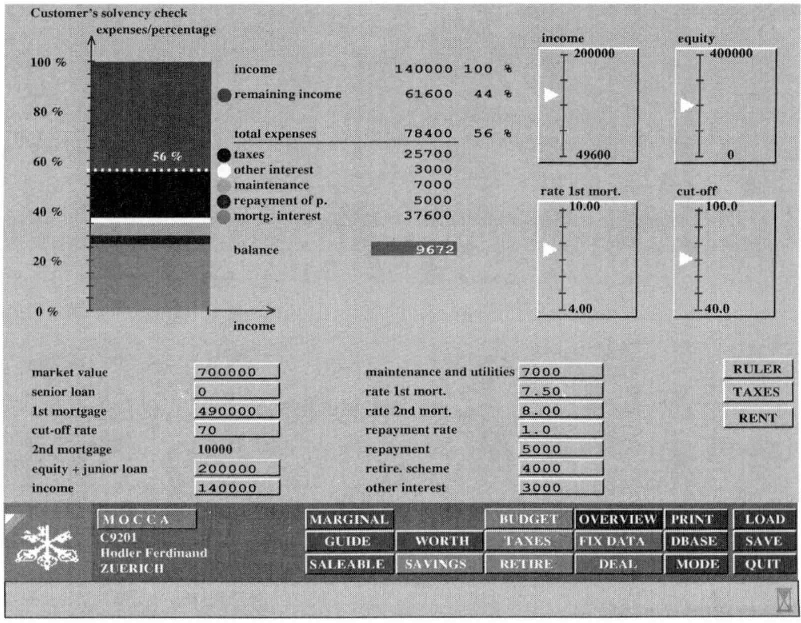

Figure 4. Solvency Check.

is a leading indicator of property risk (along with the worthiness investigation). The bank has to avoid the risk of becoming proprietor of the real estate when there is no longer any acceptable demand for the property. The importance of this risk has recently become apparent in different parts of the business. The model implemented in MOCCA is completely new—not even a rule of thumb exists, in contrast to the solvency check. It was elaborated by the expert who was inspired by the solvency check solution and the worthiness investigation. He combined them into a new model that calculates the minimum required income at different financial constellations and the quality of the property according to the worthiness model and compares them with the possible demand. In this way, any object can be classified by its market attractiveness.

With the elaboration of taxes and personal budget, important competitive advantages are achieved, requiring little effort by the staff. In addition, these elements enlarge the information base for a more competent evaluation. Although they are crucial for any solvency investigation, they had never been implemented before.

The development of all economic innovations is closely tied to the underlying technological environment, which consists of a combination and an extension of different knowledge-based techniques. The following section discusses the technological innovations that allow real prototyping with full reusability, the composition of heterogeneous instruments, and the overall automatic truth maintenance mechanism.

Technological Innovations in MOCCA

The technology described in this section enabled iterative model-oriented development (model-oriented prototyping), which was an effective and, we believe, general methodology for developing knowledge-intensive, cooperative applications (instruments). *Agent-based processing* is a concept for modeling and mastering knowledge-driven processing that claims a powerful knowledge representation by combining objects, lists, and tables. The highly iterative development of operative prototypes demands fast technical realization that is achieved by generic building blocks for the problem-solving components and the user interface. In addition, the outlined two-layer windowing system guarantees platform independence.

Agent-Based Processing

Agent-based processing is part of the executable methodology for knowledge-based application development (EMA) (Spirgi, Probst, and Wenger 1990, 1991). It combines the object-oriented, data-driven, and effect-oriented paradigms. The global processing built into MOCCA is based on this approach. Processing is executed by agents that can be seen as a cluster of conceptual rules.

An *agent* consists of an activation, a retrieval, and a processing part (figure 5). The *processing part* produces effects that change the state of the application. An *effect* is a manipulation of information in an area, for example, the internal global data area (mainly built of schemata), the database area, or the screen area. The *retrieval part* accesses all the information that is processed by methods to set up the necessary effects. All areas can be accessed. The *activation part* is responsible for the activation of the agent. A matching is done that compares internal global data with the pattern. The activation pattern, the retrievals, and the effects declare the agent exhaustively as well as the processing on a conceptual level.

In figure 5, the pattern of the activation part matches the information pieces i1, i2, and i3. The agent accesses internal global data (i4, i5, and i6) and the database area (i7). The effects, produced by the processing part, manipulate the internal global data (e1, e2, and e3), the database area (e4), and the screen area (e5).

The impact of the agent-based approach was tremendous for the prototyping, the cooperative work of the different subsystems, and the

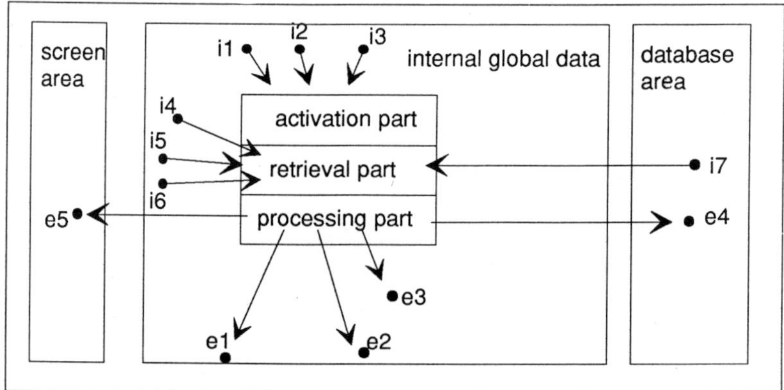

Figure 5. Structure of an Agent.

flexibility and evolution of the application.

Objects, Lists, and Tables: One Conceptual Unity

All these representations have their advantages and weaknesses. In MOCCA, they are combined in a complementary fashion to benefit from the advantages of each.

Object-oriented representation is powerful for deep object structures (many abstraction levels and concepts), but with respect to mass data (thousands of objects), it is inefficient and consumes much storage space. The strengths and weaknesses of a table are just the opposite. Therefore, both representations are used and combined. Figure 6 points out the principle. Each instance of the object DEAL (figure 6a) equals one row of the table (figure 6b).

Extending the object-oriented representation by lists improves the capability for building associations. In MOCCA, in addition to a deep structure, a shallow relational structure exists (associations 1:n, n:1, and n:m). A simple example is shown in figure 7. In the worthiness investigation, different descriptors have an impact on different aspects of worthiness. There is an n:m relation between descriptor and aspect. The relation object is called p-eval and has the attributes value and weight. Figure 7a shows the conceptual representation, and figure 7b shows the technical representation. The object p-eval has disappeared, and an attribute p-eval has been installed that relates aspect and descriptor. In EMA, this technical representation can be built automatically from the conceptual representation with the help of some guidelines. At the end, we get a list of value, weight, and descriptor. This example is only a simple one. More complex shallow structures lead to

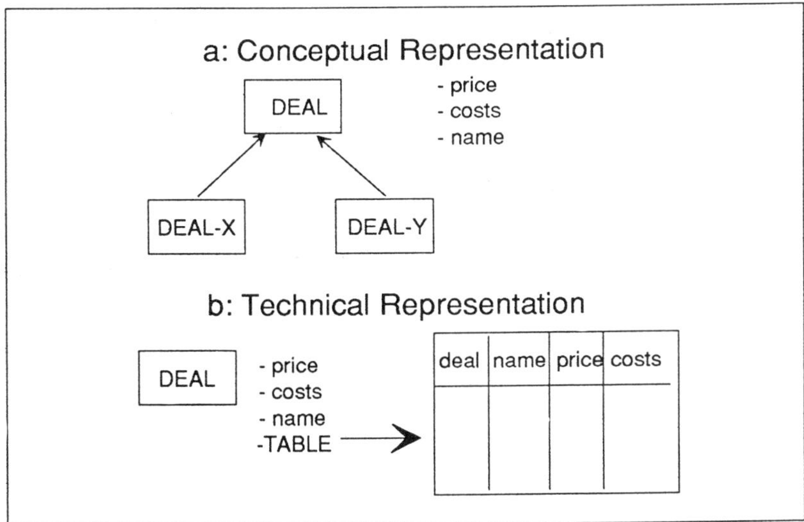

Figure 6. Combination of Objects and Tables.

more complex lists (list of lists). The conceptual unity of different kinds of data representation lets us model on a conceptual level and lets us achieve high efficiency.

Generic Application Building Blocks

The generic systems IO-GEN, IO-PRINT, and G-TECS provide the generic application building blocks for MOCCA. *Generic* means that all blocks can be instantiated and combined easily without a large effort.

IO-GEN provides the user interface building blocks. The main principle is, Point, look, and act. The user can explore the application by moving the mouse to a screen object and looking at the help line, where an explanation of possible specific actions appears. Each screen becomes self-explanatory without any help function. The user can drive the application by clicking a mouse button or giving input through the keyboard. The characteristics of every screen object can be specified by defining methods for the displaying of the object, the changing of the mouse position, and the reaction toward input given through the keyboard or mouse. With the combination of this principle with the data-driven paradigm and the IO-GEN predefined objects, it was possible to create powerful simulations in a short amount of time. With a set of graphic functions, the developer can extend the standard set of screen objects if a new element is needed. If such a new item is useful for similar topics in other applications, it is generalized and

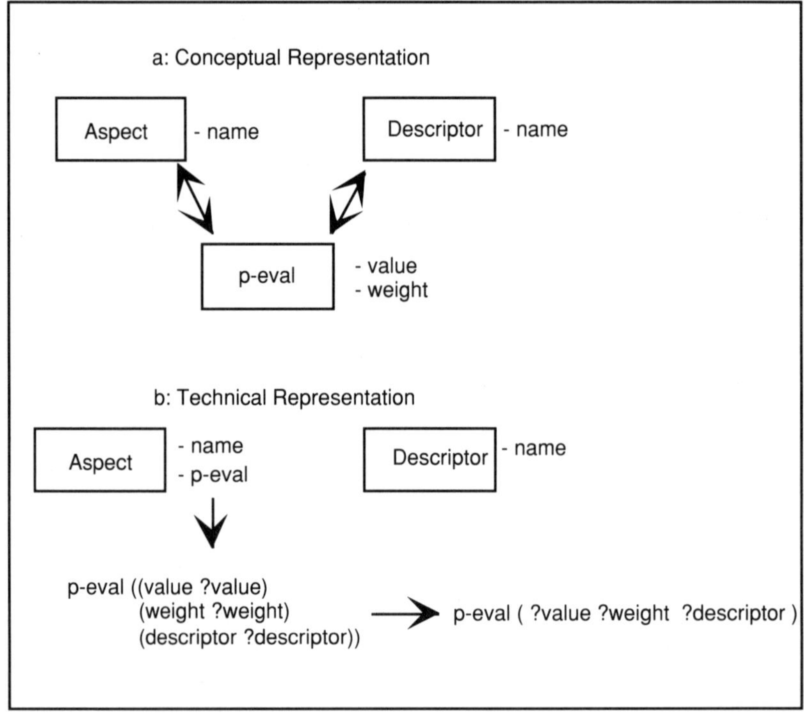

Figure 7. Relations and Lists.

added to the standard set. This procedure ensures that the user interface becomes more powerful with every application.

IO-PRINT uses IO-GEN structures for making printouts. For the developer, there is no difference between designing screens and printouts.

Information-Based Problem-Solving Techniques (G-TECs)

A problem-solving technique should be adaptable, transparent, and efficient. It should be transparent to the developer and the user. Within our applications, G-TEC (generic technique) (Spirgi, Probst, and Wenger 1990) consists of a data structure, which includes an object (name of G-TEC), the problem-solving algorithm (method); and the user interface building blocks that provide the graphics for representing information, results, and intermediate results of the problem-solving technique. The developer instantiates a certain G-TEC and gets an object that is integrated in his/her application.

CONDEV stands for condensation of evaluations. It is G-TEC that is integrated in MOCCA. It operates on a net, an example of which is shown in figure 8.

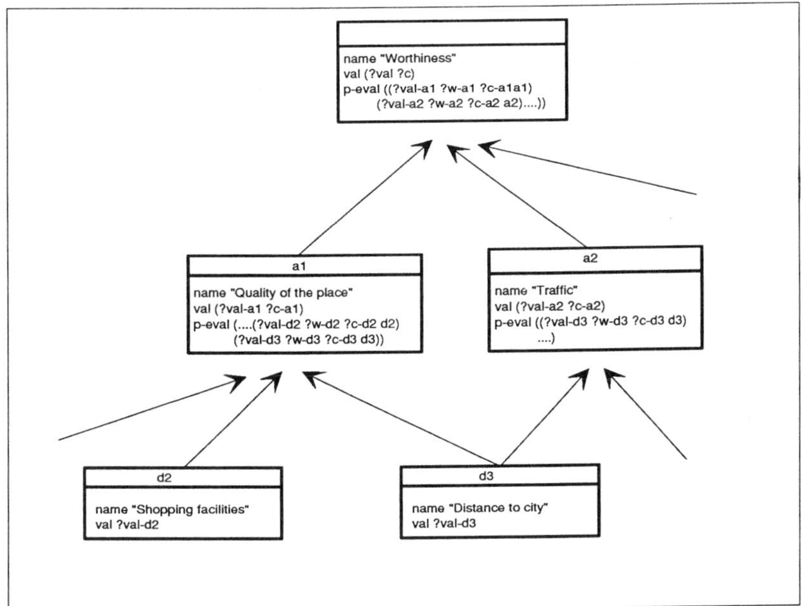

Figure 8. G-TEC CONDEV.

The input information is primarily partial evaluations, which are propagated to the nodes of the higher levels. They consist of a value and a certainty (for example, ?val-a1 and ?c-a1 in figure 8). For every node, CONDEV builds the evaluations (for example, a1@val) based on all propagated partial evaluations. It is robust against incompleteness of information and contradictory information. The worthiness check (a part of it is shown in figure 8) is a problem in MOCCA that was solved with CONDEV. The values and the weights of all descriptors (the nodes d2 and d3) are propagated to all aspects (the nodes a1 and a2); these aspects are finally propagated to the worthiness value, which produces an ideal ratio between worth of the entire property and worth of the land. To propagate the certainty in CONDEV, a simplified fuzzy measure approach was implemented. The partial evaluations of each aspect are combined to form one resulting valuation. Each additional partial evaluation modifies the resulting certainty according to its significance for the resulting evaluation.

Free Composition of Subsystems to Enable Real Prototyping

In the data-driven development environment, an application is driven by the agents that react to internal global data manipulations (blackboard

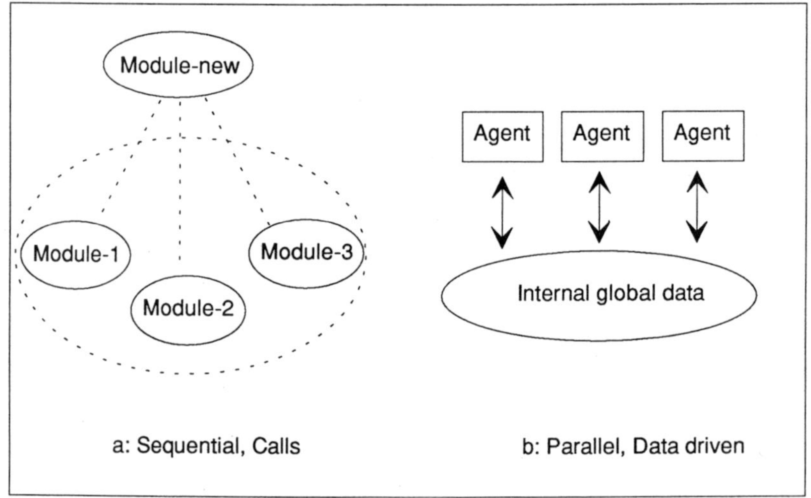

Figure 9. Data-Driven Paradigm.

principle, figure 9b). There is no need for interface programming between the subsystems (figure 9a). With this open-interface architecture, it is easy to build an application by combining independent subsystems. In MOCCA, we started to build a set of productive applications for mortgages of private properties only. In this way, we could explore the task domain in one area and see what features are important. When we started to implement the rest of the application, we could reuse these components entirely.

The basic principle is the development cycle (figure 10), which can be described as model-oriented prototyping based on a conceptual model. In each step, the missing, contradictory, and incomplete knowledge is rebuilt by verifying and validating the prototype to obtain a model that contains all the information that is important for the application. These activities are supported by EMA, which helps to formalize unstructured knowledge and support the developer in bringing the acquired knowledge into a prototype, verifying and correcting it. Building up knowledge is the main task in developing knowledge-based systems. The valuation of the customer's solvency in MOCCA is a typical result of prototyping. For many weeks, the current decision process was investigated, supported by EMA, and then replaced by a new set of decision variables. Within the prototyping process, a lot of new information, which had previously been neglected, became important (taxes, private budgets). The new solution can easily be transferred to similar problems, such as the salability investigation, that occurred during the prototyping process.

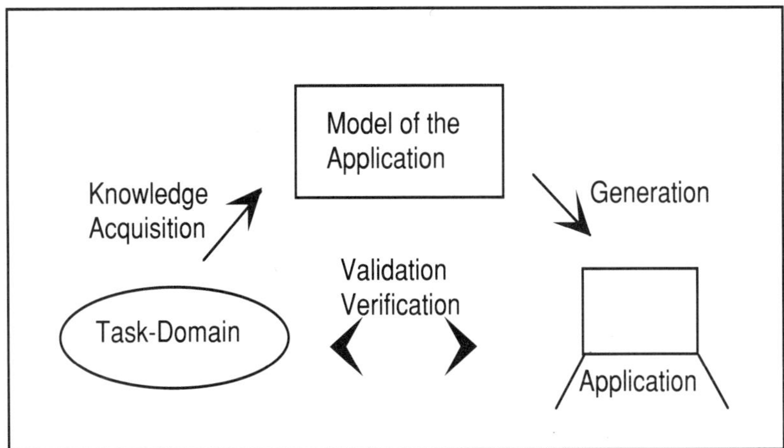

Figure 10. Application Development Cycle.

Another area of prototyping is the promoting of a new idea. For a new mortgage savings model, it was possible to develop a simulation prototype within two days that helped management decide on what terms and conditions the new product was usable and profitable.

Two-Layer Windowing System

In our windowing system, there is a distinction between operating system windowing (for example, Microsoft WINDOWS, OSF/MOTIF, OPEN LOOK, PRESENTATION MANAGER) and the application's object-oriented windowing in IO-GEN. With IO-GEN, the applications can be handled in the same way regardless of the underlying platform. Only a minimal set of graphic C routines have to be adapted to carry IO-GEN into any operating system environment. Any further development progress is instantly usable for each product on any platform because of full portability. Therefore, our products are independent of any new windowing standards that will come on the market. It allows us to concentrate entirely on the development of the applications themselves.

With the embedding of MOCCA in an operating system windowing environment such as WINDOWS 3.1, we could reuse other commercial knowledge-based systems for certain features; for example, the solvency check for commercial clients can be done by our credit-analysis system CUBUS (Wolf, Wenger, and Kirchmayr 1991).

Application Development and Deployment

MOCCA was developed in a short time by a small interdisciplinary group.

The local manager of the mortgage credit section acts as the expert responsible for all commercial aspects of the application and invests a maximum of 10 percent of his time in the development, promotion, and verification of MOCCA. Steve Hottiger acts as full-time technological project manager. For some problems, other specialists in the bank are called on for support. Important for the project's success was the technical support from other knowledge-based project managers in the group. The development environment is based on ART-IM 2.1 for DOS on an IBM PS/2.

The Project's Timeline

1990

April/May: Initial workshop conducted, where the expert and the developer explore the task domain. They develop a network of all relevant components used in the decision process. They decide to concentrate on the most important components (figure 1).

June: We start implementing the first prototypes (solvency control and worthiness investigation). The expert uses the system right from the beginning in his daily work.

October: First demonstration is given of the prototypes. A similar project in the retail banking section starts up where certain instruments will be reused.

1991

January: A small group of motivated managers from other mortgage credit sections is formed to support and introduce the new product. They are invited to contribute any input for further development.

July: The application fully supports the business section for private customers and self-contained buildings. The implementation for the other business sections (figure 2) starts.

September: The two main SBC branches introduce MOCCA.

The total personnel investment in the application is two person-years. More than 60 percent of the time was spent prototyping and developing the models. The remainder was used for customizing, demonstrating, and introducing the system.

Use and Payoff

The quantification of the payoff has to respect the different uses of the application, both monetary and nonmonetary. Qualitative advantages are mentioned to give a comprehensive idea of the use of MOCCA.

Cost savings by reducing external consultancy: MOCCA helps to separate the easy deals from the difficult ones. In this way, internal experts can be used better for the examination of crucial deals, and less external support is required.

Increasing decentralization: The comprehensive objective analysis of all critical items causes a shift of responsibility to the front staff and, thus, minimizes the effort spent on control.

Improved sales assistance: Self-explanatory and attractive instruments for all relevant bank products are basic for promoting certain products. They also contribute to a better bank image that demonstrates competence and fairness.

Reduction in risk: MOCCA provides a set of instruments to counter the increasing risks of loss. Quality is preferred to turnover.

Increased management control: MOCCA is a medium to quickly carry through any guidelines and standards in the mortgage business. Multidecision possibilities enable management to control the granting of mortgage credit.

Improved staff know-how: The easily understood model accelerates the understanding of the staff members of the crucial points of their business.

With all these factors, we estimate the profit to SBC from using MOCCA to be $2 million each year.

MOCCA is currently used by more than 20 people working in different mortgage credit sections of the bank. It is fully accepted and used daily. Supporting the front office staff, MOCCA is extremely market driven. Therefore, the maintenance of the system has to be done by the developer to ensure that the application is adapted to any important new requirements. With the open design based on the data-driven development environment and the embedding of the application in EMA, any changes can easily be performed. Furthermore, the use of EMA ensures that any developer familiar with the environment can continue the work.

Outlook

MOCCA is the mission-critical system for mortgage lending at SBC. Other applications based on the same development environment are successful in the finance and the commerce departments (for example, CUBUS). The development of highly interactive cooperative tools based on new decision patterns has a tremendous impact on the work process. Now, a number of banking specialists are motivated to work on the development of knowledge-based systems.

References

Fierz, K. 1987. *Wert und Zins bei Immobilien.* Schriftenreihe der Schweizerischen Treuhand- und Revisionskammer Band 56, 2. Auflage.

Nägeli, W. 1980. *Handbuch des Liegenschaftenschätzers,* 2. Auflage.

Spirgi, S.; Probst, A. R.; and Wenger, D. 1991. Generic Techniques in EMA: A Model-Based Approach for Knowledge Acquisition. In Proceedings of the Sixth Banff Knowledge Acquisition for Knowledge-Based Systems Workshop (KAW91).

Spirgi, S.; Probst, A. R.; and Wenger, D. 1990. Knowledge Acquisition in a Development Methodology for Knowledge-Based Applications. In Proceedings of the First Japanese Knowledge Acquisition for Knowledge-Based Systems Workshop(JKAW '90), eds. H. Motoda, R. Mizoguchi, J. Boose, and B. Gaines, 382–397. Tokyo: Ohmsha, Ltd.

Wolf, M. F.; Wenger, D. ; and Kirchmayr, K. 1991. CUBUS—An Assistant for Fundamental Corporate Analysis. In *Innovative Applications of Artificial Intelligence* 3, eds. R. Smith and C. Scott, 271—291. Menlo Park, Calif.: AAAI Press.

CRESUS: An Integrated Expert System for Cash Management

Pete Shell, Carnegie Mellon University, Gonzalo Quiroga, Juan A. Hernandez-Rubio, Eduardo Encinas, Union Frnosa S.A., Jose Garcia, and Javier Berbiela, Norsistemas Consultores S.A.

CRESUS is a unique application of state-of-the-art expert system technology to the real-world financial problem of cash management. By automating the work of company treasurers, it saves substantial amounts of both money and time every day. Real-world test cases show that CRESUS performs better and much faster than the human expert: In minutes, it generates a combination of operations that efficiently balances all banking accounts in a 15-day period. It uses user-friendly window technology to control the human-machine dialogue and has been integrated into the work environment of a major electric company in Spain. Written in Common Lisp using UNIX workstations, it was jointly developed by Union Fenosa, Carnegie Mellon University, and Norsistemas Consultores.

The Cash-Management Problem

This chapter describes our success with developing CRESUS, a cash-management expert system. In the CRESUS project, we explored the uncharted territory of automating cash-management decision making. First, we explain the motivation for turning to an expert system solution and then describe the technology itself. Finally, we explain the many benefits that CRESUS has brought us.

The cash-management decision-making process is a complex task that requires not only a highly skilled treasurer but also the availability of appropriate software tools. Each day, the treasurer has to make the following logistical decisions: how to coordinate the company's forecasted collections and payments through banking accounts; whether to borrow money or invest surplus money and how to do each; how many fund movements to make and between which accounts and with what amounts; and for each of these decisions, which financial instruments to use.

The goal is to minimize the combined cost of these operations: The credit lines used should be as inexpensive as possible; the balances of the banking accounts are preferably zero (to avoid overdrawn accounts and idle funds); and the commissions of instruments used in payments, collections, and fund movements should be the minimum.

The treasurer's job is made more complex by many factors:

First is the nature of the financial market, where the diversity, complexity, and continual change of its instruments make it difficult to choose among the many bank offers.

Second is the large number of banking accounts, collections, and payments.

Third is the interaction among the operations that causes each decision to affect the others. For example, the financial status on one day depends on the previous day's actions.

Fourth is the inherent uncertainty of collections and payments that causes continuous changes in the situation.

Fifth is the necessity of immediate response time that makes it difficult to plan the decisions.

Because of the complexities of this environment and the limitations of human memory, the treasurer must greatly simplify the problem by using several heuristics that ignore much of the interaction among the operations. When the cash flows are large, the cost to the company can be significant.

Union Fenosa attempted to solve this problem through linear programming techniques but failed. They solved the task of structuring and organizing the information but not the searching and evaluation that is inherent to optimization processes. The problem was that the search space is so large that it was impossible to simulate all the alternatives within a reasonable response time.

System Objectives

CRESUS meets all these needs through the use of AI techniques, automatically finding the set of decisions that result in the minimum cost after simulating and evaluating those possible decision combinations with the highest likelihood of obtaining this minimum cost.

CRESUS is useful not only for the daily management of the treasury problems but also as a powerful tool that allows treasurers to enhance their knowledge about the problem and infer the ideal conditions of their financial instruments. It is the only tool that we know of that automates the cash-management process.

The main objectives of this tool are the following:

First is to optimize the global cash flow by automatically generating optimal solutions. To achieve this goal, the system simulates a set of possible solutions to the current period, evaluating the cost of each and choosing the best. This approach offers an objective criterion on which the treasurers base their decisions and allows them to analyze the elements that most affect the cost.

Second is to plan future periods, taking into account the influence of each day's decision on the remaining days of the period. This approach allows the user to avoid undesired situations in the short term.

CRESUS also provides these features:

First, it presents the user with a simultaneous vision of all relevant information, globally and detailed, through X-11 WINDOW technology.

Second, it provides continuous checking for user errors and inefficiencies. When inefficiencies are found, corrective actions are suggested to the user and, if desired, automatically performed by the system.

Third, report generation allows the user to make effective management decisions and analyze their quality in terms of cost.

Fourth, it provides flexibility in managing company cash flows, with no limits on volume of information.

Fifth, it provides multilingual interaction with the user. We currently provide Spanish and English modes, and it is easy to add new languages through message files.

With all these functions, the treasurers have a powerful tool able to satisfy their needs and assure a high degree of quality in decisions that have to be made to solve the cash-management problem.

System Components

The expert system combines expert knowledge, such as constraints on how much money to borrow, pay back, or invest, cost evaluation, and operator generation, with a hybrid, multilevel *K*-best search strategy. This expert system is tightly integrated with the manual window-based cash-management component. The main modules are as follows:

Global improvements: Automatic search and execution of the best solution of the period

Flagger: Rule-based detection of user inefficiencies and suggestions for improvements

Simulator: Simulation of the user's transactions' user and global cost evaluation at any point of the period

User interface and data manager: Window-based screening of the account balances, individually and globally

Each of these functions is detailed in this section, with an emphasis on the expert system modules.

The Data Manager

The *data manager* maintains the frame hierarchy that represents the problem domain (figure 1). It provides an intelligent database (Pylyshyn 1985) by integrating a traditional database with AI techniques. This module uses a frame-based language called PARMENIDES (Shell and Carbonell 1988) to define data types and instances and allow intelligent manipulation of these instances. The data manager also guarantees data validity and consistency each time data are modified and provides file input-output (I-O) operations.

PARMENIDES also provides inheritance through a class hierarchy, demons, and user-defined relations. The data manager uses these if-added demons to interface with the other modules. When a frame is modified, it can call the simulator to infer new frame values if other frames depend on the changed value. It also automatically calls the user interface to update relevant windows to redisplay the changed data. Finally, the data manager provides these frames to the rule-based flagger module and the global improver module (see discussion later).

PARMENIDES was chosen because it not only provides powerful AI tools such as inheritance and procedural attachment, it also allows fast access to slots in frame instances, a feature that many frame languages don't have. Furthermore, it is well integrated with the FRULEKIT (Shell and Carbonell 1986) production system used in the FLAGGER module.

The Simulator

The *simulator* simulates the effects of user financial operations so that the treasurer can more efficiently plan the company's transactions. Each time that a transaction is added, modified, or deleted, the simulator computes the effects of this change and tells the data manager to

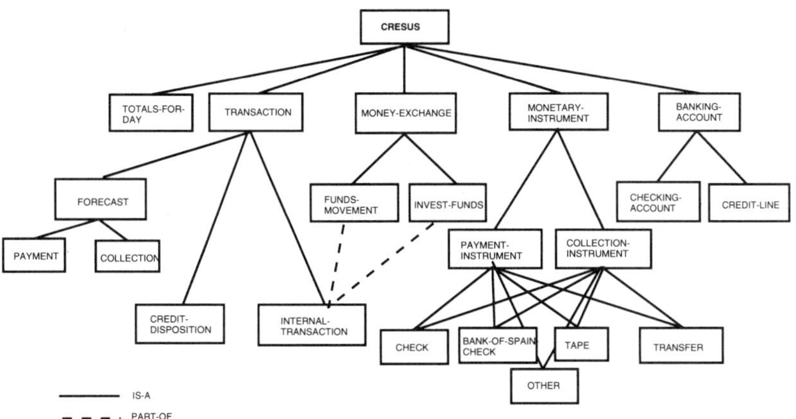

Figure 1. CRESUS Class Hierarchy (simplified).

update the relevant frames. The simulator is also responsible for evaluating the cost of the cash-management decisions.

The User Interface

The *user interface* makes it easy for the user to interact with each part of CRESUS. It is based on the X WINDOWS technology (Jones 1989), which allows the user to both make decisions and see their effect. It also facilitates a high level of integration between all the other modules.

Through this interface, the user can control and view the expert system's performance, perform data maintenance, make all types of transactions, request reports, move between different days of the simulated period, and record or play back a work session.

In figure 2, sample user interface windows are shown. These managing windows show information about abnormal banking accounts, credit-line dispositions, payment and collection forecasts, and fund movements.

The Flagger

The FLAGGER locally detects and corrects inefficiencies in the user's decisions, thereby finding local optima. By *local,* we mean that it restricts its attention to only one or two user operations at a time and only considers the current day. This approach is in contrast to the global searcher (see next subsection). The flagger is based on production rules (Forgy and McDermott 1977) that encode expert knowledge in the form of data-driven if-then pairs. The rules allow the system to be used by users with a lower degree of expertise or for training purposes.

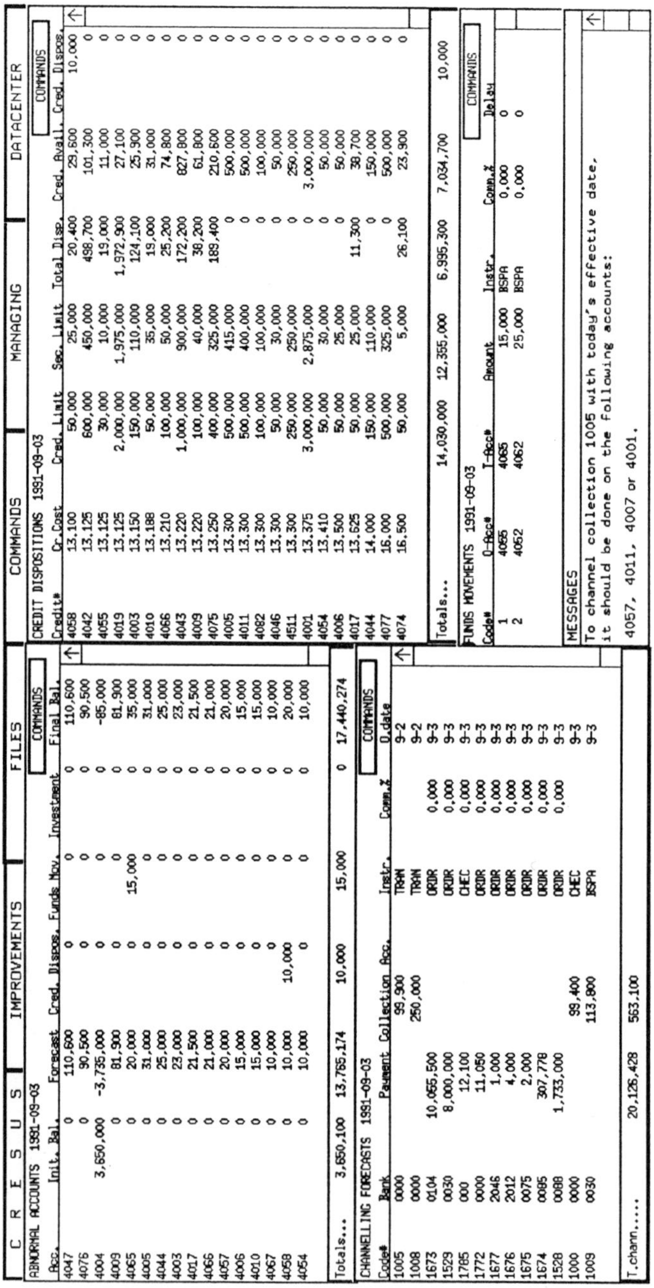

C R E S U S	IMPROVEMENTS	FILES	COMMANDS	MANAGING	DATACENTER

ABNORMAL ACCOUNTS 1991-09-03 [COMMANDS]

Acc.	Init. Bal.	Forecast	Cred. Dispos.	Funds Mov.	Investment	Final Bal.
4047	0	110,600	0	0	0	110,600
4076	0	90,500	0	0	0	90,500
4004	3,650,000	-3,735,000	0	0	0	-85,000
4009	0	81,900	0	0	0	81,900
4065	0	20,000	0	15,000	0	35,000
4005	0	31,000	0	0	0	31,000
4044	0	25,000	0	0	0	25,000
4003	0	23,000	0	0	0	23,000
4017	0	21,500	0	0	0	21,500
4066	0	21,000	0	0	0	21,000
4057	0	20,000	0	0	0	20,000
4006	0	15,000	0	0	0	15,000
4010	0	15,000	0	0	0	15,000
4067	0	10,000	0	0	0	10,000
4058	0	10,000	10,000	0	0	20,000
4054	0	10,000	0	0	0	10,000
Totals...	3,650,100	13,765,174	10,000	15,000	0	17,440,274

CHANNELLING FORECASTS 1991-09-03 [COMMANDS]

Code#	Bank	Payment	Collection	Acc.	Instr.	Comm.%	O.date
1005	0000		99,900		TRAN		9-2
1008	0000		250,000		TRAN		9-2
1673	0104	10,055,500			ORDR	0,000	9-3
1529	0030	8,000,000			ORDR	0,000	9-3
1785	000	12,100			CHEC	0,000	9-3
1772	0000	11,050			ORDR	0,000	9-3
1677	2046	1,000			ORDR	0,000	9-3
1676	2012	4,000			ORDR	0,000	9-3
1675	0075	2,000			ORDR	0,000	9-3
1674	0085	307,778			ORDR	0,000	9-3
1528	0088	1,733,000			ORDR	0,000	9-3
1000	0000		99,400		CHEC		9-3
1009	0030		113,800		BSPA		9-3
T.chann.....		20,126,428	563,100				

CREDIT DISPOSITIONS 1991-09-03 [COMMANDS]

Credit#	Cr.Cost	Cred. Limit	Sec. Limit	Total Disp.	Cred. Avail.	Cred. Dispos.
4058	13.100	50,000	25,000	20,400	29,600	10,000
4042	13.125	600,000	450,000	498,700	101,300	0
4055	13.125	30,000	10,000	19,000	11,000	0
4019	13.125	2,000,000	1,975,000	1,972,900	27,100	0
4003	13.150	150,000	110,000	124,100	25,900	0
4010	13.188	50,000	35,000	19,000	31,000	0
4066	13.210	100,000	50,000	25,200	74,800	0
4043	13.220	1,000,000	900,000	172,200	827,800	0
4009	13.220	100,000	40,000	38,200	61,800	0
4075	13.250	400,000	325,000	189,400	210,600	0
4005	13.300	500,000	415,000	0	500,000	0
4011	13.300	500,000	400,000	0	500,000	0
4082	13.300	100,000	100,000	0	100,000	0
4046	13.300	50,000	30,000	0	50,000	0
4511	13.300	250,000	250,000	0	250,000	0
4001	13.375	3,000,000	2,875,000	0	3,000,000	0
4054	13.410	50,000	30,000	0	50,000	0
4006	13.500	50,000	25,000	0	50,000	0
4017	13.625	50,000	25,000	11,300	38,700	0
4044	14.000	150,000	110,000	0	150,000	0
4077	16.000	500,000	325,000	0	500,000	0
4074	16.500	50,000	5,000	26,100	23,900	0
Totals...		14,030,000	12,355,000	6,995,300	7,034,700	10,000

FUNDS MOVEMENTS 1991-09-03 [COMMANDS]

Code#	O-Acc#	T-Acc#	Amount	Instr.	Comm.%	Delay
1	4055	4065	15,000	BSPA	0,000	0
2	4052	4062	25,000	BSPA	0,000	0

MESSAGES

To channel collection 1005 with today's effective date,
it should be done on the following accounts:

4057, 4011, 4007 or 4001.

Figure 2. CRESUS *User Interface Managing Windows.*

Each time the user makes a decision that could be optimized, one or more rules flag the user with a message that explains the inefficiency and suggests an alternate operation. If this suggestion is accepted by the user, it automatically replaces the original operation, and all windows and data structures are updated.

The action part of the production rules encodes two things: a method to explain the inefficiency to the user and a method to correct the inefficiency if the user decides to correct it.

The flagger uses the FRULEKIT production system language, a modern Common Lisp implementation of OPS5. FRULEKIT was chosen for the following reasons:

First, it is tightly integrated with the PARMENIDES frames that are used by the rest of the system. Unlike some other production systems that copy frames into their rule system, FRULEKIT matches directly on the frames themselves, and the right-hand actions apply to frames.

Second is the fact that FRULEKIT has an open architecture. It is possible to call Lisp functions on both the left-hand and right-hand sides. This structure allowed us to write our own notation for specifying what messages to present to the user and encoding knowledge about how to correct the inefficiencies.

Third is the reason maintenance facility. FRULEKIT allows the programmer to designate right-hand-side items as either beliefs or side-effects. *Side-effects* are actions that can't be taken back, whereas *beliefs* are actions that should be taken back whenever the left-hand side of the rule no longer matches. This shortcoming exists in many production systems. For example, when there is an inefficiency (for example, the user made a fund movement from account A to account B and then from B to C), a message is posted that the funds could have been moved directly from A to C. However, if this action is corrected by the user, then FRULEKIT automatically takes away the message.

The Global Searcher

This module represents the most sophisticated part of CRESUS. Instead of making only incremental improvements like the flagger, the *global searcher* constructs entirely new solutions from scratch. Thus, it attempts to find a more global optimum than the flagger. It is also global in the sense that it takes the entire period into account instead of focusing on only one day without regard to the others.

The searcher's solution comprises a set of decisions, or operators, that require the lowest global cost to balance the bank accounts. An operator can do any of the following actions: move money between two accounts, borrow or pay back money from a credit line, channel a collection or payment from or to an account, and invest money.

Before the search, the user can establish certain constraints, such as disposing of a certain amount of money from a given credit line or making a concrete collection to a given account. These constraints are respected by the system even if they are not considered efficient (that is, the system understands that they might obey some other criteria of the treasurer's).

The search space is extremely large. Solutions typically consist of a sequence of about 50 operators, and at each step of the search, on the order of 100 operators can apply. For this reason, a heuristic search is necessary because it is possible to search only a small fraction of this space. Furthermore, by partitioning the search space into subspaces with relatively little interaction, the problem becomes more tractable (this observation was first put forth by Minsky [1963]). The interaction is usually handled by encoding expert knowledge. In CRESUS, these subspaces are as follows:

First is the daily search space versus the global search space. When CRESUS searches for a daily optimal solution, it doesn't consider the global implications of each operator during this search. The global implications are considered between daily searches (see later discussion).

Second is the space of operators for a specific operator type. Inside the daily search, CRESUS only considers operators of one type at a time (the specific operator types are described at the beginning of this section). Although there is interaction between certain types of operators, this interaction is handled by putting more expert knowledge into the evaluation and generation functions. For example, the evaluation function would prefer a fund movement that balances an expensive credit line over one that balances a less expensive credit line because it would avoid having to borrow from the expensive credit line.

The searcher uses a multilevel heuristic search based on the I-BEAM search algorithm originally developed for the HARPY speech-recognition system (Lowerre 1976; Newell 1978), as we describe later. The expert's knowledge about cost evaluation and operator generation is incorporated into the searcher. Parameters affecting the search were tuned based on the performance of the searcher on typical test cases.

The global searcher is composed of the following submodules:

Searcher: This top-level module performs the searching, using all the other modules.

Generator: Its function is to generate new operators that improve a given search state.

Evaluator: It evaluates the local and global cost of a set of operators. The *global cost* is defined as the cost associated with every operator that has been applied plus the estimation of the cost needed to complete the search.

Global data manager: This module is responsible for the initial data storage and the intermediate and final results.

The global searcher performs its work in two different stages: setup and search.

In setup, the search goals are set for each day of the period: whether to borrow, pay back, or invest money and how much. These goals depend on the total balances for each day. At the end of the search, the following must be accomplished: (1) all the accounts are balanced, (2) the global cost is minimum given the conditions preceding the search, and (3) the number of operators that define the global solution is minimized.

After the setup phase, the search begins. It is divided into two different levels: within-day search and between-days search. Both the within-day and between-days searching modules are based on the I-beam search algorithm. The *beam searcher* is a breadth-first searcher that considers a number of different partial solutions simultaneously. This approach yields higher-quality results than only considering the locally best partial solution at each step because local optima are not necessarily part of the optimum global solution. The greater the number of partial solutions that are considered, the better the chance that a more optimal solution will be found. However, it is infeasible to consider every possible solution because there are so many. Thus, there is a trade-off between a high-quality solution and a large search space and between a fast solution and a smaller search space.

During a within-day search, the searcher stores the *K*-best partial solutions that it has found so far on every level of the search (*K* is known as the beam width). It always chooses to further explore the *K*-best solutions that look the most efficient based on an evaluation of the state of this solution.

For example, in figure 3, *K* is set to 5. At the first level of search, the best states are the ones labeled with evaluations of 50, 45, 40, and 40. At level 2, the best states are those labeled 80, 75, 78, 72, and 73. Note that the states with evaluations of 65, 62, 55, and 63 are not retained. This process would continue until complete solutions are found. Note that the total number of nodes on each level does not grow after level 3 because the number of states to explore is limited to *K*.

During the between-days search, the searcher performs a beam search by combining the daily searches of each day. In other words, during the between-days–search phase, the best global solution is found based on the comparison of the cost associated with each daily solution.

Because the uncertainty grows as the searcher looks forward in time, the value of *K* decreases as the day being searched increases. With this

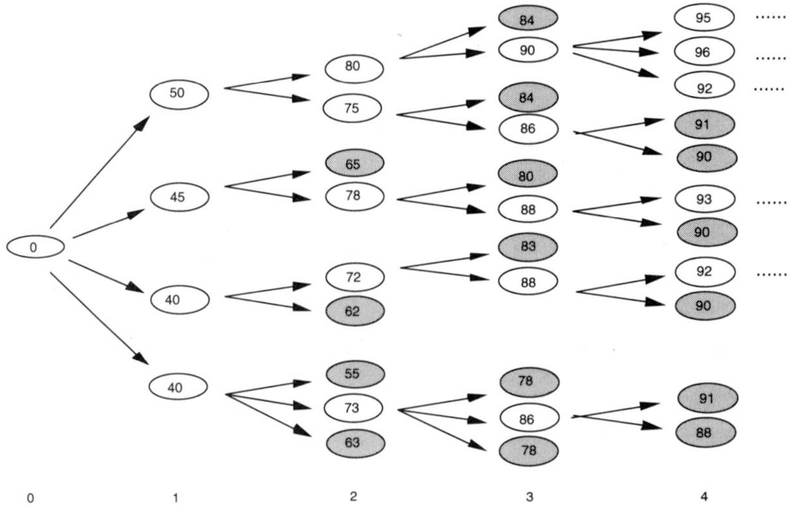

Figure 3. Sample Within-Day Beam Search (K = *5*). *Shaded nodes are not explored any further.*

algorithm, even though a particular solution might look like the best one on day *d*, the searcher evaluates the strength of this solution globally. By combining solutions over more than one day, we are globally searching for the most efficient solutions.

CRESUS Benefits

CRESUS has benefited Union Fenosa in a number of ways:

First is the time savings in the daily management of the treasury. We estimate this savings to be 70 percent of the decision-making time and 30 percent of the treasurer's total work time.

Second is the improvement in the quality of the treasurer's work. By using a tool that simulates and optimizes a priori the cash-management decisions, the treasurer is free to spend more time analyzing and searching for the best banking conditions.

Third is the augmentation of knowledge about the problem and detection of points for improvement. Because of the comparison of optimal suggested solutions with those conditioned by company policies or the conditions of certain banks, those points where the costs are concentrated arise and imply an analysis process for its improvement.

Fourth is the economic savings. The quantitative savings realized by the CRESUS searcher is significant. We compared the cost of the expert's solution using CRESUS manually with the global searcher's solution over a two-week period in January 1992. The comparison was made by computing the total cost of each solution: the cost of borrowing money, the fees associated with fund movements, and the fees for having overdrawn accounts minus the money earned by investing. The results show that Union Fenosa will save over a half million dollars a year:

	Week 1	Week 2	Projected annually
Manual use	$113,060	$34,360	$3,832,920
CRESUS searcher	$91,180	$28,740	$3,117,920
Difference (abs.)	$21,880	$5,620	$715,000
Difference (prc.)	19.35%	16.35%	18.65%

(The annual projections are computed by taking the average of the 2 weeks and extrapolating to a 52-week period.) The savings changes from week to week because a number of real-world conditions are always changing, such as the volume of the operations, the current conditions of the financial market, and the point at which the savings are measured. However, with these results, we estimate that CRESUS will pay for itself in one year.

Another benefit expected over time is the solution of the expert-substitution problem. By making it easier to extend and share the expert's knowledge with other people, CRESUS should allow us to smoothly handle times when the expert is away from the company.

Development

The application was developed starting in January 1989 and was finished by December 1990. One of Union Fenosa's main goals was to ensure that the technology would be transferred effectively to its personnel. Thus, a mixed team was formed, including personnel from both Union Fenosa and Carnegie Mellon University. The team initially included a project leader, a senior knowledge engineer, and two part-time programmers from Carnegie Mellon and a junior knowledge engineer and a domain expert from Union Fenosa.

Development Process

The development process was split into three phases:

Phase 1—Initial Prototype: During this phase, we defined the project plan, configured the development team, selected the hardware and software tools, and validated the conceptual design by implementing a prototype of the non-expert modules of CRESUS (the user interface, the data manager, and the simulator).

Phase 2—Advanced Prototype: In this phase, we scaled up the non-expert modules, designed the expert modules (flagger and global searcher), and implemented the flagger. Finally, we installed the prototype at the customer site so that the end user could validate it.

Phase 3—Final System: In the final phase, we implemented the global searcher, completed the integration of all modules, and extensively verified and validated the application.

Verification and Validation

At the end of each phase, we verified and validated the application. The initial prototype was validated by the domain expert as well as the senior manager, who was responsible for project support. At this time, we didn't pay much attention to verifying the prototype because we were mostly interested in proving the concept. After having finished the other phases, we spent about a month testing the entire application. We used several approaches. To test the simulator, we developed a record-playback option that allowed the domain expert to check for errors. To test the global searcher, we gave small test cases to test for correctness, ran it on several real-world data sets to test for quality, and wrote an auto-test program to run the searcher through several combinations of parameters.

Deployment

The application is currently being used by Union Fenosa, an electric company that during 1991 moved nearly $50 million (both collections and payments), with the number of bank operations approaching 125,000.

Deployment began in January 1991 and took 8 months of work for a team of 3 people, each dedicating 30 percent of his time to the project. The work covered everything from the study of the appropriate hardware platform to user training. Since September 1991, CRESUS has been used daily for treasury decision making in the company. Even though several people from the department are involved in the data-entry and report-making processes, the cash-management decision making is centralized by one person (the treasurer).

The first step in deploying the system was to completely study the data-collection process to feed the company data to and from the system. Because of the volume and the complexity of the study, we chose a decentralized data approach, where we built interfaces with other applications and enhanced the CRESUS data manager module to support these interfaces.

The main CRESUS software can run on any UNIX workstation with X-11 WINDOWS and is currently integrated into the environment of Union Fenosa. It runs on a SUN SPARCSTATION that is connected to a MACINTOSH II CX, a DOS Compaq 386 PC, other personal computers (PCs), and a Laser Writer printer. The PCs are used for data entry and report generation. This hardware is connected through the TOPS local area network (LAN) developed by Sun Microsystems, which offers a user-friendly environment.

This structure lets us obtain automatically, through LAN, the ASCII files generated in other environments and built with different software and combine it with data the system needs for it to function. In addition, we took advantage of the MACINTOSH to design automatic reports that directly read the simulation and optimization results of CRESUS.

With respect to user training, we can distinguish two phases: learning how to use CRESUS and gaining user confidence in the system. The first part did not present any problems because the CRESUS user interface was designed to agree with the treasurer's philosophy and work mode. A treasurer without knowledge of computers could learn to manage CRESUS in one day.

The second part required running both CRESUS and the old system in parallel for about three months. Here, the principle problems were convincing the treasurer to take advantage of the full capabilities of CRESUS and accepting its particular proposals when they conflicted with the work habits derived from the limitations of the old system.

Maintenance

CRESUS is working now, but we are continuing to enhance it. Because of feedback from the users, during the deployment phase, we discovered improvements that were needed in the user interface (such as sorting and searching functions in the data windows), the knowledge base, and the global improver module that we didn't take into account in the development phase.

The improvements needed in the global improver module warrant further discussion. The domain of the CRESUS system is variable, so that while it is being used, we need to change not only the banking account conditions (usual in the daily performance) but also the different types of banking instruments in use. For this reason, CRESUS must facilitate the creation of new instruments with different behavior. In addition, we wanted a greater sophistication of instrument use and desired to extrapolate the Union Fenosa solution to the cash-management problem to other companies. Thus, we were motivated to generalize our system further. This work is developing now, and we can already say that the knowledge base is general enough that it can be adapted to different situations.

The user interface is also general enough that it allows the user to interactively change all relevant conditions. The global searcher has been made more powerful, but some of its knowledge needs to be made more declarative so that it will be easier to modify it in the future. Finally, the maintenance and modification team, experts, and knowledge engineers are, for the most part, the same staff that developed CRESUS, which makes it easier to make the needed system changes.

Conclusions

Because this work represents the first time that knowledge engineering technology was applied to the complex problem of cash management, we had no way of knowing whether our efforts would be successful. Our experience shows, however, that it is possible to effectively automate the treasurer's decision making to save significant time and money. Other cash-management tools that we looked at claim to automate the cash-management task but in reality don't perform decision making. Instead, they typically use spreadsheet programs to simulate the effect of the treasurer's operations—equivalent to the manual part of CRESUS. We found that the bulk of the benefit is when the global searcher is utilized to automatically find less costly solutions.

CRESUS was developed for a specific utility company in Spain, but we are currently attempting to market the system to other companies in Spain. With some more work, we also hope to generalize it enough to make it useful in the rest of Europe and the United States.

Acknowledgments

We would like to thank Michael Mauldin for his useful comments on a draft of this chapter and the following people for their important contributions to the project: Daniel Borrajo, Jaime Carbonell, Mike Kanaley, Todd Kaufmann, Michael Mauldin, Chris Nuuja, and Jose Prieto.

References

Forgy, C. L., and McDermott, J. 1977. OPS, a Domain-Independent Production System Language. In Proceedings of the Fourth International Joint Conference on Artificial Intelligence, 933—939. Menlo Park, Calif.: International Joint Conferences on Artificial Intelligence.

Jones, O. 1989. *Introduction to the X WINDOW System.* Englewood Cliffs, N.J.: Prentice Hall.

Lowerre, B. 1976. The HARPY Speech-Recognition System. Ph.D. thesis, School of Computer Science, Carnegie Mellon Univ.

Minsky, M. 1963. *Steps toward Artificial Intelligence.* New York: McGraw-Hill.

Newell, A. 1978. HARPY, Production Systems, and Human Cognition. Pittsburgh, Pa.: Carnegie Mellon University.

Pylyshyn, Z. 1985. Intelligent Database Interfaces: A Survey of Some Artificial Intelligence Applications. London, Ont., Canada: University of Western Ontario.

Shell, P., and Carbonell, J. G. 1988. The PARMENIDES Reference Manual, Internal Paper, School of Computer Science, Carnegie Mellon Univ.

Shell, P., and Carbonell, J. G. 1986. The FRULEKIT Reference Manual, Internal Paper, School of Computer Science, Carnegie Mellon Univ.

Industrial Applications

DMCM
Xerox Corporation

SlurryMinder
Dowell Schlumberger

Experiment Design
Sun Microsystems and General Motors

DMCM: A Knowledge-Based Cost-Estimation Tool

Norman Crowfoot, Scott Hatfield, and Mike Swank,
Xerox Corporation

Knowledge-based systems have traditionally been implemented in *vertical application areas,* which are characterized by a deep knowledge in a narrow domain. We developed and fielded a successful knowledge-based tool that is characterized by shallow knowledge of a wide range of cost-estimation problems. Our system is used to estimate piece-part manufacturing costs and has broad knowledge of many commodities and their corresponding manufacturing processes.

We believe our design, manufacturability, and cost model (DMCM) system is also unique for the following reasons:

First, the system has enabled business process changes, such as allowing cost estimation to be done at an earlier state of the design process.

Second, the cost estimate is now continually refined. The cost estimate is updated as newer and better data become available. This process is repeated at all stages of the design.

Third, a high level of integration is achieved with existing design information stores, such as a commercial computer-aided design (CAD) system and existing corporate databases.

Fourth, a conventional, commercial database is used to provide flexible data storage and a repository for persistent objects.

Fifth, accelerated implementation allowed the application to be fielded into an integrated business process.

Sixth, simultaneous implementation of multiple cost models maximizes payback in a competitive situation.

This chapter describes our experiences in developing DMCM, including the technology used to reason in the design domain, a detailed description of the application, business process results, and long-term plans.

Knowledge-Based System Competency Center

DMCM is one of several systems developed by the Knowledge-Based System Competency Center (KBSCC) at Xerox Corporation. KBSCC is a corporate-level group of knowledge practitioners located within the Corporate Information Management Group. This department was formed four years ago, motivated by a concern that although Xerox is well known for its knowledge-based system research, this important technology was not being used for solving internal business problems.

In practical terms, *competency center* means a group responsible for identifying and adapting both research work and commercial products into workable solutions for real business problems. This process is commonly called *technology transfer*. Specifically, the center does little basic research but adapts internal and external research and applies it to internal problems.

An important, basic working concept of the center is the formation of working partnerships between developers of a new application and the important users of the application. Far too often, knowledge-based system technology is introduced with a technically well-designed application program that fails to address the structure of the business process it is being introduced to. These attempts almost invariably fail; without altering the receiving structure, technology transfer is almost always doomed.

To assist the technology transfer process, we develop each application with a partnership structure; each partnership is made up of members of the competency center, the sponsoring information-management groups, and the end users who are interested in having the application delivered. This partnership approach provides increased resources for implementation of the application. It also fosters ownership of the new product with both the future users and the long-term owners of the application process.

Task Description

Xerox is primarily known as a supplier of dry-process, plain-paper photocopiers. Indeed, the company pioneered the concept of the easy-to-use, plain-paper copier with the Xerox 914 copier in 1959.

Traditional copiers focus high-intensity light onto an original, imaging the resulting image onto a light-sensitive, electrostatically charged photoconductor through a system of lamps and lenses. The latent image is then developed with particles of toner, and the resulting image is transferred to paper. A final step fuses toner particles into the paper. Additional subsystems are commonly provided to handle the input originals and the resulting output copies.

New copier technology replaces many of the traditional light lens components with digital scanning, modulated lasers, and networked devices. Even with this modern approach, internal image-processing and paper-handling steps remain much as they have always been.

Because of the interactions of the many systems within a modern copier, their design rivals the complexity of other design tasks. Modern copiers use a wide variety of interconnected technologies, including chemical, mechanical, optical, thermal, pneumatic, electric, and software.

Ever-increasing market competition is a fact of life in our business. The process of designing and manufacturing low-cost, quality products is essential to the financial success of Xerox. As a corporation, we discovered more than 10 years ago a marked cost differential between products designed and manufactured by Japanese companies and those produced by U.S. production facilities. Analysis of these differentials demonstrated that early cost estimations are essential to cost management in that a large part of the total eventual cost is designed in at an early stage in the product development cycle.

The Original Design Process

Our design process at Xerox is much like those used in other large engineering organizations. A Product Delivery Team (PDT) is organized and charged with producing a design for a specific new copier or related family of products. The PDT chief engineer is responsible for the product delivery as well as meeting functional, quality, and cost requirements. PDT oversees the design until it is well into production.

Many specialists participate in the design of a new product. These roles are the traditional ones, such as chief engineer, cost engineer, design engineer, designer, and manufacturing engineer. These interactions are diagrammed in figure 1.

Role of Cost Estimation

The actual cost estimations for a designed part are performed by a small number of individuals (approximately 100 across the corpora-

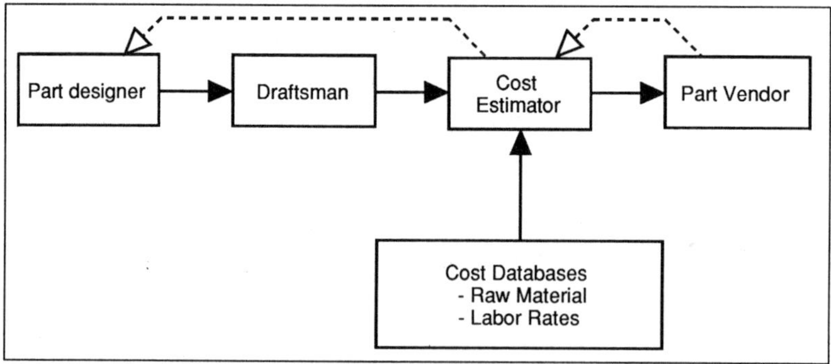

Figure 1. Original Design Process.

tion). These cost engineers match the classic profile for a domain expert. Most of them have many years of experience and specialize in a few commodities, having worked previously in such areas as manufacturing, purchasing, or the design community or as external suppliers.

Further, because the estimation resource is scarce, estimation is typically done late in the design cycle, if at all. There is no time to iterate the design with design alternatives by the time the design reaches the cost engineer.

This environment is the reason that DMCM was developed and deployed. A major design goal was to make DMCM applicable throughout the product development life cycle. In the early stages of product formulation (the concept phase), the tool provides coarse cost estimates for components and supports cost and bill-of-material roll up. In the later stages, as the design matures, the tool evaluates designs for conformance to established design standards, generates detailed cost estimates for component designs, and suggests specific external vendors based on vendor-specific knowledge.

Previous Cost Models

The use of knowledge-based systems in the engineering domain is not new. A number of general approaches to the problem are described in Brown and Chandrasekaran (1986), Dixon and Dym (1986), Dixon and Simmons (1984), Dym (1987), and Forbus (1988). Furthermore, a number of actual systems are described in Hatfield et al. (1987); O'Brien et al. (1989); and Mittal, Dym, and Morjaria (1986).

A study of some of the shortfalls of similar systems was conducted during the feasibility study phase of the DMCM project. Of course, there is the obvious problem that design is a complex domain and that manipulating geometric information is still a difficult task for a computer system. Some of the reasons that were identified during this study are described in the following paragraphs:

Failure to integrate existing databases: Many expert systems are implemented on stand-alone machines that do not communicate with existing company data resources. Although this stand-alone implementation might have been forgivable in an age when AI projects were built on specialized hardware using languages such as Lisp, it is no longer acceptable for production-quality systems.

In many systems, input data are entered through a keyboard or as one-time bulk loads of data from an existing database. In the former case, the labor intensity of the direct key entry can cause the data to become stale. In the latter case, the viability of the data is a function of the transfer cycle. In both cases, the correctness of the data erodes with time.

Such systems become outdated, and users are unlikely to spend the energy to audit data for obsolescence. Unintegrated systems are especially onerous in a domain as dynamic as cost estimation, with commodity prices constantly fluctuating.

Failure to include part geometry: Because of the stand-alone nature of many previous attempts, all part geometry information was reentered by the knowledge-based system user or was not used at all. Frequently, this duplicated information already existed in traditional CAD databases. This duplication introduces errors, additional work, and inconsistencies.

Failure to preserve the reasoning history of decisions: Reasoning systems fielded to date typically do not retain the reasoning processes that lead to their previous conclusions. Thus, one is prevented from auditing these results, comparing design decisions, and building a knowledge base of designed parts. Because of the transient nature of most commercial reasoning tools, reasoning history is lost after the estimation session is ended. Something as permanent as a database is generally not considered for reasoning patterns.

Failure to form partnerships with information-management departments: Primarily because of their stand-alone and experimental nature, previous knowledge-based system applications are not integrated into the working information-management infrastructure. Because the personnel in information-management organizations know the location and connections to databases and other information sources that are required, we included these personnel in the DMCM project at an early stage. They enhanced the success rate of fielding DMCM. Early partnership involvement with information management also allowed us to plan for long-term maintenance and support activities long before these critical processes were needed.

Too detailed knowledge of a functional area: Another concern was the great depth of knowledge encoded in many knowledge-based systems. The engineering mind set finds it more satisfying to build a wonderful system for design paper-feed rollers than to solve the general problem of parts cost estimation. Much research effort has been expended in developing these deep solutions, but few successful systems have resulted (Gael and Pirollo 1989; Gray 1988; Hoeltzel, Chieng, and Zissimides 1987; Mittal and Araya 1986; Mittal, Dym, and Morjaria 1986; Mostow 1985; Tat Chan and Paulson 1987). We believe there are systemic reasons for this failure to produce useful systems. Two things happen when using these deep reasoning approaches: (1) a few problem areas are analyzed and mechanized to the exclusion of others and (2) much time is expended in getting the model exactly right because of the detailed nature of the project. By the time the model is correct, the problem or the technology has changed.

With DMCM, we consciously chose to incorporate shallower knowledge: It requires less creativity, is more invariant, is more likely to be useful over a long period of time, and applies to a wider range of applications.

As additional design knowledge is incorporated into DMCM, we will evaluate the useful lifetime of this knowledge. In many cases, the technologies used in successive generations of products change dramatically, greatly reducing the utility of static knowledge-based systems. One can easily end up having invested two years in modeling knowledge with a three-year life expectancy.

Application Description

This section describes the DMCM application in terms of the delivery platform, the organization of the software shell and the structure of the knowledge bases used. Early results are described in Hatfield and Crowfoot (1990).

Delivery Platform

When DMCM development started, a related effort was under way within Xerox to standardize an engineering workstation. Initial requirements were unclear except that this software run on UNIX and be an open system. DMCM was developed to accommodate almost any such platform.

Hardware: DMCM was implemented for the Xerox engineering workstation environment: a set of Sun SPARC workstations connected through TCP-IP, SNA, and XNS networks to centralized database servers.

Software: Standard, commercial vendor-supplied software was used

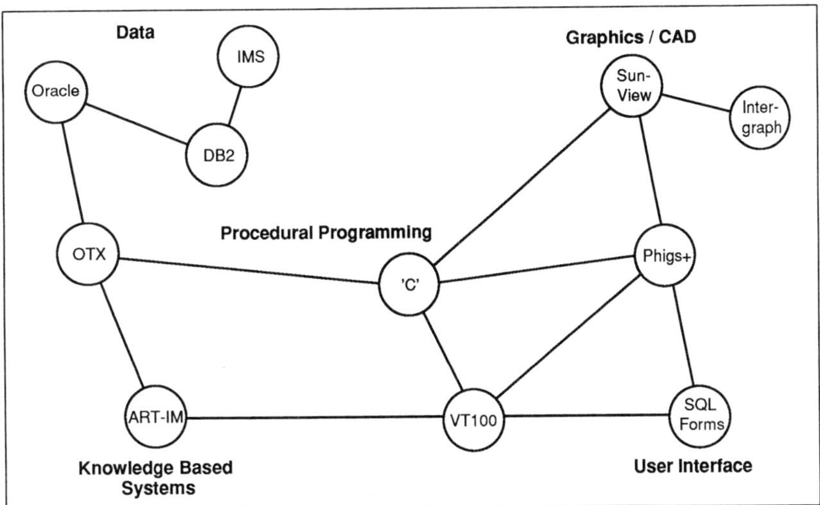

Figure 2. DMCM *Shell Organization.*

where possible. DMCM is currently implemented to run on three graphic user interface desktop environments: SUNVIEW; OPENWINDOWS, Sun's implementation of OPENLOOK; and a classic teletype interface for backward compatibility. See the section on the user interface for details.

Shell Organization

Like many knowledge-based system applications, DMCM is built using a shell that we constructed. Simply stated, a *shell* is a set of building blocks that facilitate presentation and development of the knowledge base itself. See figure 2 for an overview of the tool components that make up the DMCM shell.

Knowledge Base Structure

DMCM accommodates a variety of knowledge models partitioned by commodity. Examples of commodities include plastic injection-molded parts, sheet metal parts, and electromechanical devices. Each knowledge model is a separate, loadable module.

The primary mechanism used to describe costing knowledge is ART-IM (automated reasoning tool for information management from Inference Corporation) rules. Each commodity is costed by a set of some 100 to 200 rules. Constant tabular information, such as press capacities, are kept in facts. Alterable cost information, such as commodity costs, are maintained in a remote relational database to be fetched as needed.

Several ART-IM schemas are used to hold deduced knowledge during the course of a cost estimation. As costs are calculated, they are written to the relational database. This approach allowed us to provide knowledge about a number of commodities in a modular way, strictly separating knowledge of how a commodity functions from its specific physical attributes and current cost.

The types of knowledge that the system can deduce include the following:

How much force can a 2-inch plastic gear 1/4-inch thick typically tolerate according to Xerox design specifications?

How much money do I save if I reduce the material thickness of this part?

How large a machine press will be required to form this part? What will the cycle time be? How much might a supplier charge to use such a press?

Which supplier, A or B, would most effectively produce this shaft? What should it cost from supplier A? From supplier B?

Much of this design knowledge is represented as rules to calculate forces, quantities, and clearances. This knowledge was copied from the preferred design practice documentation within Xerox. The cost-comparison knowledge is obtained from running the calculations several ways and taking the minimum.

Little knowledge of the part's eventual use is considered because this information is generally not necessary to derive a cost. DMCM also does not currently reason over collections of parts. Examples of knowledge that is not included in the system are as follows:

Given an input torque and an output torque, consider all the possible approaches to gearing this drive assembly.

Will this base plate support the weight of the system? Is the flexure small enough to maintain the drive rollers in close enough tolerance?

How will my gear function within my design? Which way will it rotate? Have I allowed enough clearance with the meshing part?

Within each commodity, we built knowledge bases that contain logic in each of the following categories:

Geometric reasoning: Because the geometric information present in our CAD drawings is limited to wire-frame stick figures, rules are added to the knowledge bases to convert simple mouse picks into information. Examples of this conversion include determination of various part dimensions, part volume, and number of holes (see Computer-Aided Design Integration).

Cost estimating: DMCM cost estimates include raw material rates;

manufacturing rates; tooling cost; duty, insurance, and freight; and all the conversion coefficients that must be applied (for example, currency conversion).

Manufacturing process specification: To develop accurate cost estimates for a component, DMCM must understand the manufacturing process behind the component. Here, we estimate what it will take to manufacture a part in terms of raw materials, labor rates, and cycle times. These output can form the basis of the manufacturing engineer's process plan for making a part. They might also support capacity planning.

Design standards: Some of the ways that DMCM aids in disclosing design standards include knowledge of how to select appropriate materials for a given application, what standard dimensions are, and what standard finish specifications are.

Cost-saving opportunities: DMCM supports several modes of identifying cost-saving opportunities. First, the DMCM user can alter one or more parameters and rerun the cost estimate in a what-if mode. Second, the user can request a range of external vendors to be considered. DMCM automatically performs the what-if analysis and returns the minimal cost supplier. Finally, DMCM suggests alternate choices whenever it determines a lower-cost alternative. Some of these potential what-if opportunities involve lowering the cost of the part, such as by suggesting thinner materials.

Application Use and Payoff

The development and fielding of DMCM has yielded both direct benefits and indirect benefits from changes in the business process. Changes because of DMCM are happening rapidly because the process of purchasing parts is changing as a direct result.

Benefits

A cost-benefit study was performed during the DMCM concept phase. This detailed study identified many of the specific cost benefits that are now being realized. These benefits are both tangible, measurable cost savings and intangible alterations to the way Xerox does business.

The tangible benefits include (1) labor savings provided by improved efficiency in actually developing cost estimates (the demonstrated time savings for cost engineers is 50 percent, which works out to $1.1 million annually); (2) more efficient designs in terms of material use, manufacturing times, and tooling costs, yielding direct cost reductions; (3) higher-quality products as a result of better conformance to internal design standards; and (4) shorter product development cycles because of fewer redesigns and quicker cost estimations.

Tangible savings in the last three categories are measured by estimating how much closer to the industry benchmark Xerox is able to make its parts. Although it varies by commodity, the study concluded that 40 to 50 percent of the gap between Xerox and the industry benchmark could be removed with DMCM. Multiplied by the amount that Xerox spends on each commodity yields the total annual savings. Naturally, this savings is a softer value, as well as being sensitive, but it is in excess of $20 million annually.

In addition, a number of business processes have improved as a result of implementing the DMCM system. In particular, some of the benefits are (1) working inventory reductions based on using the system to drive toward standards and common parts early in the design cycle, (2) improved use and awareness of design for manufacturing considerations by disclosing manufacturing processes and requirements while the design is still on the drafting board, and (3) improved processes for source acquisition and inventory management by disclosing to the product delivery organization objective measures of cost (eventually, the DMCM cost equations will include such items as logistics costs, service costs, refurbishment costs, facilities costs, and design costs).

Process Change Agent

DMCM was sold to management based on the direct time savings it afforded the cost engineering community. However, it also benefits the whole organization by changing the purchasing cycle and the way in which piece parts are acquired. We consider DMCM to be a vital agent, creating process change. These benefits can be seen as a Trojan horse in the sense that these process changes might only be recognized after the user community has been sold by the direct benefits.

Figure 3 diagrams the desired *end goal*, or ideal state of the design process and the part-costing process. (See figure 1 for the original process.) One of the major process changes we observed with the introduction of DMCM is the increased time spent in contact between PDTs and external part vendors.

Because cost engineers have additional time, they are spending it to get better and more current cost estimates. DMCM output sheets are commonly carried into price negotiation sessions with external part vendors.

A major effort is under way to produce custom cost estimate reports for each major Xerox part supplier based on vendor-supplied costing

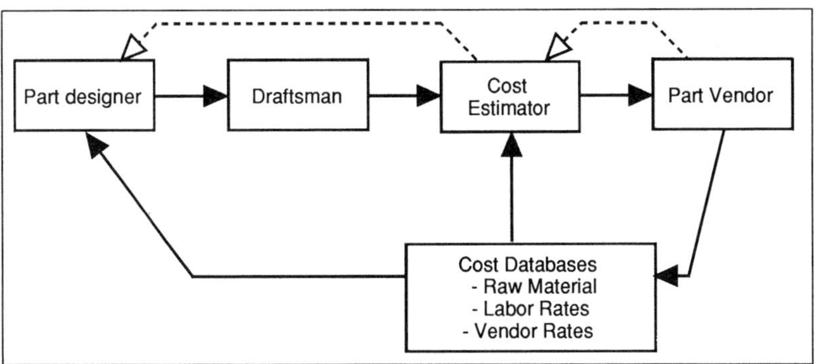

Figure 3. Altered Design Process.

information. In this manner, we can help each of our suppliers reach a higher level of quality and cost effectiveness.

These changes in the way Xerox does business are not an accidental by-product but, rather, the reason for the application in the first place. We believe strongly in planning for and expecting these process changes because they are so often associated with the acceptance of an application. It is possible and, probably, likely that these process changes will deliver more improvement than the direct benefits.

A sample of a DMCM printed report is shown in figure 4. Notice that the detailed cost estimates are given with respect to a selected vendor against a benchmark goal.[1] DMCM is able to cost an estimate against a selected set of possible outside vendors, selecting the particular vendor best capable of cost effectively producing the part.

User Feedback

The current DMCM user population within Xerox is approximately 25 cost engineers. Serious rollout began in January 1992 with the inception of monthly user classes. About 100 cost estimates are done each week with DMCM.

User feedback to DMCM is positive. In addition to the benefits observed by management, end users like the system for the following reasons:

First, access to company data is now easier.

Second, the system requires many times fewer input than prior models by using CAD files directly.

Third, they have the ability to automatically locate design violations.

Fourth, the need to constantly refer to manuals for design standards is eliminated.

COST SUMMARY	Sample-Vendor	Benchmark
Total Material Cost	0.272	0.272
Total Primary Labor Cost (USD)	0.042	0.040
Total Primary Setup Cost (USD)	0.005	0.005
Total Secondary Labor Cost (USD)	0.000	0.000
Total Secondary Setup Cost (USD)	0.000	0.000
Total Hardware Cost (USD)	0.000	0.000
Total Finishing Cost (USD)	0.113	0.113
Total Packaging Cost (USD)	0.000	0.000
Total Tooling Cost (USD)	2976	2976
Net Tool Cost Per Piece (USD)	0.07	0.07

MATERIAL COSTS	Sample-Vendor	Benchmark
Material Type	P Strips	P Strips
Parts Per Strip	18	18
Purchased Strip Size	2438x135	2438x135
Material Cost per KG (USD)	0.847	0.847
Material Weight (KG)	0.29	0.29
Material Cost (USD)	0.243	0.243
Material Markup Percent	1.10	1.10
Total Material Cost (USD)	0.272	0.272

Figure 4. Portion of Sample Vendor Report.

Fifth, they have the ability to generate hypothetical designs easily and then get objective metrics back (design cost) to evaluate alternatives.

Based on this feedback and progress to date, we anticipate that our full benefits case will be achieved.

Application Development and Deployment

DMCM was developed with four knowledge engineers working over an 18-month time frame. There were three software development phases: (1) implementation of the application shell, (2) implementation of the three initial knowledge bases, and (3) application field testing and roll-out to the field.

Implementation Issues

Shell Language: The C language was chosen for the DMCM shell for its ability to integrate with the reasoning system, the UNIX environment, and the graphics tool kit. An additional benefit is the wide degree of portability that the C language affords. C++ was not chosen because of its immature state of development. However, nothing in the DMCM im-

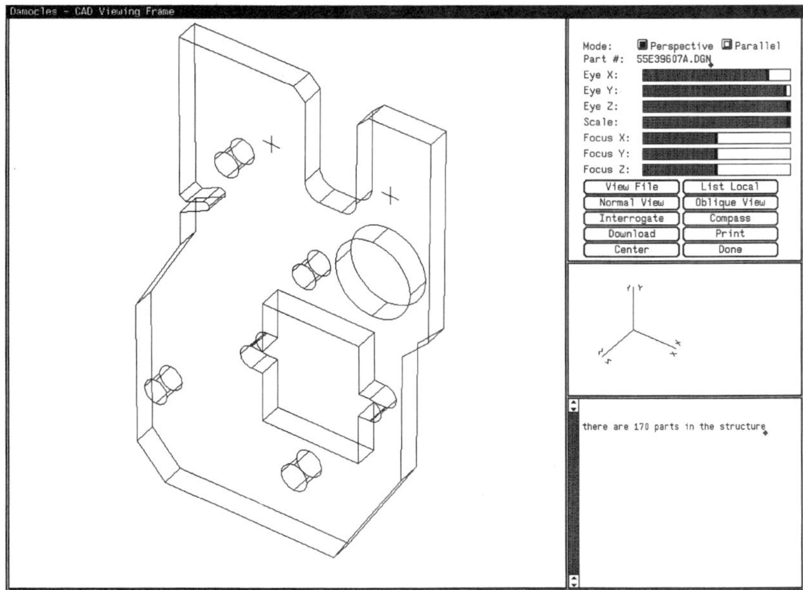

Figure 5. DMCM *Shell Integration with Computer-Aided Design.*

plementation precludes going to C++ at a later date.

Database: ORACLE is used for the relational database. The graphics and geometry presentation are implemented with Sun's PHIGS+ software.

Reasoning system: ART-IM was chosen for the AI reasoning system (Inference 1988) because of its ability to integrate with existing applications as well as the ease of extending the reasoning environment with new C-coded primitives. Such operators were added to allow remote database access; move data files through XNS, TCP-IP, and SNA connections; and support persistent objects.

AI language integration: To facilitate development of a production-quality knowledge-based system and ensure its long-term maintainability, we chose not to develop an internal language to represent DMCM's knowledge. Instead, we use a standard tool in our center, ART-IM. Using a standard tool provides our knowledge engineers with the greatest productivity and simplifies the maintenance task for the maintainers in traditional information-management departments. Use of a standard tool also affords increased flexibility in moving knowledge engineers between projects.

This tool has most of the features that are needed in an AI tool. The features we feel are important include a full-featured rule syntax for

```
(defrule obtain-thickness
  (declare (salience 11))
  (commodity "sheet metal")
  (active-design ?design ?serial)
  (cost-estimate)
  (schema ?design
          (display-file ?yn)
          (not (material-thickness ?)))
 =>
  (if (eq ?yn no) then
    (assert (schema ?design
                    (material-thickness
                     =(art-ask-float 5 5
                      "How thick do you want the material? (mm)"))))
   else
    (cad-lock 1)
    (get-dimension "Please pick on the material thickness"
                   "material thickness")))

(defrule convert-thickness-dimension
  (declare (salience 100))
  (commodity "sheet metal")
  (active-design ?design ?serial)
  ?d <- (CAD-dimensia "material thickness" ?x)
 =>
  (retract ?d)
  (assert (schema ?design (material-thickness ?x))))
```

Figure 6. Example of Geometric Reasoning Rules.

specifying rules and constraints; easy integration with the C language (a requirement for a system that is highly interconnected); a powerful object representation to support modeling of material families, designs with their features, and the like; and commercial support that includes help, documentation, and training for system maintainers.

Integration Issues

Integration with the existing infrastructure proves to be complex and challenging, even for a simple costing system. However, we believe that integration is extremely important and is fundamental to the acceptance of the system. The areas DMCM had to integrate with are detailed in the following subsections.

CAD Integration. The majority of our hardware designs are stored as simple three-dimensional, wire-frame drawings in a format described by our primary CAD vendor (Intergraph). As a part of the DMCM shell, functions are included to copy these drawings from a remote drawing

```
(defrule pl-determine-press-prices
  (declare (salience 10))
  (pl-phase price $?)
  (active-design ?design ?serial)
  (schema ?design (economics ?ver) (manuf-site ?src))
  =>
  (uiprint "\n\nGetting press rates")
  (bind ?sql (string-append
      "select machno, "
      "vnd_cycle_labor_rate + vnd_cycle_burden_rate "
      "from xp_lr_detail where "
      "machno>='HB' and machno<'HC' and "
      (sprintf "ver='%s' " ?ver)
      (sprintf "and src='%s';" ?src)))
  (query-facts ?sql "pl-press-rate-raw"))

(defrule pl-determine-press-convert-to-string
  (declare (salience 100))
  ?fact <- (pl-press-rate-raw ?id ?rate)
  =>
  (if (symbolp ?id) then
    (retract ?fact)
    (bind ?id-new (string-append ?id))
    (assert (pl-press-rate-raw ?id-new ?rate))))
```

Figure 7. Example of ART-IM *Rules Reading Database.*

archive to the workstation. The CAD drawing images are then displayed on the workstation. Many questions posed by the knowledge bases can be answered directly from the display because dimensional information is available by selecting features of the drawing with the mouse. Figure 5 depicts the CAD interaction frame that is part of the DMCM shell.

As mentioned previously, the geometric information that we obtained from the CAD drawings is largely limited to three-dimensional, stick-figure line segments. Additional information is required to reason about abstract concepts, such as width, thickness, volume, and placement. These more abstract concepts are derived from asking questions of the user and having the user answer specific questions by pointing to the appropriate feature with the mouse. The portion of the knowledge base shown in figure 6 determines the stock thickness required for a sheet metal part. The rule obtain-thickness fires when the material-thickness slot is not present within the current design schema. If a display file is not active, the user is simply prompted for the thickness value.

If a CAD display file is available for the part, the second portion of the rule requests the drawing window to be shown, and the user is prompted to click on the material thickness with the mouse. When the dimension is indicated, the shell code asserts the value as the labeled fact (CAD-DIMENSIA "material thickness" <xxx>). The second rule, convert-thickness-dimension, retracts the fact and converts the dimension information into the required slot value.

Work is under way to extend DMCM's reasoning about the parts that are presented. Research such as Cunningham and Dixon (1988), Gero (1985), Kapur and Mundy (1988), Morjaria, Mittal, and Dym (1985), and Wu has documented the importance of using geometric information in the design and analysis domains, citing a number of approaches.

Database Integration. From its earliest inception, DMCM was strongly connected with existing databases, both as a reader and as a writer.[2] The relational database server technology chosen for DMCM is ORACLE. Functions were installed in the shell to enable ART-IM rules to easily create SQL queries.

Figure 7 demonstrates how this task is accomplished. The rule pl-determine-press-prices forms a query by building a query string. This string is passed to a routine that returns each row satisfying the query as a separate fact. The second rule, pl-determine-press-convert-to-string, converts each returned press into a more useful internal form.

With a large, multinational corporation, a number of existing databases must be accessed. Grouped then under the general topic of databases were the following interface challenges:

Corporate databases: Connections were needed to approximately one dozen existing databases. Most of these databases are treated in a read-only manner. These databases are of several different styles, including IBM's IMS-DC, DB2, and ORACLE, and run on several different platforms.

DMCM-specific data: Because we controlled the placement and format of our project data, we standardized on retaining DMCM-specific data in ORACLE files resident on a departmental UNIX processor. These relational ORACLE tables hold cost information, intermediate working data, and the state of ART slots (see Implementation Issues) after a cost estimate is complete.

Persistent objects: ART-IM was augmented with persistent objects to support the reasoning process, allowing DMCM to reason over design objects later from any workstation sharing the department's database. A number of browsing activities are also supported (Nguyen and Rieu 1987; Waldron and Chan 1988). We found that moving schemata[3] between ART-IM's virtual memory and rows in the ORACLE database was a practical solution because it promoted the reuse of objects and provided multiple use, locking, and rollback and recovery of a commercial database. Our technique supports the sharing of design objects across multiple designs. All design decisions are recorded in the design schema slots so that they can be preserved in the database, reviewed, and reused. These design decisions serve as an important history for each part, preserving the initial design choices.

Query Facility: We found that working with a commercially available database such as ORACLE enhanced our productivity as developers. Tools such as the forms package SQL*Forms reduced the effort required to develop routines to browse and edit many of the records used by a complex knowledge base, such as physical material properties, standard labor rates, and currency conversions. Also available are productive approaches to generating the standard reports that users request.

Integration with IMS-DC. The principal output of DMCM is the estimated part cost. This information is entered into an existing, MVS-resident IMS database.

Early in the development of DMCM we asked the existing information-management support group to estimate the programming resources necessary to construct a remote interface into the MVS-IMS database. When this estimate exceeded one-third of the DMCM programming budget in both time and expense, we took another tack.

Because of the rapid development time frame of DMCM, we elected to interface to existing IBM 3270 transaction screens programatically. We constructed an emulator for the IBM 3278 terminal, using SUN LINK's program interface to the channel data stream. This emulator is used to log DMCM into a remote IMS-DC machine, initiate the proper transaction, complete the screen forms, and transmit the results back to DMCM with no change to existing host programs.

User Interface

The initial graphic user interface desktop environment for DMCM was SUNVIEW. We converted DMCM to operate in the X WINDOW–compliant OPEN WINDOWS environment. OPEN WINDOWS is Sun's implementation of OPENLOOK. Sun's XVIEW software library is used for its widgets. MOTIF was not chosen because of licensing considerations.

In addition, a classic teletype interface is supported for backward compatibility with older, character-mode terminals. Graphics are not supported in this teletype mode.

In many systems, a large fraction of the total development time is spent constructing the user interface. The decision was made to devote a short period of up-front time to build, debug, and document a library of calls that provide most of the DMCM user interface.

From any knowledge base or any C-language routine, the knowledge programmer can request that information be displayed to the user or obtained from the user. Furthermore, these calls have been developed to be knowledgeable about the desktop environment the user is operating in and to perform the appropriate behavior.

Additional environments can then be supported in an incremental fashion by coding a handful of user interface primitives in the new environment. Today, DMCM supports SUN VIEW and character-oriented terminals. In the near future, it will support OPEN WINDOWS PEX (X WINDOWS) with the same primitives.

Model Validation

Initial validation of the cost models was performed during a two-month field test. During this period, a set of six cost engineers estimated their designs both with DMCM and their previous methods. Many adjustments were made to the models following this test.

Because many Xerox parts are purchased externally, the cost engineering group adjusts their parameters on an ongoing basis when external bids are received. In the case of specific external suppliers, part buyers obtain shop labor rates and other cost information from the specific vendor, with the provision that this information is not to be shared with competing vendors.

Deployment

The proof of any application is in its deployment and acceptance by the user population. DMCM was initially released to the field in June 1991. Use during the first six months was primarily by the original expert departments. Three fractional, enhancement releases followed during the remainder of the year.

As mentioned earlier, the current DMCM user population is approximately 25 engineers. The estimated user population for 1992 is 60 users, with growth to 200 expected in 1993. Geographic distribution of use centers initially on Xerox domestic manufacturing centers in New York and California. International users will be located in Holland and Great Britain.

Initial rollout was hampered by the unforeseen relocation of our commodity experts into a different office facility. This move hampered the installation of network-connected workstations because of an older data communications infrastructure. This problems is one of the many real problems that were encountered and overcome.

Maintenance and Continuing Support

We feel that it is easy for a highly skilled group of bright practitioners to produce a showy concept prototype. Getting an application installed, documented, and accepted by a user community, as well as integrated into the corporation, is more difficult, which is the heart of the technology transfer problem.

Continuing Partnerships

A major theme in the development effort was continuous partnership relationships with our customers and cosuppliers. Of prime importance to us has been our cosuppliers, the information-management staff of the Xerox Product Design and Manufacturing Division.

The relationship holds the key to the technology transfer process for several reasons: Most importantly, the information-management groups manage almost all the data DMCM needed, both for its input and its output. The information-management groups also control the existing mainframe programs wrapped around these data. Information-management groups also house people wanting to develop their knowledge-based system skills. Thus, working in a continuing, close partnership with the cosuppliers in such areas as maintaining and extending DMCM into additional commodities benefits all concerned.

Resource Management. Convincing traditional information-management line managers that new resources should be allocated to these ends, getting the line items into continuing budgets, and holding these commitments against the constant buffeting of head count and budget issues are continuing problems. In a dynamic company, the personnel turnover in management positions almost ensures that a completely new cast reviews each year's budgets.

In the case of DMCM, staffing the positions was a problem because appropriate skills were lacking in the internal programmer population. External hires were placed on the project, worked on the development of the code, and then were transitioned into the information-management organization. In this position, they are (1) maintaining DMCM, (2) extending it to additional cost models, (3) continuing the product rollout, and (4) serving as the basis for a knowledge-based system competency center within the information-management organization.

Follow-On Work

The information-management knowledge-based system group continues to work closely with the corporate competency center to develop additional knowledge-based systems. Because these individuals were a part of the original development team, this work follows naturally. One follow-on project is already on the drawing board: The manufacturing operations adviser (MOA) is a system that picks up where DMCM leaves off, adding manufacturing knowledge across multiple parts to more effectively schedule a floor of manufacturing machinery.

Plans are being made to extend DMCM with additional knowledge models to cost additional commodities important to Xerox. The planned commodities include wiring harnesses and printed wire board assemblies.

Acknowledgments

We would like to acknowledge a few of the people who contributed to the development of DMCM: Mark Maletz, Lynn Heatley, Dhimant Master, Jeff Leonard, and Sergio Rubio of the Knowledge-Based System Competency Center and Vince Romano and John Beasman of the Xerox Materials Management Group were all instrumental to our success.

Notes

1. As part of ongoing quality practices, Xerox maintains a measure of industry's best practices and attempts to achieve these measures.
2. In fact, this integration with existing corporate data assets helped gain the acceptance of DMCM.
3. For the purist, *schemata* is the plural form of schema, ART-IM's term for an internal, slot-oriented data structure, or frame. A schema is roughly equivalent to the object in an object-oriented programming environment.

References

Brown, D., and Chandrasekaran, B. 1986. Knowledge and Control for a Mechanical Design Expert System. *IEEE Computer:* 19(7): 92–100.

Cunningham, J., and Dixon, J. 1988. Designing with Features: The Origin of Features. In Proceedings of the 1988 ASME International Computers in Engineering Conference and Exhibition, 237–243. New York: American Society of Mechanical Engineers.

Dixon, J., and Dym, C. 1986. Artificial Intelligence and Geometric Reasoning in Manufacturing Technology. *Applied Mechanics Reviews* 39(9): 1325–1330.

Dixon, J., and Simmons, M. 1984. Computers That Design: Expert Systems for Mechanical Engineers. *Computers in Mechanical Engineering.*

Dym, C. 1987. Issues in the Design and Implementation of Expert Systems. *Artificial Intelligence for Engineering Design, Analysis, and Manufacturing* 1(1): 37–46.

Forbus, K. 1988. Intelligent Computer-Aided Engineering. *AI Magazine* 9(3): 23–36.

Gael, V., and Pirollo, P. 1989. Motivating the Notion of Generic Design with Information-Processing Theory: The Design Problem Space. *AI Magazine* 10(2): 18–36.

Gero, J., ed. 1985. *Knowledge Engineering in Computer-Aided Design.* Amsterdam: North-Holland.

Gray, M. 1988. An Intelligent Design Machine: Architecture and Search Strategies. *Artificial Intelligence for Engineering Design, Analysis, and Manufacturing* 2(2): 105–122.

Hatfield, S., and Crowfoot, N. 1990. Knowledge-Based Systems in Cost Estimating and Design. In Proceedings of the Autofact '90, 21-1–21-10. New York: American Society of Mechanical Engineers.

Hatfield, S., Tuchinsky, P., and McWhortery, R. 1987. BRAKES: An Expert System for Engineers. In Proceedings of the Expert Systems for Advanced Manufacturing Technology Conference.

Hoeltzel, D.; Chieng, W-H.; and Zissimides, J. 1987. Knowledge Representation and Planning Control in an Expert System for the Creative Design of Mechanisms. *Artificial Intelligence for Engineering Design, Analysis, and Manufacturing* 1(2): 19–137.

Inference Corporation. 1988. ART-IM, Integrated Reasoning Tool for Information Management, DPU-C15-R2-AA, Inference Corporation, Los Angeles, California.

Kapur, D., and Mundy, J., eds. 1988. *Geometric Reasoning.* Cambridge, Mass.: MIT Press.

Mittal, S., and Araya, A. 1986. A Knowledge-Based Framework for Design. In Proceedings of the Fifth National Conference on Artificial Intelligence, 856–865. Menlo Park, Calif.: American Association for Artificial Intelligence.

Mittal, S.; Dym, C.; and Morjaria, M. 1986. PRIDE: An Expert System for the Design of Paper-Handling Systems. *IEEE Computer,* 19(7): 102–114.

Morjaria, M.; Mittal, S.; and Dym, C. 1985. Interactive Graphics in Expert Systems for Engineering Applications. In Proceedings of the 1985 ASME International Computers in Engineering Conference and Exhibition. New York: American Society of Mechanical Engineers.

Mostow, J. 1985. Toward Better Models of the Design Process. *AI Magazine.* (6): 44–57.

Nguyen, G., and Rieu, D. 1987. Expert Database Concepts for Engineering Design. *Artificial Intelligence for Engineering Design, Analysis, and Manufacturing* 1(2): 89–101.

O'Brien, J.; Brice, H.; Hatfield, S.; Johnson, W. P.; and Woodhead, R. 1989. The Ford Motor Company Direct Labor Management System. In *Innovative Applications of Artificial Intelligence,* eds. H. Schorr and A. Rappaport, 333–347. Menlo Park, Calif.: AAAI Press.

Tat Chan, W., and Paulson, B. 1987. Exploratory Design Using Constraints. *AI EDAM* 1(1): 9–71.

Waldron, M., and Chan, C. 1988. Object-Oriented System for Component Selection. In Proceedings of the 1988 ASME International Computers in Engineering Conference and Exhibition, 7–62. New York: American Society of Mechanical Engineers.

Wu, Y. 1987. Automated Design and Sketching of Mechanisms Based on Specified Design Requirements by Employing Expert System Methodologies. Ph.D. diss., Dept. of Mechanical Engineering and Applied Mechanics, Univ. of Rhode Island.

SLURRYMINDER: A Rational Oil Well Completion Design Module

E. Brent Kelly, Philippe Caillot, Robert Roemer, and Thierry Simien, Dowell Schlumberger

A critical phase of oil well completion involves positioning cement between the outer surface of a metal casing and the sides of the well. This task is done by injecting a specially formulated cement slurry down the center of the casing and up the sides of the bore hole. Designing these slurry systems is time consuming and expensive because of the variability of the conditions between wells and the variability of the raw materials and techniques used in geographically diverse locations. SLURRYMINDER is a design tool to aid field engineers in creating globally consistent cement slurry formulations and to rapidly disseminate current well-cementing techniques. We describe the implementation of this system and why AI technology was used; we also discuss corporate benefits of the system, both real and projected. We provide details on the SLURRYMINDER development process, its worldwide deployment, and our experiences in maintaining and updating it.

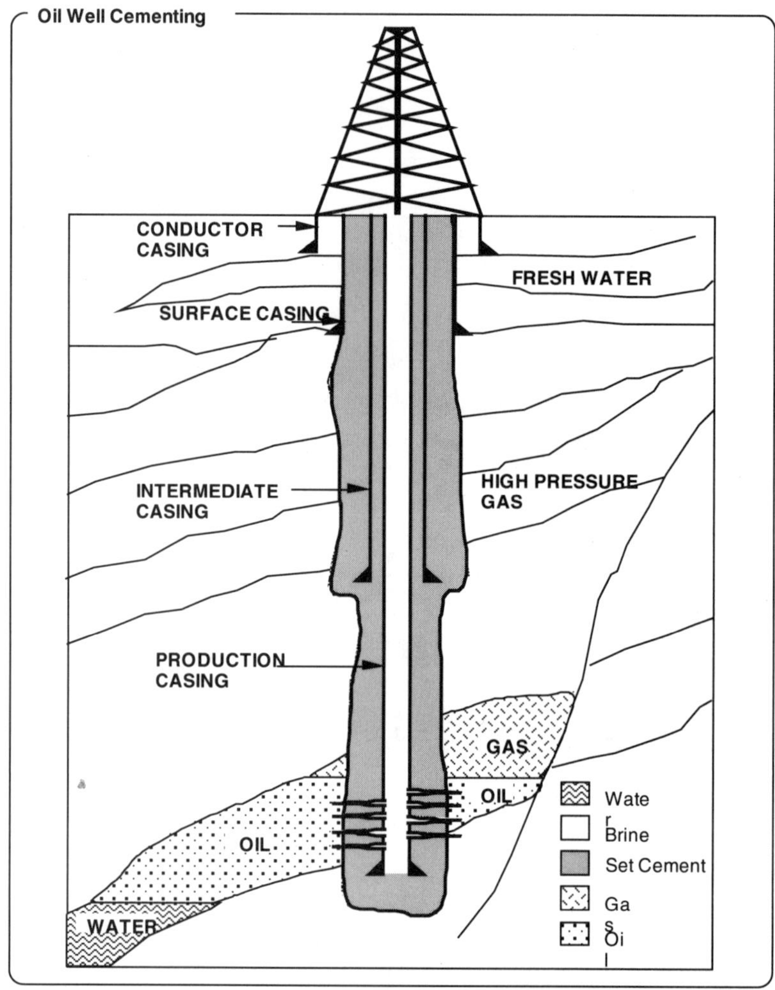

Figure 1. A Schematic Showing How Oil and Gas Wells Are Cemented. Cement slurry is pumped down the inside of the metal casing and up the annulus formed by the outer surface of the casing and the sides of the well bore hole.

Problem Description

A critical phase of oil or gas well completion involves positioning cement within the well annulus by pumping a specially designed cement slurry down the well casing and up the sides of the bore hole, as shown in figure 1 and discussed by Nelson (1990). A typical cement slurry is composed of the cement powder, some type of mix water (usually fresh water or seawater), and one or more chemical additives that give the cement certain specified physical properties during pumping and afterward when set.

Designing a cement slurry system is generally iterative in nature: An initial design is proposed, which is then followed by a series of laboratory testing and tuning steps, as in figure 2. During this testing-tuning process, additive concentrations can be modified or certain additives replaced by others until the slurry and the set cement satisfy the required physical properties, whereupon it is ready to be pumped into a client's well.

Ideally, given similar well conditions anywhere in the world, slurry designs should contain similar additives at similar concentration levels. In practice, because of the variability in the cement powder, the quality of the local additives, and local cementing tradition, slurries designed for similar well conditions often bear little resemblance to one another. This dissimilarity not only can be a source of confusion to clients, but from a global research and engineering perspective, it also makes it difficult to disseminate new cementing additive technology.

To address the slurry design problem, Dowell Schlumberger's engineering personnel embarked on an ambitious program to create a slurry design support tool. Our goals in developing this tool were twofold: (1) to ensure worldwide design consistency and quality but allow the required freedom for local practitioners and (2) to create a distribution mechanism for rapid information dissemination of an ever-evolving technology. Earlier work in designing entire cement jobs had already been done by practitioners, such as Wolsfelt, Roger, and Fenoul (1989); however, in their CEMENTEX system, no attempt was made to design the critical cement slurry systems that are actually pumped into the well.

Prior to investigating a solution to the slurry design problem using AI techniques, earlier attempts to solve the problem were made using statistical regression analysis and material characterization studies. Researchers tried to analyze existing field-design data to develop correlations between slurry performance properties and the amount of each chemical additive in the slurry mixture. Unfortunately, because of the variability in the local cement and chemical additives, the deviation in the regression parameters was so large that the parameters had no real significance, and these efforts failed. Our field engineers and laboratory technicians were, however, successfully designing cement slurry formulations daily, and we became convinced that an AI approach was the only feasible alternative remaining if we wanted to achieve a solution to this problem.

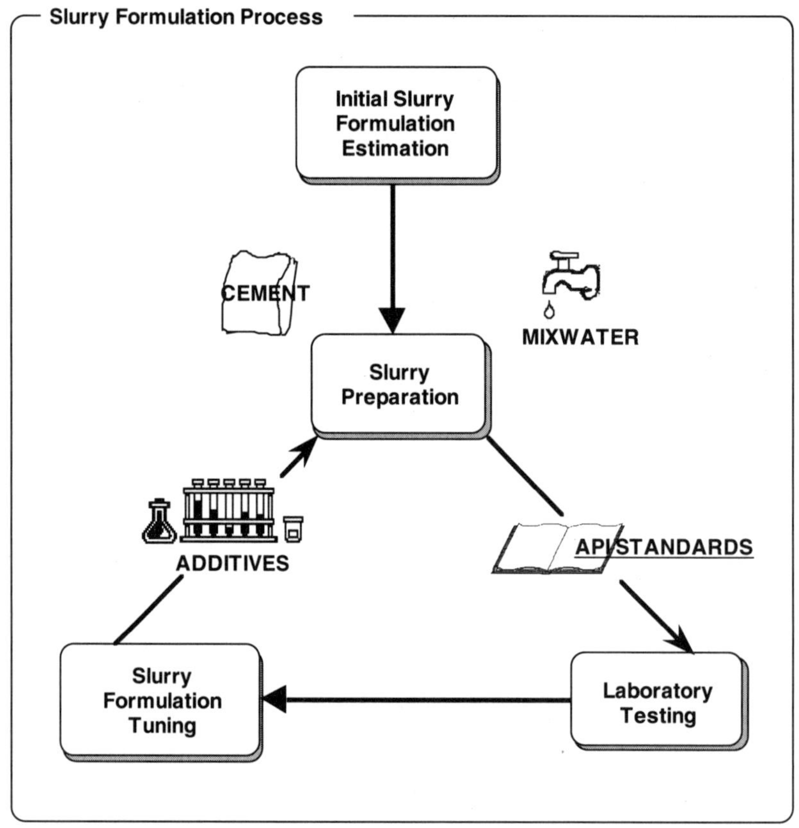

Figure 2. The Cement Slurry Formulation Process.
An inital design is formulated and given to the laboratory personnel. This design is mixed in the laboratory, and a series of standard tests defined by the American Petroleum Institute are run on the resulting slurry. If the required slurry physical properties are not achieved, the slurry formulation is tuned by modifying the concentration of one or more of the chemical additives. This tuned slurry formulation is then mixed, and the tests are rerun. This testing and tuning loop continues until the slurry satisfies the performance parameters, as specified by the client or the sales engineer.

Application Description

By nature, successful cement slurry design is a fuzzy domain where heuristic information and experience about cement and additive use is required. Compounding the problem is the fact that some of the heuristics change depending on geographic location: Design experi-

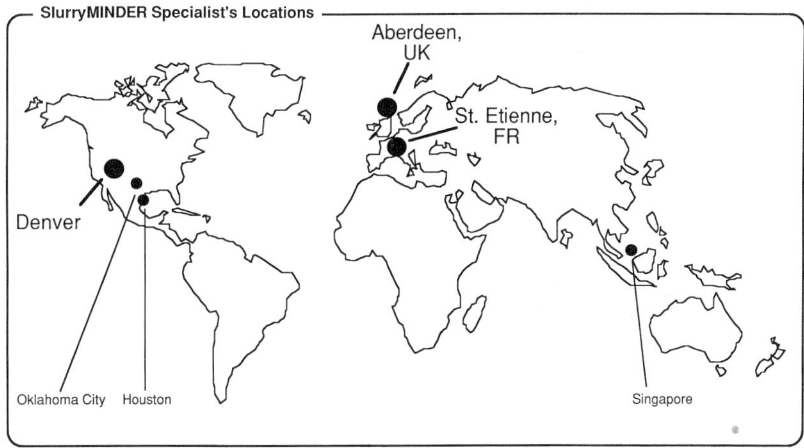

Figure 3. Cementing Specialists Who Assisted with SLURRYMINDER Development Were Located All over the World.
Primary specialists involved throughout the development process were located in Denver, Colorado; Aberdeen, Scotland; and St. Etienne, France. Additional experts providing input were stationed in Singapore; Oklahoma City, Oklahoma; and Houston, Texas.

ence in one field location might not be valid in another. As these problem characteristics became known to the development team, we concluded that solving the slurry design problem would likely require the use and integration of an extensive amount of information from a variety of sources. Having had significant experience within Schlumberger using AI techniques, we knew many of the risks and benefits associated with these technologies and opted to approach the solution to our problem through the creation of an imbedded knowledge-based system.

Development Constraints

While designing and implementing SLURRYMINDER, we were required to work under several existing constraints.

Distributed expertise and varying methodology: Our cement slurry design specialists were distributed all over the world, as illustrated in figure 3. Although they were all experts in their own region, their design methodology and design experiences were somewhat different. To rationalize these various points of view, one specialist at the engineering center in St. Etienne, France, was appointed knowledge czar, with the responsibility of converging methodologies and making strategic decisions when conflicting opinions arose.

Off-the-shelf software tools: Funding and timing constraints would not allow us the luxury of creating a custom expert system shell or developing a custom human interface tool. Hence, we were required to use software tools that were available in the software marketplace.

Existing design data: At all company locations, a cement slurry design database exists as a repository for successful slurry formulation data. We wanted to somehow incorporate the use of this local database into SLURRYMINDER so that the global methodology could be made to apply in each locality.

Computer hardware specification: In the mid-1980s, each of our 155 field locations purchased a MICROVAX II with a VT-240/241 semigraphic display. To effectively use this investment, SLURRYMINDER was required to execute on the existing field computer hardware. The implication of this decision was that the interface had to be character based.

Shell Selection Criteria

Prior to selecting a shell for use in constructing SLURRYMINDER, we performed a domain analysis to determine which kinds of knowledge were to be represented. Using this domain information and making some pragmatic decisions, we formulated the following selection criteria that we used in the evaluation and selection process:

First, it must support knowledge representation paradigms, including a robust inference engine that allows both forward- and backward-chaining production rules and an object-oriented schema system that supports multiple inheritance. The schema system must be well integrated with the inference engine pattern matcher so that the rules can effectively use the objects, slots, and slot values in their antecedent or consequent parts.

Second, it should support the concept of multiple knowledge bases, allowing knowledge decoupling and grouping.

Third, it must support the integration of user-defined procedures, functions, or routines in both the left- and right-hand sides of production rules (which implies calling-out functionality).

Fourth, it must be able to be embedded within a larger software system or program (which implies calling-in functionality).

Fifth, it must provide a development environment with the following minimum capabilities: dynamic rule and object creation through rule and object editors; browsing features to examine rules and objects within the knowledge base, including progeny graphs, rule-network graphs, and textual listings of rules and objects; breakpoints to control rule execution; and tracing features to observe rule behavior and knowledge base modification during execution.

Sixth, it must provide a small run-time kernel that can be used to execute systems created with the shell without the development environment present. In this run-time environment, system performance should improve.

Seventh, it must support a run-time kernel that does not require a bit-mapped graphics terminal or additional software packages to execute properly. The human interface should be determined by the application developers and not the selected shell.

Eighth, it must execute on a variety of hardware platforms, with knowledge bases requiring only minor modifications when changing platforms.

Ninth, it must have a significant user community to ensure its robustness and reliability.

Tenth, it must be able to operate in conjunction with future acquisition and design software written in C.

Eleventh, it must be accompanied by clearly written and professionally typeset documentation. This documentation should be written so that individuals reasonably familiar with software development can understand how to use the shell without having to ask for undocumented functions and features.

Twelfth, it must be priced so that development copies can readily be purchased by the company's engineering centers. The run-time version must be priced so that a worldwide license can be obtained economically.

Thirteenth, it must be able to be called by an Ada program or be linked with Ada program modules.

Fourteenth, it must allow communication with an INGRES database through query facilities within the shell or through the calling-out–calling-in functions.

In addition, the company or organization marketing the selected shell must do the following:

First, it must provide a hotline service staffed by qualified professionals available to answer questions regarding use of the shell. A fee can be charged for this service.

Second, it must be able to provide training either in house or at a remote location to teach individuals how to use the tool. A fee can be charged for this service.

Third, it must be reputable, with at least five years of experience in developing expert system shells or other AI software.

During the selection process, we evaluated three C-based expert system shells; our final choice was NEXPERT OBJECT from Neuron Data.

System Design

A simple representation of the SLURRYMINDER architecture is shown in figure 4. The application consists of five distinct parts: (1) human interface routines; (2) utilities for system configuration, browsing of other useful online databases, and a slurry pricing spreadsheet; (3) the reasoning mechanism for generating the list of chemical additives required in the slurry formulation; (4) the explanation and warning subsystem used to explain why a particular formulation was generated and whether there are any warnings on how to use one or more of the additives in the formulation; and (5) the query and calculation routines for generating additive concentrations and the quantities required for laboratory testing.

Knowledge Base Decomposition and Design. In attempting to create a model of how our specialists approach the slurry design problem, we became aware of four distinct levels of abstraction in their thinking processes: (1) recognition of which type of slurry system must be generated to satisfy the required performance parameters, (2) recognition based on the chemical product family that can be used in the slurry system, (3) an evaluation of whether a particular chemical family is actually required in the formulation, and (4) the actual selection of one or more of the chemical additives from a particular family that enables the slurry to meet one or more of the specified performance parameters.

Knowledge within SLURRYMINDER was decomposed into 14 separate knowledge bases, 1 knowledge base for general or kernel knowledge and the others for specific knowledge relative to one particular chemical additive family. Abstraction levels one through three are contained in the kernel knowledge base, but level four is contained within the knowledge base for each particular family, as in figure 5. Representing the current level of knowledge requires approximately 115 classes and objects and over 700 rules, with several C routines used for optimizing dynamic object creation during inferencing.

When a user queries SLURRYMINDER for a slurry formulation, the reasoning mechanism uses a backward-chaining, depth-first search strategy. We implemented an exhaustive searching strategy so that multiple types of designs can be obtained if applicable, with each type of design potentially having multiple formulations. During inferencing, competing slurry formulations are ranked according to a simple model based on how well a particular additive will perform in a given situation. Users can limit the number of solutions that are generated by SLURRYMINDER, which in certain instances can grow geometrically with the number of selectable additives at each formulation stage.

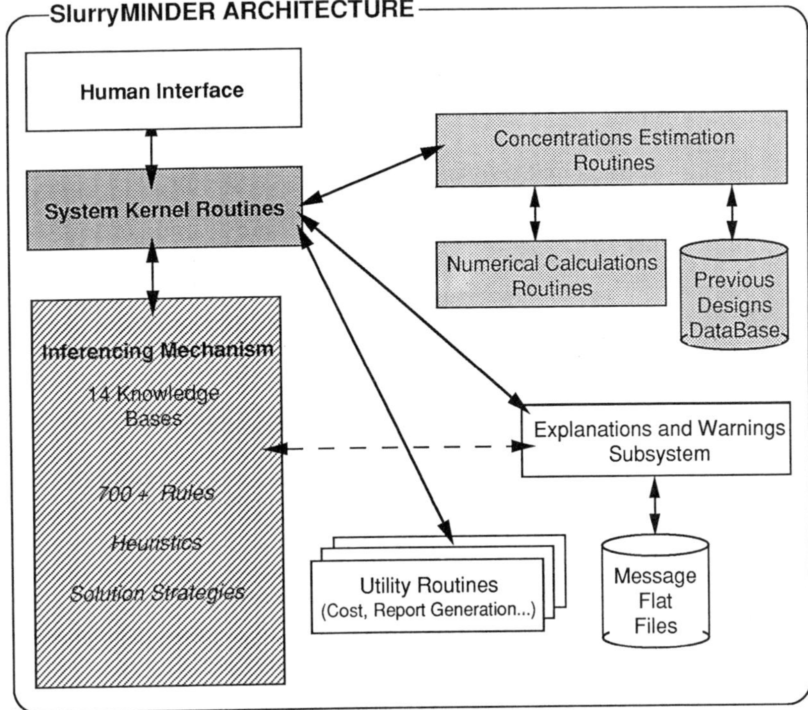

Figure 4. Simple Schematic of the SLURRYMINDER Architecture.
Five separate subsystems are connected by a set of system kernel routines: the human interface, the inferencing mechanism, the concentration routines, the explanation and warning subsystem, and some utility routines for database browsing and administration. Within the inferencing mechanism, there are 14 knowledge bases containing over 700 separate rules and solution strategies.

We designed the knowledge base so that each chemical additive family is self-validating about its applicability in a given design problem. When a family determines that its functions are required in slurry formulation, it sends a selection message to each individual chemical additive within the family. Individual additives are also self-validating; when they receive the selection message from their parent object, rules are evaluated to determine if the particular additive can be selected given the current state of the formulation and the global design pa-

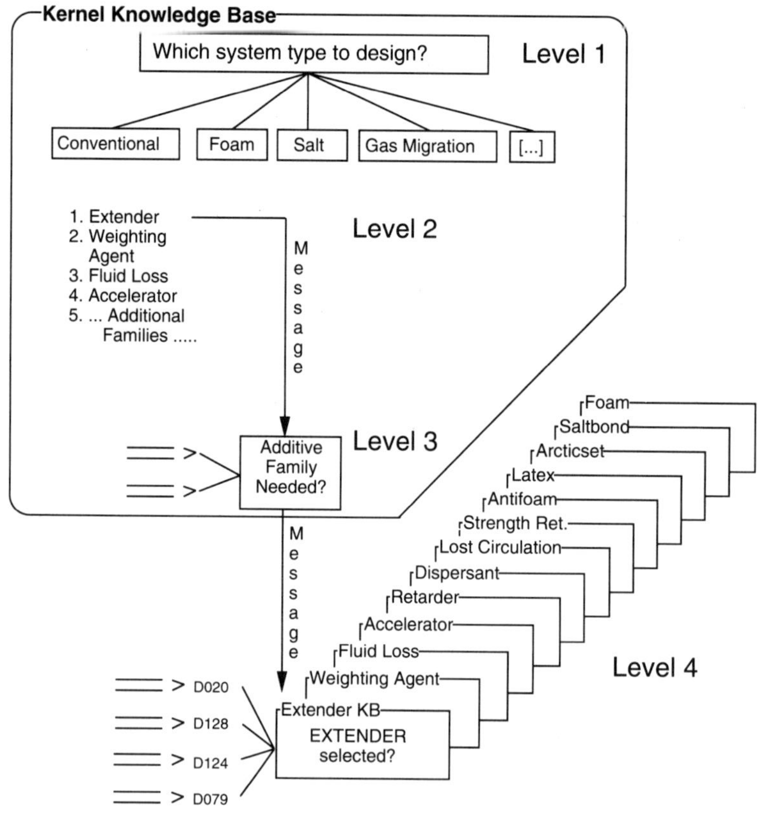

Figure 5. Knowledge-Abstraction Levels within SLURRYMINDER.
Level 1 determines which type of system to design. Level 2 is a declarative level, indicating which additive families might be included in a particular system type. Level 3 is activated by a message from level 2. Level 3 determines if the effect of a particular additive family is required given the input data and the additives already selected. If the effect of an additive family is needed, level 3 sends a message to level 4, which contains the selection knowledge for each particular additive in the family. Levels 1, 2, and 3 are contained within the kernel knowledge base, and level 4 is divided into 13 separate knowledge bases, one for each additive family.

rameters, such as well temperature or depth.

As additives are selected for use, they append an explanation code and a warning code to the current intermediate solution node, as illustrated in figure 6. These codes can then be used by the explanation and warning subsystem to extract context-specific explanation or warning messages from a flat-file database specific to the additive in question; thus, users are informed about why a particular additive was selected in a given situation. It is this explanation and warning system that provides the mechanism for rapid technology transfer within SLURRYMINDER. When new chemical products are added to the SLURRYMINDER knowledge base, they appear in the ranked formulations they obtain from the reasoning mechanism. After a particular slurry formulation is generated, the user can invoke the explanation and warning option to view an explanation of how this new additive is to be used. If more information is desired, users can branch using a hot key to a more complete online Additive Information Manual, giving complete technical details for each chemical product.

Previous Design Database Link. Users of the SLURRYMINDER prototype informed the development team that slurry formulations without additive concentrations were useless. Linking with the local design database is where SLURRYMINDER bridges the gap between a global formulation methodology and local practice.

Once the additives in a slurry formulation are selected, users have two options for generating additive concentrations: a default method or a query of their own local database, as shown in figure 7. The default method can be likened to browsing a cementing manual for general recommendations for additive concentrations, independent of the local cement and additive quality. Querying a user's local database, however, provides a connection with previous design history in the same geographic location.

When users query their local design database, interactions between the local cement and the local chemical additives are implicitly accounted for because these previous designs have already been tested successfully in the laboratory. Queries usually consist of some design input data, such as temperature and density; the targeted physical properties of the cement; and additional items for narrowing the search, such as the well name or the client name. These criteria are used to build an SQL-like query to search a series of relational tables in the database. The output of the query consists of the average chemical additive concentration value for all tests matching the query criteria, the minimum and maximum values, and the total number of tests found. Users can review this information and reformulate the query if narrower criteria are needed.

Linking with previous design experience through these local databases leverages and validates the corporate strategy for a global design methodology that can be made to apply nearly anywhere in the world. It is this coupling of expert system technology for selecting the chemical

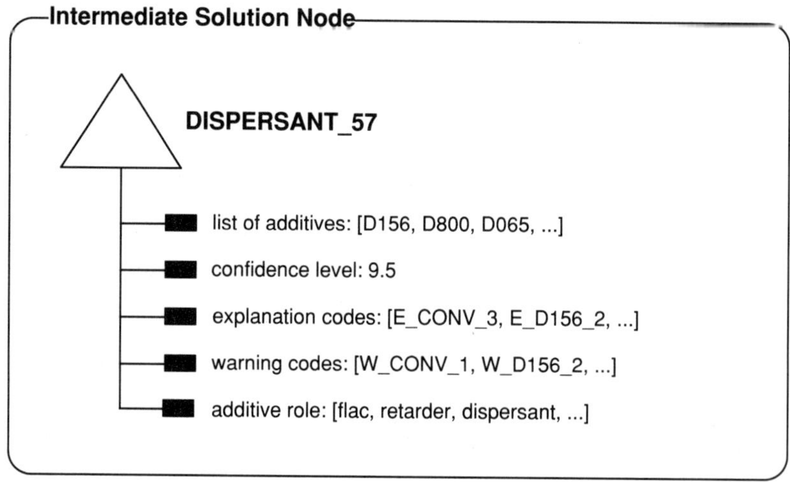

Figure 6. Each Intermediate Solution Node Contains the List of Selected Additives to This Point in the Inference and the Total Confidence Level for the Node. Explanation and warning slots contain a list of codes, the first for the type of solution the node represents and those following for each selected additive. The role of each selected additive is also represented. Node names are indicative of the type of additive most recently selected, with the node number showing the order in which this node was created.

additives with traditional database search techniques that is making SLURRYMINDER an outstanding technical success for the company.

Application Use And Payoff

SLURRYMINDER was officially released to approximately 155 field locations in 55 countries in October 1991. The system was designed for two distinct types of users: sales engineers and laboratory technicians. Sales engineers interact with clients to prepare proposals and bids for services and are usually initially interested only in approximate slurry formulations; fine tuning of the bid occurs after the laboratory technicians test and tune the slurry to obtain the exact quantities of the chemical additives needed to perform the cementing service. Laboratory technicians, however, are interested in obtaining an accurate formulation for two reasons: They want to (1) lower operating costs by reducing the number of expensive testing iterations they must perform and (2) increase their throughput. Both types of user are able to accomplish their goals using SLURRYMINDER.

Although SLURRYMINDER has only been released to our field opera-

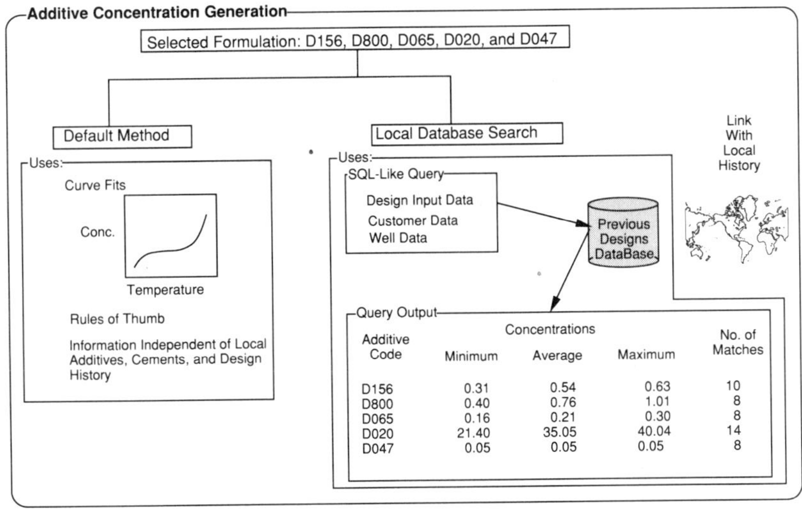

Figure 7. Additive Concentrations Can Be Estimated from Two Sources: The Local Database of Previous Designs or a Default Method.
Using the local database provides a link with local design practices and implicitly accounts for local additive and cement variations. Using the default method can be likened to reviewing a general cementing manual for recommendations, where one can find curve fits of data, rules of thumb, and concentration information that is independent of local design history and practice.

tions for a few months, it is already influencing the company's approach to its cementing business. Our European region (which provided a SLURRYMINDER beta testing location) has begun standardizing on SLURRYMINDER to assure that all laboratory personnel use this tool to perform their daily slurry designs. A specially prepared database containing over 300 tests from all parts of the region was prepared and distributed to all European locations for use with SLURRYMINDER. This region is currently delivering cement slurry designs to their customers that incorporate a uniform design philosophy and a common historical support base throughout the entire region, which includes the North Sea and the former Soviet Bloc countries. Northern Africa locations are also reporting good acceptance and design success using SLURRYMINDER.

The company maintains two training centers, one in Kellyville, Oklahoma, and the other in Nottinghamshire, England. These centers are responsible for training all new field employees and updating the skill level of the current field engineers. SLURRYMINDER training has become part of the standard training program in both centers. After several years of this one-time training, a significant portion of our design engineers and technicians will have been trained to use SLURRYMINDER, resulting in its becoming an integral part of the corporate technical structure. Thus, repetitive training costs are reduced, and geographically remote locations gain a technical marketing edge.

Expected Benefits

On a global basis, we perform approximately 36,000 well-cementation jobs annually and design approximately twice this many. For each service recommendation made by a sales engineer, we estimate that personnel savings of 1/2 to 1-1/2 person-hours will be achieved, as follows: Sales engineers typically provide design data to laboratory personnel and request that the laboratory prepare an estimated slurry formulation, without laboratory testing for bidding purposes. This process usually requires approximately 1/2 to 1-1/2 hours for each recommendation from the sales engineer and the laboratory technician. With SLURRYMINDER, the sales engineer can obtain a good initial slurry formulation in less than three minutes without requiring interaction with laboratory personnel. With a conservative basis of 12,000 formulations designed annually using SLURRYMINDER, we have an annual savings of 6,000 to 18,000 person-hours, or 3 to 9 person-years. Intangible benefits, such as better slurry designs using updated technology, which cannot be measured precisely, must also be considered.

Laboratory technicians typically perform an average of four test runs for each slurry pumped. One of our cementing specialists estimated that by using SLURRYMINDER, this number will be reduced by at least one-fourth. Normally, each laboratory test requires approximately four to six hours of expensive machine time to run. If SLURRYMINDER is used to design 12,000 jobs annually, we save worldwide approximately 60,000 machine-hours. Internal accounting audits indicate that replacement parts for the machinery required to run these tests averages about US$10 for each test run; hence, savings resulting from lower machine maintenance costs are estimated at US$120,000 annually.

Application Development and Deployment

In its current form, SLURRYMINDER is the result of a three-year effort in software and knowledge engineering. Generating the knowledge bases represents only approximately 25 to 30 percent of the total effort required to develop the entire application. Currently, we have invested eight person-years in the project.

Development Process

The SlurryMinder development process began in February 1989. Two engineers were given the responsibility for performing a feasibility analysis to determine whether a software tool could be developed to help Dowell Schlumberger rationalize and standardize its slurry design efforts on a global basis (figure 8). Earlier efforts at using statistical methods to analyze design data to distinguish definite trends in conjunction with raw material characterization studies had failed to provide the tools and the consistency the company was seeking. Hence, we began looking at expert system techniques to determine if they would be useful in solving our particular problem. Funding for the first year of the SlurryMinder project came from a special fund designed to support projects with high risk but high potential return.

As part of the five-month feasibility analysis, approximately 40 individuals in all parts of the company and at all levels were interviewed through a specially prepared questionnaire. These people represented company management, slurry design specialists, laboratory technicians, sales engineers, and some new employees with little slurry design experience. Using the results of the questionnaire and some additional information obtained through follow-up interviews, we analyzed our domain, following suggestions made by Bobrow, Mittal, and Stefik (1986) and using a methodology proposed by Slagle and Wick (1988). Our analysis concluded that the slurry design problem could be solved using expert system technology, and we recommended that we should proceed with prototype development.

The development team was given six months in which to generate a working prototype that would completely design one type of slurry system. User specifications and functional specifications for the prototype were developed in July 1989. We also obtained a portable personal computer on which to run our selected development shell for use while we worked with specialists at locations external to the engineering center. Within our company, cementing specialists are in high demand, and we felt that it would be more economical and convenient if we went to them rather than require them to come to the engineering center.

In December 1989, the prototype was demonstrated to company management and was accepted. Approval for the development version of SlurryMinder was obtained in January 1990 and was funded from the general engineering fund like all other engineering projects.

User specifications for the development version, prepared by corporate marketing and engineering personnel, were received in their final form in April 1990, and the functional specifications were ready by May 1990. Much of the knowledge base design was completed during

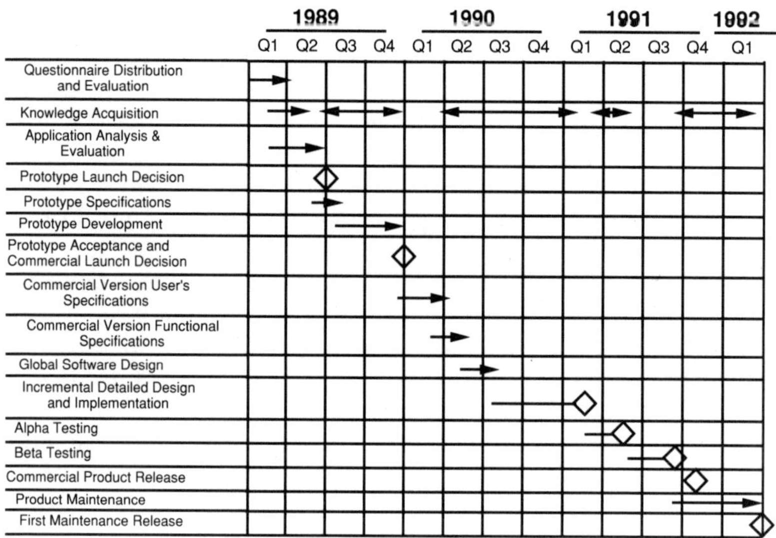

Figure 8. SLURRYMINDER Project Development Timeline.
Diamonds represent major milestones achieved in the project development process.

the prototyping phase; however, we were required to redesign the human interface and incorporate the additional functions into SLURRYMINDER, as required by the user specifications. A global software design was prepared during June and July 1990; however, the detailed design of the software proceeded incrementally with the implementation.

SLURRYMINDER alpha testing began in March 1991 and continued for three months. Our major goal during the alpha test was to ensure that the knowledge within SLURRYMINDER was correct and that it would produce good slurry formulations. As part of the alpha test, we prepared a *knowledge guide,* which is a graphic representation of the design rules within the system, as shown in figures 9 and 10. This knowledge guide can be thought of as a series of multidimensional flowcharts that can be used to follow program control during the reasoning process. Using the knowledge guide, along with the SLURRYMINDER software, allowed us to obtain 100-percent coverage of the system rules during alpha testing. Incidentally, approximately 90 percent of the SLURRYMINDER rules were modified as a result of this process, some significantly.

Beta testing began in June 1991 at three locations external to the engineering center: Africa Regional Office in Paris, France; European Regional Laboratory in Aberdeen, Scotland; and Gulf Coast Divisional Laboratory in New Orleans, Louisiana. The main goals of this testing were to ensure that SLURRYMINDER was robust in a field environment and

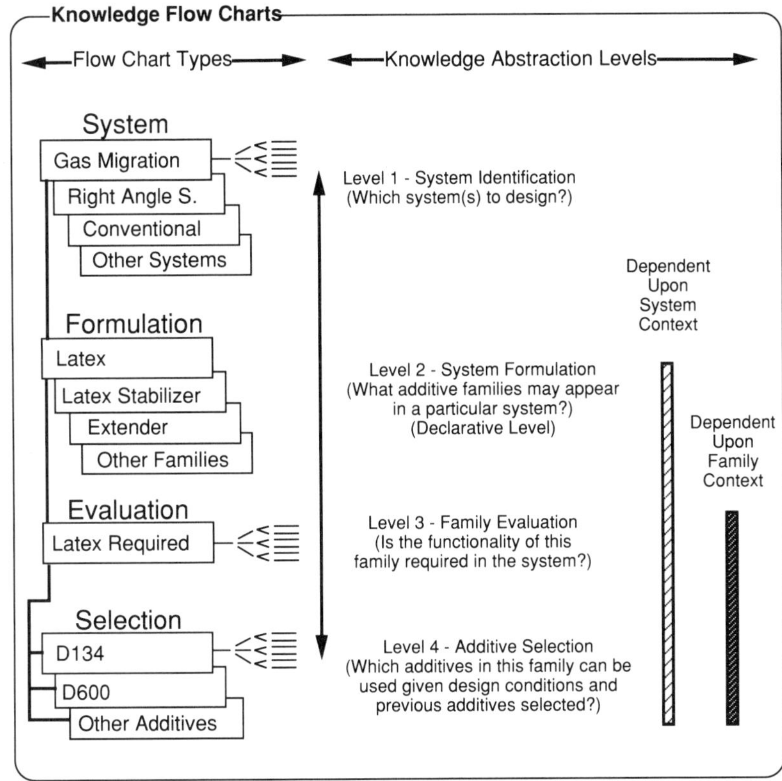

Figure 9. The Structure of SLURRYMINDER's Multidimensional Flowcharts. Prepared for experts and novices to follow SLURRYMINDER's reasoning path, each box represents an individual flowchart illustrating the conditions required to prove a particular hypothesis. The formulation level is declarative knowledge and has no explicit validation rules. The structure of these knowledge charts was designed to reproduce the knowledge-abstraction levels used in designing the knowledge representation scheme. Chart content for levels 2 to 4 is dependent on what slurry type was selected at level 1 and how the additive family is used within the selected slurry type.

that the human interface was acceptable to real users. Excellent feedback was obtained during this testing period that resulted in some significant modifications to the human interface and the mechanism for generating additive concentrations when searching the local database. SLURRYMINDER beta testing was completed and accepted in August 1991, with management approving SLURRYMINDER for worldwide deployment.

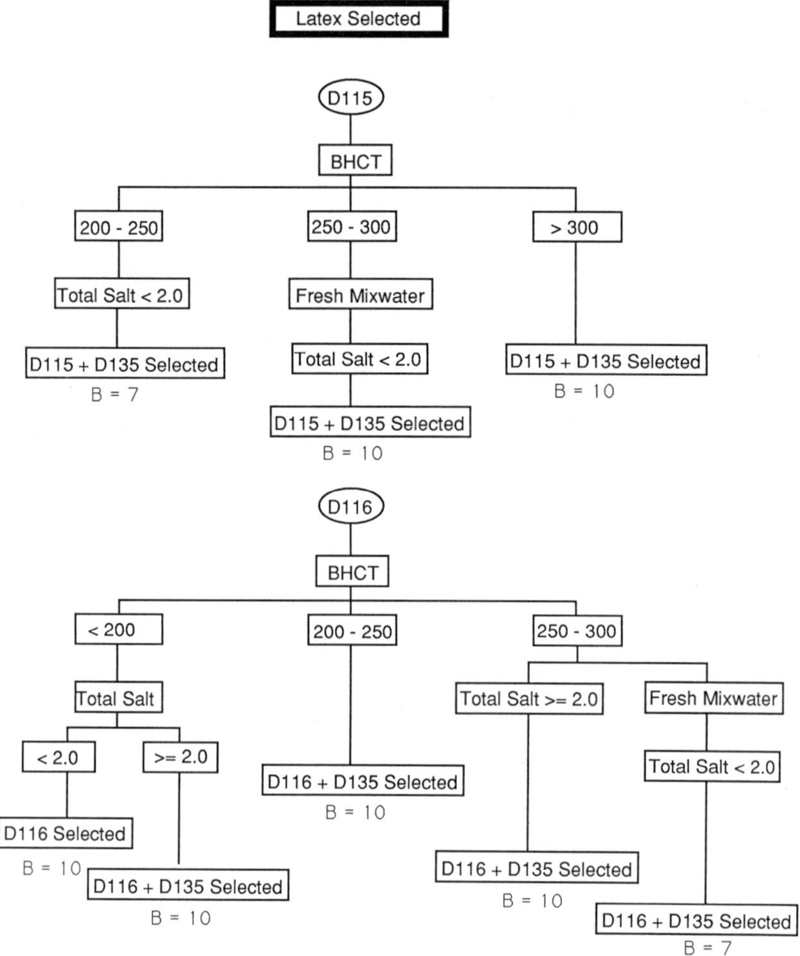

Figure 10. A Typical Knowledge Chart within SLURRYMINDER at Abstraction Level 4, Showing Detailed Conditions for Individual Additive Selection.

Deployment

In September 1991, the SLURRYMINDER executable image and accompanying data files were submitted to our corporate baseline management team in Tulsa, Oklahoma. This team is responsible for preparing a new corporate computer baseline every six months and distributing the software therein to all field locations worldwide. Because this mechanism was already in place for previously existing software, deployment to our field locations was straightforward and consisted of copying the

SLURRYMINDER files into the software baseline, testing the executable file to ensure that it performed properly in the baseline environment, and distributing a tape.

The user's manual for SLURRYMINDER was prepared using LATEX, and the corresponding printable file is contained in the documentation section of the software baseline. At any time, users in any location can obtain the latest documentation for any product in the software baseline by printing the file on their local printer.

By design, SLURRYMINDER is reasonably easy to use even for novice computer users. However, four train-the-trainer training sessions have been held; in Tulsa, Oklahoma; Aberdeen, Scotland; Nottinghamshire, England; and St. Etienne, France. Attendees at these training sessions included regional baseline managers, management personnel, trainers from our two training centers, sales engineers, and laboratory personnel. Because of the geographically diverse nature of our company, each of the individuals attending these training sessions was given the responsibility for training users in their respective regions or locations.

Product Maintenance

Within our company, software product maintenance is performed by members of the software-sustaining section at the engineering center where the product was developed. SLURRYMINDER is now being maintained by a software engineer who was not a member of the original development team. As part of the development effort and good software engineering practice, the original development team created two documents to aid in the maintenance of the SLURRYMINDER software: the SLURRYMINDER Knowledge Base Maintenance Guide and the SLURRYMINDER Software Maintenance Guide. These complementary documents respectively describe the internal logic and software structures of the knowledge bases and the rest of the software in sufficient detail to facilitate maintenance. Coupled with the Knowledge Guide (knowledge flowcharts) and the product specification documents, maintainers have significant maintenance resources available to them.

Cement slurry design is an evolving domain; we have already begun modifying the knowledge bases by adding recently developed cementing additive products and a new slurry formulation technology to SLURRYMINDER. It appears that the architecture of the knowledge bases is well suited to domain evolution because these modifications were made by an individual who was not on the original development team. New releases of SLURRYMINDER will occur every six months as the company's software baseline is updated and redistributed to all field locations.

```
                    SlurryMINDER Version 1.1C1
System Functions...          Design Slurry          Database Utilities...
                  Slurry Design Input Data Form

ADMINISTRATION                          DESIGN CONSIDERATIONS
 Lead Engineer : B. KELLY                 Salt Required     :  No
 Date Requested: 04/01/92                 NaCl Amount       :          % BWOW
 Date Required : 04/03/92                  KCl Amount       :          % BWOW
 CLIENT        : SPECIAL                  Mixwater Type     :  Sea
 RIG           : SP1                      Cement Brand      :  Cemoil
 WELL          : SP1-1                    Cement Class      :  G
 SLURRY Ident  :                          Cement Type       :  ETDS
                                          Pref. Blend Mode:    Liquid

SPECIAL WELL PROBLEMS
 Gas Zone                                SLURRY PERFORMANCE PARAMETERS
JOB TYPE                                   Slurry Density :  14.4 lb/gal
 Liner                                     Thickening Time:   6.0 hours
WELL DATA                                  Fluid Loss     :  75.0 ml
 Depth          : 12000 ft                 Free Water     :   3.0 ml/250ml
 BHST           :    235 deg.F             Comp. Strength :  5000 psi
 Temp Gradient  :    1.3 deg.F/100ft
 BHCT           :    185 deg.F
```

Figure 11. SLURRYMINDER's Primary Data Input Form.
Input data consist of well data such as depth, temperatures, and special downhole conditions; target slurry performance parameters such as density and thickening time; properties of the cement; and administration data such as well logistical information.

An Example Using SLURRYMINDER

A typical use of the SLURRYMINDER system is illustrated by the following problem: A client is drilling an offshore oil well at 12,000 feet below the surface. The temperature in the underground formation is approximately 235 °F, and the slurry density must be around 14.4 pounds to a gallon to maintain the hydrostatic head and keep formation fluids from entering the well bore. Because the rig is offshore, seawater will be mixed with the cement powder to create the cement slurry, and liquid chemical additives are preferred over solids because of limited bulk handling and storage facilities on the rig. The cement slurry must not set up for at least six hours to allow proper placement around the cement casing. This particular cement system must also isolate an adjoining formation with significant potential for gas to enter the cement matrix and corrupt the cement, allowing gas to migrate up the casing column and create a potentially dangerous situation. In a well this deep, class G well cement will be used; the particular brand available on location is easy to disperse in the presence of the salt in the seawater. The slurry should have low free water and fluid loss and should achieve a good compressive strength in 24 hours.

Design data of this nature are entered into the SLURRYMINDER input

```
-----------------SlurryMINDER Version 1.1C1-----------------
System Functions...        Design Slurry        Database Utilities...
-----------------Suggested Slurry Designs-------------------

        Cement Class: G              BHST: 235 deg.F
             Density: 14.4  lb/gal   BHCT: 185 deg.F

--------- Solution -----------------------------------------
 Rank       Type       Additive List

   1     GASBLOK  D600 + D135, D128 + D138, D604M, D008, D144, D066
   1     GASBLOK  D600 + D135, D128 + D138, D604M, D801, D144, D066
   2     GASBLOK  D600 + D135, D128 + D138, D080, D008, D144, D066
   2     GASBLOK  D600 + D135, D128 + D138, D145, D008, D144, D066
   2     GASBLOK  D600 + D135, D128 + D138, D145, D801, D144, D066

Arrow keys move between solutions; <return> key selects a solution
```

Figure 12. An Example of Slurry Additive Formulations Recommended by SLURRYMINDER.
Formulations include the list of chemical additives and the rank of each formulation. By default, the highest-ranking slurry is highlighted for further processing to obtain additive concentrations, explanations, warnings, pricing information, or a design report.

```
------------------------------ CONCENTRATIONS ------------------------------
Bulk Cement Properties                      Mixwater Properties
  Class        :       G                      Type           : Sea
  Sack Weight  :  94.0 lb                     Density        :    8.5 lb/gal
  Dry Density  : 174.3 lb/ft^3                Base Fluid     :    5.7 gal/sk
Slurry Properties                           Laboratory Calculations
  Density     :   14.4 lb/gal                 Target Volume  : 600.0 ml
  Porosity    :  63.39 %                      Cement Weight  : 458.7 g
  Yield       :   1.97 ft^3/sk                Base Fluid Wt  : 236.9 g
                                              Base Fluid Vol : 231.7 ml
---------------------- Additive Concentrations -------------------------
Additive   Conc.   Unit     Weight  Volume  Source   Tests | Original
                              g       ml                   | Design Data
D600       3.29    gal/sk   136.6   134.0   CemDABE   14   | BHCT
D135       0.13    gal/sk     5.7     5.4   CemDABE   14   | 185 deg.F
D128       4.10    % BWOC    18.8     7.1   Default    0   | BHST
D138       1.23    % BWOC     5.6     5.9   Default    0   | 235 deg.F
D604M      0.20    gal/sk     9.9     9.9   CemDABE    5   | Density
D008       0.28    % BWOC     1.3     1.3   Default    0   |   14.4 lb/gal
D144       0.03    gal/sk     1.2     1.2   CemDABE   11   |
```

Figure 13. Additive Concentrations Generated by SLURRYMINDER *Are Used to Compute Quantities Required to Prepare the Slurry Formulation in the Laboratory. Additional calculations are performed to obtain the quantity of water to use and the volume of slurry obtained from one sack of cement.*

```
——————————— Slurry Options For Selected Slurry———————————
Browse CemDABE Concentrations... Explanations Price/Cost Report Warnings
———————————Current Suggested Slurry Formulation———————————

        D600 + D135, D128 + D138, D604M, D008, D144, D066

——————————————————— EXPLANATIONS ———————————————————

  A "GASBLOK" system is considered in this context because:
  1 - of a Gas Zone in the well
  2 - BHCT is between 70F and 375F
  3 - slurry denstiy is between 12ppg and 20ppg
  4 - the total concentration of salt in the system is below 15%

  A LATEX additive is always needed in a GASBLOK system, it provides
  fluid loss control and gas migration control:

  D600 used with D135, is recommended as LATEX in a GASBLOK system
       at BHCT below 200F and with 2% or more salt in the system
       (4% D135 by Volume of Latex)

  An EXTENDER is needed because the denstiy is below 15.6 ppg (for
  a class G cement):
```

Figure 14. An Example of the Type of Explanations Generated during a Session with SLURRYMINDER.
Each explanation includes information on the criteria used to select what type of slurry to design, why a particular additive family is necessary in the formulation, and what the selection conditions are for each individual additive.

data form, as illustrated in figure 11. A series of data checks designed into the intelligent interface ensure that data entered in the fields are internally consistent. Prior to invoking the inference engine, users can specify the maximum number of solutions they would like to obtain; the default is five. This number is used internally during inferencing to prune branches from the search space; only the top candidate solutions are kept for subsequent inferencing.

We intentionally designed the inferencing mechanism to be a black box as far as users are concerned. Input data are volunteered to the inference engine, and little interaction with the user is required until the inference is complete, and the solutions have been generated.

Figure 12 illustrates the output obtained by inferencing using the data from figure 11. Five solutions were requested, with two of the solutions ranked equally as the best. Careful examination reveals that only subtle differences exist between the different solutions in this example; however, the different internal chemical additive codes have great significance to the field personnel in terms of how well these additives perform in different circumstances. Additives joined by a plus sign indicate that the first additive requires the aid of the second to provide the required functions in the slurry formulation.

After selecting one of the formulations for further processing, users have the option of generating additive concentrations, viewing explanations or warnings, generating a design report, or obtaining pricing information for the particular formulation. Figure 13 illustrates the results obtained from invoking the concentration generation mechanism, and figure 14 shows the initial explanation output screen obtained from the explanation and warning subsystem.

Acknowledgments

We would like to thank the many individuals within the Dowell Schlumberger organization for their time and efforts, so freely given to make this project a success. We also want to express our appreciation to Reid Smith of the Schlumberger Laboratory for Computer Science for reviewing drafts of this manuscript and providing insightful suggestions.

References

Bobrow, D. G.; Mittal, S.; and Stefik, M. J. 1986. Expert Systems: Perils and Promise. *Communications of the ACM* 29(9): 880–894.

Nelson, E. 1990. Well Cementing. Houston, Texas: Schlumberger Educational Services.

Slagle, J. R., and Wick, M. R. 1988. A Method for Evaluating Candidate Expert System Applications. *AI Magazine* 9(4): 44–53.

Wolsfelt, G. C.; Roger, C.; and Fenoul, R. 1989. A Cementing Job Preparation Advisor System. Presented at the Sixty-Fourth Annual Technical Conference and Exhibition of the Society of Petroleum Engineers, San Antonio, Tex., 8–11 October.

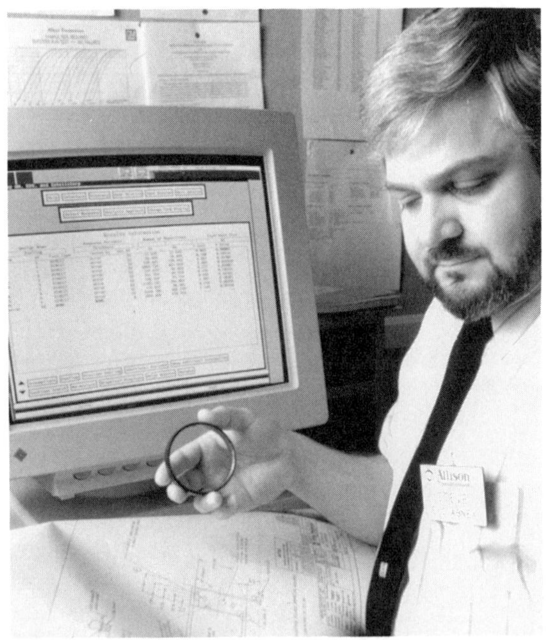
Allison

An Application of Model-Based Reasoning in Experiment Design

Andrew B. Parker,[1] Sun Microsystems, and
W. Scott Spangler, General Motors

Scientists and engineers in diverse fields such as manufacturing, medicine, and design use experiments to learn about processes and the behavior of systems. Experiments study how the settings of a series of factors affect one or more response variables. For example, an engineer trying to develop a reliable painting process for automobile components might set up an experiment to study how paint viscosity and temperature (two factors) affect a numeric measure of paint surface quality (a response variable). Because an experiment can require significant resources, the experimenter often must make trade-offs between the number of experimental trials, the order of these trials, and the expected amount and type of information gained as a result of running the experiment. *Design of experiments* is the field of statistics that addresses the problem of creating layouts (ordered lists of factor combinations, or trials, to be tested) that will provide the experimenter with statistically sound results yet account for the constraints under which the experiment must be run.

The use of experimentation in industry has grown as companies attempt to reduce manufacturing costs, explore innovative manufacturing techniques, and improve product quality and safety. In practice, however, some experimenters do not use an appropriate experiment design or use no formal design at all. Often they choose a standard design from a textbook that might not be well suited to their experimental circumstances. At best, these designs can waste experiment resources because they haven't been tuned to the experimenter's goals and interests. At worst, the experimenter might not be able to draw meaningful conclusions from the experiment or might draw incorrect conclusions.

Expert statisticians can design highly tuned experiments that focus on the specific factors or interactions that are of interest to the experimenter but keep costs to a minimum. The design process is a complicated one that often requires extensive calculations and custom computer programs. After the experimental data are collected, statisticians perform a variety of complicated analyses that also require custom programming. Experimenters in industry generally lack the statistical background to produce these designs themselves and can also lack access to statisticians who can do it for them.

In response to the growing demand for statistical expertise, statisticians at General Motors Research (GMR) developed a new approach to experiment design based on a unified mathematical model (Lorenzen and Truss 1990). The approach allows experimenters to apply a theoretically sound design methodology to satisfy a number of experimental goals and conditions. Although this methodology was successfully taught to both statisticians and nonstatisticians, it still proved time consuming and required extensive training for nonstatisticians. They decided to automate the process by building an expert system for design of experiments and the analysis of experimental results. The goal was to allow experimenters with minimal statistical expertise to produce custom, high-quality experiment designs quickly, without the assistance of expert statisticians.

Statisticians at GMR first attempted to automate their design methodology by developing C-language application programs. Although they achieved some limited success in automating some of the more tedious calculations, they soon realized that the exploratory nature of the design process would be difficult to capture in traditional computer programs. They began working with GM's Advanced Engineering Staff, who proposed an AI-based solution to be developed in conjunction with IntelliCorp, Inc., and Electronic Data Systems.

The resulting system has become known within GM as DEXPERT. DEXPERT aids an experimenter in the search for an optimal or near-optimal design. It provides manual and automated search through an infinite design space and allows the user to pursue several different design trade-offs simultaneously. It contains knowledge of numerous statistical techniques and the ability to perform all required calculations automatically. It includes graphic displays to aid the user in visualizing the design process; it also contains online help and tutorial facilities that are tailored to the user's level of expertise.

Other work in this area includes several commercially available systems for design of experiments, including CATALYST/RPE and RS/DISCOVER. Some research has been done in developing expert systems for Taguchi-type experiments (Lee, Phadke, and Keny 1989). Many of these programs simply assist users in selecting from a fixed set of standard designs. None provides the user with facilities for searching a design space or provides the rich set of design tools available in DEXPERT. Although some of these programs do use AI techniques, they use simple rule-based approaches for selecting among a fixed set of designs.

The authors attribute the successful development of DEXPERT, at least in part, to the use of model-based reasoning (Kunz 1988) in its development. *Model-based reasoning* is a development methodology that involves developing a symbolic, structural model of the application domain. The model can then be combined with a number of reasoning mechanisms and interfaces to produce several applications of the model. Model-based reasoning has allowed DEXPERT to more closely mimic the exploratory design approach used by expert statisticians. As a result, DEXPERT is complete enough to provide expert statisticians with tools that increase their productivity and improve the quality of their designs. DEXPERT provides guidance to nonstatistician experimenters to allow them to create designs comparable to those of an expert.

Experiment Design Processes

This section highlights the experiment design processes used when designing experiments manually and when using DEXPERT. Both processes use the previously cited design methodology developed at GMR. For the purposes of this chapter, the statistical content has been minimized and simplified where possible. Statistics concepts that are mentioned but not explained are included for readers with more statistical sophistication; they are not essential to the comprehension of the overall content of the chapter.

The following example illustrates the use of the mathematical model on which the GMR design approach is based: An automotive engineer wants to determine what causes variations in fuel economy in a certain type of car. He/she speculates that some of the effect might be caused by minor variations in the physical properties of the engine between one car and another. Another possibility is that the type of fuel injector used in the car might have an effect. Still a third factor might be the type of fuel used. There is also the possibility that particular combinations of two or three of these factors might be affecting fuel consumption. This last possibility is what statisticians refer to as an interaction between factors.

The mathematical model for this experiment would be the following:

$$Y = E[\iota] + I[\varphi] + F[\kappa] + EI[\iota,\varphi] + EF[\iota,\kappa] + IF[\varphi,\kappa] + EIF[\iota,\varphi,\kappa] + error[\iota,\varphi,\kappa,\lambda]\ .$$

The variable Y represents the fuel consumption for a particular trial of the experiment and is referred to as the *response variable.* The term $E[\iota]$ represents any effect on fuel consumption because of changing engines. The ι subscript ranges over the different engines used in the experiment (that is, if we use four engines numbered 1 to 4, then ι would be an integer from 1 to 4.). The EI term represents the effect of the interaction between engines and injectors (separate from the effect of changing engine or injector alone). Its subscripts $[\iota,\varphi]$ range over all combinations of the different engines and injectors used in the experiment. The *error term* represents all effects on the response variable not caused by changes in engines, injectors, or fuels. The subscripts of the error term include λ, which takes on a different value each time an $[\iota,\varphi,\kappa]$ combination is repeated. Thus, the value of the error term is expected to vary for each trial of the experiment. The error term represents the underlying variation when all experimental factors are held constant.

Manual Experiment Design

When statisticians design experiments manually, they evaluate various properties and computed characteristics of each term to determine the conclusions that could be drawn if specific settings and parameters were applied. In the example, the factor engines (E) have a variety of attributes based on the nature of the area of study. For example, it is qualitative (as opposed to quantitative factors such as temperature). This attribute cannot generally be changed by the experimenter but influences the statistical power of the experimental design. Other attributes can be manipulated by the experimenter. For example, the experimenter can manipulate the number of levels of a factor in the experiment to influence the experimental design's power. In the example, the factor engines will be studied at four levels; that is, four different engines will be tried in the experiment. The experimenter can decide to test an additional engine or choose to eliminate one of the original four from the study, if necessary, to reduce the total number of trials to be done.

In addition to the qualitative-quantitative distinction and the number of levels, a variety of other characteristics must be determined for each factor. The statistician notes these characteristics and uses them to determine a series of measures for each term in the mathematical model. The statistician then uses the mathematical model and term information to compute, for each term in the model, an equation that describes the experiment's ability to test the effect or interaction represented by that term. For a particular set of experimental circumstances (for example, each of the factors engines, injectors, and fuel studied at two levels, without repeating any combinations of trials), the statistician can compute that the experiment will detect medium-sized differences in fuel consumption caused by a change in fuel type but might not be able to determine if the interaction between engine, injector, and fuel type has any effect on fuel consumption. Computing these expected mean squares and detectable differences before running an experiment allows the statistician to evaluate the potential costs and benefits of a particular design before actually running the experiment.

Each permutation of the experimental circumstances requires the statistician to perform complex symbolic manipulation of equations, calculations, and bookkeeping for comparison between designs. These calculations can be complex, especially taking into account more advanced statistical concepts such as nesting and fractional designs. In practice, experienced statisticians don't have the time to calculate and analyze more than one or two sets of experimental circumstances for a given experiment, especially when the experiment involves several factors or complex relationships between factors.

After a design is selected, the experimenter must generate a randomized layout sheet that will be used in data collection. After the experimental data are collected, the experimenter performs a series of statistical analyses. Often, these analyses are performed repeatedly, after making assumptions or transformations based on the initial results. Finally, the experimenter creates charts and graphs, accompanied by descriptive text, to illustrate the experimental results. Each of these steps often requires the experimenter to write several custom computer programs using statistical software packages such as SAS. The design and analysis process might take a highly trained experimenter anywhere from several days to several weeks, not including the time required to run the experimental trials.

Experiment Design Using DEXPERT

When designing experiments using DEXPERT, the experimenter interacts with a window-oriented user interface. The interface provides assis-

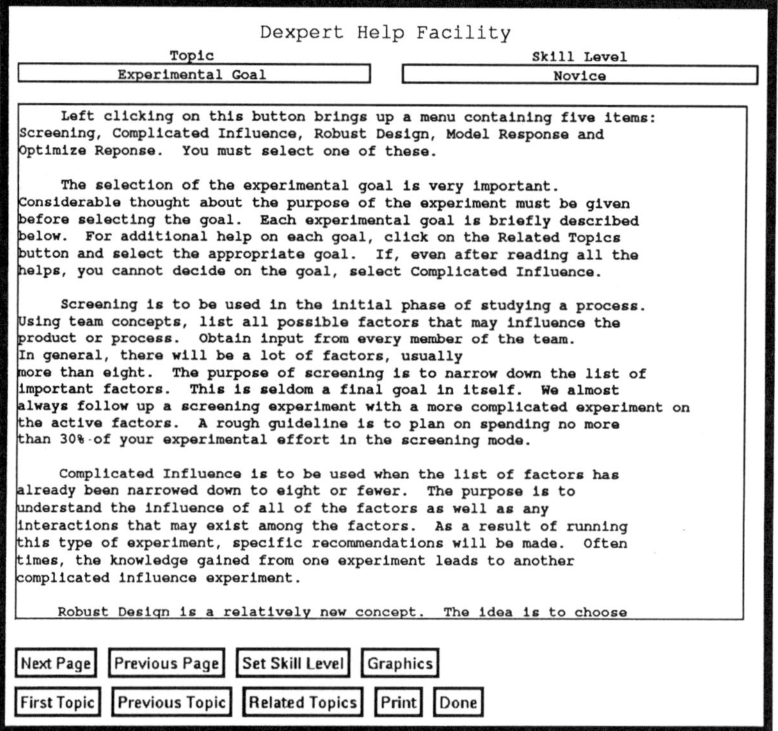

Figure 1. An Example Display from DEXPERT's Help Facility.

The user obtains help by right clicking with the mouse on fields, buttons, or menus in DEXPERT displays.

tance to the user based on the self-described level of statistical expertise: novice, intermediate, or expert. The instructions, definitions, and explanations received are tailored according to this expertise level. The user begins the DEXPERT session by specifying the high-level experimental goals as well as information about the experimental factors and response variables. DEXPERT checks for inconsistencies and assists novice users in specifying various attributes, for example, whether a factor is quantitative or qualitative. At any time, online help is available to assist the user in answering questions or understanding the displayed information (figure 1). The display shown in figure 2 summarizes the initial information entered by the user.

Based on the initial information, DEXPERT generates an initial design and computes the statistical power for each term in the mathematical model. The relevant features of the initial design are presented in a tabular format that is tailored to the profile of the user, as shown in

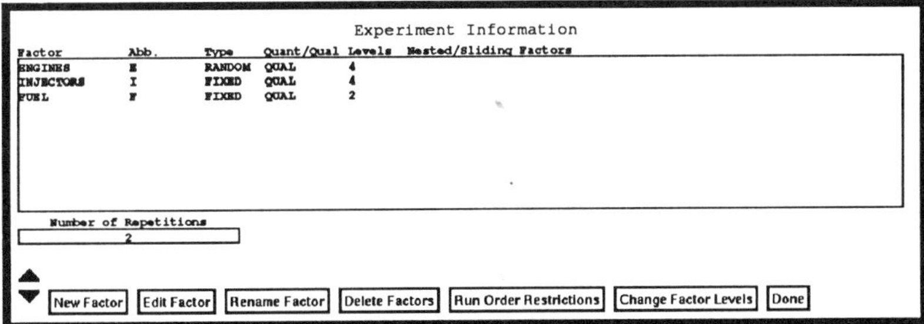

Experiment Information

Factor	Abb.	Type	Quant/Qual	Levels	Nested/Sliding Factors
ENGINES	E	RANDOM	QUAL	4	
INJECTORS	I	FIXED	QUAL	4	
FUEL	F	FIXED	QUAL	2	

Number of Repetitions: 2

New Factor | Edit Factor | Rename Factor | Delete Factors | Run Order Restrictions | Change Factor Levels | Done

Figure 2. A Display Summarizing the Information That an Experimenter Has Specified about the Experimental Goal and Factors in the Experiment.

Buttons along the bottom of the display allow the user to modify the factor information before proceeding to the design phase.

Design Name: Design 1 | Experiment Mode: Full Factorial | Number of Repetitions: 2 | Experiment Size: 64

Term	df	Test Type	Tested By	Den Df	Delta	Detectable Size	EMS
E	3	DIRECT	error	32	0.93	SMALL	s(error)+16s(E)
I	3	DIRECT	EI	9	0.68	SMALL	s(error)+4s(EI)+16p(I)
EI	9	DIRECT	error	32	0.99	SMALL	s(error)+4s(EI)
F	1	DIRECT	EF	3	0.89	SMALL	s(error)+8s(EF)+32p(F)
EF	3	DIRECT	error	32	1.32	SMALL	s(error)+8s(EF)
IF	3	DIRECT	EIF	9	0.96	SMALL	s(error)+2s(EIF)+8p(IF)
EIF	9	DIRECT	error	32	1.4	SMALL	s(error)+2s(EIF)
error	32	NONE	NONE	0	UNDEFINED	---	s(error)

Suggestions | Redesign | All/Control | Notepad

Verbal Interpretation | Show Additional Information | Print Design Information | Approve Design

Figure 3. The Initial Design Display Based on the Experimenter's Initial Specifications.

The columns that appear in the table vary based on the user's preferences and level of expertise. This example display shows all available information. Buttons along the bottom of the display allow the user to annotate the design, request suggestions or textual interpretations, or redesign using a variety of techniques.

figure 3. The user can then modify the design input (that is, redesign) to achieve the desired experimental characteristics. In addition, the user can request expert advice from DEXPERT on how to modify the design to achieve desired statistical properties. Based on the user's input about the aspects of the design needing improvement, DEXPERT generates suggestions (figure 4), which the user can apply to create a new design (figure 5). The user can also request a textual critique of the statistical power of a design (figure 6) or a comparison of two designs.

DEXPERT provides a complete set of redesign options at each design stage: The user can fractionate a design in many different ways and can specify such properties as maximum design size, terms of interest, terms not to be confounded with terms of interest, resolution, and

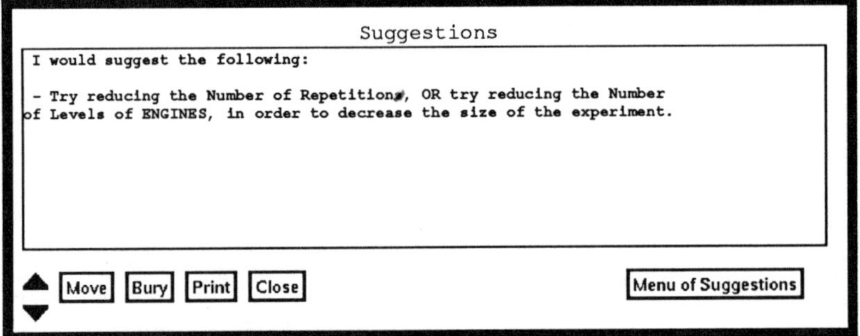

Figure 4. A Display Showing Redesign Suggestions Generated by DEXPERT *in Response to the Experimenter's Critique of the Power or Practicality of the Current Design.*

The menu of suggestions button allows the user to automatically pursue one or more of these suggestions to generate new designs.

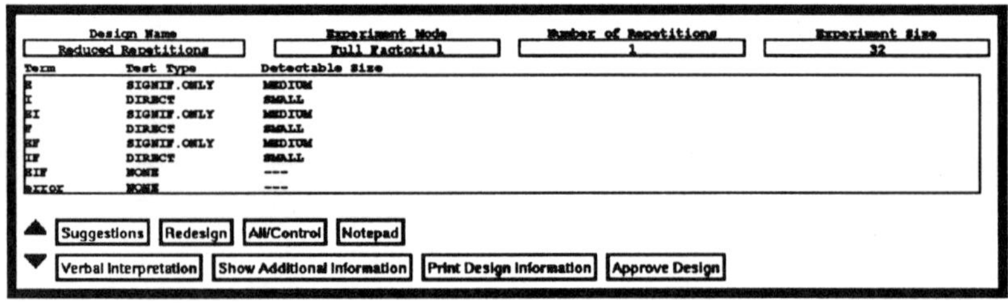

Figure 5. A Display Showing a Second Design Created by Reducing the Number of Repetitions from the Initial Design from Two to One.

In this display, the user reduced the columns of information displayed to those typically displayed for a novice user.

blocks of fractionated factors. DEXPERT allows the user to request restrictions on randomization because of experimental constraints and calculates the loss of information that results from the restriction. The user can specify that some terms or groups of terms can be assumed negligible for the purposes of the experiment. Many of these options require DEXPERT to perform substantial calculations and generate custom SAS programs—a time-consuming and often impractical task when done manually.

The experiment design process using DEXPERT allows for a much

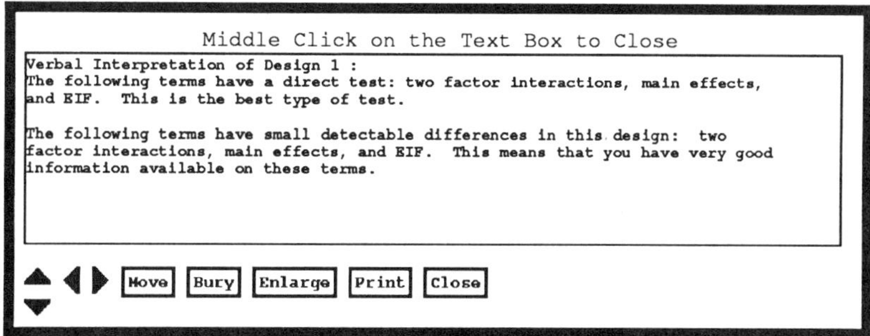

Figure 6. A Display Showing DEXPERT*'s Textual Description of the Initial Design.*

more thorough evaluation of potential experiment design alternatives. DEXPERT computes the statistical power of each design quickly. It allows for the generation of redesign alternatives from the initial design and all succeeding designs, resulting in a hierarchy of designs (figure 7). The user can also specify the desired detectable differences for each term in the mathematical model and have the system automatically search for the design with the smallest number of trials that meets the criteria. The user iterates the redesign process, often creating dozens of possible designs, until one or several satisfactory designs is generated. The user then selects a design, and DEXPERT generates the randomized layout sheet for data collection.

Once the data are collected, the experimenter returns to DEXPERT and enters it into the system interactively or through a text file. DEXPERT analyzes and interprets the results using a number of analytic and graphic methods. Figure 8 shows a standard analysis of variance table display in DEXPERT. Analysis is performed separately on each response variable. DEXPERT provides a textual interpretation of the statistical analysis on request, as shown in figure 9. It provides a number of additional analysis features such as data transformations, regression analysis, predictions of response values for particular factor-level combinations, and comparison of means. A variety of graphic analyses are provided, including main-effect plots of means (with confidence intervals), interaction plots, effects plots, residual plots, time plots, response surface plots, and contour plots, all of which can be printed as well as appear on the screen.

In contrast to the manual approach, even an inexperienced experimenter can generate a design comparable to that of an expert in 30 to 90 minutes. After collecting experimental data, the experimenter can generally complete the statistical analyses and graphs within a few hours.

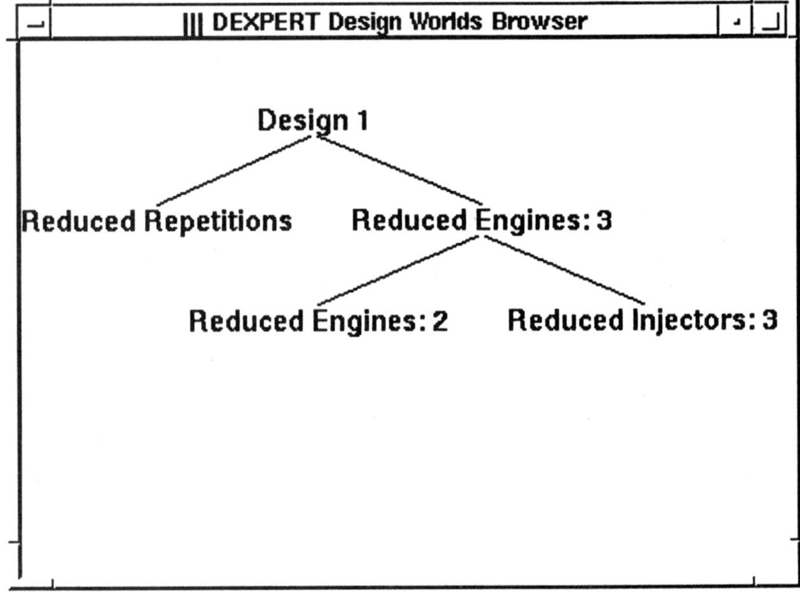

Figure 7. A Display Showing the Hierarchy of Designs Created during a Design Session.

The user can click on a design name to display or rename the design.

DEXPERT performs all calculations, generates and submits all required SAS programs, and produces a variety of printed reports and graphics.

Model-Based Reasoning in DEXPERT

A symbolic model of design of experiments theory forms the core of DEXPERT. The symbolic model represents the mathematical model that describes the experiment as well as behaviors of, and relationships between, components of the model. The reasoning components of the system manipulate the model's attributes and relationships using techniques similar to those of an expert statistician using paper-and-pencil models with calculators or statistical software packages. DEXPERT also uses the model to assist in performing analyses of the experimental results after the experimenter has collected data. The model-based approach also facilitated an interactive development strategy that allowed the system to be used early in the development cycle while more complex reasoning techniques were being added.

An object-oriented frame system is used to implement the symbolic model. Hypothetical reasoning, rule-based reasoning, and state-space

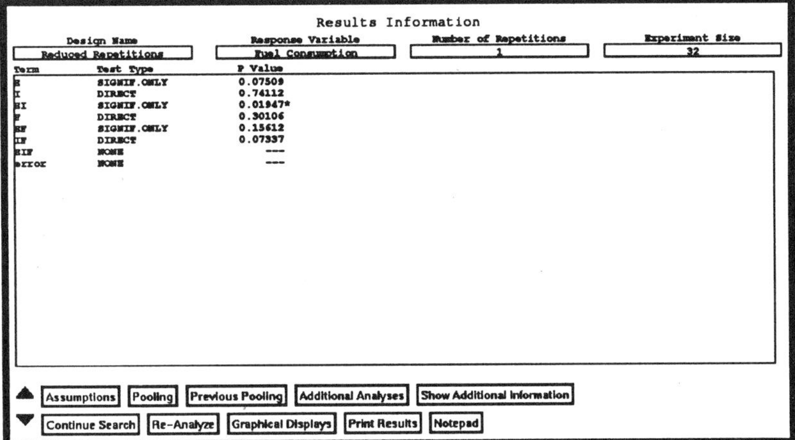

Figure 8. DEXPERT's Display of the Analysis of Variance Table for the Experimental Results.

As with the design display, columns that are not appropriate to the user's profile were omitted. A variety of additional analyses and graphic displays are available to the user through buttons along the bottom of the display.

search are utilized to implement the statistical design strategies. A variety of different user interface components interact with the model through procedural code. The reasoning and procedural components of the system interact with external routines, including C-language programs and dynamically generated SAS programs to perform some of the more difficult calculations.

Object-Oriented Frame Representation

The symbolic model is constructed using the KEE object-oriented frame system (Fikes and Kehler 1985) to represent the factors in the experiment, the terms in the mathematical model, the user's goals and level of statistical expertise, and the relationships between these components. Once constructed, this model is manipulated and evaluated using a variety of reasoning tools and procedural techniques. In addition, the user can manipulate the model or provide guidance to the system through the user interface.

For example, DEXPERT creates a frame corresponding to each factor to be studied in the user's experiment. Attributes of each factor are stored in the slots on the factor frame. In the previous example, the factor engine would have the following slot values filled in:

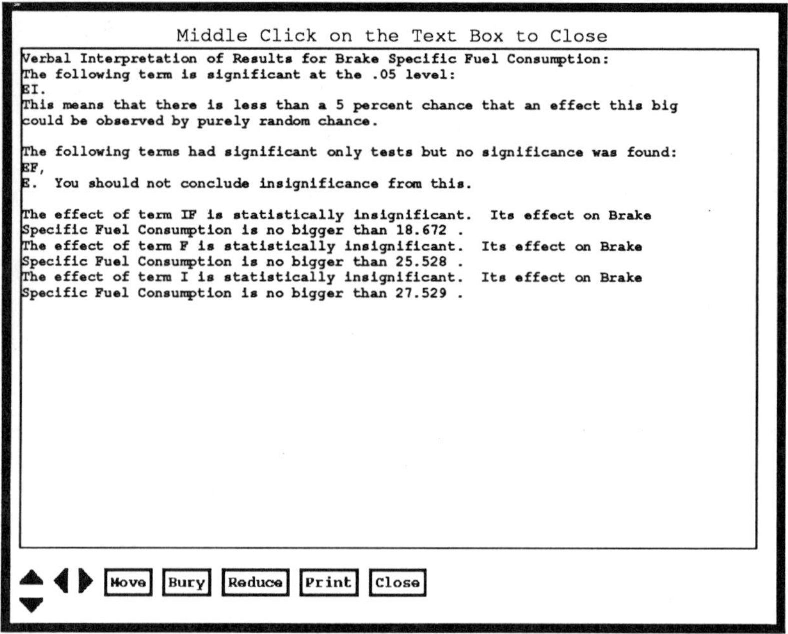

Figure 9. A Display Showing DEXPERT's Textual Explanation of the Results for the Experiment.

factor.abbreviation:	E
quantitative.or.qualitative:	QUALITATIVE
fixed.or.random:	RANDOM
number.of.levels:	4

...

DEXPERT also represents the terms in the mathematical model as frames. Attributes for each term are stored in the slots on the term frame. In addition to computed attributes, the model also maintains structural relationships between terms. For example, the tested.by relation links terms that provide statistical tests on other terms.

Hypothetical Reasoning in Multiple Worlds

One of DEXPERT's greatest strengths is its ability to search and evaluate many alternative designs. While the user searches for a design best suited to his/her needs, DEXPERT keeps the alternate designs available for comparing and for returning to previous design states. The challenge for DEXPERT was to provide many alternative designs in parallel (that is, without backtracking) to allow the user to participate in the exploration process. The complexity of the symbolic model (often consisting of hundreds of frames and thousands of attributes) made it impractical to duplicate the symbolic model for each design iteration. Instead, a context or *worlds* mechanism (Filman 1988) was utilized to represent each design as a hypothetical state of a single symbolic model. The symbolic model exists in the background, an initial state containing the frame hierarchies, slots, relationships, and methods for the user's experiment. Each design is represented as a world, offering a hypothetical configuration of this background model. World-dependent facts include relationships between factors and sets of terms in the mathematical model as well as numerous user-specified and system-computed attributes of factors or terms. The design worlds are arranged into a hierarchy that preserves the history of the design session and allows the state of the model to be inherited between parent and child worlds. As a result, only changes from a previous design need to be recorded in each new design.

During the design session, the user explores new hypothetical designs by asking the system to apply one of the redesign options to the current hypothetical world. Each such action adds a new design world to the hierarchy of designs, modifies the relationships among components within that design world, and updates any computed attributes that apply to the new model structure. The user iterates this process until satisfied that the best possible design was found. Through this mechanism, an inexperienced user can often generate and examine dozens of alternative designs during a session, where an expert statistician using manual methods might spend days investigating a small subset of these designs.

Using worlds in conjunction with the underlying model also proved valuable in implementing the analysis components. In the initial analyses, DEXPERT calculates a variety of statistical measures based on the collected data and the information stored in each term frame. Based on the initial results, the user can apply alternative analyses that might be appropriate for the user's experimental goal, or the user can refine the analysis by applying various transformations to the standard statistical techniques. Each of these alternative analyses is created as a child world of the initial analysis, inheriting the required data but storing the results of the specialized analysis locally.

Rule-Based Reasoning

DEXPERT utilizes production rules to complement the knowledge represented in the symbolic model and the state of the worlds system. The rules are partitioned into rule classes that can be invoked independently. When the user requests assistance in redesigning the experiment, the system invokes one or more rule classes to evaluate the state of the model in the current design world. The rules produce a series of redesign suggestions that are presented to the user. After acceptance by the user, these suggestions can then be applied to the current design to create a new design. The classification of rules into rule classes allowed the system to apply specialized expertise for different experiment goals as well as provide for prioritized redesign techniques.

Each rule in the knowledge base concludes with both a suggestion and a reason for the suggestion. The rule base was set up this way to address the problem of conflicting suggestions. For example, if a user wants to decrease the size of the current design while he/she improves the information available, then it would make sense to decrease the levels of engines to satisfy one goal (smaller experiment size) and increase the number of repetitions to satisfy the other goal (better information). If the system simply made these two suggestions at the same time, it might appear contradictory to the user. Relating suggestions to the user's goals provides a better understanding of the trade-offs involved in trying to achieve an experiment design that meets all the user's requirements.

Automated State-Space Search

Hypothetical worlds used in conjunction with the symbolic model facilitate DEXPERT's application of search techniques to assist the user in finding an optimal design. The design worlds correspond to nodes in a search tree that can be evaluated based on figures calculated from the state of the model. Arcs in the search tree represent the application of a subset of redesign options permissible in the user's experimental domain. When requested by the user, DEXPERT will perform a search using a search algorithm know as *branch and bound with dynamic programming* (Winston 1984). The algorithm finds the smallest design (in terms of number of trials) having the user-specified set of detectable differences by sorting the search queue in order of increasing design size. The user first specifies the attributes that are practical to vary in the context of his/her experiment. New designs are generated by incrementally changing each specified feature in the smallest design in the queue. The search terminates when one or more satisfactory designs are found, or the design size exceeds a maximum that is controlled by the user. The automated search facility is an example of how the underlying model made it easy to add another tool (a search algorithm) to the system to provide a valuable capability to the experimenter.

Textual Interpretation

DEXPERT's model-based representation of the design closely mimics conceptual and statistical models of the experiment. This representation facilitated the development of features in DEXPERT that translate the internal representations of the design conclusions into English summaries that are easy for the user to understand. By sorting the term frames in a design by their test type and their minimal detectable difference categories, DEXPERT generates a concise textual description of the properties of a particular design. A similar strategy is used to produce text that compares two different designs. DEXPERT's explanations of the experimental analysis results also demonstrate this technique. In each case, attributes and relationships inherent in the underlying model are interrogated by procedural code to produce the explanations. These features demonstrate the power of the model-based approach to add applications of the system's inherent knowledge. Although they were simple to implement, these features provide valuable assistance to the user that other experiment design packages lack.

Application History and Benefits

Development on DEXPERT began in June 1989. By January 1990, the statisticians at GMR were using preliminary versions of DEXPERT to design real experiments. A small number of engineers began prepilot use of DEXPERT in late 1990. Pilot release of the complete DEXPERT system began in January 1991, followed by a full production release in May 1991. As of this writing, over 60 sites within GM use DEXPERT on a regular basis, averaging once each week. DEXPERT has been used, primarily by engineers, to design and analyze hundreds of experiments within GM.

DEXPERT was first deployed to a small number of pilot sites that received individualized training. A DEXPERT consulting center was established, including several workstations available for general use by engineers. A short training course was developed and conducted at the consulting center; to date, over 250 engineers and statisticians from GM have completed the DEXPERT training.

Full deployment of DEXPERT required porting the system to optimized, run-time versions of the Lisp and KEE system software and subsequent ports from SUN workstations to UNIX workstations from IBM and Hewlett Packard. None of these activities proved notably difficult. It should be noted that the KEE worlds facility used to implement the design worlds was replaced by a simpler, custom-coded facility to improve run-time performance. Deployment activities also included identifying and educating the potential user community within GM, establishing an informational newsletter and support hotline for users, and coordinating the installation of hardware and software at user sites.

An estimated eight person-years of effort went into DEXPERT's development, and an additional four person-years of effort have gone into the initial deployment and maintenance efforts. The system will be maintained in the future by less experienced maintenance staff members, with assistance from the expert statisticians at GMR. The domain knowledge is expected to remain relatively static over time, with maintenance activity primarily associated with bug fixes, ports to new platforms, and minor functional improvements as requested by users.

The statisticians who used DEXPERT in early consultations with engineers kept careful records of estimated experimentation cost savings that resulted from each consulting session. During pilot testing, engineers who came to the DEXPERT consulting center to use DEXPERT were asked to quantify the savings owed to efficiencies gained from using DEXPERT. It was not uncommon for a DEXPERT session to result in cost savings of over $100,000 for a single experiment. The long-term benefits to GM associated with the use of DEXPERT are estimated to be in the millions. In addition to savings in experimentation costs, these benefits include reduced costs because of the development of more efficient manufacturing processes, lower warranty costs, and increased revenues because of improvements in product quality.

Conclusions

Although many expert systems focus on single-paradigm approaches to encoding knowledge (such as production rules), experts rarely use a single technique or type of knowledge in solving a problem. More often, an expert will draw on a large body of background knowledge that constitutes a model of the application domain and apply a variety of techniques until a satisfactory solution is achieved. DEXPERT closely approximates a design approach used by expert statisticians through its hybrid architecture. The architecture combines a symbolic model of the domain area with hypothetical worlds, production rules, search algorithms, and object-oriented programming. Because DEXPERT represents a complex model and state space in a computer program, it can manipulate the model much faster than a human expert and allows the expert to generate improved designs by exploring many more design alternatives in less time. A window-oriented interface customized for different classes of users allows experimenters with minimal statistical training to generate designs that are comparable to those of an expert. The inclusion of analysis techniques with the design capabilities allows the novice experimenter to conduct an entire study without statistical consultation or the writing of custom computer programs.

DEXPERT was developed and delivered to users in an iterative manner. Statisticians were using early versions of DEXPERT for real experiments even as it was being developed. The model-based approach made it possible to provide a core model of the fundamental concepts required for the system. Once this model was put in place, it was easy to later add new reasoning techniques and interfaces to the existing model with minimum effort.

In January 1992, the inventors of DEXPERT were honored with the Kettering Award, GM's highest technical honor. This award recognizes the benefits to GM that have been and continue to be realized by DEXPERT users throughout the company. In less than one year since its initial deployment, DEXPERT has become the standard tool for experiment design at GM.

Acknowledgments

The authors would like to thank Tom Lorenzen and Lynn Truss at General Motors Research, who developed and put into practice the statistical theory on which DEXPERT was built. It was through their vision that DEXPERT was created; they were instrumental in all phases of DEXPERT's development. Bill Corpus of Electronic Data Systems wrote substantial portions of DEXPERT. Catherine Perman worked on the design of DEXPERT in its early stages. The authors would also like to thank the following reviewers for their thoughtful comments on earlier drafts of this chapter: Laura Paterson and Tony Confrey; Robert Filman, Christopher James, and James Taylor at IntelliCorp; Bret Fisher and Mitchell Levy at Sun Microsystems; and Karon Barber at General Motors.

Note

1. Andrew B. Parker was previously a senior knowledge systems engineer at IntelliCorp.

References

Fikes, R., and Kehler, T. 1985. The Role of Frame-Based Representation in Reasoning. *Communications of the ACM* 28(9): 904–920.

Filman, R. E. 1988. Reasoning with Worlds and Truth Maintenance in a Knowledge-Based Programming Environment. *Communications of the ACM* 31(4): 382–401.

Kunz, J. C. 1988. Model-Based Reasoning in CIM. In *Intelligent Manu-*

facturing: Expert Systems and the Leading Edge in Production Planning and Control. Reading, Mass.: Addison Wesley.

Lee, N. S.; Phadke, M. S.; and Keny, R. 1989. An Expert System for Experimental Design in Off-Line Quality Control. *Expert Systems* 6(4): 238–249.

Lorenzen, T. J., and Truss, L. T. 1990. Anatomy of DEXPERT—An Expert System for the Design of Experiments, Research Publication GMR-7111, General Motors Research Laboratories, Warren, Michigan.

Winston, P. H. 1984. *Artificial Intelligence.* Reading, Mass.: Addison Wesley.

Regulatory Applications

MAGIC

Merced County Human Services Agency and Andersen Consulting

ADJUDIPRO

United HealthCare Corporation

A Truly MAGIC Solution

Rita C. Kidd, Merced County Human Services Agency and
Robert J. Carlson, Andersen Consulting

Beginning in 1988, the Merced County Human Services Agency in California realized it needed to find a solution to the rising costs of providing human services to a growing population and to the 35-percent turnover rate among its caseworkers. After selecting Andersen Consulting to provide assistance in solving its problems, the agency was helped with a little MAGIC (Merced automated global information control.). MAGIC uses an expert system designed to determine client eligibility for public aid and calculate benefits based on information in the database. Behind the scenes, MAGIC resides on Hitachi Data Systems mainframes, uses database software from Software AG, and connects a series of Hewlett-Packard (HP) minicomputers and microcomputers through an Ethernet local area network. The expert system was created using ADS (Aion development system) from Aion Corporation. In addition to increasing the services provided by the agency, MAGIC earned the 1991 Hewlett-Packard High Tech Award and is a finalist for the *Computerworld* / Smithsonian Award.

The Problem

The Merced County Human Services Agency is committed to the efficient and effective delivery of human services to needy individuals, families, and children. The nature of human services limits the ability to provide quality care to the population without automation. Problems such as large case loads, frequently changing and complex regulations, worker frustration, and error rates result in high turnover and the loss of critical knowledge and skills.

Delivering modern social services is a complex task. For example, consider the task of determining the Assistance Unit Composition. The goal of Assistance Unit Composition is to determine who in the household is eligible for assistance. The following factors are some that might or might not be considered in the assessment for eligibility: age, disabilities, U.S. citizenship, residence in Merced County, family relationships within the household, and income. Furthermore, most of these factors are interdependent (that is, income cutoffs vary with number of children, citizenship, and residence).

Because of this complexity, the agency had to keep 10 specialized classes of workers trained and knowledgeable to deliver the level of service mandated by law. Each of the five major social service programs—Aid to Families with Dependent Children (AFDC), Refugee Cash Assistance (RCA), Food Stamps, MediCal, and Foster Care—required specialized workers. Within these five social service programs, eligibility workers were further segregated into *intake workers*, who performed the initial case review and interview, and *continuing workers*, who were responsible for ensuring that ongoing eligibility requirements were met.

To compound the situation, the tools of the trade, primarily the body of law that governed the services, was changing at an accelerating rate. If the system was to be automated, it needed to support the complex decision-making process of a caseworker and would have to be easy to maintain. The system would need to support the rapidly changing regulatory environment. In California, during an 18-month period, regulations were changing at an average rate of one a day. In addition to the rapidly changing environment, the new system needed to provide some guarantee that caseworkers would administer the regulations across similar cases in a consistent manner.

Delivering human services is also a time-intensive process. In fact, most costs related to welfare systems can be measured in terms of time: how long it takes from the time a client applies for aid until the client is seen by an eligibility worker, how long it takes to process a client through an interview, and how long it takes to maintain a case each month. However, the reality of publicly funded services in Merced County is that caseworkers could not spend as much time as they needed on each case, nor could enough workers be hired to perform the tasks. The result was an inverse relationship between the amount of work pending and the productivity level of the workers. The situation created high error rates, high worker frustration, and increased worker turnover.

Prior to MAGIC, the work environment at the agency was deteriorating. Because caseworkers were overburdened, they inadvertently neglected clients, which led to adversarial administrative law hearings and a reduction of worker and client morale. Several other examples of service delivery problems are as follows:

First, clients suffered delays of three to five weeks in Merced County before the initial intake interview. Delays of as long as three months were occurring in other California counties.

Second, the process required the caseworker to spend several hours filling out multiple forms and making budget calculations for each client following the initial interview.

Third, documentation was done by hand in multitiered carbon copy forms. These forms were then filed into case folders for each case. Case folders contained hundreds of forms.

Fourth, the treatment of similar cases was inconsistent. This problem was partially the result of the specialization of application knowledge among the workers.

The Approach

The agency began its search for a solution to its problem in 1984. In 1987, those studying the problem decided that no existing system could offer what they needed to accomplish their mission. At this point, the agency developed a vision of a system that would increase service delivery costs, improve worker morale and productivity, reduce error rates, eliminate program administrative support costs, reduce the initial and ongoing training costs, and insulate the workers from regulatory volatility and complexity.

To achieve its goal, the agency employed focus groups, brainstorming sessions, national user group conferences, and visits to other states to build the vision that was to become MAGIC. At this time, all social service systems were either 3GL mainframe applications or workstation applications that covered far less territory than the agency desired. Because of the complexity of the regulations involved and the frequent updates to these regulations, an expert system approach was chosen. By using object orientation and rules, it was hoped that both the pure written regulations and the heuristics by which the experts deliver human services could be automated and maintained easily. The proposed system would not only include all the rules and regulations necessary to determine eligibility for each client but also would automatically generate legal notices, referrals, and due dates. It would remind an eligibility worker, or family assistance representative (FAR), of deadlines and aid in the actual decision-making process. Within the social services industry, an expert system solution of this scale had never been attempted.

The Technology

The MAGIC solution consists of a multiple-tier client-server architecture based on an open-system application that permits interoperability at all levels. The system resides on an Hitachi mainframe (IBM 370-series equivalent) and runs through the HP 855S minicomputer to HP 386 VECTRA personal computer workstations. Data communications is handled by an Ethernet TCP-IP network. ADABAS supplies the data management services on the mainframe host, and INGRES is used as the data manager on the UNIX-based minicomputer.

Taking full advantage of the client-server design by downsizing applications allows individual workers to capitalize on the workstation's strengths and be freed from the telecommunication and central processing unit constraints of a centralized mainframe solution. MAGIC has offloaded 70 percent of the expensive mainframe online processing to the comparatively inexpensive workstation.

The expert system was developed with ADS, an object-oriented tool that enabled developers to build and maintain a 5700-rule knowledge base. Together, the workstation and the expert system form the *expert assistant,* a combination of programs that enhances the productivity, efficiency, and effectiveness of every worker that uses it.

The expert system is designed to satisfy two goals. First, the FAR work flow must be controlled flexibly. Second, all eligibility logic and heuristics must be contained so that FAR can be a *generic worker,* or a person who could determine the eligibility and process cases for all five human services programs.

The MAGIC expert assistant guides the worker through the interview and subsequent case maintenance by establishing to-do lists of tasks that must be completed before eligibility can be finalized. In addition to the automatic generation of to-do lists, the expert assistant allows the worker to override the default consultation flow and directly select tasks to process from a menulike task list. The to-do list for the task of Assistance Unit Composition is shown in figure 1.

Once FAR selects a to-do item, MAGIC prompts FAR with questions to ask the client. The questions are tailored to the client's situation; families or individuals that have different household compositions or re-

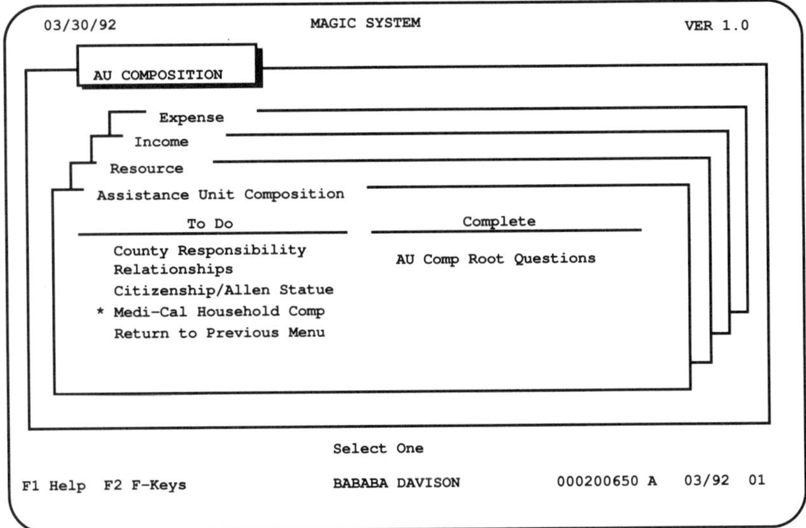

Figure 1. A MAGIC *To-Do Screen.*

quest different types of aid are treated according to their specific circumstances. The expert assistant then determines the next question to ask based on the previous client answers. These questions are dynamically formatted so that variable information can be included in the question. Answers are usually selected from lists or a standard yes-no selection. In this manner, the interview and data-collection tasks are managed for the worker and require minimal data entry. A sample question screen within the resource task is shown in figure 2.

The expert system handles to-do and question transitions through a novel use of ADS states. A *state* is the basic level of organization within the ADS tool. Rules and data elements can be owned by a state, and states can own other states, establishing a state hierarchy. Within the MAGIC system, unique state hierarchies, called modules, are defined. A *module* represents one functional task that might be executed within MAGIC. A partial list of modules within the Assistance Unit Composition task is listed in figure 3. Note that some of these modules correspond to to-do actions that FAR can select from the Assistance Unit Composition screen (figure 1). Other modules exist that govern common user utilities and the transfer of data to the minicomputer and mainframe.

Modules are composed of a parent control state and data-gathering states. *Control states* describe when the module should be called and what goals are necessary for the completion of the module. When FAR selects an item from a to-do list, usually the control state for a module

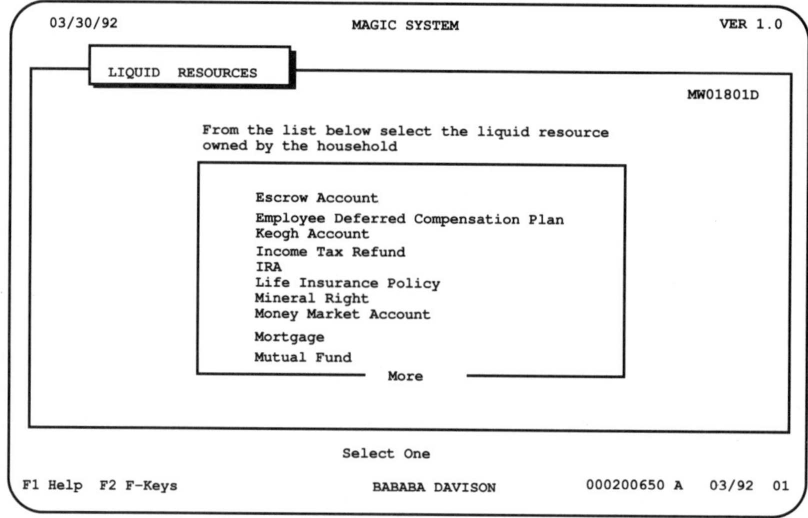

Figure 2. A MAGIC Question Screen.

is called. Control states, in turn, own *data-gathering states.* These states contain the actual questioning logic. Rules within data-gathering states are either backward or forward chaining, depending on whether the questioning is goal or data driven. Most of the data-gathering rules for the Assistance Unit Composition module are backward chaining. A sample rule and its English-language equivalent are described in figure 4.

Within MAGIC, all ADS rules, states, and objects have standardized, although cryptic, names. These naming standards are necessary given that MAGIC is one of the largest deployed ADS systems, both in terms of size (roughly 7000 data elements and object attributes; over 5500 rules) and the number of simultaneous developers. These naming standards have also facilitated the maintenance of the system.

The MAGIC system achieves significant benefits in addition to those previously outlined. One benefit is the automatic generation of notices and the statement of facts, which previously were completed manually. Among the automatically generated documents, it is important to note that many of these documents can be produced in Spanish, Hmong, and Lao, as well as English, because a large percentage of recipients are non-English speaking.

The Project

The development of MAGIC began in October 1988 when Andersen

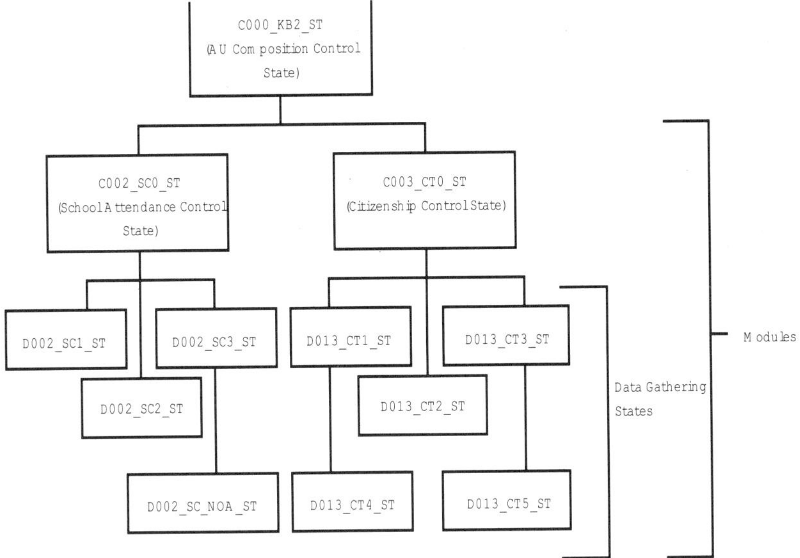

Figure 3. Some of the Modules, Control States, and Data-Gathering States for the Assistance Unit Composition Task within MAGIC.

Consulting started the requirement definition and general system design phase. The makeup of the development team for the expert assistant portion was as follows: 12 Andersen Consulting consultants, 2 Merced County programmers, 8 caseworkers, and 3 California state welfare program analysts.

The project was implemented in the following phases:

October 1989: Detailed design began, and a fast-track process was enabled that brought together design and programming.

April 1990: Began system test of the integrated knowledge base and the mainframe functions.

August 1990: Pilot started. Ten percent of the agency cases were converted to MAGIC.

January 1991: Increased cases to 50 percent of the total agency case load.

July 1991: Began converting the remaining cases to MAGIC.

A major concern was whether a distributed system could accommodate the production volumes for the largest counties in California. It was clear from the outset that each platform would have less trouble than a single mainframe in handling the volume. The main concern was the transmission between the platforms. The high-speed Ethernet TCP-IP network allayed these concerns. Operating at 10 megabits a sec-

```
IF     SIZE(INTERSECTION(HC_CASH_MNR_HH_MEM_PA,
          HC_AFDC_RP_HH_PA)) = 0                        AND
       SIZE(HC_PREG_SPEC_ND_SET_PA) > 0
THEN C1 = 0
       FOR HC_PREG_SPEC_ND_SET_PA, C1
          IF     NOT(HC_UNBRN_SET_PA INCLUDES
                 HC_PREG_SPEC_SET_PA(C1))              AND
                 HC_REQ_AFDC_PA INCLUDES HC_PREG_SPEC_ND_SET_PA(C1)
          THEN ADD HC_PREG_SPEC_ND_SET_PA (C1) TO HC_AFDC_REC_HH2_PA
END END END
```

"If no minor person is in the reporting set and there is someone in the household who is pregnant, then add that person to the recipient household"

Figure 4. Sample Data-Gathering Rule with English-Language Equivalent.

ond, the transmission between the server and the client workstation was completely transparent. For the downloading and uploading of data, eight 56-kilobyte lines were used for Merced County. In larger counties, T1 lines can be substituted without affecting the overall architecture design.

The maintainability of the rules in the system was a critical element. Concurrent with defining the regulations and proving the maintainability of the knowledge base, regulations in the system had to remain current through the development phase. Even as design was being completed, the rules were constantly changing. An arbitrary date was selected for testing, but in several cases, the necessity of immediate modifications to the expert assistant because of mandated regulation changes required updating the knowledge base. Over the last 18 months, the state of California has seen at least one regulation change each day. A few of these changes involve entirely new methods of determining eligibility for the MediCal program, involving multiple modules and many rules. Thus, to remain current with the regulations, from 2 to 5 percent of the knowledge base rules must be updated each month. Since October 1989, throughout the entire development and implementation period, the rules have been maintained to include regulation changes.

Updating rules in the knowledge base is similar to revising case structures in COBOL modules. The ADS tool provides editing tools that facilitate navigation through the rules and data structure within the knowledge base. The major advantage of the expert system is in the addition of new rules; when the data requirements are identified, new rules or regulations can be inserted into the object-oriented code with ease and efficiency. Where a structured code program might have to be restructured entirely to accommodate new logic, the expert system inference engine simply fires the rules and regulations according to the priorities and parameters that the knowledge engineer determined were appropriate.

The regulation change in AFDC provides an excellent example of how MAGIC's complex eligibility logic is easily and rapidly maintained. In August 1991, the state of California finalized and ordered the implementation of a plan that would reduce the level of assistance and change the method for computing the benefit amount for the AFDC program. Every AFDC household, over 9000 in Merced County, was affected by the new regulation. In less than two days, the knowledge engineers were able to identify the affected modules and rules. Within the next three days, the changes were coded and thoroughly tested. By 16 August 1991, well before the mandated implementation date of 1 September, the Merced County Human Services Agency was processing according to the new regulations. Merced was the first California county to do so. Several other counties were unable to implement the new regulations until November 1991. MAGIC 's rigid naming standards and modular structure were essential in helping the developers to make this change.

The Benefits

Since MAGIC was implemented, significant benefits have been achieved. Clients are now seen within 24 to 72 hours. Prior to the implementation of MAGIC, clients experienced delays of three to five weeks in Merced County. Delays of as long as three months were occurring in other counties in the state.

Following the conclusion of the interview, which normally takes about two hours, the client's eligibility and benefits are determined by MAGIC, pending any required verifications. The client is given immediate notice about his/her eligibility status and, if eligible, is advised of when to expect his/her benefits. When the worker completes the interview, he/she is done with this client's case: No further paperwork is necessary. Before the new system was implemented, caseworkers spent several hours filling out more than 700 documents and making budget calculations that were required in addition to the time spent interviewing the client.

Correspondence and fact-finding documentation are automatically generated by the expert assistant as a result of the interview. All the forms and legal notices of approval or denial are available at the nearest printer for the worker to pick up and hand to the client at the end of the interview. The laborious handwritten, multipart carbon copy forms that had to be filed into case folders are finally obsolete now that the MAGIC expert assistant handles the administrative details for the worker.

Clients with similar case circumstances receive similar treatment. It is now possible to predict the length of interviews for scheduling purposes and supervisory review.

In addition to the administrative benefits gained through MAGIC, many financial benefits were realized as well. Those financial benefits described here are goals of the agency that were developed prior to the implementation of MAGIC; they are based on the assumption that caseworkers would increase their work load from 180 to 275 households. The actual results of the system implementation is that each caseworker is now handling an average of more than 330 households. With all the cases converted to the new system, the original goals are well within the capabilities of the system. Of additional importance, error rates have declined from 3 percent to 1 percent. Monthly case maintenance has fallen from approximately 20 minutes a case to 7 minutes a case.

The goals set forth included the following:

First, the eligibility staff required to support the projected case load could be reduced by 40 percent by June 1992.

Second, approximately $1 million annually could be saved because of error reduction, equivalent to approximately $100 million statewide. This estimate is conservative and is based on a 1-percent error rate improvement; the actual error rate improvement might be closer to 2 percent. The MAGIC expert assistant has an apparent error rate of less than 1 percent.

Third is the elimination of clerical support for the eligibility workers.

Fourth is a reduction in the 700 preprinted forms inventory to about 350 forms. Most of the forms required for the intake interview, including the legal notices, are now generated on laser printers using blank stock.

Fifth is a reduction in system operating costs. States with case-load sizes similar to Merced County's have stated that their annual system operating costs range from $2 million to $3 million; Merced's cost is $500,000.

The dollar value of the savings is estimated at $6 million for the first year. In less than two years, MAGIC will have paid for itself. These estimates are conservative; they do not account for savings because of reduced staff training and improved staff morale.

These administrative and financial benefits are felt directly by the agency, but some of these benefits will be felt statewide if the MAGIC approach is introduced to other counties:

First, the cost and time to bring all 15,000 workers statewide into compliance with new regulations are the same as the cost for a single county.

Second, all counties using MAGIC will deliver the same level of service and use the same approach to eligibility determination and benefit computation, thus ensuring consistent application of all the laws.

Third, the architecture is scalable, allowing several small counties to pool their resources and use a common mainframe as a data repository yet maintain separate minicomputer servers.

Jean Toftely, a medical analyst supervisor, using the AdjudiPro reports.

ADJUDIPRO

J. P. Little and Mark Gingrich, United HealthCare Corporation

United Health Care (UHC) is a diversified managed care company, serving virtually every segment of the health-care market. Founded in 1974, UHC has become an industry front runner by offering a broad portfolio of products and services to help clients, both providers and purchasers of health care, successfully manage their health-care costs. UHC's highly integrated range of products and services includes a network of owned and managed health plans as well as specialty companies that individually address key and fast-growing cost areas of health care.

UHC's unique business mix provides an ideal research and development environment for developing, testing, and refining health-care–management products and service. Recognizing the power of knowledge-based systems, UHC's senior management hired JP Little to investigate and apply expert systems and other advanced computing technologies to the health-care industry. Success was top priority for the selection of an initial application. There were many possibilities, but the domain of claim adjudication was selected as the best choice.

Problem

Over the years, a complex coding scheme has emerged between physicians and the insurance industry for explaining the medical services provided to patients. The American Medical Association has enumerated most medical procedures and services, along with variations, in a book called the Physicians' Current Procedural Terminology (CPT) (Kirschner et al.), which is published annually. CPT is written by physicians, and they agree to code according to the guidelines stated within it. Because of the complex coding, many physicians, whether intentionally or accidentally, submit incorrect claims. For example, many times a group of procedures will be billed separately when a single comprehensive CPT code actually exists for the entire group. This practice is known as *unbundling* and costs insurance companies large sums of money because the comprehensive code usually pays less than the sum of the separate procedures.

At UHC, a complex information system known as COSMOS processes medical claims submitted by physicians and hospitals. COSMOS suspends (puts on review) many claims because of high claimed amounts and procedure-payment complexities. Departments of medical analysts must manually adjudicate these suspended claims by first classifying or categorizing the claim and then applying appropriate coding and payment guidelines (rules).

The medical analysts are typically registered nurses, have several years of clinical experience, and are hard to replace. It generally takes three to six months of training before the medical analysts achieve full productivity. As UHC grows, the work load of the medical analysts is continually increasing; new plans appear annually. Despite the increased work load, contractual agreements require expedient claim processing. To compound the problem, management pressures exist to minimize additional staffing, maximize cost savings, and standardize adjudication policies across the plans.

Additional automation of the adjudication decision process seemed necessary, but COSMOS is a large table-based COBOL system. The complexity of adding more tables for additional associations (rules) or recoding the inference process of COSMOS did not seem viable solutions for a system already so complex that it was difficult to maintain. The integration of a rule-based inference mechanism was deemed a better approach (because it was more flexible and allowed for a higher level of abstraction). Coding and payment guidelines fit well into rules, an medical procedures fit nicely into class hierarchies. COSMOS remains the vehicle for placing claims on review.

Finally, the strategic objectives of all management information system (MIS) activities at UHC include (1) managing the medical loss ratio (the cost of processing claims versus premiums received); (2) containing selling, general, and administrative expense (SG&A); and (3) selling systems externally (when it makes sense). ADJUDIPRO was de-

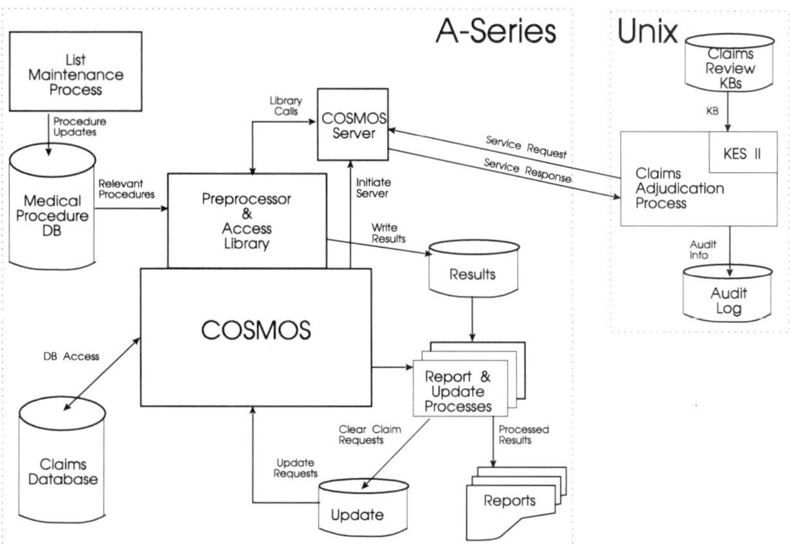

Figure 1. Current System Design.

veloped with all three objectives in mind, and the first two have been met.

System Design and Implementation

ADJUDIPRO (until recently known as the CARE system) is an intelligent augmentation to COSMOS running on a Unisys A17L mainframe. This system runs as a batch process during off-peak hours, autonomously clearing claims that the system understands 100 percent and provides medical analysts with a series of reports for those claims that still require manual intervention.

The system is logically composed of four main components: a preprocessor for collecting claims and relevant medical information, an embedded expert system component for analyzing the information, a system access component for retrieving historical claim information, and a report generator for presenting the recommendations of the expert system. Figure 1 depicts the current system design.

The principal component of ADJUDIPRO is the expert system component that is shown in figure 1 as the claims adjudication process. This component comprises the expert system shell KES-II (Template Software of Herndon, Virginia) and C code for accessing the other components of the system. A library interface to the knowledge bases provides the C code with the ability to service the information needs of the knowledge bases.

KES-II is a C-based expert system shell that runs on all relevant UHC hardware platforms (that is, personal computers [PCs], RS/6000s, a Unisys A17L, and an IBM ES-9121), with a graphic user interface supported in the PC and RS/6000 environment. The fact that knowledge bases are 100-percent portable across these platforms made KES-II the best choice. This choice enabled knowledge base development and testing on PCs and UNIX systems, and knowledge base deployment occurred on the A-Series mainframe and UNIX systems.

The ADJUDIPRO knowledge bases primarily use a backward-chaining approach to analyze the claim information. The highest-level goal is to obtain adjudication advice. At subgoal levels, ADJUDIPRO attempts to identify situations that cannot be adjudicated before attempting to deny or accept claims. These situations and important information (that is, historical claims) are logged for the reporting component. If claims are fully or partially adjudicated, reasons for decisions and payment corrections are logged for the reporting component.

The rules of the ADJUDIPRO knowledge bases fall into five categories: *ignore rules* for identifying information ignored by medical analysts, *medical analyst rules* for identifying situations that must be handled by a medical analyst, *denial rules*, *accept rules*, and *payment rules.*

Besides rules, the problem domain called for extensive use of the classification capabilities of KES-II. CPT structures medical procedure codes in a hierarchical fashion by systems of the body (for example, cardiovascular system, musculoskeletal system), which fits neatly into a KES-II class hierarchy. Also, the medical analysts' visual and mental views of the claim structure are modeled with KES-II classes (lines, claim reviews, history claims, and so on).

The system currently shares 80 classes and 10 demons between 8 different review knowledge bases. We use the demons primarily for initialization and termination processing for a claim, but the encapsulated business and medical knowledge is represented with rules. The largest knowledge base contains 168 rules (multiple surgical review), and the smallest contains 32 (radiology review). The total current number of rules between the 8 knowledge bases is 461.

ADJUDIPRO has evolved into an interesting system with roughly 26,125 lines of code: 18,000 procedural (ALGOL, C, COBOL) and 8,125 rule-based lines. Most of the procedural code was written to integrate ADJUDIPRO into the production database world and to deliver the information to the medical analysts through reports. This code is critical to the success of the system. As a stand-alone prototype, ADJUDIPRO received little attention, but as an integrated piece of the information system, it has become a required tool of the medical analysts. In today's environment, AI systems cannot survive as separate entities. If one wants to build a system that is going to have a significant corporate impact, this system must interact with corporate data.

The procedural code has formed a platform for future expert system (as well as client-server) applications at UHC. Until recently, the entire system ran on the A17L; however, because of performance considerations, the system was reimplemented as a client-server application with the computation-intensive expert system component residing on an IBM RS/6000 Model 550 running AIX. Without the client-server architecture, the operations management would not allow ADJUDIPRO to run against more than 3 of UHC's 19 health plans. This architecture reduced A-series processing requirements significantly. Initial estimates indicated the following A17 reductions: central processing use, 99 percent; input-output, 69 percent; elapsed time, 86 percent. This reduction was more significant than anticipated and is an exciting testament to the virtues of client-server.

The server process services the requests (for example, next claim, history, results) of the expert system component using the facilities of a utilities library. Logically, this library is composed of the preprocessor and system access components of ADJUDIPRO.

The server uses the preprocessor to extract the raw data for multiple surgical claims on review, appends the declarative knowledge of the medical analysts, and formats the information into KES-II syntax. Figure 2 shows a sample claim. The initial intent of the preprocessor was only to format claims data for use by the expert system; however, it quickly became apparent that vital information for claims adjudication appeared on a series of cheat sheet lists that medical analysts use daily. Also, the medical analysts identified many attributes of procedures in CPT as necessary to their decision process.

This declarative knowledge is now automated in the preprocessor. Offline, a maintenance process takes a set of lists containing procedures and their attribute values and updates a medical procedure database that is indexed by medical plan ID, procedure ID, effective date, and attribute. The preprocessor uses the database to supply the expert system component with the appropriate procedure information for each claim. Responsibility for list maintenance is currently being turned over to the users. As needed, new attributes (lists) are added to the system, requiring only modification to the knowledge base.

The server process uses the system access component when the expert system requests additional information while inferencing. Depending on the request, a response might return anything from a Boolean value to several database records. Often, more than one request is required to complete adjudication of a claim, but by only accessing data on an as-needed basis, excessive data access and processing time are spared.

The system access component also logs the expert system's results. The report-generation routines use these results to create seven reports for the medical analysts. These reports replace a single old report containing a long list of claims on review (the Age Report). One of the new reports, the Knock-Out Report, lists the claims ADJUDIPRO cannot yet handle (those with only 0- to 20-percent understanding), and the Clear Claim Report lists the claims that ADJUDIPRO can solve completely (determine payment and clear the review). The remaining new reports take the medical analysts 30 to 80 percent of the way toward adjudicating a claim. Also, the reports display additional information requested during the inference process, including relevant historical information. This information saves the medical analysts valuable lookup time because they need this information to manually process claims.

Once ADJUDIPRO can solve a particular type of claim completely and once medical analysts have performed extensive review and testing through the Clear Claim Report, a reporting routine writes claims of this type to an update file that COSMOS uses to autonomously clear claims. In other words, completely understood claims are removed from the medical analysts' claim inventory (claims on review).

Both the system access and reporting components were developed and are maintained with XGEN, a COBOL 4GL tool. This approach enabled the reuse of COSMOS components, also written with XGEN, simplifying development and maintenance. The group obtained an XGEN developer from the MIS group to write these two components.

The application of expert system technology to medical claims processing is still a new concept; however, the real effectiveness and innovation of ADJUDIPRO is the tight system integration to COSMOS, enabling quick and selective access to historical claim information during the inference process. Approximately 57 percent of the claims that ADJUDIPRO processes require historical information; however, if all historical information were provided for every claim, COSMOS and ADJUDIPRO performance would be degraded severely by excessive database access and information processing. The key is selective access.

The tight integration to the database system—combined with the declarative knowledge (cheat sheet information), the flexible reporting, the knowledge representations, and inference capabilities—has proven effective in helping us respond to enhancement requests. Several new reviews will be released during the second

```
AUDIT_NUMBER = “83114439”.
AUDIT_EXT = “00”.
PROVIDER_NUMBER = “0601487”. GROUP_PLAN = 01.
DATE_RECEIVED = “910717”.
DATE_PAID = “000000”.
HMO_ID = MSP.
INITIALS = “ “.
MEMBER_NUMBER = “5910000008415100”. assertclass MEDICINE = p01.
assertclass N_S_CRANIECTOMY OR CRANIOTOMY = p02. assertclass I_R_REPAIR_INTERMEDI-
ATE = p03. assertclass LINE = l01,l02,l03.
assertclass REVIEW = r1,r2,r3,r4. LINE:l01>proc=MEDICINE:p01. LINE:l01>modifier=” “.
LINE:l01>reason_code=32. LINE:l01>dos=”910309”.
LINE:l01>site=04.
LINE:l01>units=01.
LINE:l01>claimed= 135.00.
LINE:l01>copay= 0.00.
LINE:l01>eligible= 84.00.
LINE:l01>pcr= 0.00.
LINE:l01>fee_max= 84.00.
LINE:l01>icda=1.
LINE:l02>proc=N_S_CRANIECTOMY OR CRANIOTOMY:p02. LINE:l02>modifier=” “.
LINE:l02>reason_code=32. LINE:l02>dos=”910309”.
LINE:l02>site=04.
LINE:l02>units=01.
LINE:l02>claimed= 3350.00.
LINE:l02>copay= 0.00.
LINE:l02>eligible= 2001.00.
LINE:l02>pcr= 0.00.
LINE:l02>fee_max= 2001.00.
LINE:l02>icda=1.
LINE:l03>proc=I_R_REPAIR_INTERMEDIATE:p03. LINE:l03>modifier=” “.
LINE:l03>reason_code=67.
LINE:l03>dos=”910309”.
LINE:l03>site=04.
LINE:l03>units=01.
LINE:l03>claimed= 745.00.
LINE:l03>copay= 0.00.
LINE:l03>eligible= 0.00.
LINE:l03>pcr= 0.00.
LINE:l03>fee_max= 0.00.
LINE:l03>icda=1.
MEDICINE:p01>proc_code=”90620”.
N_S_CRANIECTOMY OR CRANIOTOMY:p02>proc_code=”61312”. N_S_CRANIECTOMY OR
CRANIOTOMY:p02>reviewable_code=true. N_S_CRANIECTOMY OR CRANIOTOMY:p02>surgi-
cal_assistant=allowed. I_R_REPAIR_INTERMEDIATE:p03>proc_code=”12037”. I_R_REPAIR_INTER-
MEDIATE:p03>no_cut_reason=repair. I_R_REPAIR_INTERMEDIATE:p03>reviewable_code=true.
I_R_REPAIR_INTERMEDIATE:p03>base_code=”12031”.
I_R_REPAIR_INTERMEDIATE:p03>base_code_assoc=only_one. REVIEW:r1>number=38.
REVIEW:r2>number=22.
REVIEW:r3>number=75.
REVIEW:r4>number=35.
REVIEW:r4>lines=LINE:l02,LINE:l03.
%
```

Figure 2. Sample Claim, Formatted by Preprocessor for Use by Knowledge Base.

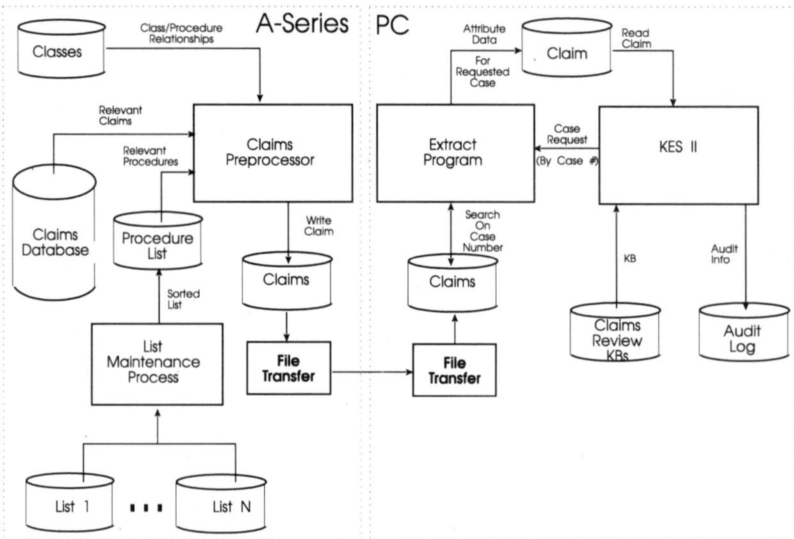

Figure 3. Phase 1.

and third quarters of 1992, bringing the total reviews to eight. This system is considered innovative in the insurance industry, and UHC filed a patent application in October 1991 to protect ADJUDIPRO.

Application Development and Deployment

This system was the first foray by UHC into AI. Although the primary objective was certainly to produce a viable system, perhaps as important was technology acceptance and the construction of a solid expert system development platform. JP Little started in January 1990 with this mission.

As previously described, there was definitely a need for further automation of the adjudication process: improving the productivity of experienced professionals, reducing the training cycle, dealing with an increasing work load, minimizing additional staffing, standardizing guidelines, and so on. The initial prototype, however, could not address the entire domain of claim adjudication. Little selected one review known as the multiple surgical review. These claims involve more than one surgery on the same date of service as well as special contractual circumstances between insurance payers and health-care providers. This problem domain was selected because of the financial importance of paying multiple surgical claims correctly and in a timely manner. Pederson (1989) was useful for identifying the problem and narrowing the scope of the domain.

The development and deployment of the system was broken into three phases. Phase 1, figure 3, was the initial prototype phase. Phase 2, figure 4, was the first phase deployed in production. Finally, the current phase, with client-server and autonomous clearing, enabled deployment across all the plans of UHC.

Phase 1

In March 1990, Little obtained the services of Mark Gingrich of the Unisys Applied Technology Group through the Artificial Intelligence Apprenticeship Program. Together, they studied CPT, policy guidelines, and other medical information to become familiar with the domain. MEDICA (formerly PHP of Minnesota and Share/Minnesota) was selected as the initial health plan for the prototype because of its size (approximately 40 percent of total claim volume) and the availability of medical analysts.

Knowledge-acquisition sessions took place with MEDICA medical analysts. These sessions took several forms. First, observation sessions and unstructured questioning were used to obtain a better yet general understanding of the problem. The medical analysts were good at explanation through examples, where they would walk through their decision process. In time, dependency-oriented techniques from the KES-II training class (Template Software 1989) were applied. Basically, with *dependency-oriented acquisition,* one attempts to identify the solutions (or types of solutions), the information used to reach the solutions, and the dependencies between the two.

Over the first few months, the knowledge-acquisition process did not go smoothly. The elicitation of knowledge is a slow, arduous task when entering a new domain. It takes a patient and introspective domain expert (that is, medical analyst) to express his/her decision process, possibly many times. It also takes the availability of an expert. Up front, promises of time were given; however, when push came to shove, ADJUDIPRO understandably took second priority. Then, Jean Toftely, a medical analyst supervisor, was identified as the expert for the prototype. With both a manager's perspective and many years of adjudication experience, Jean's availability provided an incredible boost to development productivity.

With the acquired knowledge, an initial prototype was constructed for a subset of the multiple surgical review called the "no-brainers."

These cases required a somewhat shallow level of medical knowledge, yet their volume was large enough to warrant autonomous clearing. It was assumed that the knowledge depth would grow over time. The preprocessor was developed to extract and format pending claims from COSMOS, and KES-II ran interactively on a personal computer for validation purposes.

The validation process went much more quickly than expected. To summarize, in 4 testing sessions (of 2 to 4 hours) over a 6-week period, the expert system progressed from 0 to nearly 100-percent correctness. The users were surprised at how quickly we could react to problems and create solutions.

Phase 2

Development of the production phase commenced prior to the completion of phase 1. Full deployment on the A17 seemed the most viable solution because having all processes on one machine made integration somewhat less complicated. A C programmer was added in July 1990 to develop the KES-II support code that made up ADJUDIPRO's expert system component.

One important conclusion from the prototype was that to enhance intelligent processing, access to historical claim information was necessary. Also, if access was provided to the expert system, why not report the requested information to the medical analysts; besides, this information would be useful for validation. An XGEN-COBOL programmer came on board in November 1990 to build the database-access and database-reporting mechanisms.

Once the reports were available, the medical analysts preferred working from a known format (we emulated the appearance of the Age Report) to verify the results of the expert system. The reports greatly increased the speed of the testing-correction process and enabled the implementation of formal verification procedures. To this end, the medical analysts worked from development reports for several weeks before signing off on the transmittal to production.

ADJUDIPRO was deployed in production in March 1991. Use of the ADJUDIPRO reports completely replaced the existing Age Report in June 1991. The key aspect of the deployment was the medical analysts' confidence in the accuracy of the reports.

With this confidence came a wave of requests for new features and reviews. An operational process evolved for handling the request. First, all requests were filtered through Toftely. Next, the knowledge engineers made the appropriate changes to the knowledge bases and did some rudimentary testing. After testing, the system was handed to the

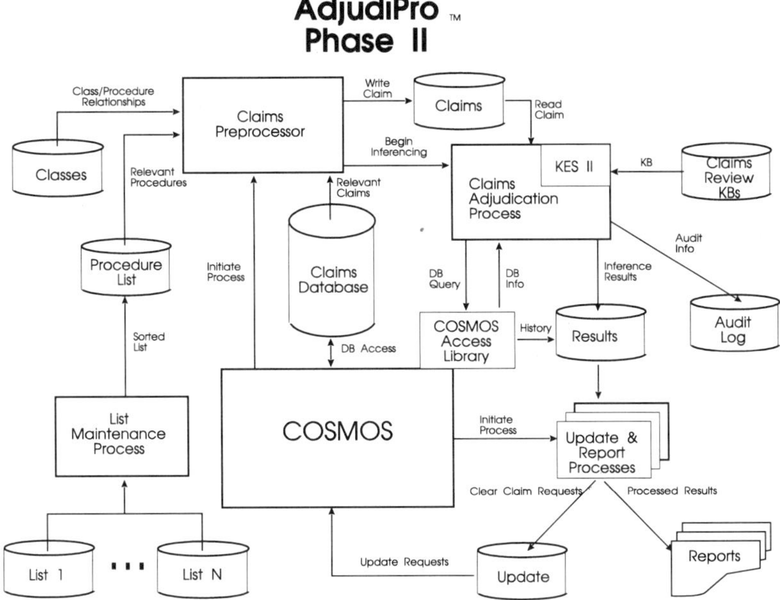

Figure 4. Phase 2.

C programmers for KES-II support code modification. They reacted to new classes, types, attributes, and so on, and produced a functional embedded system. The C programmers then handed off the system to the reporting and database programmers, who reacted to new database and reporting requirements. Finally, after testing, Toftely signed off on the transmittal to production. This process is still essentially used to introduce new capabilities.

A knowledge engineer was added in August 1991 to assume maintenance and new development responsibilities for the knowledge bases.

Phase 3

Within the wave of requests, two stood out as priorities: autonomous clearing of claims and propagation of ADJUDIPRO across all UHC plans. The ability to autonomously clear claims required total buy-in by members of the MIS group because they would develop the code; that is, MIS members had responsibility for COSMOS, so they should be responsible for updating its databases. This link meant the integration of ADJUDIPRO into COSMOS was complete, and the users were the driving force that placed its implementation as a top priority. It was a great feeling.

The second major request dictated the migration to client-server.

The UHC A17L is a large mainframe; however, COSMOS and other processes keep the machine busy. Operations keeps a close eye on processor-intensive applications, and they would not allow a new implementation that would more than double ADJUDIPRO's processor requirements. Client-server not only allowed for the processing of all plans but dramatically increased the speed of development and testing by providing online access to COSMOS data.

With all three phases, the total cost of development for ADJUDIPRO thus far has been $450,000. This figure includes salary, contract services, hardware and software, the RS/6000, and mainframe software (a C compiler, KES-II, and TCP/IP). From a labor perspective, we have invested 5.8 person-years thus far in the product.

Maintenance

Bug fixing and new features are incorporated into production as previously described. The procedural code of the system has become a flexible platform where minimal changes are required in reaction to knowledge base changes.

Knowledge bases are developed and maintained using the KES-II graphic user interface on both PCs and UNIX machines. The ability to run both offline (phase 1) and online (client-server) has provided a flexible testing environment.

Domain knowledge changes over time but has been limited to annual changes to CPT and some contract changes. Such changes between 1990 and 1992 required few knowledge base changes. Use of classes and abstraction has helped ensure that we do as little maintenance as possible. The medical analysts maintain certain auxiliary information (the cheat sheets), which changes annually with CPT.

Although maintenance has not been a problem thus far, it will be an issue in the future. Currently, all maintenance is handled by the original developers. Eventually, this responsibility will be handed to another group. The lack of automated maintenance facilities is definitely a system weakness and is an area under investigation. Some possibilities include seamless association of COSMOS database information with knowledge base attributes, natural language techniques for eliciting information from CPT, and database mining using case-based reasoning and neural networks.

Use and Payoff

The client-server version of ADJUDIPRO was deployed in March 1992. Until this time, not all the plans of UHC could use ADJUDIPRO. The user community and the Strategic Development Group are in the process of quantifying the total benefits, largely in part because they now fully understand what we can deliver and want to see more. This milestone, in and of itself, was probably the most significant in the political landscape of the project. Enthusiastic user acceptance of this new technology has created a ground swell of requests for enhancements and new applications. The users are driving the success of the project.

At this time, the most apparent quantifiable benefits of ADJUDIPRO are the cost and time savings for claims it can autonomously clear. For UHC, cost savings translate directly into improving the medical loss ratio, and personnel time savings improve SG&A. The projected cost savings for these claims are $1.6 million for 1992 and $3.4 million for 1993. A portion of the savings cannot be considered new cost savings to the company because medical analysts would have cleared these claims manually; however, there is still a time savings of 0.74 full-time equivalents (that is, 3/4 of a person) that allows the medical analysts to adjudicate other claims or perform more research. A conservative return-on-investment analysis based solely on cost savings projected over 5 years indicates a 36.3-percent return on investment.

This quantifiable portion, although not trivial, is only a fraction of the total value that will be realized over the next three to five years. No figures account for the many reviews currently in their development or testing phases, nor do the figures account for the many benefits that have not been fully quantified. These benefits primarily include the following:

Work load partitioning: The work load of the medical analysts has been partitioned to a finer level of understanding. The result is better control over the claim inventory, which is a major issue in managed health care.

Reduced online use: For claims that require checking historical claims (57 percent), ADJUDIPRO has reduced online access to the database by 83 percent. Some of the resource reduction is gobbled up during third shift when ADJUDIPRO is run, but central processing unit cycles are cheaper at that time.

Training: One of the UHC plans has used ADJUDIPRO reports to train new medical analysts and has noted that these reports greatly facilitated training.

Standardization: Prior to ADJUDIPRO, the medical analysts worked from notes in their CPT books and lists on their walls. Based on the assumption that humans make errors, this situation could be construed as a less than optimal environment for error-free work. As previously described, this information is now codified and used as input for a claim.

Architecture: The expertise of ADJUDIPRO will continue to grow as medical analysts request the automation of additional reviews. The general-purpose architecture that has evolved will provide a rapid development and deployment environment for future reviews.

Institutionalization: UHC medical and business entities are using ADJUDIPRO as a strategic tool for attacking new reviews (that is, new cost savings). Toftely was given responsibility for ADJUDIPRO as if it were another health plan that she oversees and will be accountable for cost savings.

Finally, we are in the process of positioning ADJUDIPRO as a service to sell to other managed care or indemnity companies. There are several technical and marketing challenges ahead to make it happen, but the process has begun.

Conclusion

ADJUDIPRO has opened the door for expert systems and AI technologies at UHC. Although skeptical at first, the users have embraced the technology and expect great, yet realistic results of ADJUDIPRO. New ideas for savings abound as the system and the technology gain momentum at UHC. ADJUDIPRO and advanced technologies have a bright future at UHC.

Acknowledgments

The authors of this chapter would like to acknowledge the invaluable efforts of many talented people: UHC's medical analysts; Advanced Technology's Strategic Development Team, which includes Joe Ampaabeng, Roleigh Martin, Scott McMahon, and David Williams; and Unisys's Applied Technology Group, most notably Nick Luzeski and Ed Sorensen.

References

Kirschner, C.; Coy, J.; Edwards, N.; Leoni, G.; McNamara O'Heron, M.; Pollack, A.; Ryan, C.; and Willard, D. 1992. *Physicians' Current Procedural Terminology.* Chicago: American Medical Association.

Pederson, K. 1989. *Expert Systems Programming: Practical Techniques for Rule-Based Systems.* New York: Wiley.

Template Software. 1989. Training Manual: Knowledge Engineering System. Herndon, Va.: Template Software.

Routing Applications

HUB SLAASHING
American Airlines

ARACHNE
NYNEX Science and Technology

HUB SIAASHING: A Knowledge-Based System for Severe, Temporary Airline Schedule Reduction

Trish Dutton, American Airlines

HUB SIAASHING is a knowledge-based system that recommends contingency plans for American Airlines System Operations Control (SOC) during inclement weather or other airport disruptions where severe schedule reductions must be made. The system evaluates the current situation to determine flight cancellation, delay, and overfly candidates that will provide relief at the hub airport with minimal impact on systemwide operations. HUB SIAASHING provides an expedient method for reducing the schedule by locating and ranking all possible candidate plans with explanations for these suggestions.[1]

Problem Description

SOC is the organization chartered by senior management with managing the daily operational events that have the potential to affect the safety, efficiency, or profitability of the airline. One of the major tasks for SOC is to ensure that the diverse requirements of individual departments are resolved to the best overall benefit of the airline and its customers when operational compromises are indicated by weather, mechanical problems, airport issues, air traffic control problems, fuel shortages, or other situations. The *operations coordinator* performs a control function that focuses on the macro level to ensure that American Airlines can operate as much of the schedule as possible. These tasks include monitoring the system to identify potential problem areas, identifying operating options, and coordinating irregular operations by selecting and implementing contingency plans (SABRE 1990).

When the situation is such that schedule reduction is necessary (for example, bad weather might force a 25-percent reduction in all inbound flights into Chicago for the next 2 hours), the operations coordinators devise and implement contingency plans that enable the airline to operate a maximum number of flights, provide the relief necessary, and minimize any negative impact on the airline and its customers. Prior to the deployment of HUB SIAASHING, SOC operations coordinators used printouts of several flight operations system (FOS) transactions to manually locate candidates for cancellation, delay, or overfly. They used colored markers to highlight candidates and proceeded to weed through the possibilities, ranking them manually. This process was labor intensive, taking as long as 12 hours in some cases.

FOS is a transaction-processing system containing information necessary to operate the airline, such as flight schedule data, aircraft information, and crew assignments. Because FOS is a near–real-time system, the printouts tended to become more and more outdated with each passing minute; therefore, the operations coordinators interfaced with several other departments within the airline (figure 1) to determine the current, actual situation at hand. For example, the crew scheduling area was contacted to make certain that crew legality issues could be handled if a particular plan was implemented or simply to check that the data on the printouts were up to date. The coordinators analyzed the historical market situation to ensure that they would not be canceling flights that had already been canceled. Passenger information, connections, and the possibility of reaccommodating people on later flights were researched. Discussions with maintenance took place to guarantee that aircraft could make scheduled maintenance if these aircraft were rerouted.

HUB SIAASHING automates many of the routine tasks. The search for the appropriate candidate patterns is done programmatically, saving time and allowing the operations coordinators to handle the more difficult situations. HUB SIAASHING locates the candidates for schedule reduction and assimilates much of the information necessary to facilitate educated decision making, thus minimizing the negative impact in

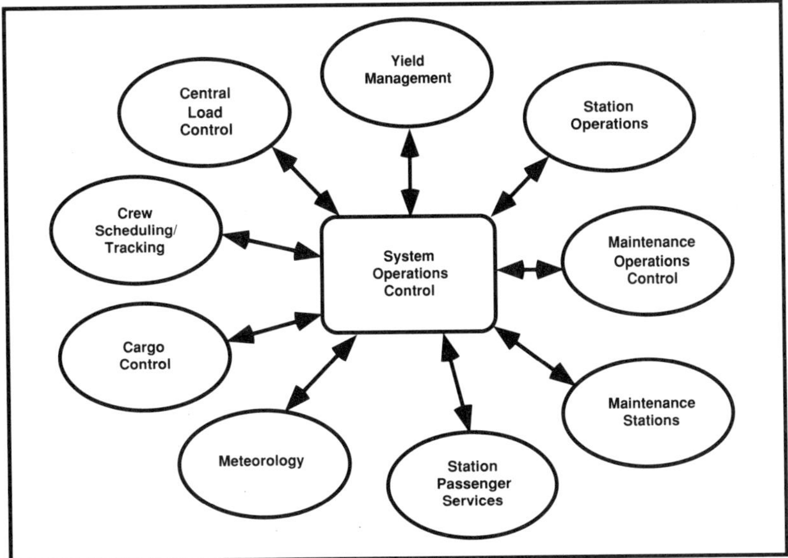

Figure 1. SOC Process Flow.

situations where it is impossible to operate all flights.

Application Objectives

The primary objective of the system is to provide a planning tool that assists the operations coordinators with decision making during irregular operations where temporary schedule reductions need to be implemented. Most importantly, HUB SIAASHING was to provide consistent planning for future events. Users are responsible for the safe and efficient operation of the airline and will not implement any plan that they do not fully understand. Therefore, the application was required to emulate the domain expertise to gain user acceptance.

This application had several additional objectives: The tool must vastly reduce the amount of time needed to implement contingency plans. It must provide explanations for the plans it suggests. The application must minimize system disruptions with regard to crew and aircraft routings. It must assist with minimizing passenger inconvenience. Any tool used in this dynamic, operational environment must be flexible and tailorable to the situation. Because most of the users are not computer literate, the application had to be intuitive to the user community. All applications deployed in SOC must use the existing hardware platform.

Importance of an AI Solution

An AI solution fit extremely well for this problem type. HUB SIAASHING uses knowledge-based technology integrated with a user interface and the corporation's computer facility. The problem is solved using rules to locate the patterns that the experts could find manually. Airlines are scheduled optimally and operated as best as possible, accounting for the weather, airport restrictions, equipment problems, and a number of other variables. A knowledge-based solution is the best technology to provide the flexibility to handle the dynamism, emulate the experts' search techniques, and provide the type of consistency necessary.

An AI solution was chosen because this technology would allow the knowledge engineers to focus on knowledge acquisition and use any number of expert system shells to provide the inferencing and knowledge representation that the domain required. The engineers were well versed in several shells on various hardware platforms, enabling them to spend more time with the experts and use rapid prototyping methodologies to quickly produce a working system. This application was successful because the use of an AI solution allowed it to meet all the project objectives in a short time frame and at little cost.

Previous Solution

An attempt was made to implement a similar system using traditional operations research techniques. The system did not suggest contingency plans; rather, it estimated the cost of canceling a particular flight segment. The users would still need to search for patterns that minimized the negative impact of reducing the schedule. The application was not well received because there was no explanation of results, it was inflexible, it used nonstandard hardware, and it did not reflect actual airline policies and decision making. The application developers did not interact with the users once requirements were defined and delivered a system that was perceived to be out of date.

Traditional approaches are inadequate for this problem because they do not allow for the flexibility required in this dynamic environment. Each event is different, and although airline policy drives decision making, the experience of senior operations coordinators is necessary to ensure that the choices selected for each situation are plans that can actually be implemented.

Traditional approaches require a longer time frame from initial concept to deployment than a rapid prototyping approach. The amount of interaction that knowledge engineers had with their users ensured that a more satisfactory solution had been found to their problem than the traditional method used in the failed attempt described earlier.

Application Description

HUB SIAASHING is meant to be used as a planning tool. It is typically used prior to actually executing schedule-reduction plans. The operations coordinators provide the application with pertinent input (for example, the hub station, time frame for the reduction, situational variables such as willingness to ferry airplanes.[2] They use the resulting suggestions and make final decisions regarding plan implementation. The users need a planning tool, not a reactionary tool. They are experts at reacting to problems and implementing appropriate corrective action but need assistance with timely planning for possible future events. Because they are tasked with making the minute-to-minute operational decisions, they tend to focus on the present, not on future problems. HUB SIAASHING assists them by providing this previously non-existent planning tool.

Environment: Hardware and Software

HUB SIAASHING is deployed on one MACINTOSH IIX with 16 megabytes of random-access memory and an accelerator card on an ETHERNET local area network (LAN) that contains over 350 individual workstations, 10 file servers, and 270 printers. The system interfaces with FOS for flight, crew, and passenger data and with MVS-TSO for market information.

SUPERCARD was used for development of the user interface. The knowledge-based system was entirely C based, written in THINK C and CLIPS (C-language integrated production system). CLIPS is a public-domain tool written by the National Aeronautics and Space Administration that was originally modeled on Inference Corporation's automated reasoning tool (ART-LISP). The shell provides a C implementation of the RETE algorithm and is portable across several hardware platforms (NASA 1991). Because the SOC hardware standard was MACINTOSH, the developers were limited to a couple of shells. Knowledge acquisition determined that the problem required a classic pattern-matching solution, easily managed with the RETE algorithm or other forward-chaining inferencing technique. Time precluded building the entire system in C; the developers were intimately familiar with CLIPS, so there was no learning curve, and using a shell simplified the development life cycle.

Architecture and Design

The application was designed with project objectives in mind, and the architecture had to ensure that it would be reliable and maintainable. It combines a knowledge base with traditional techniques such as parsing and report generation. The top-level design of the system is straightforward: a user interface and a knowledge-based system (figure 2).

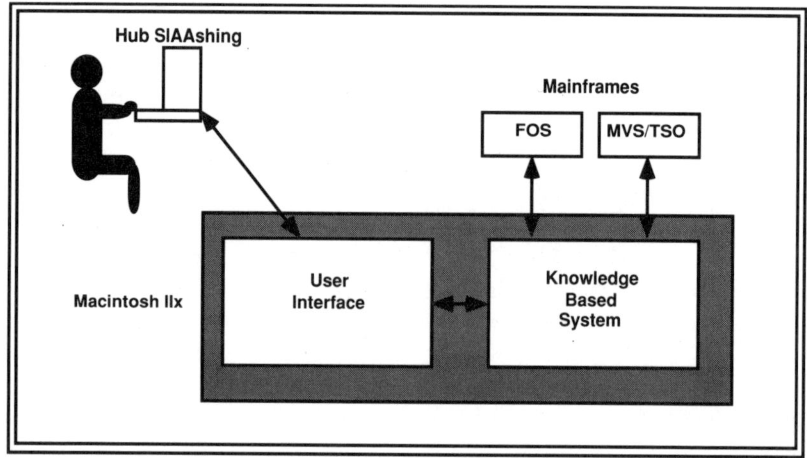

Figure 2. HUB SIAASHING *Top-Level Design.*

The user interface gathers the user's input parameters and launches the knowledge-based system. The knowledge-based system performs all other functions, including interacting with the corporation's computer facilities (specifically FOS and MVS-TSO), parsing and preprocessing data obtained from the various sources, locating the contingency plans through CLIPS rules, and formatting the results for display to the user. The knowledge-based system is divided into four major modules: the driver, the preprocessor, the knowledge base, and the formatter (figure 3). A library containing situational operands is loaded at run time, thus allowing for the flexibility so crucial to the success of the application.

The *driver* controls the processing. It makes calls to all other knowledge-based system modules, provides error-condition information, displays a status progression bar to the user, launches and controls the embedded CLIPS tool, and archives results to a file server.

The *preprocessor* performs the FOS and MVS-TSO downloading. It handles obtaining flight, crew, and passenger data from FOS, parses and abstracts the data, and builds CLIPS objects (templates). The preprocessor handles obtaining market files from TSO data sets. The functions were difficult to complete because the SOC environment uses Tri-Data Systems, Inc., NETWAY 3270 for TSO emulation, and the application programming interface for the MACINTOSH had not been completed by the vendor. The HUB SIAASHING developers were striking new ground with each line of code written.

The *knowledge base* contains rules to locate cancellation, overfly, and delay patterns in the current operating schedule and provides explana-

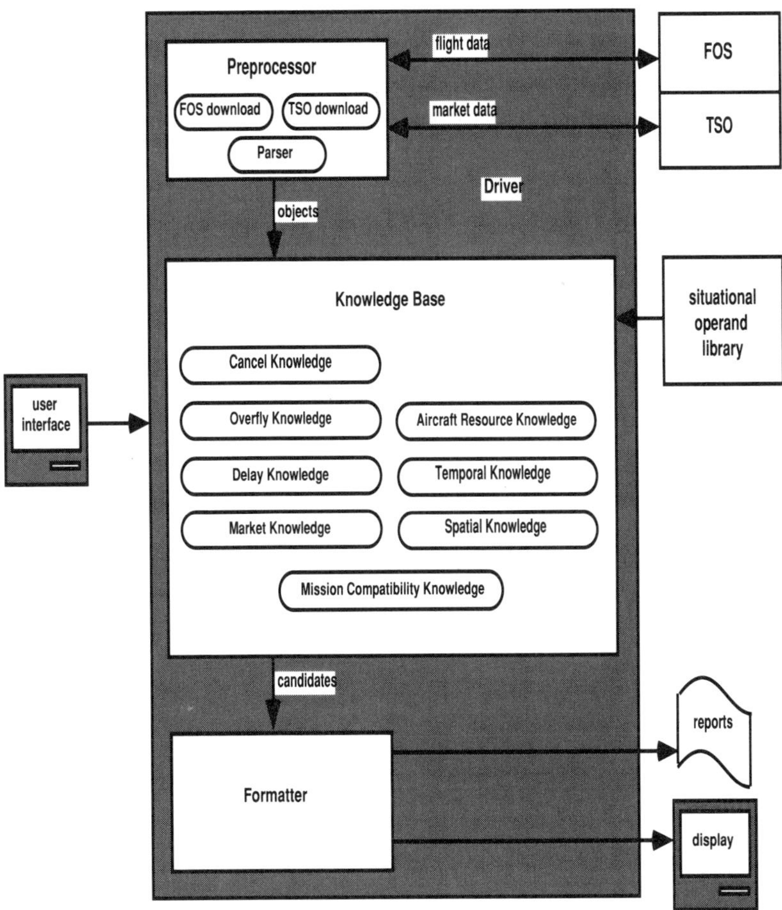

Figure 3. HUB SIAASHING *Knowledge-Based System Functional Diagram.*

tions for these suggestions. It uses airline policy, senior operations coordinator expertise, and situational operands to select and rank possible candidate plans. The rules are designed with ease of recovery from the irregular operation and minimal negative impact on systemwide operations built in. A *candidate plan* consists of flights that might be removed from the schedule, ensuring that the availability of aircraft and crews is balanced (figure 4) at all airports. For example, a basic scenario is to cancel one inbound and one outbound flight that are of the same equipment type, balance the schedule, and meet all situational constraints (figure 5).

The *formatter* prepares the results of the knowledge base for output

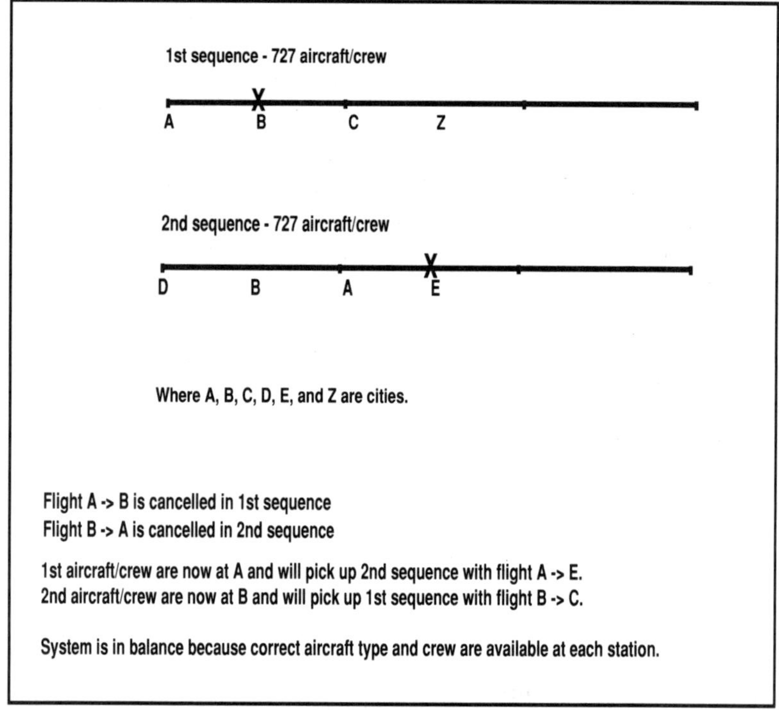

Figure 4. Example of System Balance.

to the user. Various user-tailored reports can be produced as an online display or as hard copy.

Innovations

HUB SIAASHING is an innovative application of an AI solution. Several reasons for making this statement are outlined in this subsection.

Traditional approaches used to solve similar problems at American Airlines had limited success and were not cost effective. In particular, a solution using operations research techniques was deployed with low user acceptance.

This knowledge-based system is the first for the SOC operations coordinators. It enhances the user's decision-making abilities and saves time during irregular operations by using pattern-matching and constraint-based reasoning to consistently locate schedule-reduction candidates and find a greater number of candidates than previously possible.

The system proves that a rapid-prototyping, phased approach using knowledge engineering techniques produces a quality system with high

IF

sequence pattern

<inbound flight + outbound flight>

meets passenger constraints AND

meets aircraft constraints AND

meets crew constraints AND

meets temporal constraints AND

meets spatial constraints AND

meets market constraints

THEN

possible cancellation candidate of rank X

with because-factors A B C ...

Figure 5. Typical Cancellation Rule.

user acceptance. Its development introduced a formal life-cycle methodology into SOC, where none had previously existed.

HUB SIAASHING demonstrates a novel integration between a MACINTOSH IIX workstation, the American Airlines FOS, and MVS-TSO. To my knowledge, interfacing a knowledge base on a MACINTOSH with the MVS-TSO environment had not been done before, anywhere in industry.

Application Justification

HUB SIAASHING is used by over 60 SOC personnel, including management, operations coordinators, crew scheduling personnel, and flight dispatchers. It is used on the average of one or two times each week, except in the winter when it is used almost daily.

Quantitative Benefits

The cost of a severe schedule-reduction day is measured in more than financial terms and differs with each event. It is widely known to be expensive, as much as $51,000 for each cancellation; therefore, any tool that enhances decision making is inherently beneficial. The cost of an unplanned cancellation (short notice) is three times that of a planned cancellation. HUB SIAASHING provides a tool for planning reduction in a more timely manner, thus reducing the cancellation costs.

The average length of time for implementation of schedule-reduction plans has decreased significantly. Locating plan patterns manually took an average of 8 hours; HUB SIAASHING accomplishes this task in less than 30 minutes. Each time the application is exercised to assist with an event, it saves the company over seven hours of labor costs alone. In the past, most irregular operations solutions were found while one or more operations coordinators was on overtime pay. This reduction in overtime is another labor expense savings.

The system locates candidates that would not otherwise be found because of time constraints during schedule-reduction sessions. Because the rules were designed with ease of recovery built in, it minimizes the number of cancellations required. As many as 30 percent more cancellations were required in the past to ensure the airline remained in balance.

HUB SIAASHING was developed in a short time for minimal cost. Total development cost was limited to hardware upgrades and labor. The software tools were already in house, so no additional expense was incurred.

Several application modules were slightly modified, at no cost to the user, to deploy a system for SOC crew coordinators to locate specific crew patterns. This type of code reusability is of great benefit at a time when most traditional software development costs continue to rise.

Applications deployed at American Airlines must provide return on investment within one year of implementation. HUB SIAASHING has fulfilled this obligation.

Qualitative Benefits

There are many qualitative benefits provided by HUB SIAASHING. This system allows SOC to plan at a closer temporal interval to the actual irregular operations without sacrificing the planning approach.

The system is intuitive to the user and looks and feels similar to other information sources he/she uses. The user knows exactly what the system provides and how to leverage the tool to facilitate better, well-informed decisions. By using situational operands, it is possible to manipulate the rules for optimal performance for the current situation.

Knowledge system developers forced a more formal implementation approach onto the application development group. Procedures are now in place at SOC that did not exist prior to this implementation. For example, no user sign-off procedures existed prior to the installation of the first prototype.

Application Development and Deployment

The application was developed using a rapid-prototyping, incremental-building methodology. The first version was deployed in four months, with two additional versions installed in 1991. Thus, the entire project was complete in approximately one year, each version taking three to four months to develop and deploy.

The development staff consisted of two knowledge engineers, one concentrating on the knowledge base and one focusing on communications, data preprocessing, and report generation. An application development programmer was on the staff to produce the user interface. A system analyst developed the user documentation and assisted with project management.

Knowledge Acquisition

Much of the development effort focused on knowledge acquisition and the determination of requirements. Prototypes were produced quickly and used in later knowledge-acquisition sessions for rule verification and as a tool to discover new knowledge that could be added to the knowledge base.

Engineers used interview techniques to learn of airline policy for schedule reduction. They employed bad weather simulation exercises with the expert operations coordinators to obtain actual operating rules. Crew scheduling personnel were interviewed to obtain crew situation knowledge. Yield management and operations analysis professionals were queried about market information. The knowledge engineers applied survey techniques to obtain operational commonsense information from the entire user community.

Validation and Verification

Complete validation of the application was done prior to deployment. Testing was performed throughout the development life cycle, with emphasis on close teamwork to ensure easy integration of all modules. Regression testing was performed for each version to ensure enhancements did not corrupt those functions already installed. Thorough system and user acceptance testing was performed on a test LAN that completely duplicated the production LAN environment, including use of actual data sources.

Training and User Acceptance

Because of the critical operational nature of SOC, training was accomplished one on one, with knowledge engineers training each of 66 users at the HUB SLAASHING workstation during users' regular work hours. Users had to remain on duty during training sessions. This training included the theory behind knowledge-based systems, description of each rule, concepts used in the application, and hands-on practice.

The airline policy rules were well known among the users. Rules based on the expertise of senior operations coordinators had, with few exceptions, complete user concurrence. User acceptance has been extremely good for applications deployed at SOC. The time taken to explain the application concepts to each individual has enabled them to trust the results. Now, when an event threatens a hub, the users reach for HUB SIAASHING to give them a head start at handling the situation.

Deployment

The system has been deployed formally since February 1991; although a prototype was installed in December 1990 for limited use. The current version was installed in December 1991. The application was deployed in two major steps. The first version was written almost entirely in CLIPS, containing seven basic sets of rules to locate candidates. It located simple cancellation patterns and was not situationally flexible. The final version contained 49 metarules to locate the candidate plans. The preprocessing and report-generation functions were rewritten in C rather than CLIPS. It selects more cancellation patterns as well as overfly and delay patterns. It is extremely flexible and can be tailored to the situation at hand.

The major problems encountered were system performance issues. The amount of data to be searched (American Airlines operates over 2300 flights each day) was enormous. Each flight has a flight template, at least two crew templates, market information, and passenger attributes associated with it. The RETE algorithm tends to use large amounts of memory, and it is time consuming to build the RETE network (pattern-join net). The number of possible plans, dependent on the number of flights at the hub during the time period in question, can be large. Even with the increase in functions, the second version of HUB SIAASHING was optimized to operate 45 percent faster than the first version.

Maintenance

HUB SIAASHING was designed to facilitate maintenance. The rules are generic in nature and will not require major modification. All pertinent operands are placed in tables that are input at run time to reduce the necessity of changes that require recompilation. These tables facilitate a vast range of application flexibility and have virtually no negative impact on execution speed. In the year since the first deployment, the only system maintenance has been two table updates. The users have control over many of the situational operand tables. Because the operation tends to change over time, it made good business sense to design this feature into the application.

It is anticipated that some maintenance might be required for the functions that interface with FOS and MVS-TSO, and the code was developed with this need in mind. All C code is in ANSI format and follows programming procedures outlined in the project documentation.

Conclusions

HUB SIAASHING is an innovative application that assists American Airlines with severe, temporary schedule reduction and minimizes the negative impact on our customers and systemwide operations. It is the first knowledge-based system for the operations coordinators, proves the approach is solid, and demonstrates a novel integration between the corporation's MVS-TSO facility and the MACINTOSH workstation. All project objectives were met: consistency and enhancement of decision making in this domain, flexibility, system performance, minimization of airline disruptions and passenger inconvenience, and development timeline and cost criteria.

Acknowledgments

Many thanks go to our experts Roger Beatty, John Schaefer, and Paul Prizzi; SOC managers Don Kneram, Kyle Phelps, Ed Gallagher, Doug Brown, and Paul Behm; Knowledge Systems engineers Judy Self and Bruce Kimball; Knowledge Systems managing director Lynden Tennison; and application developers Debbie Seals, Kevin Blackwell, and Virginia Dalfonso.

Notes

1. Airport disruptions are termed *irregular operations*. For example, an ice storm in Chicago forces the closure of a runway, and only 50 percent of the schedule might be operated. A *hub station* is an airport at which passengers, crews, and aircraft come together in complexes or banks to make connections (American Airlines currently has one international and six domestic hubs). A *cancellation* is a flight that cannot be operated. A *delay* is a flight that is operated later than its scheduled departure time. An *overfly* is a flight sequence that removes a stop at a hub. For example, the original sequence might be Las Vegas to Dallas–Fort Worth to Denver. An overfly would fly directly from Las Vegas to Denver, removing the stop at Dallas–Fort Worth.

2. A *ferry* moves an aircraft and crew(s) to a destination where needed. No passengers are aboard the flight.

References

NASA. 1991. CLIPS Reference Manual, Volume 1: CLIPS Version 5.0. Cape Canaveral, Fla.: National Aeronautics and Space Administration.

SABRE Computer Services SOC Operations Model, Working Paper, SABRE Computer Services, Dallas, Texas.

ARACHNE: Weaving the Telephone Network at NYNEX

Elissa Gilbert, Rangnath Salgame, Afshin Goodarzi, Yuling Lin, Sanjeev Sardana, and Jim Euchner, NYNEX Science, Inc.

The NYNEX Corporation invests hundreds of millions of dollars each year to enhance the telecommunications services provided to its customers. Extensive planning and construction are required to meet the ever-increasing demand for better service and provide the latest in sophisticated equipment throughout the telephone network. Engineering groups plan changes to network facilities five years ahead, with constant adjustments for changes to forecasted service demand, changes in the economy, changes to NYNEX company policies, or the availability of new technologies.

ARACHNE is an expert system that automates interoffice facilities (IOF) network planning in New England Telephone and New York Telephone, NYNEX subsidiaries. ARACHNE was deployed for planning the IOF networks in the New York City metropolitan area and most of New England. It dramatically reduced the overall planning time and improved the quality of the network plans. In its first production run, it identified potential capital savings of over $10 million in Massachusetts alone through expense avoidance and capital recovery.

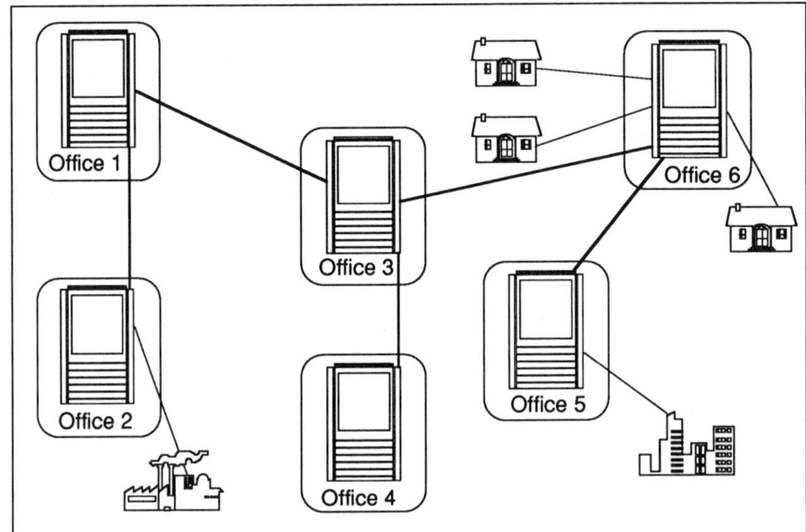

Figure 1. A Simple Telephone Network.

ARACHNE Overview

A simple telephone network is shown in figure 1. Switching equipment is located at nodes called *central offices.* These offices are connected to customer premises (forming the *local loop*) and each other (forming the *IOF network*). The physical links between nodes can be copper cables, fiber optic cables, or microwaves. The transmission on these links can be digital or analog.

ARACHNE uses a five-year forecast of expected IOF network demand—together with information specific to each central office, data about the existing network, and expert planning rules—to create a carrier program. A completed *carrier program* is a plan to meet the forecasted demand between any two central offices in the network. The plan includes transmission facilities that must be added or disconnected to satisfy the demand in an economical way together with the schedule for implementing these changes, a design for routing the services, and the equipment to be used.

We had to address several major technical and business issues for ARACHNE to be successful. Chief among these issues was the complexity of the planning domain. To be planned properly, the IOF network must be viewed as composed of several levels, corresponding to the digital services hierarchy shown in table 1. Each level of the digital hierarchy requires its own transmission equipment (for multiplexing and demultiplexing at the nodes) and uses available channel capacity at the

Table 1. Digital Services Hierarchy.

Signal Level	**Bit Rate**	**Channel Capacity**
DS0	64 Kbs	1 voice circuit
DS1 (T1)	1.544 Mbs	24 DS0
DS3 (T3)	45 Mbs	28 DS1
Optical System (HICAP)	90 Mbs–1.1 Gbs	Nonstandard

next signal level. Planning the IOF network requires providing sufficient capacity at each level.

The overall plan for any level is composed of plans for the individual links between pairs of nodes. The plan for each link involves many decisions, including *sizing* (determining needed capacity), *timing* (determining when to add capacity or when to remove excess capacity), routing onto transmission facilities at the next level, selecting the technology to use, and selecting the equipment to use. The IOF planner's objective is to come up with the most cost-effective solution for satisfying demand that takes into account such considerations as the demand, the existing capacity, engineering considerations, evolving network technologies, competitive positioning in the industry, maintenance costs, network reliability, and internal company policies.

Developing an ideal network plan is an inherently recursive problem in that the plan created at one level of the digital service hierarchy has implications for the ideal plan created at both higher and lower levels of the hierarchy. A purely algorithmic solution is not possible because the problem is nonlinear, nonnumeric, and qualitative. A purely heuristic approach cannot be used because there are no heuristics for achieving global optimization. We needed to develop a planning approach that combined heuristic and algorithmic solutions.

Another issue was the size of the network. NYNEX's network has a large number of central offices and an even larger number of links. The sheer volume of information precludes the possibility of working with all the network data simultaneously. We needed to find a way to partition the problem into manageable-sized pieces if we were going to be able to develop a solution.

Integrating ARACHNE with the existing corporate database systems was also a critical issue. NYNEX's databases record both the current and planned state of the network. ARACHNE had to be able to obtain input from these databases and return output to them. The databases involved are external products (from Bell Communications Research, Inc., [Bellcore]) and have new releases several times a year. This setup created a serious risk of obsolescence if ARACHNE could not keep pace

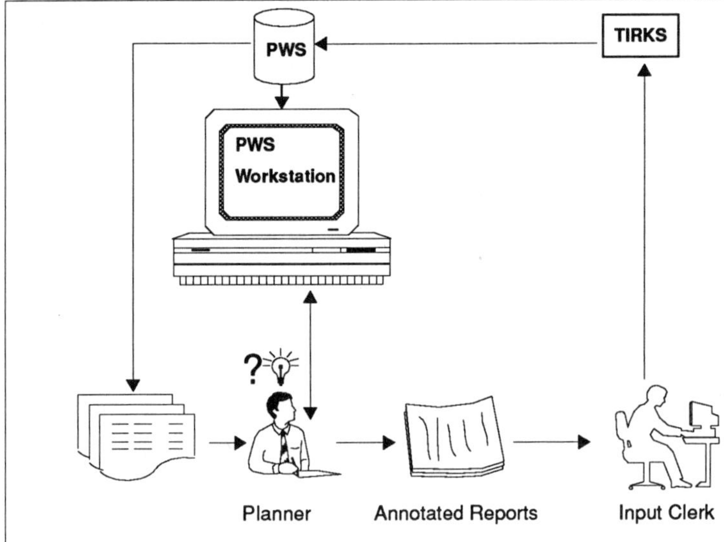

Figure 2. Planning before ARACHNE.

with these changes.

A final important issue was the impact of planning decisions. Implementing network plans can take from several months to more than a year. At any point in time, many future planning decisions are at least partially committed and have already incurred expenditures. Therefore, it is highly desirable that the plans not be too sensitive to minor changes in the business environment. ARACHNE had to be able to respond to changes as well as know when not to respond to changes.

All these issues meant that developing a working system would be a challenge; it would clearly be a long-term effort with uncertain results. However, the shortcomings of the pre-ARACHNE planning process indicated the effort would be worthwhile.

Planning before ARACHNE

The manual planning process used before ARACHNE is shown in figure 2. The trunks integrated record-keeping system (TIRKS) and the planning workstation (PWS), both Bellcore products, were used by the planners. TIRKS, an IMS-based system running on IBM mainframes, contains the facility inventory and network plans, and is a major database system used throughout NYNEX. PWS is a front end to TIRKS that serves as a reporting mechanism for the planners; it is a RAMIS-based database system also running on IBM mainframes.

NYNEX's forecasting group creates a forecast of the IOF network demand twice each year. The forecast is loaded into PWS at the start of the network-planning process. When planning was done manually, the planners reviewed reports generated by PWS for each link at each level of the network. They compared the forecasted and planned supply and altered the plan as needed. Changes were marked on the PWS reports and given to clerks for entry into TIRKS. There were several problems with this process:

Time: Manual review of the plan took months. It was difficult for planners to complete the process on time.

Quality and consistency: The planners have varying levels of expertise (many experienced personnel recently retired), which resulted in plans of inconsistent quality. There was no way to ensure that planners followed the company's guidelines and policies consistently.

Incompleteness: Because of the network's large size, the planners concentrated their efforts on planning the critical parts of the network, where there was insufficient supply to provide service for the forecasted demand. They often didn't have time to review oversupplied links that have equipment that could be disconnected and used elsewhere in the network.

Localized views: Each planner was responsible for only a limited part of the network. This approach made it difficult to ensure good global results.

Changing environment: The business, technological, and regulatory environment the telephone companies operate in changes rapidly. In the absence of automated planning tools, the planners' ability to react to change by modifying plans was limited.

All these reasons indicated that an automated planning process would have major benefits for NYNEX.

Previous Automation Attempts

To our knowledge, ARACHNE is the first and only expert system to address the domain of IOF network planning in the telecommunications industry. Although partial system support for planning existed previously, ARACHNE is the only system that addresses the complexity of the planning process and provides the flexibility required by the planning organizations at NYNEX.

PWS currently provides an automatic planning feature. However, it performs only the sizing and timing part of the planning, and it does

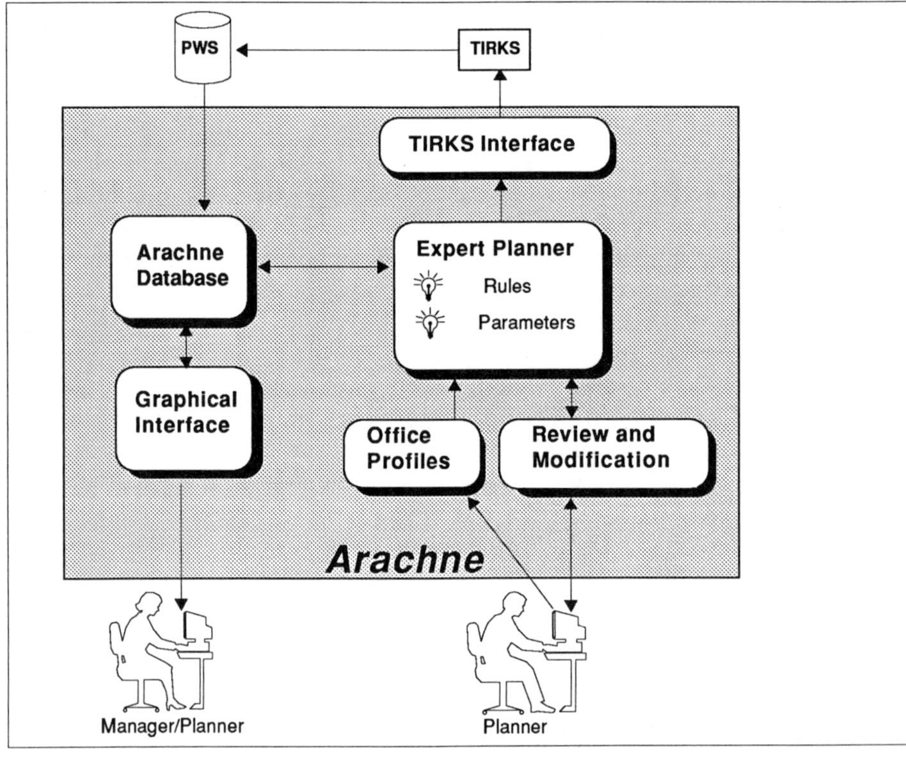

Figure 3. Planning with ARACHNE.

so in an incomplete manner. It plans to disconnect facilities only if the demand drops to zero and remains there until the end of the five-year planning period; it does not plan disconnects if demand is only reduced, not eliminated. It does not check the route used by the facilities it adds; it simply uses the old design without looking for a better design. Additionally, automatic planning in PWS is guided strictly by the forecast of network demand. However, there are known errors in the forecast that the planners must correct. Neither New York Telephone nor New England Telephone used the automatic planning feature of PWS. Because ARACHNE was tailored to the needs of New York Telephone and New England Telephone, it provides the capabilities and flexibility they require.

ARACHNE Architecture

ARACHNE was developed using a combination of traditional programming techniques and advanced technology. Figure 3 shows an overview of the system architecture. This architecture enabled us to address the issues identified earlier.

ARACHNE runs on a SUN workstation. Its major components are three expert system modules developed with Common Lisp and KEE (an expert system shell that provides both rules and objects): an internal relational database implemented in ORACLE; a C-based graphic interface for viewing the IOF network and plans; and an interface to TIRKS for uploading ARACHNE's plans, also developed in C.

ARACHNE's three expert system components plan different levels of the digital service hierarchy. One module plans the DS0 level, one module plans the DS1 level, and one module plans the DS3 and high-capacity optical system (HICAP) levels of the IOF network. These three modules are independent and communicate only through the ORACLE database. They have similar internal architectures. Each has two knowledge bases, one containing information about central office characteristics (called *office profiles*), the other containing the planning rules.

The rule base is implemented in Lisp. Early prototypes of ARACHNE used KEE's rules, but as the development process continued, we decided to stop using the rule language and implement the rules as functions in Lisp. Much of the planning must be performed in a certain order. A complex set of metarules would have been required to ensure that the rules executed in the correct order. Also, the rules are complex and require many support functions and mechanisms, also written in Lisp. They combine heuristics with greedy bin-packing algorithms and operations research techniques such as dynamic programming.

ARACHNE's planning heuristics incorporate long-term strategies to ensure that the network continues to grow according to strategic plans and not be overly reactive to local or transient fluctuations. Other heuristics guide the planning process to achieve corporate objectives such as quality of service and modernization of facilities.

The issue of domain complexity is addressed through the partitioning into three expert systems and through the combination of heuristic and algorithmic techniques. ARACHNE's DS0 and DS1 modules, where the volume of data is exceptionally large, try to achieve optimization on only the local level. The DS3-HICAP module, which deals with a smaller volume of data, is able to optimize network planning globally as well. Although this simplification does not result in a fully optimal plan, it does improve the plans produced by the network planners, who were responsible for planning geographically defined areas and were never able to address issues of global optimization. Because major capital costs are incurred at the DS3 and HICAP levels of the network, even this partial optimization is a significant benefit.

ARACHNE's combination of programming techniques addresses the

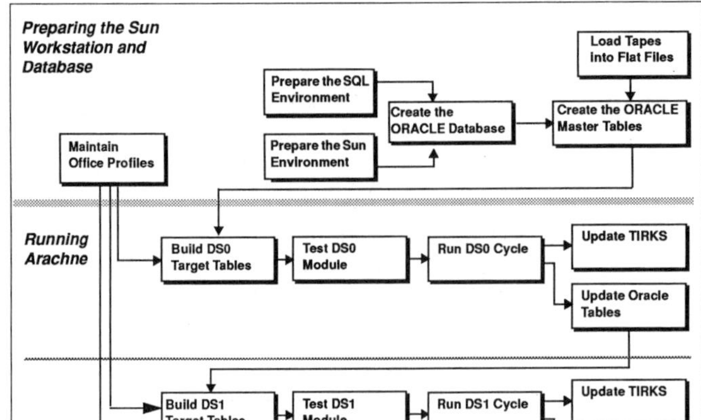

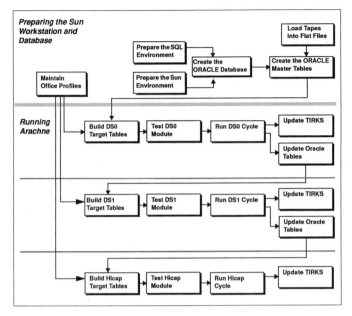

Figure 4. ARACHNE *Planning Process.*

conflicting objectives inherent in network planning: increasing overall network use while achieving local optimization. Dynamic programming techniques were employed for global optimization, but heuristics were used for local optimization. The methodology and algorithms developed at NYNEX for ARACHNE have been awarded a patent by the U.S. Patent Office ("Method and apparatus for planning telephone facilities networks," patent number 5,067,148).

The partitioning of ARACHNE into three expert systems addresses the size consideration as well. Not all nodes in the network need to be considered in all the levels of planning. Additionally, because the DS0 and DS1 modules focus on local optimizations only, they never require data about the entire IOF network simultaneously. This partitioning makes the volume of data tractable.

ARACHNE is loosely coupled with the external systems TIRKS and PWS. The expert system modules do not directly interact with the corporate databases, allowing most changes in the external systems to be addressed by ARACHNE's interface modules only. ARACHNE's input (the demand forecast and current network plans) comes from PWS as ASCII files, which are loaded into the ORACLE database. The expert systems use KEE LINK to download relevant data from ORACLE and create appropriate data structures (often KEE frames). ARACHNE generates SQL transactions to update the ORACLE database; thus, the input at the next level of ARACHNE correctly reflects the new plan. ARACHNE also creates files of transactions to be uploaded to TIRKS through screen emulation. These transactions place network plans (suggested adds, disconnects, and designs) into the corporate database where they can be accessed by other users. Planners can review, accept, reject, or modify any plans prior to updating the databases. The planners, not ARACHNE, retain the final authority and responsibility for the network plans.

ARACHNE Planning Process

Planning with ARACHNE begins after the demand forecast has been loaded into PWS. Figure 4 shows the ARACHNE planning process. At the start of the planning cycle, the ARACHNE system administrator (a member of the planning department who is responsible for running ARACHNE) collects central office information and updates the office profiles. The system administrator also sets various parameters for each module's planning. These parameters include such items as thresholds for triggering various rules.

The DS0 module is run first. For each central office to be planned, the DS0 module downloads the forecast of demand and the existing routes from ORACLE. Based on the demand, the DS0 module routes the circuits onto DS1 facilities. After the DS0 planning is completed, DS1 planning begins.

The DS1 module downloads the forecast, designs, and current and planned supply of each central office to be planned. There are four subtasks within DS1 planning: demand analysis, design analysis, augment analysis, and disconnect analysis. The *DS1 demand analysis* compares the forecasted demand to the supply in the network and proposes to add or disconnect DS1 facilities as needed to satisfy demand. When the expert system was first built, this algorithm was simple: ARACHNE always ensured the minimum supply needed to satisfy the demand. Since this time, several heuristics have been added because there is activity in the network that is not included in the forecast. One heuristic increases the forecasted demand to provide some buffer in case of unanticipated growth; the amount added depends on the forecast for that link and a parameter set by the system administrator. Another heuristic looks at current activity in the network initiated by a human being and ensures that ARACHNE does not plan contradictory actions; people have access to outside information and might have reasons for the activity that ARACHNE does not know about.

The *DS1 module's design analysis* routes the DS1 demand onto DS3 facilities. The *augment analysis* then schedules the addition of new facilities and determines their characteristics (using information from the office profiles). The *DS1 disconnect analysis* schedules any needed disconnects and selects the specific facilities to be disconnected, considering both the technology and the amount of work required.

After DS1 planning is complete, the DS3-HICAP planning module is run. At this level of planning, the volume of data is small enough to allow the KEE module to handle all the network information at once. Thus, the planning module is allowed to achieve global optimization rather than the local optimizations achieved by the DS0 and DS1 modules.

DS3 planning has three parts: demand analysis, design analysis, and demand allocation. The *DS3 demand analysis* looks at the utilization of each DS3 link (measured as demand/capacity) and attempts to keep it within a certain range. There is a tolerance period during which the use can be outside this range, limiting the volatility of ARACHNE's plans. DS3 facilities are added or disconnected, as required, to keep the use within the desired range.

The DS3 design analysis routes the DS3 facilities ontoHICAP facilities using information from the profiles and a recursive algorithm guided by a set of heuristics to determine the ideal route. The routing algorithm has two phases, which are applied iteratively until equilibrium is reached (both recommend the same route). The first phase augments the topology of the network by creating new links between central offices. The second phase improves capacity use by carrying out local or nonlocal optimizations.

The *DS3 module's demand allocation* adjusts the HICAP demand for new or disconnected DS3 facilities. Then, the HICAP level is planned. HICAP planning has three parts: demand analysis, technology selection, and routing onto fiber. The *HICAP demand analysis* provides the minimum supply to meet DS3 demand and determines which HICAP technology will be used (*technology selection*). Two designs are formed for the HICAP facilities using the same recursive algorithm and heuristics as the DS3 routing. One design is called the *service route* and is the best route; the other, a *protection route*, uses entirely different fiber cables and enhances network reliability. After the HICAP routes are created, the fiber level of the network is planned, requiring a demand analysis and the addition of new fiber, as needed.

Development and Deployment Experience

ARACHNE's development took approximately 2-1/2 years. An estimated

15 person-years of developer time, plus 2 to 3 person-years of expert time, have been spent developing and supporting ARACHNE. The three expert system modules were developed in parallel. Each module had a different programmer, although the experts were shared across modules. The modules finished development at approximately the same time, although the DS3-HICAP module took slightly longer because of its greater complexity.

ARACHNE was developed through an informal prototyping methodology. The experts were located in Massachusetts, but the developers were in New York, so extensive telephone contact, as well as occasional meetings, was used to refine the rule base. The prototypes were tested several times during the development process, and numerous corrections and enhancements to the rules resulted from the experts' review of the modules. In some cases, the experts agreed that ARACHNE was correctly applying rules they themselves used, but once they were able to see the impact of the rules on a more global scale, they realized that the rules did not produce the best plan. New rules were created and experimented with until the experts were satisfied. Thus, ARACHNE's development did not merely capture expert knowledge; it enriched and enhanced this knowledge as well.

One drawback to the informal prototyping process and the lack of a formal specification or requirements document was that it was difficult to tell when development was done. When the experts and their managers saw the capabilities of early versions of the system, they requested more and more functions. Coding the extra functions delayed our testing of the final release, system version 1.0. Finally, we were told by the managers that they liked the system, and they wanted—needed—to use it immediately.

Therefore, we were forced to deploy ARACHNE before the system had been tested to our satisfaction. The individual modules had been tested, both through unit testing of the Lisp code and function testing with the experts, but no integration testing or validation of the database updates had been done (these tasks had been scheduled for the end of the development process, which never came). We proceeded extremely cautiously because of the incomplete testing and because procedures for running ARACHNE had not been finalized, formalized, or documented.

The first two runs of ARACHNE became combined test-production runs. Test cases were selected prior to the runs after a careful review of the domain. Each module's plans were reviewed for about a week, and rule changes, including several major ones, were implemented on site. Only after the experts were satisfied with ARACHNE's plans for the selected cases was it run for the entire region and its output uploaded to the corporate database. Approximately six weeks were spent on each of these ARACHNE runs. By the third use of ARACHNE (July 1991), planner confidence in ARACHNE was high. Only a few hours were spent reviewing output, no major code changes were considered, and planning each level required only a few days. The most recent runs have been similarly short, with planning concluded within three weeks.

The initial development of ARACHNE focused on New England Telephone. Following its first run there, our emphasis shifted to modifying the rules as needed by New York Telephone. The two companies use similar but not identical rules. Currently, there is one set of code, with parameters specifying whether to use the New York or New England rules. Some rule changes under consideration for New York Telephone might eventually lead to two distinct sets of code. Two code sets is a serious maintenance issue that has not yet been resolved.

Another serious issue that has not yet been resolved concerns ARACHNE's basic structure. Although the current architecture successfully addresses the design challenges identified three years ago, changes in the planning process have added dependencies between the different levels of the IOF network as well as among links within a level. It is not certain that we will be able to address these issues within the current architecture.

Impact of ARACHNE

Following each run, a significant effort was made to analyze the impact and benefits of the ARACHNE plan.

ARACHNE has had significant monetary benefits for the telephone companies. Operational savings of $2 million have been identified. However, the major savings from ARACHNE result from reduced capital expenditures (ARACHNE suggests new construction only where needed) and opportunities for capital recovery identified by ARACHNE (the company can remove unused equipment and use it elsewhere in the network). In its first run at New England Telephone, ARACHNE identified $10 million in potential capital savings; total savings identified to date are over $20 million. Quantifying the actual benefits is difficult because the planning environment is so dynamic that the plan created by ARACHNE might not be carried out fully because of changes in the forecasted demand.

Other monetary savings are anticipated. ARACHNE's speed of planning allows a long lead time for equipment recommendations, thus reducing the likelihood of incurring premium charges for unanticipated rush jobs. The reduction of errors also saves costs because less rework is required. The reduced planning load results in work force savings.

In addition to providing financial benefits, ARACHNE's plans improve the quality of the network. The improvements to existing planning rules, the introduction of new planning rules, and the consistent and exhaustive application of the best planning rules resulted in superior carrier programs. The new designs created by ARACHNE improve a network measurement called *routing efficiency*, making better use of the existing base network, and improve network use. These improvements should eventually reduce network maintenance costs. Through the designs it creates, ARACHNE also promotes routing diversity in the network, improving its reliability.

ARACHNE also assists with the introduction of new technologies and new services. The rapid dissemination of new planning rules and strategies shortens the interval between the availability of new technology and its effective use in the network. Company policies, such as replacing copper cable with fiber and the use of optical systems, were incorporated into ARACHNE's planning strategies and implemented throughout the network.

ARACHNE has had a qualitative impact on the planning process itself. Because of ARACHNE, the planners feel they are able to make decisions based on quality rather than expedience. Because ARACHNE's plans are accurate and are completed quickly, better annual budget estimates can be prepared; the reduced planning interval allows the construction program to be more closely aligned with the forecast. Planners are able to react more quickly to internal and external changes. They now have time to review the impact of the plans on the network and make changes and are able to concentrate on solving new problems and investigating new network technologies. The reduced planning time yields a longer lead time for allocating resources and carrying out the plans.

The planners have begun to use ARACHNE for tasks in addition to the routine planning. Although ARACHNE does not currently have true what-if functioning, the planners identified a way to use ARACHNE to help them perform a study of network survivability and diversity issues. We anticipate that such studies will become more common in the future as the users become more experienced with the system.

Conclusion

Although the major development of ARACHNE is complete, there is a strong possibility of continuing work. Some work is necessary simply to keep up with the changing environment; for example, a new technology, SONET, is being introduced into the network in 1992 and requires different planning strategies. Other potential work includes the implementation of true what-if capability to allow the planners to experiment with different rules. We are also investigating demand forecasting; because the forecast drives the planning process, an improved forecast has obvious benefits. A generalized network-planning platform is also being considered.

We also plan to expand the use of ARACHNE throughout NYNEX. Its first use was in the state of Massachusetts and the New York City metropolitan area. New England Telephone has since expanded its use to Rhode Island, New Hampshire, Vermont, and Maine, and New York Telephone is considering its use in upstate New York. Some rule modifications might be necessary at that time.

ARACHNE's success is largely owed to its hybrid approach to problem solving. Its effective combination of heuristics and algorithmic approaches enables it to efficiently augment capacity in a network without a fixed topology. It has now become a routine part of the planning process, and we anticipate enhancing its capabilities to ensure that its benefits will continue to be realized in every planning cycle.

Acknowledgments

ARACHNE could not have been developed without the active support and participation of engineers and management from both New England Telephone (Bruce Spinney, John Curran, John Switzer, Deborah Druvins, William Uliasz) and New York Telephone (Craig Soloff, Andy Jingeleski, Arnold Woo, Chitra Alesi, Mike Algeri, Joe Bartone, Ken Monahan). Other members of NYNEX Science and Technology who participated in the development effort are Ivy Eisenberg, Larry Finkel, Pierre-Yves Guillo, John Martin, Gary Sevitsky, Erik Urdang, and Poh-Yee Wong (from the National Computer Board of Singapore).

Software Development

ICICLE
Bellcore

Sequence Control
Toshiba Corporation

Knowledge-Based Code Inspection with ICICLE

Laurence R. Brothers, Velusamy Sembugamoorthy, and Adam E. Irgon, Bellcore

ICICLE[1] (intelligent code inspection in a C language environment) is a multifaceted software system developed with components from several technologies, including AI, computer-supported cooperative work (CSCW), and software technology. It is intended to support the process of formal code inspection within the software development cycle. This chapter reports on ICICLE in the context of its successful deployment at Bell Communications Research, Inc. (Bellcore) for code inspection and discusses its design and operation with particular emphasis on its AI components.

The Problem: Code Inspection

In this section, we review software development and the telecommunications industry. We also analyze the techniques of code inspection, manual and intelligent.

Software Development and the Telecommunications Industry

Modern telecommunications companies are heavily dependent on software in virtually all aspects of running their businesses. When a customer calls the telephone company and asks for telephone service, customer service representatives use a host of software systems to determine the customer's current status, verify information about the customer, determine what services the customer might want (often supported by sales advice expert systems), and initiate the customer's order. Initiated orders are sent to other software systems that provision the order, selecting and configuring the facilities and equipment that can implement the customer's requested services. Other systems monitor and operate the network on an ongoing basis: electronic switching systems connect calls; software routes calls in the network dynamically; and software systems monitor the health of the network, providing alarms as needed and in some cases fixing problems automatically.

The systems used to run the day-to-day business of the telephone companies are referred to collectively as operations support systems (OSSs). Development of OSSs is a major part of the services of Bellcore, which was created at AT&T's divestiture in 1984 to provide centralized services to the divested Bell Operating Companies.

This ubiquity of software in telecommunications results in a strategic edge for companies deploying advanced software systems. At the same time, bugs in telecommunications software systems can be catastrophic, as the recent network breakdown in the New York metropolitan area illustrated (Russell 1991). The loss of customers' goodwill because of network outages such as this one can have enormous financial impact on a company. At best, the act of fixing bugs in telecommunications software systems is expensive; we estimate that in 1990, Bellcore spent approximately $65 million fixing bugs. Accordingly, the pressure to make software development quality and productivity gains is powerful.

Manual Code Inspection

In an influential paper, Fred Brooks (1987) argued that no techniques will fundamentally transform software development quality and productivity. Rather, gains will be incremental, as in the case of code inspection. *Code inspection* is a phase of software development intermediate between implementation and testing. It is a rigorous, formalized process that is rapidly replacing informal code reviews in companies such as IBM (Dobbins 1987; Fagan 1976), AT&T Bell Labs (Ackerman 1984), BellNorthern Research (Murray 1985), and Bellcore because it offers significant software quality and long-term maintenance benefits.

Inspection involves using the knowledge of a team of expert developers, designers, and application-domain experts to achieve reduction of errors and more understandable software. Ideally, code inspection should be performed on all new or significantly changed code, a goal Bellcore has set. Such inspection pays off handsomely in software quality gains but also carries a heavy cost. Code inspections are painstaking, time consuming, and knowledge intensive. Code inspectors must apply a wide variety of knowledge, including design, programming, and application-domain knowledge. In general, it is difficult to find a code inspector who is an expert in all these areas. Often, even experienced code inspectors suffer from cognitive overload.

The nature of code inspections makes them expensive and often unpopular with software developers. The tendency of software development projects to be behind schedule has been well documented (Brooks 1975). In addition, customer demands for new, increasingly sophisticated services supported by rapidly changing technology put software development organizations under pressure to develop systems faster, cheaper, and better, often at the expense of code inspection.

Code inspection is broken into several phases, the two most important of which are comment preparation and the code-inspection meeting.

Comment Preparation: Using the distributed materials, code inspectors individually analyze the code and prepare comments relating to bugs and deviations from coding standards, requirements, and design specifications.

Code-Inspection Meeting: On the scheduled day, the inspection team meets, discusses the comments prepared earlier, analyzes the code wherever necessary, and finalizes the list of comments. Also, certain statistics such as the number and types of errors found and time spent are obtained. These data are used for monitoring the effectiveness of code inspection in the organization.

Several difficulties are associated with these two phases. In comment preparation, the problems are mainly cognitive, focusing on the inability of a single developer to understand source code written by another in a limited amount of time and once understanding the code to be able comment on it. In the code-inspection meeting, the problems are mainly secretarial and administrative: The rigorous and formal requirements of the code-inspection procedures described by Fagan (1976) and Ackerman and his colleagues (Ackerman 1984; Ackerman, Buschwald, and Lewski 1989) are desirable for the reasons they discuss but also make actual participation in such meetings unpleasant and tedious. These problems are not insuperable, but together, they have combined to make code inspection unpopular in many development organizations and have reduced the overall value of the activity where it does take place.

Intelligent Code Inspection

Given the previously described difficulties with code inspection, our task was simple: to provide systems that seek to eliminate the negative aspects of the process yet accentuate the positives.

ICICLE (Brothers, Sembugamoorthy, and Muller 1990; Rich 1986) is a software system developed at Bellcore that augments and improves on manual code inspection by computerizing many of the problem-solving tasks that underlie code inspection. For some years, C has been the programming language of choice in Bellcore, and accordingly, ICICLE is for C program inspection. ICICLE has been designed to accommodate other languages, such as C++, as they increase in popularity.

Ideally, a code-inspection system should have the following virtues:

First, from the point of view of the user, a code inspector, it should make code inspection much more palatable as a task and easy to perform, reducing cognitive load and secretarial tedium, thus increasing the likelihood that it will actually be done.

Second, from the point of view of the manager of a development project, it should reduce the time and resources needed to inspect code and improve the overall quality of inspections by automating a range of tasks previously done manually and assisting inspectors in better performing some tasks that are not amenable to complete automation.

These goals can be accomplished by targeting the two difficult phases of code inspection with specific functions:

First, during comment preparation, code inspectors employ informal static debugging techniques to detect coding errors. The inspectors also work to understand the code and check whether the code meets the requirements and design specifications. A computer-aided code-inspection environment should provide tools to aid static debugging, checking coding standards violations, browsing through various kinds of code-inspection knowledge (such as manual pages, library function specifications), and above all integrate these tools in a user-friendly human interface.

Second, during code-inspection meetings, the team of inspectors meet to reach consensus on problems with the program under inspection. A good computer-aided code-inspection system should support this cooperative effort by computerizing the communications between inspectors, enabling the team members to maintain their focus of attention without being required to resort to paper listings, permit comment integration and recording with a minimum of effort, and also make the secretarial and administrative burden of the meeting as light as possible.

ICICLE Design and Architecture

In this section, we discuss the design and architecture of ICICLE. We examine the integration of multiple technologies for code inspection; ICE, the expert system within ICICLE, the human interface for comment preparation; and the automation of the code-inspection meeting by ICICLE.

Integrating Multiple Technologies for Code Inspection

As a result of the analysis previously described, we realized the need to combine components from several technologies.

To support the efforts of an individual code inspector to understand the code, we needed to provide a sophisticated human interface capable of browsing and navigating source code in different interconnected files. We also needed to be able to present the results of the analyses of software tools such as cross-referencers in an understandable and easy-to-use fashion. The effect of human program understanding in the comment-preparation phase is the compilation of a set of comments about the code. With a knowledge-based debugging tool and conventional debugging tools such as LINT (Johnson 1983), we could provide an automatically generated set of comments. Some of these comments pertain to problems in the code that might otherwise have been overlooked by the human inspector, and other comments might help the inspector to better understand what the original programmer was trying to do.

The activities of the inspectors during the code-inspection meeting are primarily administrative and secretarial in nature but can also occasionally involve some of the same activities as in comment preparation. To support the conduct of the code-inspection meeting, we had to provide groupware to enable inspectors to carry out all the meeting procedures online but still retain the capabilities of the interface used for comment preparation.

The architecture that supports these multifarious activities is shown in figure 1. ICICLE's current components include the following: (1) a human interface for effective presentation of information and interaction with the user (also manages annotation and comments, as provided by either the human user or other automatic subsystems, and contains connections to various software tool interfaces) (2) groupware for supporting the cooperative effort of code-inspection meetings, (3) software tools for static debugging and providing useful program-understanding aids such as cross-referencing information, and (4) an expert system to represent expert developers' knowledge for detecting programming errors and violations of coding standards.

ICICLE's architecture is modular. Because all the analysis tools are interfaced with the human interfaces through text files, it is easy to add new analysis tools (for example, complexity analysis tools, program

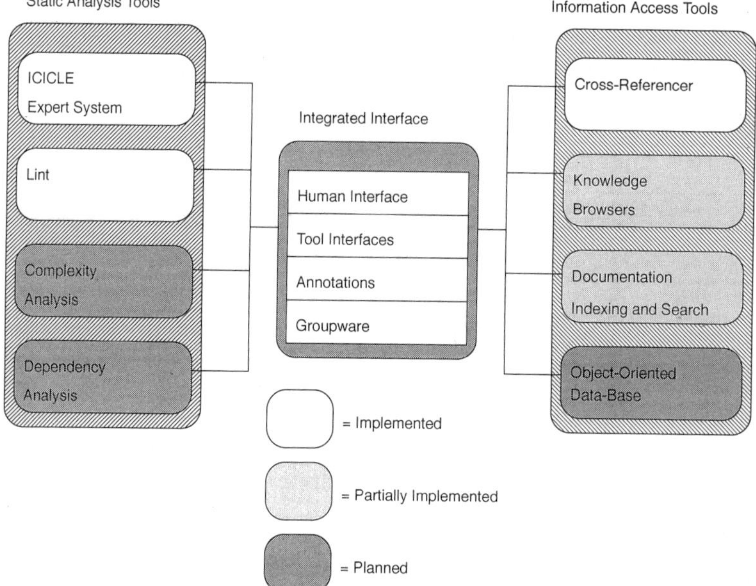

Figure 1. ICICLE Architecture.

slice analyzers). Even if some or all of the analysis tools fail for a given source code module (perhaps the program is syntactically incorrect or in an unusual language dialect), ICICLE still provides all the functions necessary to perform a code inspection, albeit with reduced efficacy.

The primary innovations offered by ICICLE are embodied in (1) the expert system for automatic detection of bugs in C programs, (2) ICE (the ICICLE C expert), (3) a CSCW system for code-inspection meeting support (we refer to this as ICICLE groupware), and (4) the integration of these technologies to enable all the complex and demanding activities of code inspection to run online through the medium of a single system.

ICE: The ICICLE C Expert

Certain classes of relatively simple errors and warnings can be captured by bug-detection tools such as LINT or DAVE (Lukey 1980). To detect more complex errors, one needs to acquire and represent the heuristic rules that expert developers use. Because of the easy modifiability of the rule base and the availability of explanation facilities, rule-based systems provide an excellent framework to represent not only these rules but also those for detecting violations of coding standards. Examples of rule-based debugging systems are FALOSY (Osterweil and Fosdick 1976), MESSAGE TRACE ANALYZER (Gupta and Seviora 1983), and Harandi's (1983) system. The first two systems require the program to be run and are therefore unsuitable for code inspection. Code inspection requires syntactically correct code but is not intended to perform run-time analyses, which are usually performed by a separate testing group. Koenig (1989) compiled more significant debugging knowledge than that represented in Harandi's system. ICICLE has rules to detect many of the characteristic problems reported by Koenig.

ICE contains a YACC[2]-based C grammar parser, which can efficiently accept C code and output a Lisp-readable annotated parse tree in the form of a series of S-expressions. The parser is by no means as complete a parser as, for example, those used by C compilers. Because code presented for inspection must compile without errors, the grammar and actions can be fine tuned to provide exactly the information required by the rules of the expert system component and need not provide robust explanations of syntactical and lexical errors.

ICE's primary inference mechanism is a rule-based system written in ART, a commercial multiparadigm expert system shell, along with auxiliary routines in Lisp. The output of the parser is decomposed into schemata suitable for assertion into the frame knowledge base used by the expert system. The shell's relational pattern-matching inference engine is capable of detecting specific patterns or templates of parse tree nodes corresponding to potential errors, dangerous coding uses, and coding standards violations. If this structural (syntactic) matching is not sufficient to detect some errors or violations, additional Lisp routines can be triggered to perform semantic analysis of the area of the code being focused on by the pattern-matching step. For example, syntactic analysis can find an instance of a pointer being dereferenced, but further semantic analysis is required to determine if dereferencing the pointer is likely to lead to a segmentation fault.

Cliche recognition (Wills 1990; Harandi and Ning 1990; Johnson 1986) is an emerging technology for identifying the function or intention of a piece of code by recognizing a pattern associated with the function. Detection of the intention of a programmer goes a step beyond mere semantic analysis into the more difficult area of pragmatics. This technology can be used to recognize patterns of C traps and pitfalls. It provides a higher-level language-independent framework (for example, PLAN CALCULUS [Rich 1986]) to represent patterns of code and semantic and program-understanding knowledge (for example, the representation in PAT [Harandi and Ning 1990]). Tutoring systems such as PROUST (Johnson 1986) and TALUS (Murray 1985) have also experimented with frameworks to represent debugging knowledge. Compared to the pattern-matching and object-oriented languages available in rule-based system shells such as ART, these higher-level frameworks

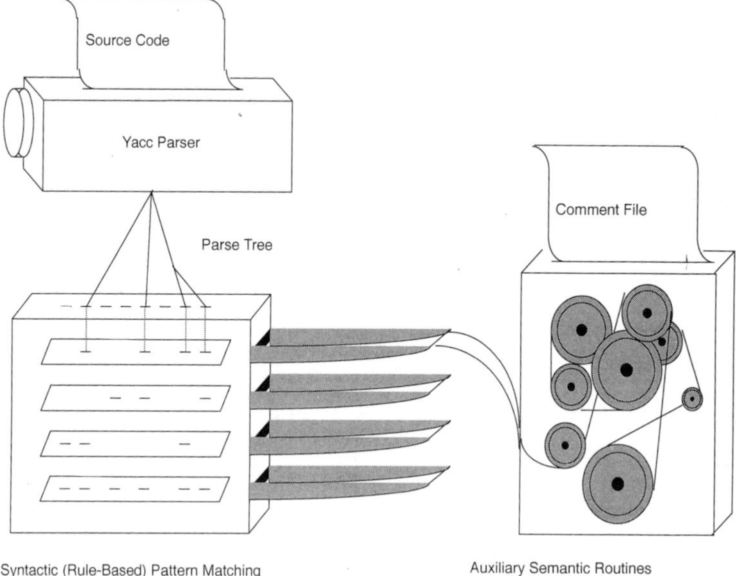

Figure 2. ICE Architecture.

make it easier to represent knowledge to catch complex traps and pitfalls that involve sophisticated patterns (delocalized plans [Letovsky and Soloway 1985]) and semantic information dispersed across many procedures and modules. However, none of the reported cliche-recognition systems is scalable to large, real-life application systems implemented in languages such as C (Harandi and Ning 1990; Rich and Wills 1990). Hence, we decided to use an integrated frame- and rule-based expert system shell to implement ICE.

Although, in general, detection of the intention of a programmer is difficult, several of ICE's rules are designed to detect simple cliches. For example, a common use of the C for loop is to iterate through a fixed-size array. ICE rules can detect possible errors in array bounds and iterator direction based on the expected template provided by this programming cliche. ICE rules do not attempt to detect higher-level cliches, such as sorting functions or access methods; such analysis is beyond the representational and computational capacity of the system. Figure 2 shows the interrelationship of the YACC parser, the parse tree, the pattern-matching rules, and the auxiliary semantic routines.

ICE currently contains about 45 programming heuristics, implemented as a rule-based system. These heuristics can catch many of the traps and pitfalls compiled by Koenig (1989). They fall into several classes:

Standards violations: An example is a failure to initialize automatic variables. These rules are mainly syntactic and, thus, have complete certainty that their firing is correct. Standards violations generally do not reflect actual bugs but are enforced by development organizations to ensure consistent good programming practices across different modules and systems.

Definite programming errors: These errors are serious coding errors, for example, an attempt to dereference the null pointer. These rules are also sure that they are flagging real errors. Most of these rules operate on a fairly small scale, for example, a single expression or operation.

Possible programming errors: Frequently, the system is unable to determine whether a dangerous coding situation is definitely an error; these situations are flagged as such. For example, a for loop that runs from 1 to n (instead of 0 to n - 1) might be correct, but it is atypical enough to flag for further attention. Usability testing has demonstrated that the flagging of false positives is not a problem for users or the system. Because of the high cost of bug correction after code inspection, even a high ratio of false positives to actual bugs detected is acceptable.

All these situations are flagged differently and are displayed as such through the user interface.

Human Interface for Comment Preparation

In the process of code inspection, various ICICLE features come to the fore in different phases. Both comment preparation and the code-inspection meeting require support for automated analysis, human program understanding, and various secretarial and organizational tasks such as recording and filing annotations, but the style of system use is markedly different during the two phases.

The ICICLE human interface was implemented using the XVIEW tool kit for the X WINDOW system. The functions of X permit easy operation of applications on remote displays, helping to enable the CSCW interface functions. ICICLE can operate on any display device that runs X as long as at least one machine can run the X VIEW client or a client with similar functions.

The human interface has two modalities of operation: comment preparation and code-inspection meeting. The latter mode subsumes the functions of the former, with the addition of groupware to automate the cooperative effort of the meeting. Figure 3 is a screen dump of the ICICLE human interface in its most basic configuration.

The output of comment preparation is a file that contains all com-

```
ICICLE: Scribe
Quit)  Save Comments)  Review Comments)  Module Overview)  Describe Selection)  Man Pages)  Options)  Refresh Screen)
Describe: setbuf

Pop)  Push)  Goto)  Find Next Transferred Comment)
File: l.llfile.c           Stack: 0)
Line: 1
There is a setbuf man page. Click on Man Pages to view
setbuf has been indexed. Click on Describe Selection to view
There is a errno man page. Click on Man Pages to view
errno has been indexed. Click on Describe Selection to view

    46  llfile(ct_f, outct_f,st_f)
    47
    48  FILE *ct_f;
    49  FILE *outct_f;
    50  float *st_f;
    51  {
   ⊘=52      struct FCIF_TAG fcif;
   ⊘-53      int retcode;
    54      int old_level = 0;
   ⊘-55      float temp_st;
    56      char buf1[132],buf2[132];
    57      char tagval[MAX_TG_VL];
   ⊘-58      char *tv_ptr;
    59      int i=0;
    60      /* reset buffering */
 T ?-61      setbuf(ct_f,buf1);
   ?-62      if (errno)
   ⊘-63        return(FAILURE);
   ?-64      setbuf(outct_f,buf2);
   ?-65      if (errno)
   ⊘-66        return(FAILURE);
    67
    68      /* initialize statistic */

Defer)     ✓ Selected Comment
Ignore)    ❏ All in Window
Transfer)  ❏ All of type selected
T l.llfile.c line 61; WARNING:  setbuf on a local variable may lose data on program termination
D l.llfile.c line 62; WARNING:  probably incorrect use of errno to detect error condition
I l.llfile.c line 63; VIOLATION:  statement in this position should be compound
Explanation)       ✓ Edit comment     Line #: 61
Propose Comment)   ❏ New Comment      Comment: setbuf on a local variable may lose data on program termination
Done)
```

Figure 3. ICICLE Human Interface.

ments and annotations made by the human user and ICICLE components such as ICE and LINT. This file is used as one of several input to the code-inspection meeting. Each inspector is required to review the module individually and prepare separate sets of comments and annotations in separate comment files.

Groupware for Code-Inspection Meeting Support

Figure 4 shows a typical code-inspection meeting situation. During the code-inspection meeting, active analysis of the module's source code is secondary to the discussion of the validity of comments and annotations compiled during the previous comment-preparation phase. Nevertheless, many of the functions required during comment preparation might be needed during the meeting. ICICLE automates the conduct of the code-inspection meeting by supporting the various secretarial and administrative roles assigned to the inspectors during the meeting.

The groupware of the basic ICICLE product requires each inspector to be present, with a personal workstation or terminal in the same room for the duration of the meeting (usually about two hours). To accommodate the requirements of distributed work groups and also afford the possibility of using ICICLE for informal code-review sessions, we ex-

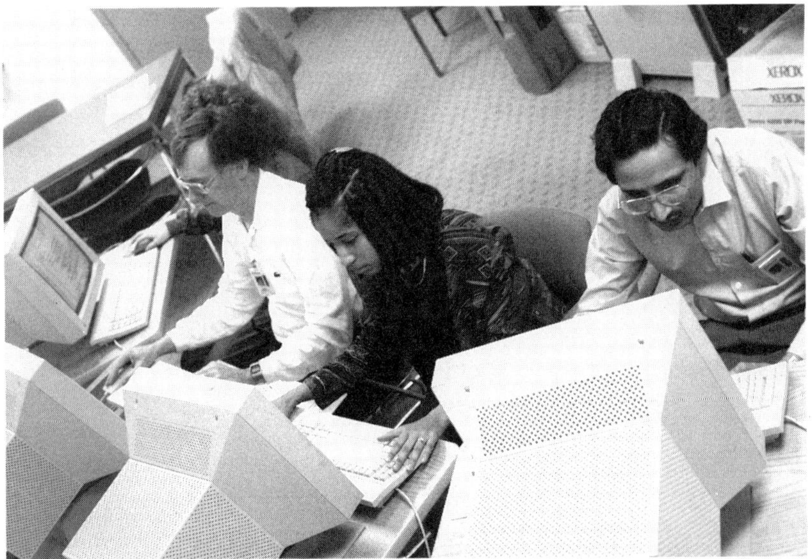

Figure 4. A Bellcore Code-Inspection Meeting.

plored the use of multiple media (voice, image, and video) in the groupware interface to permit inspectors to carry out inspections from their separate offices or across internetworked local area networks between remote sites. ICICLE groupware obviates the need for paper at the meeting (although paper listings and documents can still be used as an auxiliary aid) and greatly enhances the efficiency of code-inspection meeting procedures by streamlining secretarial and administrative procedures through computer support.

For further discussion of ICICLE's groupware and usability testing results and other human-computer interaction issues, see Brothers, Sembugamoorthy, and Muller (1990).

ICICLE: Development, Maintenance, and Use

In this section, we discuss details of ICICLE's development, maintenance, and use.

ICICLE Development

The ICICLE project was started as a research prototype intended to explore issues of code inspection by means of an intelligent assistant approach to program understanding. We understood immediately that many other research prototypes (Harandi and Ning 1990; Johnson

1986; Letovsky and Soloway 1985; Rich and Wills 1990; Harandi 1983) in the field had encountered scaling problems in dealing with such large and difficult phases of software development as specification, design, and implementation (see Sembugamoorthy et al. for more details). We chose, therefore, to focus initially on the relatively isolated phase of software engineering known as code inspection, which we felt existing techniques and hardware could address in real-world situations. Further impetus for our work was the realization that the ordinary code-inspection process was entirely manual and not computer assisted in any way, so that our efforts would not have to conform to a rigid set of expectations in our planned user community (nevertheless, we tried to continue to uphold the principles of the old style of code inspection where this approach was reasonable).

The project was initiated in response to an internal Bellcore policy to include code inspection for all new software. We anticipated that many software developers would be unfamiliar with code inspection and that given the scale of Bellcore's software development efforts, even a slight savings of time or a slight improvement in effectiveness could save many millions of dollars. Later, positive results from usability testing and the joining of our efforts with those of the Bellcore Advanced Software Environment (BASE) development group continued to support our work.

Our initial feasibility prototype took approximately 1-1/2 staff-years for two developers (L. Brothers and V. Sembugamoorthy) to complete. From the beginning, we had the cooperation of a major Bellcore software development group without whose assistance the system could never have been constructed. Developers from this organization permitted us to observe their manual code inspections and also took part in usability testing and field trials of various ICICLE prototypes.

Once our experimental prototype had been tested (approximately 2-1/2 total staff-years, or 1-1/2 calendar-years, of research and development from project initiation), it was time to turn ICICLE into a deployable software system. Approximately three more staff-years, or another year of real time, including the efforts of developers from BASE as well as our own group (Knowledge-Based Systems Development), led finally to the development of the ICICLE software system, which has been deployed internally for several months.

At every stage of ICICLE's development, we followed the principles of user-centered design, with particular emphasis on usability testing. Software developers who have used the ICICLE system have reacted almost uniformly positive to the introduction of the system despite the radical changes it brings to the code-inspection process. As the ICICLE product continues to be used for real code inspections, many changes, both small and large, are being planned to improve the code-inspection process.

ICICLE Maintenance

ICICLE is currently being maintained as an internal software system by BASE. Because every organization has a different set of coding standards and might or might not approve of certain use rules within the ICE expert system, ICICLE must be configured slightly differently for each development group it is deployed for. Fortunately, this configuration is made easy by the alteration of a pair of setup files that define which rules are to be used and also permit development organizations to add certain coding standards of their own. An additional issue is the use by different development organizations of a variety of database languages such as SQL preprocessors. Another configuration item requires such preprocessors to be accessible to the ICE analysis scripts so that all source code can be analyzed to the greatest extent possible.

Current development directions include a transition from ART, a Lisp-based product, to a C-based shell of comparable power. ICICLE will also be ported to use the MOTIF[3] tool kit and will be extended to cover additional languages and environments beyond C and UNIX. BASE treats ICICLE as a component of its general product BASIS, which addresses all phases of the software development process; every one of these components will have to be actively maintained by a staff of developers for the lifetime of the product to support the changing needs and situations of Bellcore software developers.

ICICLE Use

At present, BASE is still deploying ICICLE to its initial client group. Once use patterns are analyzed, and requests for maintenance are received, BASE will update ICICLE's components accordingly. As of this writing, ICICLE has been deployed to several Bellcore development organizations, covering hundreds of potential and actual users. During the course of its development, other development groups were invited to help test the system, and the needs and concerns of different groups were thereby addressed.

Because many Bellcore development organizations use traditional dumb terminals connected to minicomputers or mainframes, ICICLE introduction has been slowed by the need to purchase special equipment (workstations and software licenses). Fortunately, many of these organizations have begun to actively convert their operations to workstation and PC-based configurations, so we anticipate accelerated deployment of ICICLE in the near future.

Looking Back at ICICLE

Here, we examine the impact of ICICLE on Bellcore and the code-inspection process as well as the lessons we learned during its development.

Impact of ICICLE

As anticipated, Bellcore's code-inspection goals were difficult to meet, partially because of the problems attributed to the old regime of manual inspections. Even modest gains in inspection rates and efficiency would be major gains for the productivity of Bellcore's software development organization because of the organization's size.

We characterize the scale of Bellcore's software development effort with the following statistics from 1990: Bellcore produced 18.1 million lines of new or significantly changed code and spent 68,000 hours inspecting 20 percent of this code manually. Inspections resulted in an average fault-detection rate of 7 for every 1000 lines of code inspected. The cost of correcting defects detected during code inspection averaged in the hundreds of dollars. The cost of correcting defects detected during software use averaged $20,000. The correction of defects (not found during inspection or testing) cost $65 million in Bellcore development costs (from a budget of about $400 million), excluding potentially enormous costs from lost productivity in the user community.

Gains from the use of ICICLE fall into the following areas. For each area, we describe our experience to date:

More inspections done: Surveys of ICICLE users indicate an overwhelming preference (over 90 percent) for inspections using ICICLE as opposed to manual inspections. A major barrier to increasing inspection rates is developers' distaste for inspections. Comments from users of ICICLE indicate that it removes many of the most onerous aspects of inspections. ICICLE is currently used on five major software projects. The current version of ICICLE processes Kernighan and Ritchie C. In the near future, versions of ICICLE for ANSI C and C++ will be deployed, making further gains in inspection rates possible.

More errors found: We know that ICE detects errors that many developers are unfamiliar with; we have observed inspectors being surprised by errors detected by ICE. Because analysis tools such as ICE and LINT are capable of automatically finding many classes of errors, ICICLE users are freed to concentrate on more sophisticated and subtle problems, which they otherwise would not have time to look for. This analysis by people is further enhanced by the finely tuned human interface described earlier. Specific data on additional errors found with ICICLE have not been obtained to date because tight development schedules have not allowed for the needed comparative studies. With conservative assumptions of one additional error found with ICICLE for every 1000 lines inspected and just 5 percent of these errors remaining in deployed code, the use of ICICLE could have saved Bellcore approximately $3 million for 1990, when only about 20 percent of the code was inspected.

Less time taken for inspections: We know that ICICLE saves a lot of paper shuffling during comment preparation and inspection meetings and that it eliminates most of the secretarial drudgery and bookkeeping associated with manual inspections. Because our analysis of time spent in manual code-inspection meetings revealed that a large portion of meeting time was wasted in paper shuffling, we believe that ICICLE can be used to save meeting time. Clearly, however, the discovery of more errors for every 1000 might have a countervailing effect on this statistic because more comments will have to be analyzed, discussed, and resolved. Thus, instead of merely reducing meeting time, ICICLE might be said to increase the value of meeting time, however much time is spent.

Impact on the code-inspection process: Following our analysis of ICICLE use (for more detail see Brothers, Sembugamoorthy, and Muller [1990]), we determined that computerized code inspection can significantly alter the nature of the special roles (moderator, reader, and scribe) assigned for traditional code-inspection meetings. For example, because the scribe has much less work to do in an ICICLE-moderated inspection meeting and because the moderator performs no special functions within ICICLE, we suggested that these roles be merged. Such a merger would permit smaller inspection teams, consequently allowing the performance of more inspections or less cost in staff time. If the size of average inspection teams was reduced from four to three, and the number of inspections stayed constant, Bellcore could save approximately $1.5 million in inspection costs.

As discussed previously, ICICLE is intended not merely to improve metrics such as the number of code inspections and the errors found but, more importantly, to increase the value of code inspections as such. As ICICLE permeates our software development organization more thoroughly, we expect a consensus to emerge among developers about the value of ICICLE in each of these areas and to obtain better statistics to demonstrate this success.

Lessons Learned

As a result of our work, we have gained insights into numerous issues regarding the application of AI techniques to problems in software engineering. Following are some of the most significant. Not all these insights are new or original, but inasmuch as other efforts in the field have sometimes neglected them, we can repeat them here with new emphasis:

Scalability: Unless research prototypes are designed with eventual deployment among real user populations for real problems in mind, they will remain, at best, studies. We were forced to abandon several promising directions that seemed valuable in prototype form because of the improper amount of resources they would consume when scaled to real-world situations. For example, we had hoped to represent a significant amount of project-specific knowledge within ICICLE to expand the reasoning capabilities of ICE and also provide more sophisticated assistance for program understanding. However, the knowledge-acquisition problem forced us to retreat from the representation of knowledge to the presentation of information in its stead.

Ripeness: In the area of code inspection, we found a phase of the software development process that was ripe for exploitation. Because it was entirely manual and at the same time regarded as exceedingly difficult and onerous, we could introduce radical changes into existing procedures without social engineering among the target user population, and we could almost guarantee from project inception that our system would be received favorably. Even systems that can objectively be demonstrated to provide performance that is superior to existing systems might fail if the user population does not perceive the need for the new systems or if the cost of changing over is too great.

Problem integration: Our system was designed from the start to address all major aspects of code inspection, from individual comment preparation to group code-inspection meetings to form and report generation. ICICLE would have been much less valuable had it only supported part of the process, even had this support been even stronger for this phase than the actual system now provides. We were forced to integrate multiple technologies to provide a product capable of dealing with the whole problem of code inspection.

Problem isolation: Despite our need to address the whole problem of code inspection, we were able to avoid having to construct a system to deal with the manifold other problems of software development in general. Had our system been required to address other issues in requirements, specification, design, implementation, or maintenance, we would have been unable to ever deploy a usable system.

Additionally, we learned some less abstract lessons about the specific systems we developed and deployed:

Human interface: Regardless of the success of the ICE software analysis expert system, the human interface is undoubtedly the most critical component. An intelligent assistant program, at least in the style of ICICLE, can be rendered worthless by a human interface that makes interaction with the program difficult or otherwise provides less than optimal performance. We were frequently forced to alter the human interface in response to requests by usability testers and based on our observation of users' interactions with the system.

ICE: Although our rule-based framework enabled us to quickly write and modify both simple and powerful rules for error detection, we eventually found that we had employed this complex pattern-matching system in a few cases to discover errors that could have been more efficiently found by much simpler systems. In fact, we now use a simple SED-based[4] system to detect certain categories of errors that were unnecessarily written in a form much more wasteful of resources. We found that in this case, it was important to trade off simplicity and consistency of approach for efficiency and eventually achieved an order-of-magnitude increase in performance. Of course, most rules continue to operate within our expert system shell language, but we have been forced by concerns for efficiency to constantly reevaluate our choice of rules and rule formats.

Groupware: Through detailed task analysis, we were able to construct a groupware system based on a limited set of primitive operations nonetheless capable of supporting all our communications requirements for the code-inspection meeting. Despite its small size and relative simplicity, the development of the ICICLE groupware took an unexpected amount of development, testing, and refinement. The interaction of multiple users, combined with the synergetic increase in the interaction complexity of other ICICLE subsystems operating in a groupware, made the system unusually hard to develop and test. Nevertheless, we consider this ICICLE component one of the most valuable ICICLE subsystems.

Software tools: We had hoped to directly employ many vendor tools to either detect errors or assist users with program understanding. Unfortunately, we found most such software tools to be either too inflexible to use for our purposes or too isolated and self-contained to connect to our tool framework. We still plan to adopt more such tools but have found our choices more limited than we had expected.

Our work on ICICLE has not only been of use in the development of a system to help users to accomplish a difficult and time-consuming task, it has also reinforced our beliefs in the basic principles of applied research and exploratory development. Our diligent task analysis, integration of diverse technologies, and, above all, our commitment to the philosophy and procedures of user-centered design helped to ensure that our research hypotheses could be developed into a working software system capable of dealing with serious problems in the software development life cycle.

Acknowledgments

We are grateful to Carl Lewis and other members of the Bellcore Provisioning Order Control System Development Department who provided critical assistance in usability and field testing of various ICICLE versions. ICICLE could not have been deployed without the work of Reva Leung, Bob Kayel, and Eric Jung of the Bellcore Advanced Software Environment Department. The continued encouragement and support of our own management, namely, Chris Riley, Dave Kessell, and Bob Martin, was essential to our success.

Notes

1. ICICLE currently runs under UNIX on Sun Microsystems workstations using the ART expert system shell and the X WINDOW system. The human interface was built using the XVIEW tool kit.
2. YACC, yet another compiler compiler, is a common UNIX tool.
3. An example is ART-IM.
4. SED, the stream editor, is a commonly available filter language available on UNIX systems.

References

Ackerman, A. F. 1984. Software Inspections and the Industrial Production of Software. In *Software Validation*, ed. H. L. Hausen. New York: Elsevier.

Ackerman, A. F.; Buschwald, L. S.; and Lewski, F. H. 1989. Software Inspections: An Effective Verification Process. *IEEE Software.* 6(3) (May): 31–36.

Brooks, F. 1987. No Silver Bullet: Essence and Accidents of Software Engineering. *IEEE Computer.*

Brooks, F. 1975. *The Mythical Man-Month.* Reading, Mass.: Addison-Wesley.

Brothers, L.; Sembugamoorthy, V.; and Muller, M. 1990. ICICLE: Groupware for Code Inspection. Presented at the Computer Supported Cooperative Work Conference, Los Angeles, California, October.

Dobbins, J. H. 1987. Inspections as an Up-Front Quality Technique. In *Handbook of Software Quality Assurance*, eds. G. G. Schulmeyer and J. J. McManus, 137–177. New York: Van Nostrand Reinhold.

Fagan, M. E. 1976. Design and Code Inspections to Reduce Errors in Program Development. *IBM Systems Journal* 15(3): 182–211.

Gupta, N. K., and Seviora, R. E. 1983. An Expert System Approach to Real-Time System Debugging. In Proceedings of the First Conference on Artificial Intelligence Applications, 282–288. Washington, D.C.: IEEE Computer Society.

Harandi, M. T. 1983. Knowledge-Based Program Debugging: A Heuristic Model. In Proceedings of the 1983 Softfair, 282–288.

Harandi, M. T., and Ning, J. Q. 1990. Knowledge-Based Program Analysis. 2(1) (January): *IEEE Software*: 74–81.

ohnson, W. L. 1986. *Intention-Based Diagnosis of Errors in Novice Programs.* San Mateo, Calif.: Morgan Kaufmann.

Johnson, S. C. 1983. LINT, a C Program Checker. In UNIX Programmer's Manual, vol. 2. Murray Hill, N.J.: Bell Labs.

Koenig, A. 1989. *C Traps and Pitfalls.* Reading, Mass.: Addison-Wesley.

Letovsky, S., and Soloway, E. 1985. Strategies for Documenting Delocalized Plans. In Proceedings of the Conference on Software Maintenance, 144–151. Washington, D.C.: IEEE Computer Society.

Lukey, F. J. 1980. Understanding and Debugging Programs. *International Journal of Man-Machine Studies*: 189–202.

Murray, W. R. 1985. Heuristic and Formal Methods in Automatic Program Debugging. In Proceedings of the Ninth International Joint Conference on Artificial Intelligence, 15–19. Menlo Park, Calif.: International Joint Conferences on Artificial Intelligence.

Osterweil, L. J., and Fosdick, L. D. 1976. DAVE: A Validation Error Detection and Documentation System for FORTRAN Programs. *Software Practices and Experience* 6: 473–486.

Rich, C. 1986. A Formal Representation for Plans in the PROGRAMMER'S APPRENTICE. In *Readings in Artificial Intelligence and Software Engineering*, eds. C Rich and R. C. Waters. San Mateo, Calif.: Morgan Kaufmann.

Rich, C., and Wills, L. M. 1990. Recognizing a Program Design: A Graph Parsing Approach. *IEEE Software*. 7(1) (January): 82–89.

Russell, G. W. 1991. Experience with Inspection in Ultralarge-Scale Developments. *IEEE Software*: 25–31.

Sembugamoorthy, Y., and Brothers, L. 1990. ICICLE: Intelligent Code

Inspection in a C-Language Environment. Presented at the Computer Science and Applications (COMPSAC) Conference.

Wills, L. M. 1990. Automated Program Recognition: A Feasibility Demonstration. *Artificial Intelligence* 45:113–172.

When the Public Network Dies. 1991. *Networking Management*: 31–35.

Automatic Programming for Sequence Control

Hiroyuki Mizutani, Yasuko Nakayama, Satoshi Ito, Yasuo Namioka, and Takayuki Matsudaira, Toshiba Corporation

Industrial plants are controlled using sequence control programs running on programmable controllers. Sequence control program design has been carried out manually, and an increase in applications of programmable controllers has caused a shortage of programmers. Therefore, automatic programming systems are strongly required in this field.

Controllers receive operation signals from plant operators and current plant states through sensors, then select actions that have to be executed. Sequence control programs consist of a large amount of control logic (about 100K program steps) for such decisions. The following problems were found in previous manual designs of sequence control programs:

First, control logic is often omitted.

Second, programs might include some mutual contradictions.

Third, information that is necessary to complete one program step is distributed in several different kinds of specification document. It costs too much time for program designers to understand specifications.

Fourth, alteration of control specifications often occurs, resulting in a wide range of program modifications.

The purpose of the automatic programming system (CAD-PC/AI) described in this chapter is to reduce these difficulties to increase productivity and improve the quality of sequence control program design. Moreover, it aims to facilitate a systematic accumulation of design knowledge.

There are two kinds of design knowledge used in generating sequence control programs: One is knowledge about the environment in which the programs work. The other is the specific programming knowledge for plant control.

We found through an analysis of designers' behavior that knowledge about the environment (that is, plant) plays an essential role throughout the entire life cycle of software development: requirement analysis, specification validation, implementation, testing, and maintenance. This knowledge constitutes a model of the plant that is to be controlled and leads us to propose a model-based automatic programming paradigm. Under this paradigm, the plant model supports every task in the software life cycle.

The second significant kind of knowledge is for refining specifications to target program codes. It appears that two kinds of programming knowledge are involved: One is to find reusable program parts suitable to given specifications. The other is to select a program skeleton and refine it in a stepwise fashion, according to the specifications, into concrete programs when program parts cannot be reused.

We chose the knowledge-based approach to develop CAD-PC/AI. The significant innovations are as follows:

First, it is one of the first knowledge-based systems in the plant control program design domain in which knowledge about the environment, as well as programming knowledge, is crucial.

Second, it demonstrates a new technology for making a knowledge base widely applicable, that is, the generic-specific modeling technique and model transformation discussed later.

Problem and Approach

A plant system includes operators, operation devices, programmable controllers, plant machines, actuators, sensors, and products, as shown in figure 1.

Control programs in conventional problem-oriented languages (for example, LADDER DIAGRAM) are written at the signal level—input-output (I-O) signals of programmable controllers—as shown in figure 2.

Because these programs have become increasingly complex to implement, they are still being manually designed; as a result, the process has begun to suffer from several of the problems that were

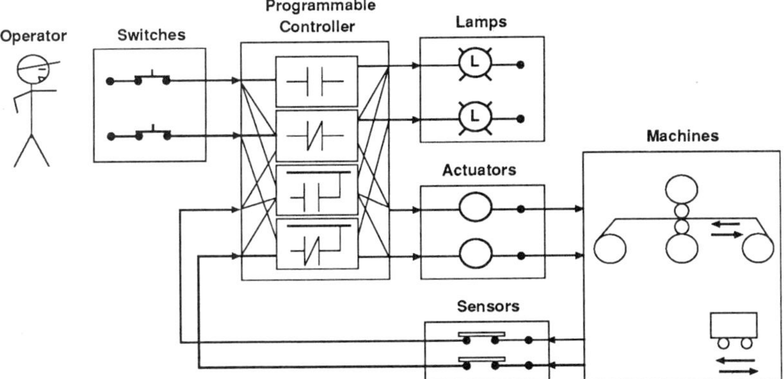

Figure 1. Conceptual Block Diagram for Plants.

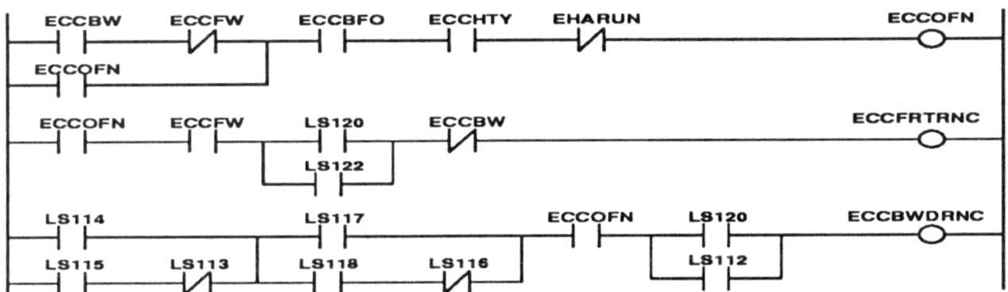

Figure 2. Example of Control Programs Written in LADDER DIAGRAM.

previously mentioned.

At the first stage of automatic programming system development, we established the software life cycle that we describe here. It was set up similar to conventional design processes so that designers would be able to easily transfer to the new system and maintain it. Because of this policy, it was necessary to simulate designers' conventional thinking on the computer system. Therefore, AI techniques were considered promising.

Previously, automatic programming research was based on the theorem-proving approach (Manna and Waldinger 1980), the program-transformation approach (Fickas 1985; Darington 1981; Green and Westfold 1982), and the knowledge-based approach (Barstow 1985; Lubars and Harandi 1987; Smith, Kotik, and Westfold 1985; Neighbors 1984). We selected the knowledge-based approach, where an informal high-level specification would be attainable, and prototyping would be easy; moreover, a conventional program-parts database could be used.

MACHINE	OPERATION	ITEM	MV TYPE				MAGNET ELECTION			VOLT
			DS3P	DS2P	SS2P	OIL/AIR	A	OFF	B	
NO.1CONVEYOR	FORWARD - BACKWARD	DMV1000	○			OIL	FORWARD	STOP	BACKWARD	DC100V
NO.1CONVEYOR	HIGH SPEED - LOW SPEED	DMV1001			○	OIL	HIGH SPEED	LOW SPEED		DC100V

Figure 3. Example of Machine Specification.

Requirement Analysis Phase

Requirement analysis means deriving detailed specifications from brief requirements given in terms of the structure and operation of the plant. There are two aspects to requirement specification: One is *machine specification* (figure 3), which gives a static description of the plant in terms of actuators, sensors, operation devices, interlocks, and so on. The other is *control specification* (figure 4), which sets out the operations that the plant is required to perform.

In figure 4, a box represents an action, and a horizontal bar represents a transition. We set composite-action–level specifications as informal high-level specifications. *Composite action* is an abstract description of possible machine actions or states that can be broken down into some set of serial or parallel primitive actions or states. Detailed specifications, such as speed and subsidiary actions, are not described at this level. For example, "move forward" can later be broken down into "move forward at low speed until some conditions become true, and then move forward at high speed." This high-level specification brings control design closer to the designers' conceptual level, making design more natural.

In the new automatic programming system, a generic model constructs a specific model by interpreting machine specifications. These models are discussed later. The generic model determines a structural representation using the general knowledge of the functional structure of such plants. At the same time, it derives the detailed machine behavior using the general knowledge about machine operations and translates incomplete and ambiguous control specifications into detailed specifications.

Specification Validation Phase

The conventional testing method is based on a comparison of the actual behavior of the programs with the user's intent. It is carried out using a special-purpose plant simulator after implementation is complete. If mismatches are detected, the implemented programs must be modified.

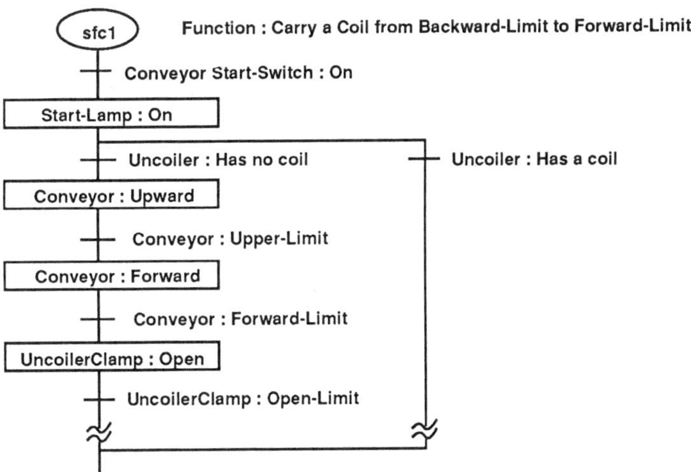

Figure 4. Example of Control Specification.

In the new system, the plant model supports specification validation. A symbolic simulation is performed using the detailed machine behavior, as represented by transitional relations between machine actions and states in the specific model.

Implementation Phase

Implementation is carried out by selecting suitable program parts and modifying them according to the specifications. Sequences that cannot be covered by program parts are refined using the program pattern in a stepwise fashion to create detailed programs. The specific model provides the knowledge necessary for these refining processes.

Maintenance Phase

Maintenance should be implemented by modifying the specifications and reimplementing them by replaying the development.

The plant must satisfy two requirements:

Task independent: The model must support the entire design process previously mentioned. There are different kinds of tasks in the design process. General-purpose modeling techniques must be developed to support every task. The knowledge-compilation technique (Chandrasekaran and Mittal 1983; Araya and Mittal 1987; Brown and Sloan 1987; Keller et al. 1989) was suggested based on a similar idea. Knowledge compilers facilitate knowledge reuse, and the same knowledge can be used for more than one purpose.

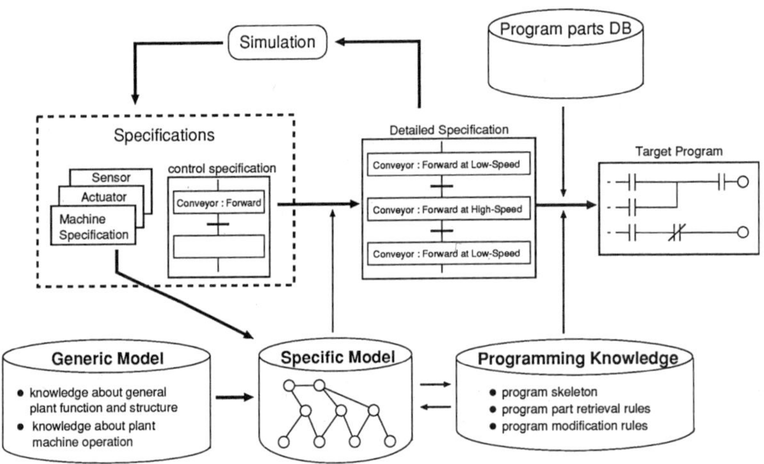

Figure 5. CAD-PC/AI Flow Diagram.

Application independent: The model must support general automatic programming for plant control. A common problem exists in conventional domain-specific expert systems: The knowledge base must be revised for each application because most of these systems rely on a large amount of ad hoc knowledge. To overcome this problem, modeling techniques must be developed that support every application in a specific domain, such as plant control.

System Description

Under this paradigm, we built the automatic programming system (Ono et al. 1988; Nakayama et al. 1990; Mizutani et al. 1991), as shown in figure 5. It works on the AS4000 workstation. We developed and used a knowledge description language in Lisp. It has facilities for frame representation, rule representation, and object-oriented programming. Program parts are stored in a relational database (RDB), and the knowledge description language has an SQL interface. Designers input specifications through a dedicated editor.

Model-Based Approach

We propose the modeling techniques that are outlined in the following subsections.

Generic and Specific Models

The plant model is composed of two parts: One is a generic model that contains knowledge used by system designers in the requirement analysis phase of control systems for a particular class of plants. It includes the functional structure of such installations, types of machine behavior, and expertise about plant control. The generic model is constructed by collecting the practical knowledge of experts and generalizing it. The same model is applicable to all plants of the same type; for example, the generic model of a steel plant is used for a hot-strip mill, a tandem cold mill, a processing line, and so on.

The other part is a specific model that contains knowledge used in the specification validation and implementation phases. This knowledge includes the structure, machine behavior, and constraints of a single target plant. This specific model is derived from the generic model according to the specifications of the target plant.

Extended Semantic Network

The generic model is represented in an extended semantic network that contains conditional relations in addition to the conventional semantic network. The conditional relations are associated with certain conditions. When the conditions are valid with regard to the specifications, the relation is reflected in the specific model. This representation makes the model flexibly accessible.

Furthermore, it has an object-oriented facility. The model-derivation procedures, mentioned previously, are represented as methods. Conditional relations in the generic model are instances of classes and, as such, are able to inherit the methods. As a result, appropriate specific models are built by interpreting the generic model with regard to the user-defined specifications of the target plant.

Model Transformation: The Design Process

The design process was considered as an iterative model transformation from abstract level to detailed description. In Gero (1990), a *design prototype* is a conceptual schema for representing a class of generalized functions, structures, behaviors, and relationships that are derived from alike design cases. In addition, routine design is viewed as a design prototype instance refinement.

The sequence control program design described in this chapter is a routine design, and the generic model can be considered one of the design prototypes. Figure 6 shows the model transformation in CAD-PC/AI. The refinement in the transformation is guided by input specifications. The generic model represents general knowledge about plant

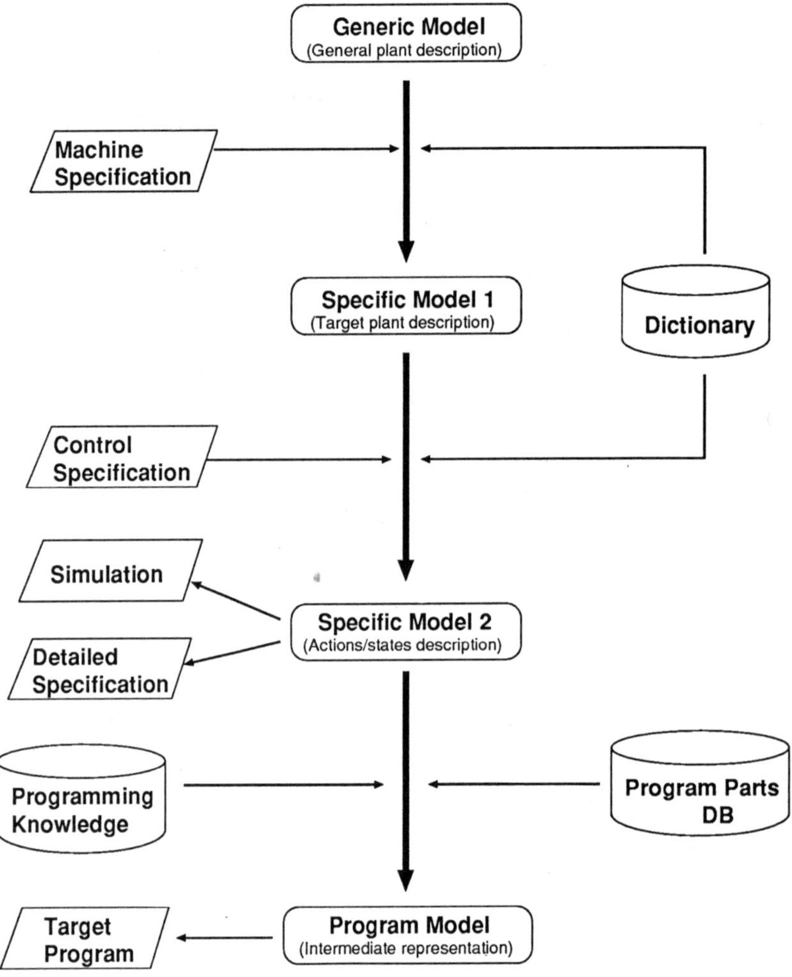

Figure 6. Model Transformation and Refinement in CAD-PC/AI.

functions, structures, behaviors, and relationships as well as expertise about plant control. The general knowledge is independent of the individual target plant. Interpreting a machine specification, CAD-PC/AI understands how the structure, represented in the generic model, is implemented in a target plant. In other words, the functions, structures, and behaviors become associated with target plant machines in the specific model 1 in figure 6, so that expertise about plant control becomes applicable to the target plant.

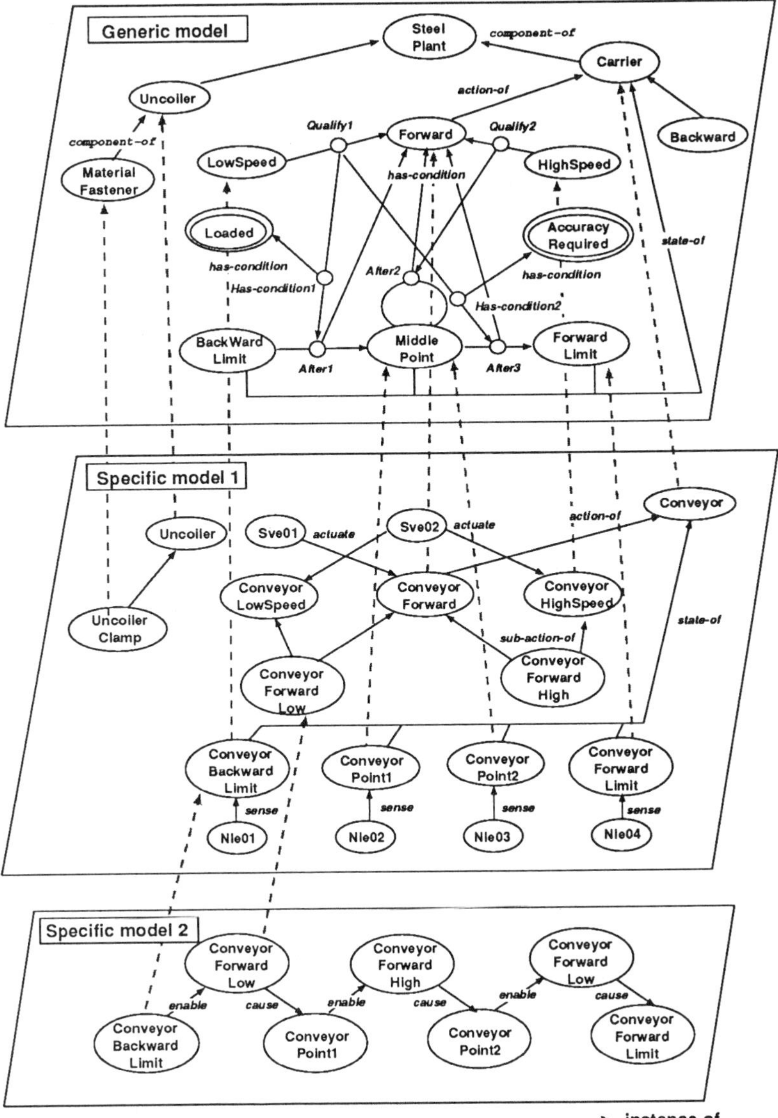

Figure 7. The Plant Model.

In the next step, specific model 1 is transformed into specific model 2 along a high-level control specification, that is, a composite-action–level specification. Detailed machine behaviors, as represented by transitional relations between machine actions and states, are specified and stored in specific model 2. They are further refined to the program model (intermediate representation) using programming knowledge and program parts.

Designers validate specific model 1 with views of a simulation and a detailed specification format. If the transitional relations between machine actions and states are not just as the designers intended, higher-level specifications are modified.

Plant Model

Figure 7 illustrates a portion of the model of a steel plant. The generic model contains general knowledge concerning the class of a plant. SteelPlant is shown as the composition of two machines, Carrier and Uncoiler. Forward is one of several possible actions of Carrier. The relation Qualify specifies the possible control speed for Forward, which can be executed at either LowSpeed or HighSpeed. BackwardLimit, MiddlePoint, and ForwardLimit are possible states of Carrier, with After specifying transitional relations conditioned by Forward. For example, a partial description of the class Forward is as follows:

```
[ Forward
        SUPER:                  MachineAction
        OPPOSITE:               Backward
        ACTION-OF:              Carrier
        CONDITION-OF:           After1, After 2, After 3
        Qualified-by 1:         LowSpeed
        Qualified-by 2:         HighSpeed
        method:                 [...]
] .
```

Qualify, After, and Has-condition are conditional relations. They are defined as a class in terms of domain primitives, and they have conditions and methods for constructing specific models. Qualify1 is one of the instances of the conditional relation Qualify. Qualify and Qualify1 are as follows:

```
[ Qualify
        SUPER:          Relation
        ORIGIN:         MachineAction
        DESTINATION:    MachineAction
        Has-condition:  Relation
        method:         [...]
];
```

```
[ Qualify1
        INSTANCE-OF:     Qualify
        ORIGIN:          LowSpeed
        DESTINATION:     Forward
        Has-condition1:  After1
        Has-condition2:  After3
] .
```

Qualify1 is related to After1 and After3 by the conditional relations Has-condition1 and Has-condition2. Has-condition1 has the condition Loaded, and if Loaded is true, Has-condition1 is actual. Has-condition2 has the condition AccuracyRequired, and if AccuracyRequired is true, Has-condition2 is actual. Thus, when a carrier is loaded at the beginning of an action, or accuracy is required at the end of an action, it must be driven at low speed. Loaded and AccuracyRequired are condition frames that have methods to infer the actual states of the target plant. Thus, the generic model has general knowledge that is independent of the target plant.

The specific model consists of two consecutive models. The first specific model (Specific model 1 in figure 6) contains concrete descriptions of the target plant structure. After the environment of the target plant is specified, the specific model is constructed and is referred to in all subsequent phases of the software life cycle. The basic structure—for example, the physical construction, control relations, and interlocks—is generated by interpreting machine specifications using a dictionary that contains the basic vocabulary of plant control. The machine Conveyor is an instance of Carrier, and UncoilerClamp is an instance of MaterialFastener. The machine Conveyor has the action ConveyorForward driven by the actuator Sve01. The states ConveyorBackwardLimit, ConveyorPoint1, and so on, are detected by the sensors Nle01, Nle02, and so on. A partial description of ConveyorForward is as follows:

```
[ ConveyorForward
        INSTANCE-OF:        Forward
        ACTION-OF:          Conveyor
        ACTUATED-BY:        Sve01
        HAS-SUB-ACTIONS:    ConveyorForwardLow
                              ConveyorForwardHigh
        START-INTERLOCK:    UncoilerStop
        RUN-INTERLOCK:      (AND ConveyorLowerLimit
                              (OR  (NOT  ConveyorCoil Touch)
                                   (AND  ConveyorCoil Touch
                                         Uncoilerclamp CloseLimit)))
         MUTUAL-INTERLOCK:ConveyorBackward
] .
```

The second specific model (specific model 2 in figure 6) contains a transitional relationship between actions and states of machines in the target plant. Relations between actions and states are constructed by interpreting and refining a control specification using a dictionary and expertise about plant control. ConveyorForwardLow and ConveyorForwardHigh are concrete actions of Conveyor. The relations cause and enable specify the transitional relationship between actions and states of Conveyor. The cause links an action to a state. It specifies that the execution of a specified action results in a specified state. The enable links a state to an action. It specifies that a specified state enables a specified action.

Specification Validation

The symbolic simulation (Fox 1987; Reddy and Fox 1986) enables designers to validate specifications by testing for errors or omissions. The description of the machine action, the machine state, and the transitional relations between them in the specific model represent the detailed machine behavior of the target plant. The system simulates an expected machine behavior by tracing these transitional relations, that is, cause and enable relations.

Stepwise Refinement

The action-level specifications are refined into programs by referring to programming knowledge. The programming knowledge is implemented in an object-oriented style of programming, with objects representing a particular piece of programming knowledge. The programming knowledge for a machine operation sequence is:

```
[ MachineOperation
      SUPER:  ProgrammingKnowledge
      PATTERN:        (BETWEEN
                              StartOrderAcceptance
                              < StopSensor
                              : (AND RunInterlock
                                        MutualInterlock))
                      -> (ON MachineOperation)
] .
```

It has a program pattern that means "in a period between accepting a start order and detecting a stop sensor, provided the interlock conditions hold, output an on signal to the actuator that drives the target machine." The object sends a message to lower-level objects that possess their own programming knowledge (StartOrderAcceptance, StopSensor, RunInterlock, and MutualInterlock) until an intermediate representation is obtained. The intermediate representation of a part of a program is as follows:

```
[ ConveyorForward
  (BETWEEN (AND StartOrder UncoilerStop) ; StartOrderAcceptance
        < ConveyorForwardLimit              ; StopSensor
        : (AND (AND ConveyorLowerLimit
                (OR (NOT ConveyorCoilTouch)
                      (AND ConveyorCoilTouch
                          UncoilerclampCloseLimit))) ; RunInterlock
                (NOT ConveyorBackward)) ; MutualInterlock
  )
  -> (ON ConveyorForward)
] .
```

Each element is replaced by controller I-O signals, and finally, the fragment is converted to a target LADDER DIAGRAM and SEQUENTIAL FUNCTION CHART, established languages for writing control programs.

Part-Retrieval Method

Program parts are retrieved by keys that consist of the operation device type, the machine type, the actuator type, and the sensor type. The retrieval function is implemented by the production system, which uses rules in the programming knowledge base. Retrieved parts are customized in accordance with the combination of operation devices and the number of actuators.

Program parts are designed to be as small as possible, basically so that they can be widely applicable. Furthermore, macrodescriptions are provided in the program parts to enhance their flexibility.

Programmable controller languages usually use static storage allocation, and most of their variables are global. Variables in different retrieved program parts are required to be appropriately identified. This automatic programming system attaches attributes, such as machine names and operation names, to each newly created variable for maintaining identity.

Discussion

CAD-PC/AI has been in practical use since October 1990 in the sequence control program design divisions in the Toshiba Corporation. Programmable controllers are being applied to a wider range of work, and their functions are being upgraded and diversified. Thus, a design support system was strongly required in these divisions. During the first stage of development, we decided that the design processes using CAD-PC/AI should be close to the conventional ones. The sequence control program design process was considerably analyzed, and the life cycle discussed previously was established. We then decided what activities in the life cycle could be supported by AI technology. This policy was one reason that the system was deployed smoothly.

We used CAD-PC/AI to generate sequence control programs for steel plants as follows:

Wire and rod mill plant	2.5K program steps
Continuous pickling line	6.5K program steps
Continuous galvanization line	90K program steps
Continuous galvanization line	15K program steps

The first case was for validating the CAD-PC/AI prototype. The quality of generated programs was compared with those designed manually. Some problems were found with the knowledge bases, the lack of program parts, and the inconvenient human interface. After these problems were altered, three practical jobs were implemented using CAD-PC/AI. The generated programs are now running in a real plant control situation in Japan. For example, the third case breaks down as follows:

System size	
Number of frames	2900 frames
Number of program parts	190 parts
Number of part-retrieval rules	320 rules
Specification	
Number of records (machine specifications)	17K records
Number of steps (control specifications)	5.5K steps
Target program	
Target plant	Continuous galvanization line
Programmable controller	PCS-5000 (4 sets)
Program size	90K steps

It would have taken about 100 person-months to complete the target program using the conventional technique. The total cost for software development, including specifications and testing, was reduced by half using this system. The generated program was checked by both design experts and a plant simulator. The achieved quality was satisfactory. The reasons for these advantages are as follows:

First, the plant model enables designers to easily describe machine actions and states for specifying control programs.

Second, the plant model supports specification validation by explaining the expected machine behavior represented in the specific model, helping the designers notice mistakes in earlier design stages.

Third, maintenance activity much more closely parallels the original development. In this domain, plant operations are sometimes changed, which, in turn, affects the control program specifications. When machine specifications are altered, the specific model is constructed again. When control specifications are altered, the resulting programs are regenerated by replaying the development process. Thus, maintenance is performed by altering the specifications and repeating the original development process, not by patching programs.

The generic model represents general knowledge about a class of plants, and it can be used for several different applications. A single generic model was shared between the last three applications. This applicability is important for widespread use of the system.

CAD-PC/AI doubled design productivity. It took about 20 person-years to develop CAD-PC/AI: 3 person-years by the experts, 10 person-years by the system engineers, and 7 person-years by researchers. At the first stage of the development, three researchers were apprenticed to a design division for a few months to learn the design skill by themselves. It helped these researchers to communicate with the experts throughout CAD-PC/AI research and development.

The system made the quality of programs generated by the experts and others relatively uniform. However, it cannot be said that a systematic accumulation of design knowledge was accomplished because only the original developers can maintain the knowledge bases consistently. Maintenance has been continued by the original developers (researchers and system engineers) in accordance with the designers' requirements. Enabling designers to easily extend knowledge bases is the basis for further work.

References

Araya, A., and Mittal, S. 1987. Compiling Design Plans from Descriptions of Artifacts and Problem-Solving Heuristics. In Proceedings of the Tenth International Joint Conference on Artificial Intelligence,

552–558. Menlo Park, Calif.: International Joint Conferences on Artificial Intelligence.

Barstow, D. R. 1985. Domain-Specific Automatic Programming. *IEEE Transactions on Software Engineering* SE-11(11): 1321–1336.

Brown, D. C., and Sloan, W. N. 1987. Compilation of Design Knowledge for Routine Design Expert Systems: An Initial View. In Proceedings of the ASME International Computers in Engineering Conference, 131–136. Fairfield, N.J.: American Society of Mechanical Engineers.

Chandrasekaran, B., and Mittal, S. 1983. Deep Versus Compiled Knowledge Approaches to Diagnostic Problem Solving. *International Journal of Man-Machine Studies* 19:425–436.

Darington, J. 1981. An Experimental Program Transformation and Synthesis System. *Artificial Intelligence* 16:1–46.

Fickas, S. F. 1985. Automating the Transformational Development of Software. *IEEE Transactions on Software Engineering* SE-11(11): 1268–1277.

Fox, M. S. 1987. Constraint-Directed Search: A Case Study of Job-Shop Scheduling. San Mateo, Calif.: Morgan Kaufmann.

Gero, J. S. 1990. Design Prototypes: A Knowledge Representation Schema for Design. AI Magazine 11(4): 26–36.

Green, C., and Westfold, S. J. 1982. Knowledge-Based Programming Self-Applied. *Machine Intelligence* 10.

Keller, R. M.; Baudin, C.; Iwasaki, Y.; Nayak, P.; and Tanaka, K. 1989. Compiling Special-Purpose Rules from General-Purpose Device Models, Technical Report, KSL-89-49, Knowledge Systems Laboratory, Dept. of Computer Science, Stanford Univ.

Lubars, M. D., and Harandi, M. T. 1987. Knowledge-Based Software Design Using Design Schemas. In Proceedings of the International Conference on Software Engineering, 253—262. Los Alamitos, Calif.: IEEE Computer Society.

Manna, Z., and Waldinger, R. 1980. A Deductive Approach to Program Synthesis. *ACM Transactions on Programming Languages and Systems* 2(1): 90–121.

Mizutani, H.; Nakayama, Y.; Sadashige, K.; and Matsudaira, T. 1991. A Knowledge Representation for Model-Based High-Level Specification. In Proceedings of the IEEE Conference on Artificial Intelligence Applications, 124–128. Los Alamitos, Calif.: IEEE Computer Society.

Nakayama, Y.; Mizutani, H.; Sadashige, K.; and Matsudaira, T. 1990.

Model-Based Automatic Programming for Plant Control. In Proceedings of the IEEE Conference on Artificial Intelligence Applications, 281–287. Los Alamitos, Calif.: IEEE Computer Society.

Neighbors, J. M. 1984. The Draco Approach to Constructing Software from Reusable Components. *IEEE Transactions on Software Engineering* SE-10(5): 564–574.

Ono, Y.; Tanimoto, I.; Matsudaira, T.; and Takeuchi, Y. 1988. Artificial Intelligence–Based Programmable Controller Software Designing. In IEEE AI'88 Proceedings of the International Workshop on AI for Industrial Applications, 85–90. Los Alamitos, Calif.: IEEE Computer Society.

Ramana-Reddy, Y. V., and Fox, M. S. 1986. The Knowledge-Based Simulation System. *IEEE Software* 3(2): 26–37.

Smith, D. R.; Kotik, G. B.; and Westfold, S. J. 1985. Research on Knowledge-Based Software Environments at Kestrel Institute. *IEEE Transactions on Software Engineering* SE-11(11): 1278–1295.

Index

Colophon

Editorial and Production Management by
The Live Oak Press, Palo Alto, California.

Copyedited by Elizabeth Ludvik.

Cover design by Spectra Media.

Composed in New Baskerville and Futura by
The Live Oak Press

Output on a Linotronic 300 by G&S Typesetters,
Austin Texas.